RECALLING DEEDS IMMORTAL

UNIVERSITY PRESS OF FLORIDA

Florida A&M University, Tallahassee
Florida Atlantic University, Boca Raton
Florida Gulf Coast University, Ft. Myers
Florida International University, Miami
Florida State University, Tallahassee
New College of Florida, Sarasota
University of Central Florida, Orlando
University of Florida, Gainesville
University of North Florida, Jacksonville
University of South Florida, Tampa
University of West Florida, Pensacola

RECALLING DEEDS IMMORTAL

Florida Monuments to the Civil War

WILLIAM B. LEES AND

FREDERICK P. GASKE

University Press of Florida

Gainesville · Tallahassee · Tampa · Boca Raton

Pensacola · Orlando · Miami · Jacksonville

Ft. Myers · Sarasota

VIVA FLORIDA 500.
1513-2013

A Florida Quincentennial Book

Frontispiece: Confederate veterans at the 1891 Pensacola monument, ca. 1910. Florida Photographic Collection, State Archives of Florida, image no. RC06184.

Portions of text excerpted from the Florida Civil War Heritage Trail are used with permission of the Florida Department of State, Division of Historical Resources. For further information, call 1.800.847.7278 or visit www.flheritage.com.

Many additional photos of the monuments shown in this book are located at the Web site maintained by the Florida Public Archaeology Network at Destination: Civil War—Monuments. Visit http://www.flpublicarchaeology.org/civilwar/monuments.

Printed in the United States of America on acid-free paper

This book may be available in an electronic edition.

19 18 17 16 15 14 6 5 4 3 2 1

Library of Congress Control Number: 2014937651
ISBN 978-0-8130-4996-0

The University Press of Florida is the scholarly publishing agency for the State University System of Florida, comprising Florida A&M University, Florida Atlantic University, Florida Gulf Coast University, Florida International University, Florida State University, New College of Florida, University of Central Florida, University of Florida, University of North Florida, University of South Florida, and University of West Florida.

University Press of Florida
15 Northwest 15th Street
Gainesville, FL 32611-2079
http://www.upf.com

CONTENTS

List of Figures · vii

Preface and Acknowledgments · xv

INTRODUCTION · 1

1. RECONSTRUCTION AND BEYOND: Different Memories · 17

2. REMEMBERING CONFEDERATE SACRIFICE AND VALOR AFTER RECONSTRUCTION · 49

3. REMEMBERING THE UNION SOLDIER AND SAILOR · 163

4. REMEMBERING HALLOWED GROUND · 189

5. MONUMENTS ERECTED AFTER THE CIVIL WAR CENTENNIAL · 259

CONCLUSION · 293

Notes · 307

Bibliography · 339

Index · 355

FIGURES

1. Walton County Confederate monument, ca. 1916 · 2
2. Monument to the Thirty-Second Indiana dead from the Battle of Rowlett's Station, Kentucky · 5
3. Bartow monument at the Manassas Battlefield · 6
4. Monument to Hazen's Brigade at Stones River Battlefield · 7
5. Surrender monument at the Vicksburg Battlefield · 8
6. Groveton monument commemorating Union soldiers at the Battle of Second Manassas · 9
7. Envelope editorializing the human cost of the Civil War · 14
8. Key West's Clinton Square Union monument in 2012 · 36
9. Key West's Clinton Square Union monument, ca. 1870 · 37
10. Key West's Clinton Square Union monument, ca. 1910 · 37
11. Walton County Confederate monument, ca. 1960 · 39
12. Walton County Confederate monument in 2009 · 41
13. Original St. Augustine Confederate monument, ca. 1875 · 43
14. Second St. Augustine Confederate monument in 1891 · 44
15. Confederate monument in St. Augustine's Plaza de la Constitución in 2012 · 46
16. State capitol in the 1890s showing the Leon County Confederate monument · 53
17. Leon County Confederate monument in 1958 after a rare winter snow · 55
18. Leon County Confederate monument in front of the restored state capitol building · 57

19. Confederate monument on the grounds of the Jackson County Courthouse, Marianna, in 1880s · 59
20. Confederate monument at Marianna Courthouse, ca. 1897 · 60
21. Marianna Confederate monument in front of the current Jackson County Courthouse in 2008 · 61
22. Quincy Confederate monument, ca. 1908 · 63
23. Quincy Confederate monument in front of the current Courthouse in 2009 · 64
24. Pensacola Confederate monument, ca. 1903 · 70
25. Confederate veterans at the Pensacola monument, ca. 1910 · 71
26. Confederate monument in Pensacola's Lee Square in 2009 · 72
27. Monticello Confederate monument in early 1900s · 74
28. Monticello Confederate monument in front of the current courthouse in 2010 · 75
29. Jacksonville's Hemming Plaza Confederate monument, ca. 1910 · 78
30. Jacksonville's Hemming Plaza Confederate monument after the Great Fire of 1901 · 81
31. Confederate monument in Jacksonville's Hemming Plaza in 2008 · 81
32. Dedication of monuments in St. Petersburg's Greenwood Cemetery in 1900 · 83
33. Confederate monument in St. Petersburg's Greenwood Cemetery in 2011 · 84
34. Monument to the crew of the CSS *David* in Jacksonville's Evergreen Cemetery in 2013 · 85
35. Gainesville Confederate monument in 1919 · 89
36. Gainesville Confederate monument in 2011 · 90
37. Dedication of Ocala Confederate monument, 1908 · 93
38. Ocala Confederate monument at its new location in Veterans Memorial Park in 2011 · 95
39. United Daughters of the Confederacy and veterans at Madison Confederate monument in early 1900s · 96
40. Madison Confederate monument in city park in 2011 · 98
41. Lakeland Confederate monument in 1915 · 100
42. Confederate monument in Lakeland's Munn Park in 2009 · 101

43. Confederate monument at the Hillsborough County Courthouse, Tampa, prior to its relocation in 1953 · 104
44. Detail of Hillsborough County Courthouse Confederate monument showing paired soldier statues · 105
45. Orlando Confederate monument at its original location, ca. 1915 postcard · 108
46. Orlando Confederate monument at its original location in a city intersection, ca. 1915 · 109
47. Orlando Confederate monument overlooking Lake Eola and the modern cityscape in 2009 · 110
48. Miami Confederate monument at its original location on the grounds of the Dade County Courthouse, ca. 1922 postcard · 111
49. Miami Confederate monument in Confederate Circle in the Miami City Cemetery in 2009 · 112
50. Brooksville Confederate monument in 1926 on the grounds of the Hernando County Courthouse · 115
51. Brooksville Confederate monument in 2008 · 115
52. Loring monument on the grounds of Government House in St. Augustine in 2008 · 117
53. Confederate monument in Key West's Bayview Park, ca. 1930s postcard · 120
54. Southernmost Confederate monument in Key West's Bayview Park in 2012 · 121
55. Dedication of Bradenton Confederate monument, 1924 · 122
56. Bradenton Confederate monument in front of the Manatee County Courthouse in 2009 · 124
57. Confederate monument on the grounds of the Putnam County Courthouse in Palatka in 1925 · 126
58. Palatka Confederate monument in 2008 · 126
59. Dedication of Robert E. Lee/Dixie Highway monument at Bradfordville, 1927 · 129
60. Robert E. Lee/Dixie Highway monument in its current location in 2010 · 131
61. Monument to Evander M. Law at his former home in Bartow in the 1930s · 133

62. Monument to Evander M. Law at its current location in 2013 · 134
63. United Daughters of the Confederacy fountain in the Lone Oak Cemetery in Leesburg in 2013 · 136
64. Confederate monument at the Gamble Plantation Historic State Park in 2011 · 137
65. Southern terminal monument of the Stonewall Jackson Highway in St. Petersburg in 2012 · 139
66. Monument honoring General "Stonewall" Jackson in Jefferson County in 2013 · 140
67. Confederate monument in Woodlawn Cemetery in West Palm Beach in 2012 · 142
68. DeLand monument, honoring Confederate veterans buried in Oakdale Cemetery, as it appeared in 2011 · 144
69. Robert E. Lee monument in downtown Fort Myers in 2011 · 146
70. Temporary Confederate monument at Live Oak, 1909 · 149
71. Monument to General J. J. Dickison in Jacksonville's Evergreen Cemetery in 2013 · 150
72. Confederate monument in Confederate veterans plot in Tampa's Woodlawn Cemetery in 2009 · 152
73. Florida Confederate women's monument, Jacksonville, ca. 1930s postcard · 156
74. Florida Confederate women's monument in Confederate Park, Jacksonville, 2009 · 157
75. Statue for Florida Confederate women's monument on cover of 1915 *Confederate Veteran* magazine · 158
76. Proposed alternate Florida Confederate women's monument in Jacksonville, ca. 1915 postcard · 159
77. Monument to alleged oldest Florida Confederate veteran, Bill Lundy, in Crestview in 2011 · 161
78. Dedication of St. Cloud Grand Army of the Republic meeting hall in 1914 · 168
79. Lynn Haven Grand Army of the Republic meeting hall and Union monument, ca. 1922 · 170
80. Union monument in Jacksonville's Evergreen Cemetery in 2010 · 172

81. Union monument in St. Petersburg's Greenwood Cemetery in 2011 · 175
82. Grand Army of the Republic monument in Orlando's Greenwood Cemetery in 2011 · 176
83. Union monument erected by Woman's Relief Corps in St. Cloud's Mt. Peace Cemetery as it appeared in 2012 · 177
84. Union veterans in front of Lynn Haven Grand Army of the Republic monument in 1928 · 179
85. Grand Army of the Republic monument in Lynn Haven park in 2012 · 180
86. Union monument and veterans plot in Tampa's Woodlawn Cemetery in 2009 · 182
87. Dedication of Grand Army of the Republic monument in Miami in 1939 · 184
88. Fund-raising medal for 1930s Miami Grand Army of the Republic monument · 185
89. Southernmost Grand Army of the Republic monument in Miami's Woodlawn Park Cemetery in 2012 · 186
90. Monument erected at Olustee Battlefield in 1991 to honor the Union dead · 193
91. United Daughters of the Confederacy monument in Oaklawn Cemetery in Lake City in 2008 · 195
92. Confederate veterans of the Battle of Olustee at dedication of the battlefield monument in 1912 · 198
93. Olustee Battlefield monument during dedication in 1912 · 199
94. Confederate monument on the Olustee Battlefield in 2005 · 200
95. Olustee Battlefield gate pillars showing urn and 1912 monument in background · 201
96. Dedication of Lake City Confederate monument to the Battle of Olustee in 1928 · 203
97. Confederate Battle of Olustee monument in downtown Lake City in 2008 · 204
98. Monument honoring General Alfred Holt Colquitt at Olustee Battlefield in 2005 · 206

99. Dedication of the monument honoring Brigadier General Joseph Finegan at the Olustee Battlefield in 1951 · 207
100. Confederate monument to the Battle of Marianna, ca. 1920s · 209
101. Confederate monument commemorating the Battle of Marianna as it appeared in 2008 · 210
102. Confederate pillar monument at Natural Bridge Battlefield before being covered with mortar stucco · 212
103. Confederate pillar monuments at Natural Bridge Battlefield in 1958 · 213
104. Dedication of the Confederate monument at Natural Bridge Battlefield in 1922 · 215
105. Monuments to the Battle of Natural Bridge as they appeared in 2008 · 216
106. Confederate veterans at the Gamble Plantation in the 1920s after its purchase by the United Daughters of the Confederacy · 219
107. Monument to yellow fever victims of the Ninetieth and Ninety-First New York Infantry at Key West · 222
108. Unveiling of the Judah P. Benjamin monument in Sarasota in 1942 · 224
109. Confederate monument commemorating the escape of Judah P. Benjamin as it appeared in 2011 · 225
110. Confederate monument at the Yellow Bluff Fort State Historic Site in 2008 · 227
111. Florida monument in the McGavock Confederate Cemetery, Franklin, Tennessee, in 2013 · 234
112. Monument in the Florida section of the Stonewall Confederate Cemetery in Winchester, Virginia, in 2011 · 237
113. State shafts surrounding the central monument at the Groveton Confederate Cemetery in Virginia in 2013 · 239
114. Florida monument at the Chickamauga Battlefield, Georgia, in the 1930s · 241
115. Florida monument on the Chickamauga National Battlefield in 2012 · 242
116. Florida shaft in the Confederate section of Blandford Cemetery in Petersburg, Virginia, in 2013 · 245

117. Confederate monument erected by the United Daughters of the Confederacy on Florida Circle in Vicksburg, Mississippi, as it appeared in 2012 · 247
118. Members of the Florida commission at Devil's Den, Gettysburg, Pennsylvania, in 1895 · 250
119. One of two Florida markers erected by the Gettysburg National Military Park Commission as it appeared in 2013 · 250
120. Dedication of the Florida monument at the Gettysburg Battlefield in 1963 · 252
121. Florida monument on the Gettysburg Battlefield in 2012 · 253
122. Unveiling of the Confederate monument at Arlington National Cemetery in 1914 · 256
123. Confederate monument erected in Crosby Lake Cemetery near Starke as it appeared in 2013 · 261
124. Confederate monument placed in Tampa's Oaklawn Cemetery in 1975 · 262
125. Union monument in Tampa Oaklawn Cemetery placed at an unknown date · 263
126. Monument commemorating Union attack on Tampa in Oaklawn Cemetery · 263
127. Confederate monument to "South Florida Bulldogs" erected in Bartow in 1982 · 265
128. Monument in Crawfordville dedicated to the service of Confederates from Wakulla County · 266
129. Confederate monument erected to commemorate those lost on the explosion of the *Chattahoochee* · 268
130. Monument to former slaves of Madison County · 269
131. Monument to the Second Regiment U.S. Colored Troops in Fort Myers · 270
132. Grand Army of the Republic monument placed in St. Cloud's Veterans Park in 2000 · 272
133. Jacksonville monument commemorating Confederate losses in local skirmishes · 273
134. Monument plaza of a Confederate "Flags across Florida" monument near White Springs · 274

135. Monument to Confederate and Union veterans buried in the Sebastian City Cemetery · 277
136. Monument in St. Cloud to Confederate veterans buried in Osceola County · 278
137. Monument to "Our Confederate Ancestors" near Perry · 280
138. Confederate monument placed in Marianna's Riverside Cemetery at the interment site of Battle of Marianna casualties · 281
139. Monument placed in Plant City to commemorate the First Battalion of the Confederate Special Cavalry · 282
140. Florida monument erected in 2008 in the Tullahoma Confederate Cemetery · 284
141. Confederate monument in the Gilchrist County Veteran's Park in Trenton in 2011 · 286
142. Monument in Magnolia Springs Cemetery to replace an earlier monument that is now missing · 288

PREFACE AND ACKNOWLEDGMENTS

Throughout the South, issues relating to how the Civil War is remembered lie just under the surface. There are some who joke, perhaps only half in jest, that the war isn't quite over yet. In keeping with the "Lost Cause" interpretation of the Civil War, they promote an idealized view of the antebellum South, argue that states' rights, tariffs, and taxes rather than slavery caused secession, and maintain that soldiers of the South were simply better than those who fought for the North and lost only because of the Union's overwhelming resources in men and matériel. There are those who hang on to the Confederacy as if this is what defines the South above any other quality. From our perspective as this book goes to press, the promotion of the Lost Cause narrative by the United Daughters of the Confederacy and other Confederate heritage groups has been an incredibly effective information campaign because it continues to permeate southern society. The erection of monuments throughout the South was, and continues to be, an integral part of this campaign of promoting the Lost Cause narrative.

Debate over how to commemorate the Civil War through monuments and other symbols is not new; it is embedded in the history of monument building from Reconstruction onward. Interesting to us is that the debate is just as vital today as it seems to have been a century or more ago. A recent proposal to place a Union monument on state-owned land at the Olustee Battlefield, in sight of the grand 1912 Confederate monument, raised furious opposition on the 150th anniversary of this battle. The anger expressed by those who felt that such a monument would, at best, diminish the message of the Confederate monument or, at worst, insult the dignity of Florida's Confederate heritage forced a postponement on deciding where, and even if, such a monument should be erected and spurred a Florida legislator to introduce a bill to require legislative approval before a monument is placed on state park land.

Erecting monuments, placing portraits of Robert E. Lee in schools and other public buildings, sponsoring textbooks, and naming schools for Confederates was all part of the work of the United Daughters of the Confederacy to vindicate the Confederate cause. In 1959, the Daughters were successful in having a new high school in Jacksonville named for Confederate officer Nathan Bedford Forrest. Forrest is surrounded by controversy regarding his treatment of black Union soldiers, and he was also instrumental in the initial formation of the Ku Klux Klan. With a student body that is now predominantly African American, the Duval County School Board voted to change the name of the high school, effective July 2014, but not without strong opposition from some in the community who argued that the Forrest name represented southern heritage and not racism. Confederate flags flying over Civil War monuments on public property continue to spark controversy in cities and towns throughout the South, as do the simple existence of Confederate monuments on the grounds of municipal buildings.

The Lost Cause may have lost much of its prominence in the "New South," but it is still anchored deeply in southern culture. However, as cracks appear in the Lost Cause ideology, we are fearful that Confederate Civil War monuments will be a casualty. Many of these are, of course, embodiments of the Lost Cause narrative, but they are also eloquent sentinels of a significant period in our history that, like the Civil War itself, has defined who we are as a nation and what we will become. This book will, we hope, promote an understanding of the human context behind Civil War monuments and help to secure their place in a cultural landscape that will someday not be totally bound by the story of the Lost Cause.

* * *

We owe a debt of gratitude to the scores of individuals who helped us during the course of research on this book. Some are unknown by name, such as the police officer in Lynn Haven who helped Dr. Lees find the Union monument in that city. Others are affiliated with historic sites and archives and made them accessible to us. We want to thank Martha Atkinson, Blandford Church and Cemetery, Petersburg, Virginia; Jeffrey A. Burgess, Barrancas National Cemetery, Pensacola; Eric Jacobson, the Battle of Franklin Trust, Franklin, Tennessee; Rebecca B. Saunders, Bay County Public Library, Panama City; Dale Cox, Civil War author and blogger; George Haskins, *Fieldguide to U.S. Public Monuments and Memorials* Web site; and Dr. Eugene Flemm, of Dunedin, Florida, for sharing his information on Florida monuments. With the Florida

Public Archaeology Network, we thank Barbara Hines (North Central Region), Sarah Miller and Ryan Harke (Northeast Region), Gregg Harding (formerly with East Central Region), Sarah Nohe (Southeast Region), and Rae Harper (formerly with West Central Region). Finally, we thank Laura Bass, Miriam Gan-Spalding, Deborah Mekeel, Adrienne Serra, and N. Adam Watson at the Florida State Archives, State Library of Florida; Sandy Boyar and Kathryn Travis, Goodwood Museum and Gardens, Tallahassee; John Rooney Jr., Historic Petersburg Foundation, Virginia; Sue Tindel, Jackson County Clerk of Circuit and County Courts, Marianna; Jim Burgess, Manassas National Battlefield Park, Virginia; Will Wilson, Vicksburg National Military Park; Tom Hambright, Monroe County Public Library, Key West; Bruce Graetz, Museum of Florida History, Tallahassee; John Coski, the Museum of the Confederacy, Richmond, Virginia; Robert Trapp, Natural Bridge Historical Society; Jacki Wilson, Pensacola Historical Society; Roger Heiple, Sons of Union Veterans; Charles Tingley, St. Augustine Historical Society; Lucille McClure, St. Cloud Heritage Museum; Marta Jones, St. Petersburg Museum of History; Sidney Johnston, Stetson University, DeLand; Claude Kenneson, Tallahassee Historical Society; Sue F. Cowger and Sandra Genetin, United Daughters of the Confederacy; Diane Merkel, Walton County Heritage Association, DeFuniak Springs; John Hendricks, West Nassau Historical Society; Jeffrey Lahurd, Sarasota County History Center; and Jeff Grzelak, Seventh Connecticut Infantry Reenactment Group.

If we have omitted anyone from this list we apologize and thank you nonetheless. We also want to acknowledge Dr. David Coles and David S. Gregory for their thoughtful and very useful review of our draft manuscript for the University Press of Florida and Meredith Babb, Sonia Dickey, and Nevil Parker of the Press for their help with our project. We are grateful for the careful attention paid to our manuscript by freelance copy editor Jonathan Lawrence.

Dr. Lees would like in addition to thank his family, and especially his colleague-wife Monica Beck but also children Emily, Beck, Kellen, and Hallie, for patience during the writing and revision of this book and for being usually willing travel companions on many expeditions to visit Civil War monuments in Florida and throughout the eastern United States. It was a journey that spanned five years, but it is now complete.

INTRODUCTION

> We are told by the historian of an earlier age that whenever the renowned men of the Roman commonwealth looked upon the statues of their ancestry, they felt their minds vehemently excited to virtue. It could not have been the bronze or marble that possessed this power, but the recollection of great actions which kindled a generous flame in their souls, not to be quelled until they also, by virtue and heroic deeds, had acquired equal fame and glory.
>
> **John J. Dickison, "Military History of Florida" (1898)**

In 1871 the Walton County Female Memorial Association erected a monument at the Euchee Valley Presbyterian Church (see figure 1). Engraved on its surfaces are the names of ninety-four Confederate soldiers from Walton County who died during the Civil War. They died in battle, hospital, camp, and at prisoner-of-war compounds in places throughout the South and in northern states as far away as Missouri, Illinois, Ohio, and New York. These soldiers went away to war and never returned, and in most cases their graves are far from home. For many, their place of burial is unknown. The families of these soldiers were deprived of a "proper" death, which in the mid-nineteenth century was supposed to happen at home in the presence of loved ones.[1] Also missing was a proper funeral as well as a grave in the family or local cemetery that could be visited and honored. The Euchee Valley monument became a substitute for the grave, and it served to assist family and community in mourning and remembering these tragically departed souls.

The Walton County monument is thus a physical symbol coded with meaning intended to help us remember—what memory scholars call a "mnemonic device."[2] At first this memory was one familiar to the community.

Figure 1. 1871 Walton County monument at Eucheeanna, ca. 1916 photograph. Courtesy of Mark Curenton, Apalachicola, Florida.

People in Walton County knew the men listed on the monument or their families, knew that most of these soldiers had fought and died far from home, and knew that neither they nor their bodies had returned to Florida. They understood why the monument helped with the mourning, and they knew this stone was important if these young men were to be remembered. They also probably knew a bit of the history of the monument and its creation, which is a story in its own right, with its own meaning.

The Walton County monument still stands, albeit in a different location, some 150 years after the war, and more than 140 years since it was dedicated. The stone remains, and while the inscription's overt meaning can still be garnered, the intimate knowledge of and connection with the men named on the monument and the events of the Civil War and its immediate aftermath has ended.

Today, the Walton County monument stands alongside many others in Florida that commemorate Confederate and Union participation in the Civil War. Joining these is a handful of monuments outside the state that tell of the participation of Florida regiments in the war's western and eastern theaters. These monuments were erected for specific reasons and with specific inspiration. Each has an individual story, often of great interest and importance and with its own deep meaning, which is not necessarily conveyed by the monument itself. Though each is unique and has aspects that set it apart from others, they were not developed in isolation. They were erected following patterns of history that rolled out of the Civil War and that have evolved and changed through time.

A changing roster of interested groups served as the main advocates and sponsors of these monuments. At one time these patterns and players were more clearly understood by mainstream society, but today this familiar knowledge has also faded. Civil War monuments in Florida are thus not just an assortment of sometimes fantastic outdoor sculpture, although they are indeed that also. They cannot be fully understood or appreciated without the benefit of the local, statewide, and national context of their times. Civil War monuments are very clearly more than the sum of their parts.

Our purpose in this book is to reconnect these seemingly random dots on the map that are Florida monuments to their individual stories and to the broader patterns of Civil War and postbellum history of which they have been a part and which affected their creation. We believe this is an intriguing story that deserves to be told, even though information used to piece this story together is scattered, sometimes conflicting, and found in obscure places if it can be found at all. We also believe the story of Florida monuments illustrates the war's lasting legacy in a state that by the end of the nineteenth century was growing rapidly, due largely to the influx of new residents from the northern United States—the Sunshine State's former adversary. Ironically, this influx was in part inspired by favorable reports of the state made by Union veterans who had spent time during the war on the Florida coast from Pensacola to the Keys to Fernandina.[3]

Finally, we think it important to confront the importance of Civil War monuments, which are part of our community landscapes and public spaces and cemeteries in the twenty-first century. This is especially true for Confederate monuments, given the ramifications of the appropriation of Confederate history and symbols by groups whose motives are questioned by many. How do we reconcile this appropriation and repurposing of symbolism borne on Civil War monuments with the intention of those who created these monuments, or were the intentions of their creators just the same as those we question today? Related here is our desire to confront, even if we cannot totally explain, the reasons behind the continued placement of monuments to the Civil War on our landscape, especially a new genre of monument that we feel is more concerned with honoring Confederate descendants than with commemorating and remembering the Civil War, Civil War soldier dead, and Civil War veterans.[4]

Nowhere should it be forgotten that the Civil War monuments in and about Florida are a result of a tragic moment of our national heritage that ultimately ended the institution of slavery in the United States and changed the nation and our collective narrative in so many other ways. Soldier, sailor, civilian, and slave died in the process; the nation was torn apart economically and socially; and more than a century was spent trying to go forward as one nation when half had won a major victory and the other half had suffered defeat.

We do believe that the Civil War monuments erected between the close of the Civil War and its centennial, as well as some erected more recently, remain important today. This importance relates to the commemoration of significant events of the Civil War and of the soldiers and sailors who took part, which at some level was a reason behind each of these monuments. For the twenty-first century, however, a new level of importance consists of understanding and remembering the difficult passage of this country between 1860 and at least World War I. We have emerged a nation that has finished much of the work of the Civil War—though some is certainly still a work in progress—and we are becoming the nation that our founders may have actually envisioned but were powerless to create in the context of their times.

* * *

The erection of monuments commemorating the Civil War began early in the conflict. Shortly after the December 17, 1861, Battle of Rowlett's Station, Kentucky, Union private Christian Friedrich August Bloedner carved a monument out of limestone to mark the graves and commemorate the death of thirteen fellow members of the Thirty-Second Indiana Volunteer Infantry (see figure 2). The Thirty-Second Indiana was composed largely of German immigrants, and Bloedner, a stonecutter, carved the inscription in his native tongue. In addition to listing those buried on the battlefield, the monument is dedicated to the "men of the 32nd First German Indiana Regiment sacrificed for the free Institutions of the Republic of the United States of North America."[5]

Little did Private Bloedner know that his would be one of the first of many thousands of monuments constructed to commemorate the Civil War. He would probably be equally mystified that monuments to the Civil War are

Figure 2. 1862 monument to the Thirty-Second Indiana dead from the 1861 Battle of Rowlett's Station, Kentucky, in the Cave Hill National Cemetery, 2004 photograph. Library of Congress, Prints and Photographs Division, image no. HALS KY-8-2.

part of the landscape of most if not all of the states that now make up our reconstructed nation and that they are still being erected today.

Bloedner's monument may be the most personal of the few monuments erected during the Civil War, but the others were also immediate responses to great human loss. On September 4, 1861, a monument was erected to Confederate brigadier general Francis Stebbings Bartow on the Manassas Battlefield by members of his brigade at the approximate spot where he was killed (see figure 3). What is apparently the base of this monument can still be seen at Virginia's Manassas National Battlefield Park, but the six-foot marble column dedicated to Bartow is believed to have been vandalized and destroyed by Union soldiers when they occupied the area in 1862.[6]

In 1863, after being heavily engaged and suffering substantial losses at the Battle of Stones River, Tennessee, members of Union general William Hazen's brigade erected a monument on ground that they had heroically defended during the battle. Made of limestone blocks, the monument is itself a ten-foot-square block (see figure 4). It is within the brigade cemetery containing the graves of forty-five officers and men killed in the battle and is dedicated "TO THE MEMORY OF ITS SOLDIERS WHO FELL AT STONES RIVER, DEC. 31ST 1862 'THEIR FACES TOWARDS HEAVEN, THEIR FEET TO THE FOE.'"[7]

Figure 3. 1861 Bartow monument at Manassas Battlefield, ca. 1872 lithograph. Library of Congress, Prints and Photographs Division, image no. LC-USZ62-17069.

Figure 4. 1863 monument to Hazen's Brigade at Stones River Battlefield, 1860s photograph. Library of Congress, Prints and Photographs Division, image no. LC-B811-2649.

In July 1864, members of the Union garrison of occupied Vicksburg, Mississippi, erected a marble obelisk on the battlefield commemorating the Confederate surrender on its first anniversary (see figure 5). Known as the "surrender monument," it was placed on the location between the Union and Confederate lines where Union general Ulysses S. Grant and Confederate general John C. Pemberton discussed terms of surrender.[8]

These few monuments are significant in signaling the impact that the battles and the Civil War in general had on the soldiers involved. Their rarity is symbolic as well, and certainly speaks to the press of war and the eventual realization that the acreage of hallowed ground was becoming staggering as the war progressed.

In 1865, after the surrender of the major Confederate armies but while some Rebel troops remained in the field in the far west, the U.S. War Department ordered two monuments erected at the Manassas battlefields, one on Henry Hill to commemorate the first battle, in July 1861, and another at Groveton to commemorate the second battle, in August 1862 (see figure 6). Both were dedicated "IN MEMORY OF THE PATRIOTS WHO FELL" and expressed an incipient commitment by the federal government to Civil War commemoration.[9]

Figure 5. 1864 surrender monument at the Vicksburg Battlefield, 1910s photograph. Library of Congress, Prints and Photographs Division, image no. LC-D4-73332.

Figure 6. 1865 Groveton monument commemorating Union soldiers at the Battle of Second Manassas, 1860s photograph. Library of Congress, Prints and Photographs Division, image no. LC-B817-7299.

Except for the end-of-war monuments at Manassas, which were erected when the outcome of the war was certain, these wartime monuments were erected by Confederate and Union armies in the field, both of whom believed they could win the war. As the spring of 1865 drew to a close, there was no question that this dynamic had changed and that the United States would become a nation at peace but divided by status of victor and defeated. How the nation dealt with this reality speaks to the heart of how the Civil War was remembered through the building of monuments.

* * *

By the summer of 1861, Florida and ten other states had seceded from the Union to form the Confederate States of America. In less than five years they were defeated and occupied territories. At the end of the Civil War as many as 850,000 Union and Confederate soldiers and sailors had died of battlefield wounds or, more commonly, diseases such as chronic diarrhea and malaria.[10]

This included some five or six thousand dead from Florida, a sizable number compared to the state's free population at the start of the war of only 78,679 persons. Northerner or Southerner, most were buried far from home in hurriedly dug and poorly marked graves. By war's end, the landscape and economy of each of the states of the Confederacy were devastated along with parts of several border states with divided loyalties and the western lands of the Indian nations known collectively as the Five Civilized Tribes.

When the last musket fell silent in the summer of 1865, the great armies of the South went home, as did most of the Union soldiers and sailors who formed one of the largest armies the modern world had ever known. Confederates went quietly back to a place they hardly recognized, while many of the Union ranks assembled for grand parades through a conquered Richmond or through the streets of the nation's capital before heading home.[11] But even for the victorious, home was forever changed because of voids left by those who had died and because of the brutal experience of four long years of civil war.

The experience of war was in many ways the same for soldiers from North and South alike. It was an experience forever welded to the loss they had witnessed and had themselves suffered. Between 1861, when Confederate soldiers erected a monument to their fallen Brigadier General Bartow, and 1865, when the Fifth Pennsylvania Heavy Artillery erected monuments on the battlefields of First and Second Manassas, soldiers and citizens North and South had come to realize that the Civil War was the most profound event they or their country would likely ever experience.[12]

When we look at today's landscape and see the thousands of monuments to the Civil War erected within the lifetime of the war's veterans, it is clear that none wanted future generations to forget their shared sacrifice. But as scholars of social memory have pointed out in a growing body of literature about the Civil War, the meaning of that sacrifice differed for the victor and the defeated during the lifetime of the veterans and is therefore not the same for those living today.[13]

One outcome of the war was the imminent reunification of a country torn apart by a seeming act of self-destruction. The states and their populations formerly in rebellion were devastated by this outcome, and they were soon suffering an armed occupation that was often under the watchful eye of U.S. Colored Troops recruited from newly freed slaves. In the occupied South, any attempt to honor or commemorate the Southern cause or its soldier dead was regarded as a continuation of the act of treason that had started the rebellion.

Another outcome of the war was that many thousands of Union and Confederate soldiers lay buried in places generally far from home, often in what was still perceived as enemy territory, and in inadequate and poorly marked graves. Veterans and the wives, mothers, fathers, siblings, and children of those dead soldiers feared the neglect or outright desecration of these graves at the hands of former foes. They did not want the sacrifice of their fellow soldiers or loved ones to be forgotten or, perhaps worse, to have been in vain. Possessing the power to do so, the federal government and loyal Union states ensured that their dead were accounted for and properly buried, many in newly created national cemeteries, and ensured that Confederate soldiers—who, in their view, died as traitors—would receive no such due. Although southern states stepped up to do their part, the nation remained divided through openly different respect for and treatment of the soldier dead.[14]

For Union veterans, the Grand Army of the Republic (GAR) appeared shortly after the war's end as the preeminent veterans association of that conflict. Founded in 1866, the GAR had long-reigning influence on veterans. Through impressive numbers (more than four hundred thousand members in 1890), they had a very effective voice in defining the nature of commemoration through influence on federal programs to provide care of the remains of Union dead, to care for living Union veterans, and to commemorate national battlefields such as Antietam, Chickamauga, Vicksburg, Shiloh, and Gettysburg. For decades following the war, the reconstructed nation's programs of commemorating the soldier dead did not include soldiers of the Confederacy, partly due to the efforts of the GAR.[15]

In the Reconstruction-era South, preservation of Confederate war graves was allowed by occupying federal forces, but commemoration of the Confederacy itself was treated as an act of continued rebellion. A major force in southern commemoration therefore became local Ladies' Memorial Associations (LMAs), which were originally dedicated to the care of soldier graves. Between seventy and one hundred such associations were established throughout the postwar South. These groups undertook efforts to provide proper burials for Confederate dead, including the establishment of numerous Confederate cemeteries.[16]

As time went by, these associations undertook more overt forms of commemoration. Many of them eventually merged into the United Daughters of the Confederacy (UDC) after the formation of that organization in 1894. The UDC, along with the United Confederate Veterans (established in 1889), took charge of commemorating the southern dead and the memory of soldier sacrifice that was separate from that being championed by the federal government, Union states, and the GAR.[17]

Unable to celebrate victory, the southern commemoration wrapped itself around the bravery and valor of the soldier and the righteousness of the cause for which the South had fought. Just as the death of Abraham Lincoln had solidified northern grief around a theme of the righteous cause of the nation and the righteous duty of its soldier dead, the deaths of Confederate leaders Robert E. Lee in 1870 and Jefferson Davis in 1889 did much to fuel the origin story of the new South. At the forefront of this commemoration was the narrative of the "Lost Cause," in which the valor of the southern soldier and the right and just cause for which he had fought and died was promoted.[18]

Although Florida is often left out or marginalized in national Civil War narratives, it contributed troops and provisions to the Confederacy and suffered itself from battle, blockade, economic privation, and the loss of its native sons in far-off theaters of war. Florida was involved in a significant way in the war, and it was equally involved in the social forces that shaped the way the victors and the defeated commemorated their different realities within an increasingly reunited country.

When the war ended, about a third of Florida's Confederate soldiers were buried in the western and eastern theaters of war in which they had participated. The state's economy was, like that of other southern states, in ruin, but it rebounded at the end of the nineteenth century at the hands of lumber and fishing industries and increasingly due to a boom in tourism and retirement that drew more and more people to Florida. Ironically, the growth in population included many Union veterans, many of whom were members of the GAR. Despite their increasing numbers, the landscape of monuments within Florida remained overwhelmingly Confederate.

On the national stage, the few monuments erected during the war and the thousands that followed were diverse in form and message, yet they can be grouped into two broad categories: those that consecrate ground hallowed by human sacrifice and those that we call community monuments. The former are best exemplified by those found on battlefields; they typically reference accomplishments and sacrifice by military units, such as regiments, or individuals, generally officers. The monuments erected at Rowlett's Station, Stones River, Vicksburg, and Manassas fall within this category. The Rowlett's Station and Stones River monuments consecrate the sacrifice of particular units—the Thirty-Second Indiana and Hazen's Brigade, respectively; the Bartow monument at Manassas commemorates the loss of an individual Confederate officer who was among the first to die in battle; the Vicksburg surrender monument marks a place of significant victory for the Union; and the Manassas monuments consecrate the sacrifice of all Union participants in First and Second Manassas. The reasons for the consecration of the ground on which they were placed were clearly expressed in each. Postwar monuments in this category were often erected by or with the assistance of state governments, often at the behest of veterans or veteran organizations such as the GAR or groups like the UDC.

Because they are not constrained by commemoration of hallowed ground, community monuments are more diverse, although they often also reference sacrifice of particular individuals, military units, or engagements of the Civil War. City parks, the grounds of county courthouses, and veteran plots in cemeteries were common places for community monuments. The Walton County monument, for example, discussed at the beginning of this introduction, references the ultimate sacrifice of ninety-four individual Confederate soldiers yet is placed far from where these soldiers died.

More common are community monuments dedicated to the general sacrifice of soldier dead or veterans. These were an important postwar work of the LMAs, the UDC, the GAR, and similar groups. Some of these monuments (in Florida most often Confederate) extol the virtues and the unequaled valor of soldiers and sailors and the righteousness of the cause for which they fought.

The following chapters present a narrative of Florida monuments to the Civil War, focusing on the century between the war's close and its centennial commemoration in the 1960s. We also discuss more recent monument building. Chapter 1 considers the Reconstruction period. Although only a handful of monuments were erected in Florida prior to the end of Reconstruction in 1877, we singled out this period because of its significance for what followed. The meaning of Civil War monuments is not easily understood without an understanding of Reconstruction-era policies and practices. Commemoration of the war through creation of monuments became part of the new social battleground over how the war was remembered. Some have argued, in fact, that monument building in the late nineteenth century made reconciliation more difficult until well into the twentieth century.[19]

Despite the initial reconciliatory intentions of Lincoln and others, Reconstruction soon became increasingly difficult for the South. Lincoln's assassination and the loss of his leadership on the issue were keenly felt. Also,

Figure 7. Civil War–era commemorative envelope reflecting Northern sentiments of the great human cost of the Civil War. Courtesy of William B. Lees.

after the euphoria of victory had subsided, the war's grim effects began to sink in for those in the loyal northern states, including an increasing bitterness regarding the treatment of Union prisoners of war held in the South at places such as Andersonville, Georgia (see figure 7). Policies and practices were established that for decades established a federal double standard for the treatment of Civil War dead and Civil War veterans. Although perhaps understandable from the point of view of Union veterans, their families, and the states they served, this position did nothing to help southerners feel that they had been received back into the nation—even after their state governments had been recognized and their congressional delegations seated.

Following the review of monuments erected during Reconstruction, the next three chapters cover monuments constructed from the end of Reconstruction through the Civil War Centennial. The Confederate community monuments discussed in chapter 2 are by far the most numerous Civil War monuments in Florida. Found in cemeteries, parks, and on courthouse grounds throughout the state, these were generally the work of local LMAs at first, but during the twentieth century the UDC became their primary sponsor. The underlying purpose of these monuments quickly became one of vindication of the South through promotion of the Lost Cause narrative. This development is evident in the evolving messages engraved on these monuments and, by corollary, with a lessening of this rhetoric during the latter part of the twentieth century as the UDC increasingly believed they had achieved reconciliation with honor for the Confederate soldier dead and veterans, as well as vindication for the South.

As chapter 3 details, despite the movement of many Union veterans to Florida after the war, including to Union veteran communities at Zephyrhills, St. Cloud, and Lynn Haven after 1900, Union monuments are uncommon in the state. The message carried on these is muted compared to Confederate monuments of the same period and Union monuments in the northern states. They are largely confined to cemeteries, with only one found in a city park.

Chapter 4 examines monuments constructed to consecrate hallowed ground. The first section of this chapter looks at such monuments within Florida. Despite the existence of locations in the state that could easily be favored for placement of Union monuments, there is only one dating after the end of Reconstruction and prior to the Civil War Centennial that consecrates Union hallowed ground. In fact, efforts to incorporate commemoration of Union participation on at least one Florida battlefield in the early twentieth century—the 1864 Battle of Olustee—became a battle in its own right that was won by the UDC and its supporters. The second section reviews monuments commemorating Florida's Confederate soldiers that were erected in other states. Four of these monuments are in cemeteries, and three are on battlefields. A number of monuments in other states also commemorate Florida along with other states of the Confederacy. Of the battlefield monuments, only one was erected during the lifetime of Florida veterans, at Chickamauga, with the other two being recent additions at Vicksburg and Gettysburg.

Chapter 5 reviews the period from the war's centennial to the present and considers both Union and Confederate monuments. The erection of some

Civil War monuments during this period tells a significant part of the history of the war in Florida, such as those dedicated to the Second U.S. Colored Troops at Fort Myers, to the CSS *Chattahoochee* in Chattahoochee, and to the Confederate "Cow Cavalry" at Plant City.

The conclusion considers why monuments continue to be erected to this day, the changing nature of Civil War monuments in Florida, and the importance of these monuments for our current and future society and cultural landscape. As we become further removed from the people and events of the Civil War, and as the focus of our state's education becomes more on math and science and less on civics and history, Civil War monuments and other physical markers of our heritage are increasingly at risk yet retain a great and fundamental importance.

Civil War monuments were once central to everyday life in the communities in which they were placed. Although they retain a significant message for the future, that message may be different from the one that was originally intended. While respecting the original message and those who caused it to be embedded on monuments, and while honoring all of those affected by the Civil War, it is important to add this new message to the narrative of historic Civil War monuments. The message is one of understanding the struggle that the United States underwent following the Civil War to reconcile victory and loss and to move the nation forward from the brink of destruction. These monuments are now not so much about the Civil War as they are about our struggle to regain a national identity after the loss of a generation of our native sons.

1

RECONSTRUCTION AND BEYOND

Different Memories

They died far from the home that gave them birth.

Inscription on monument in St. Augustine, Florida, 1872

President Abraham Lincoln's fourth Annual Message to Congress,[1] on December 6, 1864, closed with the following sentence: "In stating a single condition of peace I mean simply to say that the war will cease on the part of the Government whenever it shall have ceased on the part of those who began it."[2] In April 1865, General Robert E. Lee and what remained of the Army of Northern Virginia, including the remnants of the Florida Brigade, had retreated from Petersburg, Virginia, and were trapped by Lieutenant General Ulysses S. Grant's substantial forces near Appomattox Courthouse, Virginia. Resigned to the futility of further resistance, Lee asked Grant for terms of surrender, and on April 9 he surrendered his troops. The surrender terms allowed Confederate officers and enlisted men to receive paroles and return home. Officers could retain a horse, sidearm, and personal baggage, and enlisted men could keep a horse if they had one but forfeited all other military material. Today, Lee's surrender at Appomattox has become synonymous with the end of the American Civil War, but other important commands had to follow suit before hostilities would truly come to an end.[3]

After learning of Lee's surrender, General Joseph E. Johnston surrendered the Army of Tennessee on April 26 to Major General William Tecumseh Sherman at the James Bennitt (Bennett)[4] farm at Durham Station (modern Durham), North Carolina. After a complicated negotiation, Johnston accepted terms of surrender similar to those accepted by Lee.[5] Reporting on Johnston's surrender, the *New York Times* proclaimed, "With the surrender of JOHNSTON the last formidable fragment of the rebel armies is extinct, and truly, indeed, the last days of the rebellion are rapidly approaching."[6]

On May 4, at Citronelle, Alabama, Lieutenant General Richard A. Taylor surrendered his small command, and on June 2, General E. Kirby Smith accepted the terms of surrender for the Army of the Trans-Mississippi aboard the USS *Fort Jackson* in Galveston Bay, Texas. Most units of his Trans-Mississippi command had already dissolved and returned home after Lieutenant General Simon Buckner agreed to terms on May 26 in New Orleans. Both Taylor and Smith surrendered to Major General E. R. S. Canby with terms similar to those extended to Lee. One Confederate commander in the West, Brigadier General Stand Watie, a Cherokee, stubbornly refused to come in despite knowledge of the surrender of Smith, under whose command he served. Watie finally surrendered on June 23 at the town of Doaksville in the Choctaw Nation (what is today Choctaw County, Oklahoma). With the surrender of Lee, Johnston, Taylor, Smith, and Watie, the Civil War had come to an end.[7]

THE WAR'S END IN FLORIDA

By the time of these surrenders, many of the key places along Florida's long coast had long been under control of Union forces. Fort Pickens in Pensacola, Fort Taylor in Key West, and Fort Jefferson in the Dry Tortugas had, in fact, never left Union control and had been crucial in the establishment and maintenance of the Gulf Blockading Squadrons starting in 1861. After its occupation in November 1861, Egmont Key was a base of operations for the Union blockading fleet for the remainder of the war. In 1862 the Union permanently occupied Fernandina and Fort Clinch (March), St. Augustine and Fort Marion (March), and Pensacola and Forts Barrancas and McRee (May), and temporarily occupied Apalachicola (April). Jacksonville changed hands four times beginning in 1862, but by the end of the war it was firmly in Union hands. In 1864 Union forces temporarily occupied Tampa, Manatee (Bradenton), and, on two occasions, Palatka on the St. Johns River. By early 1864, Union troops had taken control of Fort Myers and Cedar Key.[8]

From these occupied Florida communities, Union forces actively recruited enlistees for newly formed regiments of U.S. Colored Troops and, for service in the Union navy, from escaped slaves who had taken refuge at those places. The First and Second Florida Cavalry Regiments, which served in the Union army, recruited white Unionists and Confederate deserters. Regardless of these successes, Union attempts to gain significant advantage in the interior of the state failed when an invasion launched from Jacksonville in February 1864 ended in Union defeat at the Battle of Olustee. In March 1865 a Union campaign directed at Fort Ward on the St. Marks River and probably ultimately at Tallahassee failed when the Confederates defeated a force composed largely of African American troops at the Battle of Natural Bridge.[9]

For Florida, the surrender of General Joseph Johnston on April 26, 1865, was of particular importance. Johnston didn't merely surrender his army in the field; he also surrendered all Confederate troops in the Carolinas, Georgia, and Florida. Stacking arms at the Bennitt Farm with Johnston's Army of Tennessee were the remnants of the First Florida Infantry Regiment Consolidated (First, Third, Fourth, Sixth, and Seventh Florida Infantry and First Florida Cavalry) and Abell's Light Artillery. In Florida, Major General Sam Jones, commander of Confederate forces in the state, had initially called for continued resistance after Lee's surrender. However, Jones received word on April 29 of Johnston's surrender, which, under the terms of that settlement, included the capitulation of Confederate troops in Florida. The Civil War in Florida was over.[10]

Following Johnston's surrender, Brigadier General Edward M. McCook and his staff entered Tallahassee on May 10 in order to establish federal control and authority in Florida and to accept the formal surrender of all Confederate troops in the state. On May 10, after the surrender of Tallahassee, Captain Charles G. Campbell lowered the Confederate flag at Fort Ward, and on May 12, McCook's Union troops took possession and raised the United States flag over Florida's last coastal fort to surrender and the target of the Union campaign that had ended in failure only two months prior. In a ceremony in Tallahassee on May 20 marking the formal transition of power, McCook announced the Emancipation Proclamation and raised the United States flag over the state capitol. By early June, all regular Confederate units in the state had formally surrendered, and organized armed insurrection in the state was at an end.[11]

Johnston's Surrender and Lincoln's Reconstruction

When Johnston surrendered his command, it came at the end of an involved negotiation over not just military surrender but also political issues related to the restoration of the Union. Important, however, is that his surrender came on the heels of the April 14 assassination of President Lincoln; Sherman had in fact shared a telegram about the assassination with Johnston when they first met to discuss surrender on April 17. There is no doubt that this tragic event had profound implications for the outcome of these negotiations.[12]

A year earlier, the Union invasion of the interior of Florida that ended in defeat at the Battle of Olustee had both military and political goals.[13] With a victory in this campaign, Lincoln had hoped that pro-Union residents would help to establish a reconstructed government along the lines proposed in his December 8, 1863, proclamation. In a January 13, 1864, communication with Major General Quincy A. Gilmore at Hilton Head Island, South Carolina, Lincoln had stated, "I understand an effort is being made by some worthy gentlemen to reconstruct a loyal State government in Florida. . . . I wish the thing done in the most speedy way possible, so that when done it will be within the range of the late proclamation on the subject."[14] Although Lincoln was interested in a reconstructed Florida as a means to garner more support for his reelection, there can be little doubt that he also wanted to begin in Florida the process of reconstruction that had already begun in Arkansas, Louisiana, and Tennessee. The failure of the 1864 Union military campaign in Florida ended these hopes.

Under Lincoln's leadership, work to extend into peacetime protection of the freedom granted to slaves by the wartime Emancipation Proclamation and to extend freedom to all slaves in the nation had resulted in Congress's passing the Thirteenth Amendment on January 31, 1865. This amendment provided that "Neither slavery nor involuntary servitude, except as a punishment for crime whereof the party shall have been duly convicted, shall exist within the United States, or any place subject to their jurisdiction." Although not yet ratified by the required number of states at the time of the surrender of the Confederate armies in the spring of 1865, it was clear to all of the southern states that the former slaves would be free, regardless of their subsequent political and social status.[15]

In early April 1865, General Johnston had been in communication with President Jefferson Davis and Secretary of War John C. Breckinridge, who were in nearby Greensboro, North Carolina, after evacuating the capital at Richmond. Although Davis initially wanted Johnston to continue the fight, after learning of Lee's surrender he allowed Johnston to meet with Sherman to discuss terms. They met on April 17 at the Bennitt Farm near Durham Station. Sherman and Johnston met again the following day and signed conditional terms of surrender that disbanded Confederate armies under Johnston's command. Southern regiments would return to their respective state capitals, where they would deposit arms in state arsenals, and each officer and enlisted man would sign an oath of allegiance. Also, current Confederate state governments would be recognized upon the taking of loyalty oaths by state officers and legislators, except where Union governments had been established in states during the course of the war, in which case the U.S. Supreme Court would determine which were legitimate. Additional terms reestablished federal courts, restored individual political rights and rights of property, and provided a general amnesty for the individuals and states participating in the rebellion. Basically, execution of oaths of allegiance by Confederate soldiers and by officers and legislators of the states in rebellion would restore the Union to a status very much like the one before hostilities had erupted four years earlier.[16] A meeting between Sherman and Lincoln at City Point on March 27 may have influenced the conciliatory nature of these terms. Lincoln discussed reconstruction, although these terms went well beyond what he had contemplated by offering, among other things, to recognize the legality of the state governments of the Confederacy.[17]

Sherman sent the terms agreed to by General Johnston to President Andrew Johnson for approval. Coming on the heels of Lincoln's assassination, and given the extremely conciliatory nature of the proposal, Secretary of War Edwin M. Stanton and the president quickly rejected this agreement.[18] Johnson dispatched General Grant to Raleigh, North Carolina, where he arrived on April 24 to prepare to resume hostilities against Johnston's army. Grant instructed Sherman to attempt to negotiate a military surrender from Johnston modeled after terms agreed to by Lee a few days earlier. Sherman and Johnston met again on April 26 and agreed to those terms.[19]

It will never be known if Lincoln would have, had he lived, accepted terms for the surrender of Johnston which included political reconstruction as well as military surrender, and if reconstruction might have been based on the original agreement signed by Johnston and Sherman. He certainly would have modified the conditional terms forwarded to Washington to include freedom for slaves and nonpayment of the Confederate debt, among other things.[20] In the end, the terms of Johnston's surrender were similar to those agreed to by Lee for the Army of Northern Virginia, and questions of personal rights and the political reintegration of the states in rebellion were left unresolved.

President Johnson's view of reconstruction was certainly harsher than Lincoln's, even after Lincoln had been hardened by four years of brutal and costly war. Johnson believed that state governments were essentially intact because secession had not been legally possible and that it was instead necessary to deal with those individuals who had subverted the state governments. He was intent on unseating the power of the landed southern aristocracy, whom he felt was responsible for the late war. He believed in protecting the freedom of former slaves but did not believe that this "laboring, landless, and homeless class" deserved much more in the way of civil rights. Johnson's meetings with delegations of Radical Republicans and African Americans shortly after he took office did not change his beliefs.[21]

On May 29, 1865, Johnson issued two proclamations that made clear his approach to reconstruction.[22] The first was an amnesty proclamation for the non-loyal individuals in the states in rebellion, and the second outlined the path to restoration of North Carolina to the Union. Johnson saw his first proclamation as being derived from that which Lincoln had issued in December of the previous year and providing a swift pathway for national reunification.[23] Johnson's proclamation differed in one important way, however, in that it excluded fourteen "classes of persons" from being able to receive amnesty and pardon. These fourteen classes included officials of the Confederate government, officers of the Confederate army and navy, governors of the states in rebellion, all non-loyal persons with taxable property over $20,000, and many others who in one way or another directly aided in the rebellion. This provided that the hierarchy of the Confederate government and military and members of the landed aristocracy would not participate in the reconstructed state governments or serve in posts, including Congress, of the federal government.[24]

Johnson's second proclamation concerned "Reorganization of a Constitutional Government in North Carolina."[25] This proclamation appointed a provisional governor and charged him with convening a constitutional convention. Delegates to the convention must have been eligible to vote in the state prior to the 1861 secession and were required to take and subscribe to the oath of amnesty as set forth in the first proclamation, which of course excluded the landed aristocracy and many officers and officials in the Confederate military and civil government. Similar instruments followed this proclamation in June and July for Mississippi, South Carolina, Florida, Georgia, Alabama, and Texas.[26]

The provisional governors appointed by the proclamations were required to convene conventions to adopt new constitutions that would abolish slavery, renounce secession, and repudiate the Confederate debt. Johnson appointed William Marvin as the provisional governor of Florida on July 13, 1865. On October 10 Marvin convened the state's constitutional convention, and by the time it was adjourned on November 7 the delegates had annulled the ordinance of secession, prohibited slavery, repudiated the Confederate debt, and extended protection of the courts to former slaves. Suffrage remained restricted to white males over the age of twenty-one. Similar conventions, with similar results, were held in other former Confederate states that fall.[27]

Believing they had satisfied requirements to restore their relationship within the federal government, Florida and other southern states dispatched their delegations to the Thirty-Ninth Congress, which convened on December 4. Despite Johnson's early intentions, these delegations included many former Confederates, including many officers and officials. Congress was highly critical of Johnson's executive actions and refused to recognize these newly reformed governments or seat their delegations. In 1866 Johnson further angered Congress when on February 19 he vetoed an extension of the Freedmen's Bureau, authorized on March 6, 1865, which was in charge of all relief and educational activities for refugees and freedmen, and on March 27, 1866, when he vetoed the Civil Rights Act of 1866, which declared all persons born in the United States except Native Americans to be citizens.[28] Although Congress overturned Johnson's veto in both cases, to protect these civil rights from future congressional action and from the Supreme Court it also, on June 13, 1866, passed the Fourteenth Amendment, which extended citizenship to all persons born or naturalized in the United States, denied seats in Congress and many other offices to certain individuals engaged in insurrection or rebellion, and repudiated debts incurred by the states in rebellion. Congress further made ratification of this amendment a condition of a state's reintegration into the Union. Final adoption of the Fourteenth Amendment did not occur until July 1868.[29]

Johnson's policies and the confrontation with Congress led the way for Radical Republicans to gain super-majorities in both houses during the 1866 midterm elections, and on March 2, 1867, Congress passed, over the president's veto, "An Act to Provide for the More Efficient Government of the

Rebel States" (Reconstruction Act of 1867). This act established five military districts within the former Confederacy in which an appointed military governor would oversee martial law and new state constitutional conventions. Election of delegates to these conventions was through universal male suffrage. The convention was to ratify the Fourteenth Amendment and guarantee black male suffrage as a condition for restoration of a full relationship within the Union, upon final approval of Congress. Due to resistance from the southern states, Congress imposed further pressure with three additional Reconstruction Acts passed in March 1867, July 1867, and March 1868. Having ratified the Fourteenth Amendment prior to the March 2 Reconstruction Act, Tennessee was the first state, in July 1866, readmitted to full status within the Union. Florida attained readmission to full political status in 1868 along with Alabama, Arkansas, Louisiana, North Carolina, and South Carolina. Virginia, Mississippi, Texas, and Georgia followed in early 1870. This did not end, however, military oversight of some states of the former Confederacy, including Florida.[30]

In May 1868 the Republican Party nominated Ulysses S. Grant as its presidential candidate. Grant's election in November of that year ended the stalemate that had existed between Democratic president Andrew Johnson and the Republican Congress. Between his election and inauguration in March 1869, Congress passed the Fifteenth Amendment to the Constitution, which guaranteed male suffrage regardless of race, color, or previous condition of servitude. Ratification came one year later, on February 3, 1870. In addition to supporting legislative solutions to reconstruction, Grant used the military to protect the rights of African Americans living in the South.[31]

National interest in reconstruction began to wane in the 1870s, and Republican control in southern states began to weaken and was eventually lost to the Democrats. The first states to revert to conservative Democratic rule were Virginia and Tennessee in 1869, and the last were Louisiana and Florida in January 1877.[32]

Grant's presidency concluded after two terms, and in 1876, in a very close and contested election in which both the Republican and Democratic candidates claimed victory, complex political maneuvering resulted in an equally complex political deal that placed Republican Rutherford B. Hayes in the White House in exchange for an end to federal policies of Reconstruction, including removal of federal troops from Florida, South Carolina, and Louisiana. Prior to leaving office, Grant ordered the withdrawal of federal troops from Florida. In that same election, Democrats gained control of the

Florida Legislature, signaling an end to Reconstruction policies in the state. The Thirteenth, Fourteenth, and Fifteenth Amendments protected African American freedom and voting; unfortunately, with the end of federal Reconstruction and the return of Democratic rule in Florida and other southern states, the freedoms and the social and economic progress that had been fought for by the Republican Congress under President Johnson and by the strongly Republican Congress under President Grant were eroded by new state laws and regulations that went unquestioned for generations by the federal government.[33]

ECONOMIC AND HUMAN COST OF WAR FOR FLORIDA

Within this context, Florida struggled to recover economically. Despite the loss of property in the form of slaves, which constituted slightly less than half of the state's population at the start of the Civil War, Florida had suffered less from destruction of economic infrastructure than had many other southern states. Nonetheless, actions, especially along the Florida coast, had left the state's economy much diminished. The Union navy's blockading squadrons had relentlessly attacked industry along the coast and had protected emancipated slaves in refugee camps.

As they withdrew from coastal towns, Confederates often destroyed economic resources so that they would be of no use to the Union forces who would soon occupy these places. In West Florida, for example, as part of the Confederate withdrawal from Pensacola in the spring of 1862, orders came to Lieutenant Colonel William H. Beard of the Confederate First Florida Infantry to "burn every saw-mill, planing-mill, sash factory, every foot of lumber, and all boats of every description. If there is any cotton at any of the places you will not fail to destroy it."[34] These properties on the Blackwater and Escambia Rivers represented one of the state's most advanced industrial districts. Burned were sawmills and gristmills, houses, stores, wagons, and boats of every description. In a letter to Florida governor John Milton in April 1862, one local resident bitterly complained, "The effect of this unnecessary wanton and atrocious vandalism reaches much beyond the individuals who have suffered. This Milling business was the only support of Milton, St [Santa] Rosa County and contributed in no little degree to the prosperity of Pensacola. The sudden and utter destruction of the basis of that which it has cost 30 years to build up and establish completely annihilates the population of St [Santa] Rosa County and inflicts a stab upon Pensacola she will not recover from for many years."[35]

Large portions of the state between the areas occupied by Union forces and those controlled by the Confederacy became virtual no-man's lands. Soldiers and looters stripped houses of anything of value, and fields became overgrown. Except for occupying Union troops, residents virtually abandoned once-thriving towns, which suffered accordingly. Union brigadier general Alexander Asboth's description of Pensacola in 1863 provides a typical report of the destruction: "The houses are nearly all deserted, and deprived not only of their furniture, but mostly of doors and windows, the streets covered with high weeds and bushes."[36] On a journey from Alabama to seek refuge with the Union blockading squadron off Choctawhatchee Bay in the summer of 1863, Wade H. Richardson described passing through an uninhabited wilderness with abandoned and burned houses that stretched some fifty miles inland of the coast in West Florida, "where roads had grown up with wire grass. They had not been used for two or three years, and only by the scars on the trees could we tell where a road had been."[37] Finally, and profoundly, the state's 61,745 African Americans listed as slaves on the 1860 U.S. Census—roughly half of Florida's population in that year—were now free but with an undefined social status.

Along with economic loss was the loss of a generation of the South's native sons. Roughly a third of Florida's soldiers had died during the conflict, many in far-off places such as Virginia, Maryland, Pennsylvania, Mississippi, and Tennessee. Private Confederate cemeteries established throughout the South after the war served as the final resting place of the dead from nearby camps, hospitals, and battlefields. Among these are cemeteries at Winchester and Petersburg, Virginia, at Franklin, Tennessee, and at Vicksburg, Mississippi, which contain Florida soldiers. Other cemeteries established during the war, such as the one at Tullahoma, Tennessee, are the final resting place for other Florida soldiers. Three Confederate soldiers from Florida who died in action around Washington, D.C., lie buried in the Confederate plot in Arlington National Cemetery (a rare exception to the general prohibition of interring Confederates in national cemeteries).

Established in 1866, the Stonewall Confederate Cemetery in Winchester contains a Florida plot with thirty-six individual graves and a monument to Florida dedicated in 1902 (described in chapter 4). These soldiers of the Second, Fifth, and Eighth Regiments of Florida Infantry died between September and December 1862 and were probably wounded in the nearby September

1862 Battle of Antietam, Maryland, and subsequently died in hospital in the Winchester vicinity. In Petersburg, the local Ladies' Memorial Association, organized in 1866, received a portion of that city's Blandford Cemetery for Confederate reinterments. The Florida section contains ten Florida soldiers identified by name and others unknown from the siege of Petersburg as well as a Florida shaft monument erected between 1917 and 1919 (see chapter 4).

Established in Franklin in 1866, the McGavock Confederate Cemetery has a Florida plot containing the graves of four Florida soldiers killed at the Battle of Franklin. This plot includes a monument erected in 1890 dedicated to these four soldiers (described in chapter 4). A cemetery in Tullahoma, Tennessee, near the 1862–63 winter camps of the Confederate Army of Tennessee, contains the remains of Confederate soldiers buried beginning in 1862. Included here are the graves of some fifty Florida soldiers and a monument to their memory dedicated in 2008 (described in chapter 5).

In Vicksburg, the Soldiers' Rest Confederate Cemetery, established in 1866, contains nineteen Florida soldiers from the First, Third, Sixth, and Seventh Regiments of Florida Infantry who died between November 15, 1862, and February 25, 1863. These Floridians were with the Army of Tennessee and probably died in Vicksburg hospitals after their capture during the 1862 campaign in Kentucky. Probably transported to Vicksburg as part of a negotiated prisoner exchange, these Florida soldiers may have arrived with wounds or illness that proved to be fatal.[38]

The Florida soldiers buried in Winchester and Petersburg, Virginia, in Franklin and Tullahoma, Tennessee, in Vicksburg, Mississippi, and in Washington, D.C., are only a handful of the approximately five to six thousand who died during the war and were laid to rest far from their homes. Although many Florida soldiers had died in these far-off places, some also died in their native state. In addition, sons and fathers of Confederate families from other states, such as Louisiana, Mississippi, and Georgia, had died in Florida during the war, along with Union soldiers from far-off northern states and loyal Union men and former slaves from Florida who had served in the Union armies or navies. At war's end, soldiers and sailors were buried everywhere in Florida where Confederate or Union troops had camped for any length, where they were in garrison, or where skirmishes or battles had occurred.

At Fort Barrancas, where troops from Florida and several surrounding southern states gathered after secession to challenge the Union garrison at Fort Pickens across Pensacola Bay, seventy-two Confederates (twelve unknown) were buried in what has since become the Barrancas National

Cemetery. Buried nearby are 533 known and 369 unknown Union soldiers (including 252 members of the U.S. Colored Troops) and 112 known and 225 unknown officers and sailors of the Union navy. Some of these soldiers and sailors certainly died during the Union occupation of Pensacola after the Confederate withdrawal in May 1862, but many were postwar reinterments of soldiers who died in West Florida at Marianna, Bayou Chico, Gunboat Point, Santa Rosa Island, East Pass, Apalachicola, San Juan Island, and Saint Andrew Bay and were moved from their original graves to Barrancas in the late 1860s.[39] The War Department removed and reinterred 468 more burials within the Barrancas National Cemetery after the Key West Post Cemetery, which contained numerous Union Civil War dead, closed in 1927.[40] Following the Civil War, Union soldiers were similarly relocated from cemeteries in eastern Florida and reburied in Beaufort National Cemetery in South Carolina.[41]

Graves of soldiers who died of battle wounds and disease during the Civil War are common in community and private cemeteries in Florida. Buried in a common grave on the battlefield, Union dead from the February 20, 1864, Battle of Olustee remain there today, although the precise location of this mass grave has been lost to time. A large plot in Oaklawn Cemetery in nearby Lake City contains the graves of 155 unknown Confederate soldiers, most of whom were wounded in the Battle of Olustee and died later in Lake City hospitals. In 1901 the UDC erected a monument in this plot to commemorate these men (described in chapter 4). Another thirty-one Confederate soldiers wounded at Olustee were taken to hospitals in Madison, where they died. The graves of these soldiers are in the city's Oak Ridge Cemetery.

On March 1, 1864, in the Jacksonville vicinity, a Union force killed seven Confederates in a day-long skirmish. A monument in a small cemetery in western Jacksonville commemorates these Confederates (described in chapter 5). Casualties of the September 27, 1864, Battle of Marianna were buried in Riverside Cemetery. In marked graves are several Confederate casualties, and a short distance away is the lone grave marker of Lieutenant Isaac Adams, a member of the Union Second Maine Cavalry. The Confederate casualties remain at Marianna; the remains of Lieutenant Adams and the other Union casualties were relocated to the Barrancas National Cemetery after the war.

During the Civil War, the town of Quincy served as an important Confederate supply depot and hospital station. In Quincy's Eastern Cemetery an iron fence surrounds a plot known as the "Soldiers Cemetery," which contains an unknown number of unmarked graves of wounded and sick Confederate soldiers who died in the city's hospitals. The Old City Cemetery in nearby Tallahassee, which dates to 1829, contains plots for both Confederate and Union soldier dead. The Confederate plot contains the remains of soldiers sent to hospitals in Tallahassee from nearby camps and battlefields who died of their wounds or from sickness. Located in the western side of the cemetery, reserved at that time for persons of color, is a plot of Union soldiers that may have included some wounded from the Natural Bridge and Olustee battles who later died in Tallahassee hospitals. Fifteen members of the Eighth U.S. Colored Troops died in Tallahassee hospitals of wounds from Olustee. They may have been buried in Old City Cemetery, along with three members of the Third U.S. Colored Troops who died in Tallahassee during the occupation of that city in the summer of 1865 following the Confederate surrender. These soldiers were moved to the Beaufort National Cemetery in 1868, probably by J. P. Low operating under a contract with the U.S. government. The U.S. soldier dead remaining in Old City Cemetery are apparently from the U.S. Seventh Infantry, stationed in Tallahassee during Reconstruction, who died of disease prior to 1871.[42]

Throughout the state, Confederate and Union soldiers were buried at or near where they were stationed in places such as Confederate Fort Ward at St. Marks, at Fort Clinch and camps in Fernandina, at Jacksonville and Key West, at Fort Marion in St. Augustine, at Fort Myers and Cedar Key, at Confederate defenses along the Apalachicola, and at innumerable camps and contested landscapes in Florida. The locations of many of these graves, especially those of Confederate soldier dead but Union dead as well, are now lost to time. At the close of the Civil War, however, these graves of defender and invader were a stark reminder of what had just happened. These were the graves of fathers, brothers, and sons who died far from home and whose families did not have even the simple satisfaction of a tragic homecoming.

It was this national and local political, economic, and social context that Floridians faced beginning in the summer of 1865. Whether or not they had remained loyal to the Union, their state had been defeated in war, the victorious Union army had become an army of occupation, the social contract of 1860 was destroyed and its replacement was nowhere in sight, and homes and fortunes were ruined. Everywhere—in new cemetery and old—was the stark evidence of the staggering loss of the nation's youth in the graves of soldiers both Confederate and Union, from Florida and other southern states and from the Union states of the North.

The reality of death and destruction was accompanied by the concurrent reality that the reconstruction envisioned by Lincoln was not to be. Despite President Johnson's attempts to reintegrate the southern states into the Union and to restore many rights to the citizens of the South through executive powers, when Congress reconvened in December 1865 that dream came to an end as well. As 1866 came to the South so did congressionally mandated Radical Reconstruction, fueled by a perhaps previously underestimated anger among the people of the northern states about the war's human and fiscal costs. The road back to normal status within the Union, for both the southern states and their people, had become a very long one indeed.

A NEW CRISIS OF HUMAN LOSS

In Florida, and throughout the country, the emergency of war quickly gave way to an emergency of another nature: what should be done about the graves of the hundreds of thousands of soldiers who had died as a result of battle or disease? Some who had died in battle remained unburied at war's end, some were in shallow mass or individual graves on battlefields, some resided in somewhat more formal graveyards at campsites or prisoner-of-war camps, and some lay properly buried in local cemeteries. Many of these graves were not marked with the name of the interred individual. Those that were marked were generally marked poorly on inscribed wooden headboards. With every passing day the names on these markers grew ever more faint, or the markers were lost entirely due to weather or simple neglect.

To compound the crisis, the death and burial of the vast majority of Civil War casualties had broken the convention of the day, where death was to occur at home in the presence of loved ones and was to be a fitting end to life and beginning of whatever came next.[43] Death in the Civil War ranged from those that were unattended due to the exigencies of the battlefield, to those attended to by comrades in arms (which occasionally included relatives), to those attended to in field hospitals (which may have been operated by the enemy). In some instances bodies traveled home for burial, but more typically all a family could hope for was a letter detailing the honorable death of a loved one written by a friend, officer, hospital attendant, or chaplain. In other cases, a name printed in a newspaper was all the notice one received, and in many cases the family never knew the fate of a loved one who simply never came home.

To confront this crisis of faith and family, the North and the South reacted in different yet not unrelated ways. By far the majority of soldier graves were on battlefields, around hospitals, and on campgrounds in the southern states. For families of Union soldiers, their dead were not only far from home but lay buried on a landscape that was the home of their former enemy. Whereas a fitting cemetery existed on the major battlefield fought in a northern state—the Battle of Gettysburg—there was immediate desire for similar treatment of the Union dead buried in the southern states. There was an abiding fear that graves of loved ones would be at best forgotten and neglected and at worst desecrated by a southern population made vindictive by their defeat in war.[44]

A major proponent of proper burial of the northern war dead was the Grand Army of the Republic. Founded in 1866 as one of a number of Union Civil War veterans organizations, the GAR became the preeminent Union veteran association. At its height it wielded extraordinary power in national politics and did much to define the national narrative about the legacy of the Civil War. Both sides were caught off guard by the numbers of soldiers and sailors who died during the conflict, but efforts to improve the burial of the dead began early in the war, and by 1862 the United States had begun to establish national cemeteries to hold the bodies of Union dead. At the end of the war, however, only slightly more than one-quarter of the estimated Union dead lay in proper graves. Starting in 1866, the federal government issued contracts for the reburial of these Union dead; this continued until 1870 when most of this work was completed. Although the GAR did not cause this work, which was finished before it became an effective and significant organization, the GAR was interested in ensuring that the Union dead in national cemeteries would receive the honor they were due and that this honor would not be bestowed on their former Confederate foes.[45]

From the outset, the general sentiment in the North and the specific efforts of the GAR worked to restrict the federal program of reburial of Civil War soldier dead to include only those who had served in the military of the United States to the specific exclusion of soldiers of the former Confederacy. Although Congress began seating representatives from the former Confederate states in 1868, the GAR was successful in preserving a national policy on treatment of the Civil War dead focused solely on those who had been loyal to the Union during the war. Certainly with backing of the GAR, the system of national cemeteries created to hold Union Civil War dead, which were visibly placed throughout the former Confederacy and made prominent through deliberate development of their memorial nature, became symbols of federal power and statements of the Union victory in the Civil War.[46]

By contrast, southern efforts to properly care for their dead remained localized, and remained so despite the readmission of the states to the Union because of the continued exclusion of Confederate soldiers in federal reburial programs. During the war, Ladies' Aid Societies had helped provision and outfit locally raised regiments, and later they assisted in supplying and operating hospitals caring for sick and wounded soldiers. As the war came to a close, these societies soon focused on ensuring proper burial of Confederate soldier dead and eventually on commemorating the dead and memorializing the cause for which they had fought. With this postwar focus, these societies generally became known as Ladies' Memorial Associations (LMAs), and in Florida they were often organized at the county level.[47] An exception in name was the Walton County *Female* Memorial Association, which erected the first Confederate monument in Florida in 1871.

In addition to political and economic reconstruction, then, proper and respectful care of the war dead emerged as a central theme of the postwar years. The federal government's failure to adopt policies that provided for respectful care of all of the war dead did much to make regional reconciliation difficult. The South saw itself as a defeated nation that had been invited back into a Union whose government would accept no responsibility for the respectful treatment of its war dead or ultimately of its disabled and aging veterans. To add insult, this postwar Union lavished national treasure on the respectful treatment of the Union war dead, on living Union veterans, and on the commemoration of the Civil War itself.

FLORIDA'S RECONSTRUCTION-ERA MONUMENTS

It was in this context that commemoration through erection of monuments began in Florida. The few monuments erected during this time are both instructive of this period and provide witness to the emergence of a narrative of the Lost Cause that would become overt after the end of Reconstruction in 1877. Only four monuments dedicated to the Civil War were erected in Florida before the end of Reconstruction. They are a monument marking the graves of Union dead on the Olustee Battlefield, a monument to Union soldiers and sailors at Key West, and monuments to the Confederate soldier dead in Walton County and in St. Augustine.

Olustee Battlefield, 1866

At the Battle of Olustee (also known in Confederate accounts as the Battle of Ocean Pond), fought on February 20, 1864, Confederate forces repulsed an attempted Union thrust through Florida in the state's largest Civil War engagement. After the war, in 1866, a detachment of U.S. Army soldiers ordered to the Olustee battleground sought to determine the location and condition of the remains of the Union soldiers hastily buried by the Confederate victors. Bones, including 125 skulls, were collected and reburied in a mass grave on the battlefield, around which a whitewashed wooden fence was erected. There they also erected a "wooden monument twelve feet high" that was painted white with inscriptions cut into it which were in turn painted black. The inscription letters were "one inch long" and were "cut a fourth of an inch deep into the wood." On the monument's south side, the inscription read "To the memory of the officers and soldiers of the United States army who fell in the Battle of Olustee, Feb. 20, 1864"; on the west side it read "Our Country"; on the north side it read "May the living profit by the example of the dead"; and on the east side it read "Unity and peace." The U.S. Army's reburial report does not specify the design of the monument. This wooden monument did not last long, as a Union veteran of the battle, observing the battlefield from the platform of a passing train in 1873, noted that a portion of the "weather-stained and broken down fence" was all that remained.[48]

In the ensuing years, the precise location of the Union mass grave was lost. An archaeological survey conducted in 1994 was unable to locate this important feature of the battlefield. In May 1991 the Union Army District of Florida (a Civil War reenactment organization) erected a granite representation of the original wooden monument at a location thought to be close to the original (see figure 90 in chapter 4). The new monument consists of a large granite cross on a base and a one-stepped foundation. Inscriptions from the original monument are engraved on the base. Inscriptions on the foundation note that it is a replacement for the original 1866 monument, list the Union units in the battle, and list the monument's sponsor and the date of its erection.[49]

Although the original 1866 monument and its location are lost, this monument was the result of early efforts to provide for proper burial of Union soldier dead in Florida. The army detachment deemed the mass grave to be better than the probably shallow and poorly marked graves that had been prepared by the Confederate burial details. The wooden monument not only marked the location of these graves but also memorialized the sacrifice of these soldiers who had died for their country.

Key West, 1866

The oldest extant Civil War monument in Florida is a Union monument erected in Key West in 1866, only one year after the end of the war. This is not only one of the older Civil War monuments in the country but also one of the furthest south.

By the time of the Civil War, Key West was Florida's second-largest city, with an economy based largely on maritime activities, including wrecking, or maritime salvage activity, of ships grounded or sunk on the nearby Florida Reef. Due to its strategic location astride the Caribbean and deep channels that provided protected anchorage, the U.S. military had maintained a presence on the island since 1822. In 1845 construction began on a massive brick fortification to protect the harbor, which was named Fort Zachary Taylor in 1850.[50]

This fort was part of the United States' comprehensive "Third System" of coastal fortifications.[51] Construction of these forts began in 1816, and most were completed before the Civil War. These large masonry forts were built along the nation's coastline to protect important harbors, cities, interior waterways, and navy yards from seaborne attack. Due to advances in naval ordnance during the Civil War, masonry fortifications such as Fort Zachary Taylor, as well as Florida Forts Barrancas (Pensacola), Clinch (Amelia Island), Jefferson (Dry Tortugas), Marion (St. Augustine), McRee (Pensacola), and Pickens (Pensacola) were obsolete at the war's end.

Despite the Southern sympathies of many of its residents, Key West remained in Union possession throughout the Civil War. Quick action by the small Union army force in Key West at the beginning of the war secured Fort Taylor and prevented its falling into the hands of Florida militia, as had happened to most other federal fortifications in the state (Fort Jefferson and Fort Pickens also remained in Union hands throughout the war). Key West served as an important Union supply base and naval fueling depot during the war. The headquarters of both the Union navy's East Gulf Blockading Squadron and the Union army's District of Key West and Tortugas were located there.

Over the course of the war nearly three hundred captured Confederate blockade runners came before the Key West prize court and were condemned for sale at auction. Although Key West was never the scene of fighting, Union forces stationed there suffered numerous casualties from disease, particularly typhoid and yellow fever. New York regiments, for example, lost over one hundred men to disease during a one-year tour of duty in Key West.

With the end of the war and the discontinuance of the East Gulf Blockading Squadron in 1865, "the officers forming the 'Navy Club' of Key West voted to apply the proceeds arising from the sale of the property, etc., to the erection of a monument in Key West in memory of those of their comrades who had fallen" during the war. With "a nucleus of twelve hundred dollars [which] was thus obtained," the Navy Club had the monument erected in Clinton Square in downtown Key West in 1866.[52]

Made of gray granite, the monument consists of an obelisk shaft on a pedestal and base that rests on a one-stepped foundation and is approximately seventeen feet in overall height (see figure 8). The pedestal has a pediment that juts out from all sides of the monument just below the shaft. A bas-relief image of two crossed cannons over an anchor with an attached rope decorates the front, or west, face of the shaft. The front face of the pedestal contains an inset space engraved with "ERECTED 1866, By the Navy Club of Key West, To the Memory of the Officers, Sailors, & Soldiers, of the Army, Navy, & Marine Corps of the United States, who lost their lives in their Country's service upon this station from 1861 to 1865."

A nineteen-inch-tall ornamental wrought-iron fence encircles the base of the monument. A bronze plaque on the front gate of this fence reads "ERECTED BY J. V. HARRIS CONFEDERATE VETERAN." Jeptha Vining Harris was an assistant surgeon in the Confederate navy from Mississippi who moved to Key West after the war and died there in 1914. Historic photographs first show the iron fence beginning in the early 1900s. An early photograph (ca. 1870) shows the monument in an ill-defined grassy plaza but surrounded by an octagonal fence probably made of wood (see figure 9). A bit later, a wooden picket fence that enclosed the entire plaza replaced the octagonal fence. An early photograph of the new adjacent Custom House, constructed in 1891, shows Clinton Square and the monument without a fence but surrounded by a low masonry retaining wall and sidewalk. A photograph taken in the early twentieth century, probably about 1910, however, shows the ornamental iron fence encircling all of Clinton Square (see figure 10). The iron fence was removed at a later date, possibly due to poor condition, but part of it was repurposed as a much smaller fence around the base of the monument, as a comparison of the current fence with historic photographs shows. A modern fence that mimics the pattern and placement of the original iron fence now surrounds Clinton Square.[53]

Figure 8. 1866 Union monument in Key West's downtown historic district as it appeared in 2012. Photograph by William B. Lees.

Left: Figure 9. 1866 Union monument in Key West in undefined Clinton Square surrounded by wooden fence, ca. 1870 photograph. Monroe County Public Library, Florida History Department Images, image no. MM00032458.

Below: Figure 10. 1866 Union monument in Key West showing iron fence around Clinton Square, ca. 1910 photograph. Monroe County Public Library, Florida History Department Images, image no. MM00001458.

Envisioned and erected by a private club of military officers and at least partially funded by receipts from the sale of government surplus property, the Key West obelisk is interesting in an overall comparison of Civil War monuments. The members of the Navy Club erected the monument virtually as the last act of their service in Key West during the war. Unlike monuments to follow, this was not erected by veterans looking back on the war many years later to honor the memory of their fallen comrades. Although certainly not intended as part of the original monument, the addition in about 1900 of a fence donated by and dedicated to a Confederate makes Clinton Square a bit unusual. Probably forever clouded by the passage of time is whether this fence was an act of reconciliation or defiance on the part of Confederate veteran Harris.

Walton County, 1871

The oldest Confederate monument in Florida was erected in Walton County in the Florida Panhandle in 1871 by the Walton County Female Memorial Association. On August 17 of that year, a crowd of "about one thousand" attended the dedication of a monument to the Confederate dead of Walton County erected at the Euchee Valley Presbyterian Church. Featured speakers included local Confederate veterans W. C. McLean and John L. McKinnon. Dinner for the attendees followed the ceremony.[54]

Anthony Barret[55] of New Orleans constructed the monument. An 1871 newspaper article reports the cost of this monument to be $1,000.[56] However, a perhaps more reasonable figure of $250 is found in more recent accounts of its construction.[57] Born in Germany, Barret was a sculptor and marble yard owner known for his cemetery statuary.[58] The sixteen-foot-tall monument consists of an Alabama marble obelisk and pedestal topped by a pediment with a granite urn containing a clenched fist with the index finger pointing upward, as clearly shown in figure 11.[59] The monument rests on a three-stepped masonry foundation.

The front pedestal face of the monument contains an ornate bas-relief decoration consisting of two crossed cannons over a stack of cannonballs with a flag on a staff furled over one of the cannons. On the shaft above the decoration are the words "TO THE MEMORY OF THE CONFEDERATE DEAD OF WALTON CO. FLORIDA. ERECTED BY THE LADIES OF THE WALTON COUNTY FEMALE MEMORIAL ASSOCIATION. 1871." Another pedestal face contains portions of the 1844 poem "The Place Where Man Should Die" by the Irish poet

Figure 11. 1871 Walton County Confederate monument on the grounds of the Walton County Courthouse in DeFuniak Springs, ca. 1960 photograph. The original urn with its pointing-fingered hand tops the obelisk. Florida Photographic Collection, State Archives of Florida, image no. RC16411.

Michael Joseph Barry (1817–89): "WHEN THE SPIRIT FREE DESERTS THE BODY AS IT MUST[,] WHAT MATTER WHERE THE LIFELESS FORM DISSOLVES ITSELF AGAIN TO DUST. 'TWERE SWEET INDEED TO CLOSE OUR EYES WITH THOSE WE CHERISH NEAR; AND WAFTED UPWARDS BY THEIR SIGHS, SOAR TO SOME CALMER SPHERE; BUT WHETHER ON THE SCAFFOLD HIGH, OR IN THE BATTLE VAN[,] THE FITTEST PLACE WHERE MAN CAN DIE, IS WHERE HE DIES FOR MAN."

The other two pedestal faces contain the names of ninety-four Confederate dead from Walton County. The listed names include one colonel, two captains, four lieutenants, and eighty-seven enlisted men, most of whom served in the First, Sixth, and Seventh Florida Infantry Regiments. Two of the names were added to the monument sometime after May 1986.[60] On the base is engraved the name of the monument's sculptor, "A. BARRET. N. ORLEANS."

Soon after the monument was erected at the Euchee Valley Presbyterian Church, a dispute arose among the monument's sponsors as to its proper location. The monument was subsequently relocated by some of the monument sponsors to the Walton County Courthouse in Eucheeanna, about two and one-half miles to the west, at that time the county seat and the site of an 1864 skirmish during the Union expedition against Marianna.[61] Not long after that, the rival faction relocated the monument back to the church and threatened "violence to any one who should interfere with them." The vying parties took the issue to court. The circuit court of the First Judicial Circuit ruled in favor of the faction supporting the church location. Upon appeal, the Florida Supreme Court, in 1874, ruled for those favoring the county courthouse location, and the monument was again relocated to Eucheeanna.[62] A historic photograph (ca. 1916) of the monument at Eucheeanna shows it resting on a pyramidal brick foundation which, due to its rough appearance, may be unfinished (see figure 1 in the introduction).[63]

In 1886, DeFuniak Springs became the county seat. In 1927 the monument was relocated to the Walton County Courthouse grounds in DeFuniak Springs with funding provided by a $1,000 appropriation from the Florida Legislature (see figure 12).[64] The three-stepped masonry foundation was apparently added after its final relocation. The monument's original pediment, with the urn and clenched fist with a finger pointing skyward, was still present until at least the mid-1980s but then disappeared, presumably taken by vandals. In the meantime, the Walton County Heritage Association, a local historic preservation organization, raised $3,500 to have the urn-and-hand portion of the monument replaced with a new one in 2014.[65]

Figure 12. 1871 Walton County Confederate monument as it appeared in 2009 in front of the county courthouse in DeFuniak Springs. Since then, the missing urn-and-hand ornament has been reproduced and now tops the obelisk. Photograph by William B. Lees.

The monument dates to the middle of Reconstruction and is dedicated to local Confederate dead whose names are inscribed on the monument. Some of these soldiers died early on in Florida's Camp Walton, but most died out of state from disease, in battle, or from wounds suffered in battle. For example, soldiers named on this monument died in, or as a result of wounds from, the battles at Perryville and Cumberland Mountain, Kentucky, in 1862; Murfreesboro, Tennessee, in 1862; Marietta and Chickamauga, Georgia, in 1863; Missionary Ridge, Tennessee, in 1863; and Franklin, Tennessee, in 1864. Others died at hospitals in Atlanta, Georgia; Sparta, Tennessee; Lexington, Kentucky; and Vicksburg, Mississippi. Several died of disease in Union prisoner-of-war camps such as Camp Chase, Ohio; Jefferson Barracks, Missouri; Elmira Prison, New York; and Alton Prison, Illinois. Most lie buried in distant fields and cemeteries, many certainly in unmarked or unknown graves. Lacking a grave in a local cemetery, this monument would have been the only way for local commemoration of individual loss.

Overall, this monument does not speak to or commemorate individual valor of the soldier or the cause for which he fought; the closest to this is the line from the poem inscribed on the monument, "The fittest place where man can die, is where he dies for man." Had this monument honored Confederate valor or the Confederate cause, Reconstruction-era federal authorities would probably have denied placement of this monument on public property.

St. Augustine, 1872, and 1879

On the eve of Florida's secession from the Union in early January 1861, state militia seized the massive coquina Fort Marion (Castillo de San Marcos) at St. Augustine without violence from the lone U.S. Army sergeant assigned to the post. Confederate forces occupied the city and its fort until March 1862, when they evacuated the area as Union warships approached. Many of the city's residents also fled to Confederate-held regions in the state's interior. For the duration of the war, St. Augustine was under Union control and was used mainly as a rest center for Union troops. Confederate forces made no attempt to retake the city, although they occasionally skirmished with Union troops sent to the city's outskirts to gather firewood and other supplies.[66]

In 1872 the Ladies' Memorial Association of St. Augustine requested permission of the mayor and city council to erect a monument to the Confederate dead in the city's central public square, the Plaza de la Constitución. However, the U.S. military commander of the District of Florida in St. Augustine, Colonel John T. Sprague, objected to the erection of a monument in

Figure 13. 1872 Confederate monument erected on private property in St. Augustine, ca. 1875 photograph. Florida Photographic Collection, State Archives of Florida, image no. SV0950.

the public plaza so soon after the war, and the city government denied the request. Catholic bishop Augustin Verot, known as the "Rebel Bishop" for his defense of the Confederate cause during the war, offered the association an area in the yard of his home on private property owned by the Catholic Church, which was accepted.[67]

The monument was erected in April 1872 by Joseph Llambias of St. Augustine, a coquina and concrete worker, on the east side of St. George Street between Bridge and St. Francis Streets (see figure 13). At its dedication on May 10, 1872, the anniversary of Confederate general Stonewall Jackson's death, the featured speaker was Wilkinson Call of Jacksonville, a Confederate veteran who had participated in the Battle of Olustee and was later a U.S.

Figure 14. 1879 Confederate monument in Plaza de la Constitución in St. Augustine, 1891 photograph. Florida Photographic Collection, State Archives of Florida, image no. RC19686.

senator.[68] Constructed of stucco over coquina, the monument consisted of a center "broken shaft" column rising above the pedestal, symbolic of a life cut short. Historic photographs show that it had two marble crosses flanking the shaft (one on either side of tiered three-stepped columns atop the wide pedestal), a marble plaque inserted in the front of the shaft, and three larger marble plaques inserted in the front pedestal face.[69]

In 1879, two years after the end of Reconstruction, the LMA gained permission from a much more friendly and sympathetic city council to erect a

Confederate monument in the plaza. The old monument was dismantled and rebuilt in the plaza in a larger and substantially different form (see figure 14).[70] Marble plaques and probably the coquina from this original monument were used in rebuilding the new monument. On November 1, 1879, the city and the LMA signed a ninety-nine-year lease for a twenty-by-twenty-foot plot on the plaza for one dollar per year. In 1883 the city conveyed the monument plot to the LMA, for which the association paid the remaining $95 on the ninety-nine-year lease. The city afterward donated this money back to the association.[71]

Twenty-five feet tall, the monument consists of a stucco-over-coquina obelisk shaft and pedestal on a larger pedestal and base, probably also stucco over coquina, which rests on a one-stepped foundation (see figure 15). In 1883 a marble finial consisting of a smaller obelisk with a bas-relief image of a soldier's head on one side was placed on top of the monument. Soon after its addition, this finial was damaged, possibly by a lightning strike or from the 1887 fire that destroyed many structures in and around the plaza. It was replaced in 1888 with concrete cannonballs stacked in a pyramid design that grace the monument to this day.[72]

On the front (west) face of the obelisk shaft is a marble plaque engraved with "OUR DEAD." In an inset space on the pedestal below this is a shaped marble plaque engraved with "IN MEMORIAM OUR LOVED ONES WHO GAVE THEIR LIVES IN THE SERVICE OF THE CONFEDERATE STATES." The bottom pedestal contains a marble plaque in an inset space with the engraved names of twenty-three of the forty-six Confederate dead from St. Augustine. The east upper pedestal face contains a marble plaque in an inset space engraved with "ERECTED BY THE LADIES MEMORIAL ASSOCIATION OF ST. AUGUSTINE, FLA. A. D. 1872." while the lower pedestal face contains a marble plaque in an inset space engraved with the names of the other twenty-three Confederate dead from St. Augustine. Many of the names of the dead engraved on the two marble plaques are of Hispanic origin, speaking to the cultural and ethnic diversity of the community at the time of the Civil War.

The south upper pedestal face contains a marble cross in an inset space, and the lower pedestal face contains a marble plaque in an inset space engraved with "THEY DIED FAR FROM THE HOME THAT GAVE THEM BIRTH BY COMRADES HONORED AND BY COMRADES MOURNED." An identical marble cross in an inset space is located on the north upper pedestal face, while the lower pedestal face contains a marble plaque in an inset space with an adaptation of the last words of General Stonewall Jackson before dying of

Figure 15. 1879 Confederate monument in St. Augustine's Plaza de la Constitución in 2012. Photograph by William B. Lees.

his wounds from the 1863 Battle of Chancellorsville, Virginia: "THEY HAVE CROSSED THE RIVER AND REST UNDER THE SHADE OF THE TREES."

Almost immediately after its erection, the monument became a tourist attraction. Author Constance Fenimore Woolson in 1874 and the noted poet Sidney Lanier, a Confederate veteran, in 1875 visited the monument in its original location and mentioned it in their writings. Woolson's article also included a drawing of an amputee on crutches, presumably a Confederate veteran, observing the monument.[73] With its new and more prominent location in the plaza, the monument became even more visible to the city's visitors. Travel guides in the 1880s prominently mentioned the monument, and President Grover Cleveland visited the monument during his 1888 visit to the city.[74] In a public display of mourning upon the death of Jefferson Davis in 1889, virtually the entire monument was elaborately draped in black.[75] Surrounding the monument on its four corners are four Civil War–era artillery pieces from Fort Marion, two 32-pounders and two eight-inch Columbiads. In 1900 the U.S. War Department presented the cannons to the City of St. Augustine.

The inscriptions on the original 1872 monument, and hence the message, are presumed to be the same as on the monument that now stands in the Plaza de la Constitución, because it seems clear that although the form of the monument changed, the same marble plaques were used on both. In addition to honoring the individual soldier dead of St. Augustine, not unlike that done on the 1871 Walton County monument, the St. Augustine monument commemorates their service to the Confederacy and also references Confederate hero Stonewall Jackson. In addition, the original form of the monument, including the motif of the broken column, may symbolize not only the lives of soldiers cut short by war but the Confederacy itself. It is not surprising that a Reconstruction-era city council overseen by a military district headquartered in St. Augustine denied this monument, which paid homage to the Confederacy, a place on city property. Contrast this to the Walton County monument, which did end up on public property based on a decision of the Florida Supreme Court, and a window opens into the complexity of commemoration in Reconstruction-era Florida.

* * *

The work of local Ladies' Memorial Associations in the commemoration of the Civil War in Florida would continue through the remainder of the nineteenth century. The ability of these associations to more freely choose both their means of commemoration and the message of commemoration increased immediately upon the end of Reconstruction. It is important to understand, however, that the foundation of postwar sectionalism had been firmly set during Reconstruction. This would affect both the narrative of the Civil War and the success of regional reconciliation for many years to come, if not to the present day.

2 REMEMBERING CONFEDERATE SACRIFICE AND VALOR AFTER RECONSTRUCTION

Defeat has not made "all our sacred things profane." The war has left the South its own memories, its own heroes, its own tears, its own dead. Under these traditions, sons will grow to manhood, and lessons sink deep that are learned from the lips of widowed mothers.

Edward A. Pollard, *The Lost Cause: A New Southern History of the War of the Confederates* (1867)

The end of Reconstruction in Florida in 1877 saw a continuation of the activity by local Ladies' Memorial Associations (LMAs). The task of securing proper burial for the soldier dead being largely over, the work of the women increasingly became remembering and honoring the dead. An important focus of this effort remained Confederate Memorial Day, which typically began with a parade in which veterans were prominently featured and ended at the local cemetery where the graves of the Confederate dead were decorated. Beginning in 1866, Confederate Memorial Day was recognized in the South as a day to remember the soldier dead, but it was held either on the day that General Joseph E. Johnston surrendered, April 26, or the date of the death of General Thomas "Stonewall" Jackson, May 10. The former date was more prominent in the lower South, including Florida, while the latter was more common in the Carolinas. In time, Jefferson Davis's birth date, June 3, was added to the mix, and by 1916 ten southern states recognized this date as a public holiday.[1]

Another important function of the Ladies' Memorial Associations and of local monument associations, also typically organized by women, was the erection of monuments. As was the case with the monuments placed in Walton County and in St. Augustine during Reconstruction, these monuments initially were simple expressions of loss. They were also a means to memorialize soldier dead buried on distant battlefields and campsites. As time passed and as southerners increasingly sought ways to raise their status as citizens in a nation that was reunited only through their defeat in war, the message conveyed by monuments began to change with the evolving rhetoric of the Lost Cause. The Lost Cause was a narrative or social memory that owes its genesis to the likes of Robert E. Lee and Jubal A. Early, who sought from the very end of the war to vindicate the Confederacy.[2] With time, the Lost Cause narrative was carried on by southern women active in memorial associations that sought to transform the Confederacy's defeat and the status of the South's soldiers as traitors into something more palatable or "usable."[3] In simple terms, this narrative involved recasting the Civil War as a constitutional contest in which the South fought to protect states' rights as guaranteed in the Tenth Amendment to the Constitution and in which the soldiers of the Confederacy were American patriots whose devotion to cause, honor, and valor should be a source of continuing pride for all and a role model for southern children of succeeding generations.

Beginning in 1890, some LMAs in the South changed their name to "Daughters of the Confederacy." This new name was inspired by a nickname given to Winnie Davis, the inspirational spokesperson of the Lost Cause and daughter of Jefferson Davis.[4] Although other LMAs and monument associations continued to function alongside this updated incarnation, its appellation became the root of a new nationwide Confederate legacy organization.

Correspondence between Caroline Meriwether Goodlett of Kentucky and Georgian Anna Davenport Raines about the need for a collaboration of Confederate Ladies' Associations led, in 1894, to the creation of the National Association of the Daughters of the Confederacy. This organization's goals were broad and included memorial, historical, benevolent, educational, and social aspects. These goals built upon the work of the LMAs but added, among other things, a focus on caring for aging Confederate veterans and ensuring that "correct" histories of the Civil War would be available throughout the South and especially in the schools. They sought to ensure through education that the youth of the South would understand the role of the Confederacy as a defender of the Constitution and would view its soldiers as American patriots whose dedication, devotion, and bravery were above reproach. A year after the founding of the national association, the name was changed to the United Daughters of the Confederacy (UDC).[5]

Also known as the Daughters, this new national organization was different by design. On the one hand, it was formed to ensure that a consistent message about the Confederacy was delivered at the local level; on the other hand, it sought to harness the power, including political power, of a national association to achieve national goals focused on vindication of the Confederacy. Local chapters continued to function alongside other Confederate associations such as the LMAs, monument associations, auxiliaries to Confederate soldiers' homes, and camps of Confederate veterans, but the UDC gradually became the prominent voice of the Lost Cause because of its root purpose of preserving "Confederate culture." In 1903, less than a decade after its founding, the UDC had 35,000 members, and by 1912 that number had grown to approximately 80,000. In 1918, during the U.S. involvement in World War I, the organization claimed 100,000 members.[6]

Like LMAs, local associations of Confederate veterans also proliferated in the decades following the Civil War. Although the premier Union veterans organization—the Grand Army of the Republic (GAR)—was formed in 1866, it was not until 1889 that its Confederate counterpart, the United Confederate Veterans (UCV), was formed by consolidating more than five hundred local Confederate organizations throughout the South.[7] The mission of the UCV was to "Unite in a general federation all associations of Confederate veterans, soldiers and sailors, now in existence or hereafter to be formed; to gather authentic data for an impartial history of the war between the States; to preserve relics or mementos of the same; to cherish the ties of friendship that should exist among men who have shared common dangers, common sufferings and privations; to care for the disabled and extend a helping hand to the needy; to protect the widows and orphans; and to make and preserve a record of services of every member, and as far as possible of those of our comrades who have preceded us in eternity." The UCV became inactive during the 1940s. Although the UCV and the UDC shared numerous goals, the veterans were much less interested in erecting monuments than were the Daughters.

A few private individuals contributed to the landscape of Civil War monuments in Florida. These individuals acted at the turn of the twentieth century during the heyday of monument erection by the LMAs and the UDC, but they were not constrained nor directed by the mission of these groups. One very late monument was placed by a civic organization to honor the supposed oldest Confederate veteran in Florida, and it is unique among those erected in the century following the close of the Civil War.

MONUMENTS ERECTED BY LADIES' MEMORIAL ASSOCIATIONS AFTER RECONSTRUCTION

Ladies' Memorial Associations erected several monuments in Florida between 1871 and 1899. The first of these were erected during Reconstruction: in Walton County in 1871 and in St. Augustine in 1872 (discussed in detail in chapter 1). Dismantling the Confederate monument erected in St. Augustine in 1872 and erecting a new monument utilizing the same dedicatory marble plaques in the public plaza immediately following the end of Reconstruction symbolized a new era of memorialization in Florida and the South. Local communities could now, without fear of federal military oversight, place monuments in prominent public places and could define what messages those monuments would convey. The Reconstruction-era monument in Walton County had simply honored the memory of local soldier dead, but the St. Augustine monument, in addition to honoring its dead, had also made reference to the service of these soldiers to the Confederacy and to a Confederate general seen as a martyr by many southerners. For reasons previously established, the Confederacy would increasingly receive center stage in the monuments that followed in their demonstration to the following generations that the sons of the South had not died in vain.

Tallahassee, 1881

At the beginning of the Civil War, Tallahassee, Florida's capital, was a small but prosperous city in the center of north-central Florida's cotton plantation system and an important railroad center. In March 1865 a Union force landed on the coast of the Gulf of Mexico near the St. Marks Lighthouse and proceeded north to seize Fort Ward at the blockade-running port of St. Marks. If successful, the campaign would have likely then led to a movement to capture Tallahassee. However, the Union advance was halted by defeat at the Battle of Natural Bridge about ten miles south of Tallahassee, and the Union force was compelled to retreat to the coast for evacuation. As a result, Tallahassee remained the only southern capital east of the Mississippi that was not captured during the Civil War.[8]

On April 26, 1881, Confederate Memorial Day, a monument to the Confederate dead of Leon County was dedicated on the grounds of the state capitol in Tallahassee where the Ordinance of Secession had been approved on January 9, 1861 (see figure 16). Sponsored by the Ladies' Memorial Association of Leon County, the monument cost $515 and was manufactured by the

Figure 16. Alvan S. Harper photograph of the capitol building in Tallahassee during the 1890s showing the 1881 Leon County Confederate monument immediately left of the columns. Florida Photographic Collection, State Archives of Florida, image no. HA00103.

Thomas Delahunty Marble and Granite Works located in the Laurel Hill section of Philadelphia. An unusual aspect of the monument project was the participation of "two well-known colored men," Curtis Hill and Tallahassee city councilman George Fitzgiles, "each of whom has contributed both money and the labor of his hands" to its erection.[9]

The dedication ceremony program of hymn singing, prayer, and speeches was witnessed by "a large assemblage" of participants, including the Governor's Guards (a local militia unit), the Tallahassee Brass Band, and "a selected choir of a dozen or more of Tallahassee's best voices." Prominent local attorney and political leader Frederick T. Myers served as master of ceremonies. The featured speaker was Judge William P. Byrd, who proclaimed that "while we rejoice in the peace of our country, let us ever remember the heroic deeds of those for whom this monument was proudly dedicated."[10]

Standing seventeen and one-half feet high, the monument consists of a white flat-topped marble shaft, pedestal, and base on a gray granite foundation (see figure 17). The shaft is topped by a handled marble urn on a footed base. The urn contains a bas-relief image of "the face of a cherubim" with wings on one side and a carved flame flowing from its top.[11] One handle of the urn has been partially broken off since its original erection. The east pedestal face contains a marble tablet inscribed with "TO RESCUE FROM OBLIVION AND PERPETUATE IN THE MEMORY OF SUCCEEDING GENERATIONS THE HEROIC PATRIOTISM OF THE MEN OF LEON COUNTY WHO PERISHED IN THE CIVIL WAR OF 1861–1865. THIS MONUMENT IS RAISED BY THEIR COUNTRY WOMEN."

The other three faces of the monument are decorated with tablets inscribed with the names of Civil War battles in which Leon County troops participated. The north pedestal face lists "FLORIDA BATTLES. PENSACOLA. OLUSTEE. NATURAL BRIDGE. &c." The west pedestal face lists "VIRGINIA BATTLES. WILLIAMSBURG. SEVEN PINES. RICHMOND. COLD HARBOR. MANASSAS. SHARPESBURG [*sic*]. FREDERICKSBURG. GETTISBURGH [*sic*]. CHANCELLORSVILLE. WILDERNESS. YORKTOWN. &c." The south pedestal face lists "WESTERN BATTLES. SHILOH. FARMINGTON. 1ST BATTLE OF CORINTH. GREEN RIVER. PERRYVILLE. CHICKAMAUGA. MISSIONARY RIDGE. RESACA. GILGAL CHURCH. GILGAL CHURCH [repeated]. CASSVILLE. KENNESAW. MT. DECATUR. ROUGH AND READY STATION. JONESBORO. FRANKLIN. &c." The manufacturer's name is engraved on the base: "T. DELAHUNTY. LAUREL HILL. PHILADA."

The monument's erection caused some controversy in Tallahassee. Only a year after the war had ended, in 1866, a Florida Southern Woman's Memorial Association was formed in Tallahassee with one of their purposes being the erection of a monument at the state capitol to all of Florida's Confederate war dead.[12] Surprisingly, the women's fund-raising efforts were initially criticized by three Tallahassee clergymen who believed it was "inappropriate female behavior" and that "only men could perform such an act of public consolation." In a series of letters published in the Tallahassee newspaper in February 1867, the women and the ministers exchanged heated criticisms of each other's positions. Despite the criticism from the ministers, the association continued

Figure 17. 1881 Leon County Confederate monument in its current location in Tallahassee prior to the restoration of the capitol building to its 1902 appearance; photograph taken in 1958 after a rare winter snow. Florida Photographic Collection, State Archives of Florida, image no. RC00586.

its fund-raising efforts, including a "Calico Ball" in the capitol building that also raised funds for widows and orphans of Confederate soldiers.[13]

Despite some initial success, fund-raising efforts were slow in the immediate postwar period, and after several years the effort was abandoned. Funds that had been collected for the purpose of building the monument were returned to the various county memorial associations that had contributed.

With the end of Reconstruction in 1877, the idea of erecting a monument to all of Florida's Confederate dead at the state capitol was revived, and fund-raising efforts began again in the late 1870s. By 1879 a design for a twenty-eight-foot-high monument costing $1,700 had been selected, and the monument was to be erected "when a sufficient sum of money should be raised."[14]

The Leon County Memorial Association's decision to erect a monument to the county's Confederate dead at the state capitol, rather than contributing to the statewide monument, caused some resentment and hard feelings. In her memoirs, published in 1926, Susan Bradford Eppes, one of the state association's leaders, stated that "in 1882 [*sic*] a few women ordered a marble shaft and, without consulting the [statewide] Association, had an inscription carved upon it, which gave us the heartache and made us feel that our work had been in vain." She went on to describe the erected monument as a "small and insignificant" and "plain and badly executed . . . shabby shaft."[15] In 1937 she was still highly critical of it and encouraged the UDC to "take steps to have the small monument with incorrect wording, removed from the Capitol grounds and a monument befitting the grounds erected."[16] In 1940 she criticized "the mismanagement of the fund which erected not only an inferior stone, but one incorrectly dated and inscribed."[17]

Efforts to raise funds for a monument to be erected in Tallahassee in honor of all Florida Confederate war dead were continued in the 1880s by a committee chaired by Mrs. Edward A. Perry of Pensacola. Her husband had commanded the Florida Brigade in the Army of Northern Virginia for much of the Civil War and was elected governor of Florida in 1884. He died shortly after leaving office in 1889. By 1890 some $3,000 had been raised for the project, almost all of which had come from Pensacola and Escambia County. After her husband's death, Mrs. Perry stepped down from her fund-raising activities and turned the project over to the Ladies' Monument Association in Pensacola. Since almost all of the donations had been raised in the Pensacola area, the decision was made to use the funds for erecting a monument in Pensacola rather than Tallahassee. That monument, dedicated in June 1891, is discussed in more detail later in this chapter.[18]

The Tallahassee monument was originally erected in front of the west steps of the state capitol. As shown on an 1885 bird's-eye view map of Tallahassee, it was located in the center of a circular green created by sidewalks on the landscaped capitol grounds. Construction of a new west wing of the capitol in 1921–23 made it necessary to move the monument to the northeast corner of the grounds, where it stands today (see figure 18). The new location was recommended by a committee of the UDC to the Board of Commissioners of State Institutions on December 17, 1921. They also suggested at the time that an inscription be put on the monument noting its relocation, but this was not done. In 1933 the Anna Jackson Chapter of the Florida UDC received a $1,000 state appropriation to renovate the monument.[19]

Figure 18. 1881 Leon County Confederate monument in front of the restored capitol building in Tallahassee in 2008. Photograph by William B. Lees.

Remarks given at the monument's dedication recounting "heroic deeds" and the words engraved on the monument referring to "heroic patriotism" of the soldier dead show a trend toward remembering the soldiers of the Confederacy not as warriors of a defeated nation but as those who had fought the good fight for a just and honorable cause. Given the impressive monuments erected by the State of Florida at the Olustee and Natural Bridge Battlefields and other imposing monuments erected in other communities in the state, it is surprising indeed that the monument in Tallahassee about which Mrs. Eppes was so disappointed is the only Confederate monument in the state's capital.

Marianna, 1881

During the Civil War, Marianna was an important commercial center for products grown in the rich agricultural lands of Jackson County. The well-appointed antebellum houses and mansions that remain in town to this day speak to the affluence of those with land and property prior to the outbreak of hostilities. During the war the community also served as a Confederate military center with a training camp, hospital, storehouses, and government stables. In September 1864, Marianna was the scene of a small but bitter battle when a Union force of seven hundred troops from Pensacola overwhelmed a force of some three hundred Confederate defenders composed mostly of reserve forces and local Home Guard militia.[20]

The Ladies' Memorial Association of Jackson County was formed in the early 1870s with one of their goals being the raising of funds for a monument in honor of the county's Confederate war dead. In 1877 the Jackson County Board of County Commissioners granted the LMA a space on the grounds of the county courthouse for the monument.[21] In late 1879 the association held a ceremony for the laying of the monument's cornerstone. The featured speaker was former Confederate brigadier general Jesse J. Finley, who had commanded the Florida Brigade in the Army of Tennessee.[22] Although the monument's foundation was completed in March 1880, sufficient funds to purchase and install the monument were not available until the following year. In September 1881 the Ladies' Memorial Association ordered the monument, and on November 30, 1881, the complete ornate Confederate monument was dedicated (see figure 19).[23] As in other southern communities, the Marianna monument was the focal point for Confederate observances, and an 1897 illustration shows it draped in banners and wreaths for such an occasion.[24]

Figure 19. 1881 Confederate monument in front of Jackson County's first brick courthouse, Marianna, 1880s photograph. Florida Photographic Collection, State Archives of Florida, image no. N034614.

Distinctive bas-relief emblems used on the faces of this monument identify it as having been manufactured by the Monumental Bronze Company of Bridgeport, Connecticut. This company was established in 1879, shortly before the erection of the Marianna monument, and produced sculptures and monuments of white bronze until 1914. White bronze is actually pure zinc, which, distinctive to the Monumental Bronze Company, was finished by sandblasting to give it the appearance of stone.[25]

The seventeen-and-one-quarter-foot-high monument consists of an obelisk shaft with a decorative pointed finial and decorative base on a pedestal and base that currently rests on a two-stepped masonry foundation. The monument has apparently never been surrounded by a fence or other landscaping.[26] The front, or east, face of the monument contains a detailed bas-relief of a Confederate soldier on horseback on the obelisk base, an inscription in raised letters on the pedestal that reads "IN MEMORY OF THE CONFEDERATE SOLDIERS OF JACKSON COUNTY, FLORIDA," and the dedication

Figure 20. 1881 Confederate monument at the Marianna Courthouse. Illustration in the 1897 publication *The Confederate Soldier in the Civil War, 1861–1865*, edited by Ben LaBree.

date in large raised letters and numbers on the monument base, "NOV. 30, 1881." The north obelisk base contains a bas-relief of two crossed swords in their scabbards, and the pedestal contains a quotation in raised letters from the poem "March of the Deathless Dead" by Father Abram J. Ryan (1838–86): "WE CARE NOT WHENCE THEY CAME, DEAR IN THEIR LIFELESS CLAY! WHETHER UNKNOWN, OR KNOWN TO FAME, THEIR CAUSE AND COUNTRY STILL THE SAME—THEY DIED—AND WORE THE GRAY." Father Ryan was a Catholic priest who served as a Confederate chaplain during the Civil War and is known as the "Poet-Priest of the South."

The west face of the obelisk base contains a bas-relief of a bust of a Confederate soldier wearing a kepi, while the pedestal contains the words "IN GOD

Figure 21. 1881 Marianna Confederate monument in front of Jackson County Courthouse in 2008. Photograph by William B. Lees.

WE TRUST" in raised letters. The south obelisk base contains a bas-relief of three upright crossed rifles, and the pedestal contains another quotation from "March of the Deathless Dead": "OF THE WARRIORS TRIED AND TRUE, WHO BORE THE FLAG OF OUR PEOPLES TRUST, AND FELL IN A CAUSE, THOUGH LOST, STILL JUST, AND DIED FOR ME AND YOU."

The monument as it appears today may differ from its original construction. The 1897 illustration shows a building in the background that we presume is the courthouse, and hence we believe the photograph faces south and shows the north face of the monument (see figure 20). Although the monument is draped in ribbon and wreath, what we believe to be the north face shows the bas-relief of the soldier's head, while today this bas-relief graces the west face. Wreaths block details of the base, but it appears that at some point the orientation of the monument was changed or part of the monument was incorrectly reassembled.[27] In 1908 a "severe storm" caused the monument to topple and break "in two pieces."[28] In the early 1960s the monument was temporarily moved while the new county courthouse was constructed (see figure 21).[29] Either of these events may have caused this change to all or part of the monument.

This Marianna monument, contemporary with the Tallahassee monument, was intended to remember the soldier dead of Jackson County. The use of the line from Father Ryan's poem referring to "a cause, though lost, still just" documents an increasingly overt validation of the sacrifice of the soldier dead.

Quincy, 1884

During the war, Quincy was the location of the Confederate military headquarters for the Middle Florida District. In one of the few rail construction projects in Florida during the war, the line from Tallahassee was extended to Gee's Turnout, just four miles from Quincy, in 1862. The city also served as a Confederate commissary depot and hospital station with the Episcopal church, Gadsden County Courthouse, Quincy Academy, and private homes used as makeshift medical centers after the Battles of Olustee in 1864 and Natural Bridge in 1865. A plot in the city's Eastern Cemetery contains the unmarked graves of many of the soldiers who died in Quincy hospitals.[30]

On May 15, 1884, a monument to the Confederate dead was dedicated on the grounds of the Gadsden County Courthouse in Quincy with a program of prayers, band music, and speeches (see figure 22).[31] Funds for the monument were raised by the Ladies' Memorial Association of Gadsden County

Figure 22. Gadsden County Courthouse in Quincy ca. 1908; 1884 Confederate monument is visible to left of courthouse under a tree. Florida Photographic Collection, State Archives of Florida, image no. RC03958.

through "entertainments, private subscriptions, etc."[32] This monument was erected in front of the second courthouse to stand in the square in Quincy. The first courthouse was erected in 1827 and burned in 1849. It was replaced in 1850 with a brick structure that was in turn replaced by the modern courthouse, constructed in 1911–12. The monument does not appear to have been moved during construction of the new facility.

The featured speaker at the dedication ceremony was former Confederate brigadier general Edward A. Perry of Pensacola, who had commanded the Florida Brigade in the Army of Northern Virginia from 1862 to 1864. In November 1884, Perry was elected governor of Florida, a position he held until 1889. The day's festivities ended with a performance of Gilbert and Sullivan's opera *Iolanthe* at Wilson's Hall in Quincy by singers and musicians from North Florida.[33]

Constructed by James Clark and Company of Louisville at a cost of "about $1,000," the monument was erected by J. F. Barbour of Thomasville, Georgia, and John T. Howard of Quincy. The approximately seventeen-foot-high monument consists of an Italian marble pillar partially covered with carved

Figure 23. 1884 Quincy Confederate monument in front of the 1912 Gadsden County Courthouse in 2009. Photograph by William B. Lees.

"heavy drapery representing the Confederate flag" on an ornately decorated Italian marble pedestal and base that sits on a two-stepped granite foundation (see figure 23).[34]

The front, or north, pillar base is decorated with "C.S.A." in large raised letters with a bas-relief image of two crossed swords in their scabbards in an inset space below. The pedestal face on this side contains a large bas-relief image in an inset space of a Confederate soldier. The soldier is wearing a wide-brimmed hat, cape, coat, and cartridge box. He is holding his musket muzzle down with one hand on the gunstock. In the background are two crossed flags on staffs, a wagon wheel, a drum, two cannons, and two stacks of cannonballs. Above the soldier in raised letters is "ESTO PERPETUA," Latin for "Let it be perpetual" or "May she live forever." Below this on the pedestal base is "OUR FALLEN HEROES" in large raised letters.

An inset space on the south pedestal face contains the following in raised letters at its top: "SACRED TO THE MEMORY OF THE CONFEDERATE SOLDIERS FROM GADSDEN CO. FLORIDA WHO DIED IN THE DEFENSE OF THEIR COUNTRY." This is followed by a quotation in raised letters from the 1847 poem "The Bivouac of the Dead" by Mexican-American War and Confederate Civil War veteran Theodore O'Hara (1820–67): "ON FAME'S ETERNAL CAMPING GROUND THEIR SILENT TENTS ARE SPREAD AND GLORY GUARDS WITH SOLEMN ROUND THE BIVOUAC OF THE DEAD." Lines from this poem, which O'Hara wrote to honor his fellow soldiers from Kentucky who died in the Mexican-American War, are found on Confederate monuments throughout the country and are also found on a gate at Arlington National Cemetery and on markers in many other national cemeteries. Below this in raised letters is "ERECTED BY THE LADIES OF THE MEMORIAL ASSOCIATION OF GADSDEN CO. FLORIDA." On the pedestal base in large raised letters and numbers is "APRIL 26, 1884" (Confederate Memorial Day), apparently the date the monument or its cornerstone was erected.

A circular inset on the west pedestal face is decorated with a bas-relief image of a crescent moon and star surrounded by laurel leaves with a ribbon, which a contemporary newspaper article described as the "seal of the Confederate states."[35] Although the items in this image were widely used motifs during the Civil War, and this exact image can also be found on the cover of an 1867 printing of Edward Pollard's *The Lost Cause*, this is not the official Great Seal of the Confederate States, which was adopted in 1863.[36] A circular inset on the east face is decorated with the unofficial Florida state seal image used during the Civil War.[37] It consists of a bas-relief image of an eagle with wings spread holding four arrows in one talon and an olive branch in the other. Above the eagle in a semicircular pattern are thirteen stars, and below is a bed of cactus.

Like the monuments in Florida that came before, this one is devoted to the memory of the county's soldier dead. At the same time, it does not elevate the cause of these departed Confederates to the same level as does the monument erected a few years earlier in Marianna. Whether the ladies of Marianna were more vocal on the justness of the cause because of the Battle of Marianna, which raged through their town and saw a church and dwellings burned, can only be left to speculation.

Pensacola, 1891

At the onset of the Civil War, Pensacola was an important shipping port on the Gulf of Mexico, a railroad transportation center, and a center for commercial brick and lumber mills. It was also an important military center with a large U.S. navy yard and three masonry forts that protected the entrance to the harbor—Forts Pickens, McRee, and Barrancas. After Florida seceded in January 1861, Union forces withdrew from the navy yard and Forts McRee and Barrancas to the more defensible Fort Pickens. In early 1861 national attention was focused on Pensacola, as the very real possibility existed that hostilities might erupt there first. Instead, the first fighting occurred at Fort Sumter in Charleston Harbor in April 1861.[38]

For the remainder of 1861 and into early 1862, Pensacola was the scene of several military actions as the reinforced Union garrison at Fort Pickens refused to surrender. Two Union raids from Fort Pickens were directed against the Confederate-held navy yard in September 1861, and the Confederates retaliated in October 1861 with a night attack against the Union regiments encamped east of Fort Pickens. In the ensuing Battle of Santa Rosa Island, Confederate forces overran and destroyed a Union camp and then withdrew to their boats while fighting off a counterattack. Massive multi-day artillery duels erupted in November 1861 and January 1862.[39]

The stalemate continued until May 1862, when Confederate troops withdrew from Pensacola to reinforce their hard-pressed forces in Tennessee. On departing, they burned the navy yard and the mills and ships on the Blackwater and Escambia Rivers that flow into Pensacola Bay. Pensacola and its military facilities were quickly occupied by Union forces, who retained control for the rest of the war. It served as an important center of operations for the West Gulf Blockading Squadron and as a base for Union army operations into the surrounding areas. Union forces engaged at the Battle of Marianna in 1864 were dispatched from Pensacola.[40]

In 1889 a city park on Gage Hill overlooking Pensacola and the bay, which in 1887 had been renamed for General Robert E. Lee, was "placed under the charge of the ladies of the Confederate Monument Association with power to erect a Confederate Monument upon said square."[41] This group evolved into the Ladies' Confederate Memorial Association, which was formed on August 15, 1890, in Pensacola to take over earlier fund-raising activities originally intended for a monument in Tallahassee. Since almost all of the initial donations for that monument had come from the Pensacola area, it was decided to locate the monument in Pensacola rather than Tallahassee. Three months later, a contract was awarded to J. F. Manning and Company of Washington, D.C., to manufacture the monument at a cost of $5,000.[42]

While work on the monument proceeded, the ladies' association continued to raise the necessary remaining funds with a series of activities, including public lectures, benefit suppers, musical programs, auctions, "elocution" performances, and horse races. The dedication ceremony was originally scheduled for June 3, 1891, the anniversary of Jefferson Davis's birth, but construction delays forced it to be rescheduled for June 17. Railroad companies provided free passes to troops in uniform for travel to the event and offered private citizens a discounted rate of one cent per mile. As a result, some three thousand visitors to the city that day swelled the dedication ceremony crowd to an estimated ten thousand people.[43]

The dedication ceremony was preceded by a parade through the city of state militia companies, civic organizations, fire companies, city officials, Confederate veterans and even Union veterans, ladies' association members, schoolchildren, and a float carrying fifteen girls representing the states of the Confederacy (eleven seceded states, three border states, and West Virginia). The parade concluded at the monument for a program of prayers, music, and speeches. Featured speakers included three Confederate veterans: Governor Francis P. Fleming, prominent local businessman William D. Chipley, and former Florida House Speaker Robert W. Davis. Chipley and his wife had played prominent roles in promoting and raising funds for the monument. As the band played "Dixie," the monument was unveiled by Jennie Henderson of Tallahassee, granddaughter of Florida colonel George T. Ward, who was killed at the 1862 Battle of Williamsburg, Virginia, and for whom Confederate Fort Ward at St. Marks, Florida, had been named.[44]

Constructed of Virginia granite and some fifty feet in total height, the monument is surmounted by an eight-foot-tall statue of a Confederate soldier modeled from the circa 1888 painting *Appomattox* by John Adams Elder. A similar bronze statue, also clearly based on Elder's painting, was erected in Alexandria, Virginia, in 1889. In both statues, the booted soldier stands with his arms crossed, carries a wide-brimmed hat in one hand, and wears a haversack across his torso. Below the statue is a long shaft and pedestal with a three-stepped base. Originally erected on a short grassy knoll, the monument is currently surrounded by a large raised square concrete apron encircled by a wide brick walk added in the 1960s during a major reconfiguration and landscaping of Lee Square.[45]

The front, or south, pedestal face contains a panel with raised letters: "A.D. 1861. A.D. 1865. THE UNCROWNED HEROES OF THE SOUTHERN CONFEDERACY, WHOSE JOY WAS TO SUFFER AND DIE FOR A CAUSE THEY BELIEVED TO BE JUST. THEIR UNCHALLENGED DEVOTION AND MATCHLESS HEROISM SHALL CONTINUE TO BE THE WONDER AND INSPIRATION OF THE AGES." On the base below in large raised letters are the words "OUR CONFEDERATE DEAD." The east pedestal face contains a tribute to the recently (1889) deceased Jefferson Davis in raised letters: "JEFFERSON DAVIS, PRESIDENT OF THE CONFEDERATE STATES OF AMERICA. SOLDIER. STATESMAN, PATRIOT, CHRISTIAN. THE ONLY MAN IN OUR NATION WITHOUT A COUNTRY, YET TWENTY MILLION PEOPLE MOURN HIS DEATH."

The other monument sides contain tributes to two prominent Confederates with Pensacola connections. The north pedestal face contains a panel in raised letters: "STEPHEN R. MALLORY, SECRETARY OF THE NAVY OF THE CONFEDERATE STATES OF AMERICA." This is followed by a quotation from the 1712 play *Cato, a Tragedy* by the English playwright Joseph Addison (1672–1719): "TIS NOT IN MORTALS TO COMMAND SUCCESS; BUT WE'LL DO MORE, SEMPRONIUS, WE'LL DESERVE IT." Mallory was born in the West Indies, and his family settled in Key West in 1820 when Mallory was a young boy. He lived there until after the Civil War. A U.S. senator before the Civil War, Mallory served the Confederacy as secretary of the navy from 1861 to 1865, the only individual to serve in the same cabinet position throughout the existence of the Confederacy. After being imprisoned for almost a year by federal authorities following the war, he moved to Pensacola to practice law. He died in 1873 and is buried in Pensacola's St. Michael's Cemetery.

The west pedestal face contains a tribute panel with raised letters to another Pensacola resident: "EDWARD AYLESWORTH PERRY, CAPTAIN OF THE PENSACOLA 'RIFLES,' COLONEL OF THE SECOND FLORIDA REGIMENT, GEN-

ERAL OF THE FLORIDA BRIGADE IN THE ARMY OF NORTHERN VIRGINIA. AMONG THE FIRST TO VOLUNTEER IN THE DEFENSE OF HIS ADOPTED STATE. FAITHFUL IN EVERY POSITION TO WHICH HIS MERIT ADVANCED HIM. HIS LIFE AND DEEDS CONSTITUTE HIS BEST MONUMENT." Born in Massachusetts, Perry moved to Alabama and then Pensacola in the 1850s. During the war he served with the Second Florida Infantry in Virginia, and in 1862 he was promoted to brigadier general. Perry commanded the Florida Brigade in the Army of Northern Virginia until 1864, when he was severely wounded at the Battle of the Wilderness. After the war he returned to Pensacola and was elected governor of Florida in 1884, serving one term. Perry died in 1889 and is buried in Pensacola's St. Johns Cemetery.

As part of their mandate under the 1889 city ordinance "to fence and to improve and ornament" Lee Square, the ladies' association purchased eight hundred cannonballs and two cannons in 1891 to place around the monument.[46] Eventually, four colonial-period cannons, dating from the seventeenth and eighteenth centuries, were placed around the monument.[47] Photographs from the late 1800s and early 1900s show the cannonballs stacked in two pyramids at the southeast and southwest corners of the monument outside a square walkway enclosing the surrounding low mound.[48] The cannonball stacks in the photos are an impressive nine across at the base and nine rows in height, which would have required 284 cannonballs each, so the ladies' association apparently had quite a few to spare.

A photograph published in 1897 shows the full stacks of cannonballs, but a circa 1903 image shows the top cannonball to be missing, cannons buried muzzle down up to their trunnions at the southeast and southwest corners, and a stepped sidewalk in front of an iron fence around the low mound on which the monument sits (see figure 24). A yet later photograph (between 1905 and 1915) shows four cannons mounted on masonry pedestals at each corner (presumably two of these were the cannons previously buried), a greatly diminished stack of cannonballs on the left, and a surrounding sidewalk redone to be level. A photograph of Confederate veterans at the monument also illustrates this period (see figure 25). Eventually the cannonball stacks disappeared entirely, a post-and-chain fence replaced the iron fence (which in turn disappeared), and by the mid-twentieth century Lee Square had become neglected and overgrown to the point that the monument was hardly visible.[49]

In 1903 the ladies' association transferred responsibility for stewardship of the park to the Pensacola Chapter of the UDC. With the increase in the

Figure 24. 1891 Confederate monument in Lee Square, Pensacola, ca. 1903 photograph. Library of Congress, Prints and Photographs Division, image no. LC-D4-16277.

importance of automobile traffic, and with Lee Square located in the middle of the main approach to downtown Pensacola from the north, some city officials, beginning in the 1930s, proposed that the square be modified for better traffic flow with streets constructed through the park. This proposal, which would allow more efficient movement of traffic on Palafox Street, was controversial. From the 1930s through the early 1960s, various proposals to modify the park with new streets running through it were met with successful opposition spearheaded by the UDC and others concerned with preservation of the park's integrity. By 1963 the proposal had become so controversial that the

Confederate Monument Association was resurrected to oppose the project, and one city council member even suggested tunneling under the park rather than building streets through it. However, in 1964 the city council voted to repeal the 1889 ordinance that had placed Lee Square under the Confederate Monument Association's management, and the streets were finally constructed through the park. The monument itself remained, and as part of the street project the park was landscaped to its present configuration (see figure 26). Park improvements included the installation in 1964 of brick steps bearing the names of the thirteen Confederate states (eleven seceded states and two border states) leading up the east slope to the monument from a parking lot.[50]

Today, Lee Square is maintained by the City of Pensacola's Public Works Department as a city park. Of related interest, Lee Square is believed to have been the site of Fort McClellan, an earthwork fortification constructed by Union troops after their occupation of Pensacola in 1862. This fort, in turn, may have incorporated elements of the earlier British Fort George and Spanish Fort San Miguel, which were located in the area.

The Pensacola monument is significant in that it was the culmination of an effort that originally was intended to erect a Florida monument to the

Figure 25. Confederate veterans at the 1891 Pensacola monument, ca. 1910. Florida Photographic Collection, State Archives of Florida, image no. RC06184.

Figure 26. 1891 Confederate monument in Pensacola's Lee Square in 2009. Photograph by William B. Lees.

Confederacy in Tallahassee. The Pensacola monument is the first that focused on Florida and the Confederacy rather than on the soldier dead of an individual county. The development of this monument came at an important time, between the death of Jefferson Davis in 1889 and his final burial in Hollywood Cemetery in Richmond in 1893. Davis's death, like Robert E. Lee's in 1870, did much to galvanize the memory of the Confederacy in the South and to foment the growing narrative of the Lost Cause. Significant on this monument is the statement that Davis died without a country (his citizenship was restored posthumously by a joint resolution of Congress signed by President Jimmy Carter in 1978) and that his death was mourned by twenty million Americans, presumably of the South. This, coupled with the statement engraved on the monument about the Confederate soldiers, "whose joy was to suffer and die for a cause they believed to be just," shows clearly that this is a monument celebrating the righteous cause that was the Confederacy.

Monticello, 1899

During the war, Monticello's function as a Confederate supply center was based on the rich Middle Florida agricultural lands of Jefferson County, which produced cotton and foodstuffs, and on its manufacturing facilities. It was the site of a small shoe factory, a small woolen factory, and the Southern Rights Manufacturing Association's cotton mill, the state's only cloth mill. Located a little over a mile east of the community, the mill was known as the Bailey Cotton Mill, after William Bailey, a Jefferson County planter and the major organizer and investor in the mill. It provided cloth, yarn, and thread to the Confederate commissary throughout the war. In 1861 a spur of the Pensacola and Georgia Railroad was extended to Monticello, increasing the community's wartime importance.[51]

Fund-raising for a Confederate monument in Monticello began as early as 1882.[52] By 1886, $175 of "about $1,000" needed "to erect the desired monument" had been raised.[53] However, it was not until 1899 that the Ladies' Memorial Association of Jefferson County erected the monument on the Jefferson County Courthouse grounds (see figure 27). The monument was dedicated on May 17, 1899, with state senator Charles B. Parkhill, the son of a Confederate soldier, serving as the featured speaker.[54] His father, Captain George W. Parkhill of the Second Florida Infantry, was killed in the Battle of Gaines Mill, Virginia, in 1862. Charles Parkhill would also later be a featured speaker at the dedication ceremonies for the Confederate monuments in Brooksville (1916), Bradenton (1924), and Palatka (1924). When the monument was erected, the original 1841 courthouse was still standing, but in 1909 it was replaced with the courthouse that now graces the community's downtown.

This marble monument consists of a pillar on a pedestal and base that rests on a two-stepped granite foundation (see figure 28). After the 1904 death of Kate Dilworth Scott, who had organized the local LMA, "a bronze tablet

Figure 27. 1899 Confederate monument, Monticello, early 1900s photograph. Florida Photographic Collection, State Archives of Florida, image no. N029071.

Figure 28. 1899 Monticello Confederate monument in front of the 1909 Jefferson County Courthouse in 2010. Photograph by William B. Lees.

commemorating her many services to the Confederate cause" was placed on the monument. Historic photographs show a small plaque on the north side's marble base that is no longer present. Holes where this plaque was once attached are still visible. A photograph of the monument from the early 1900s also shows that it was surrounded by a wrought-iron fence that was gone by the 1940s. The fence that now surrounds the monument on three sides was erected by the Kate Dilworth Scott Chapter of the UDC in 1996 and was clearly based on the fence seen in the early historic photograph.[55]

The top of the pillar is ornately decorated with a sword in its scabbard, a laurel wreath, and a draped Confederate battle flag. The front, or north, face of the pillar base is decorated with "C.S.A." in large raised letters, and the pedestal cornice contains a bas-relief image of a crossed anchor and cross in an inset space. Below this is a panel engraved with "ERECTED 1899 BY THE LADIES' MEMORIAL ASSOCIATION OF JEFFERSON COUNTY FLA." On the pedestal face is "OUR FALLEN HEROES" in large raised letters. The south pedestal face is decorated with a large bas-relief image of the Confederate battle flag.

The west pedestal face is engraved with a dedicatory verse: "LET THIS TESTIMONIAL OF WOMAN'S DEATHLESS FIDELITY TO MAN'S IMPERISHABLE VALOR SPEAK TO THE SONS AND DAUGHTERS OF THIS SOUTHLAND FOR ALL TIME TO COME. LET THIS MUTE BUT ELOQUENT MARBLE TESTIFY TO THE ENDURING HARDNESS OF THAT LIVING HUMAN WALL OF FLORIDA SOLDIERY THAT STOOD DURING FOUR LONG YEARS OF PITILESS WAR—A BARRIER BETWEEN OUR HOMES AND AN INVADING FOE. LET THE YOUNG SOUTHRON, AS HE GAZES UPON THIS SHAFT, REMEMBER HOW GLORIOUSLY FLORIDA'S SONS ILLUSTRATED THEIR SUNNY LAND ON THE RED FIELDS OF CARNAGE. AND HOW WOMAN—FAIR AND FAITHFUL—FRESHENS THE GLORY OF THEIR FAME."

The east pedestal face is also engraved with a eulogizing verse: "FAR MORE INDESTRUCTIBLE THAN POLISHED STONE OR TEMPERED BRONZE IS THE MEMORY OF THOSE WHOSE LIVES WE HERE COMMEMORATE SUBLIME IN LOVE OF STATE; BRILLIANT IN EXECUTION OF HEROIC DUTY; CONSCIOUS OF RIGHTS BEYOND CONTROVERSY; PATIENT UNDER THE RAVAGES OF PESTILENCE; UNSUBDUED BY MERCILESS HARDSHIPS IN PRISON; GLORIFYING AN UNSUCCESSFUL CAUSE BY MATCHLESS DEEDS AT ARMS; ENRICHING A THOUSAND HILLS WITH CRIMSON CREST—DYED WITH PRECIOUS BLOOD; BOWING IN SUBMISSION TO GOD ALONE;—THESE BE OUR HEROES."

Information regarding the contractor who fabricated this monument is limited. There are, however, striking similarities between this monument and the one erected in 1884 in Quincy, which was fabricated by James Clark and Company of Louisville. For example, the design of the dedication "OUR FALLEN HEROES" on both monuments, while not precisely the same, is so similar as to suggest the same company was responsible for both.

Although far more modest than the one erected in Pensacola in 1891, and not evoking the name of Jefferson Davis, this monument carries on the thread of memorialization first seen in Pensacola. No longer focused on the soldier dead of a community, this monument waxes poetically on "execution of heroic duty, conscious of rights beyond controversy" and "bowing in submission to God alone." Clearly, as the nineteenth century came to an end, Floridians' view of Confederate soldiers still living, as well as memories of those who had passed, was of soldiers of a just cause who were victorious in defeat.

MONUMENTS ERECTED THROUGH THE GENEROSITY OF PRIVATE INDIVIDUALS

Confederate monuments in Florida were not erected entirely or primarily with private funds until the end of the nineteenth century. There are five such private monuments: one is a remarkable monument in Jacksonville erected in 1898; another, less spectacular but intriguing in its own right, was constructed in St. Petersburg in 1900; two are the first monuments erected on the Natural Bridge Battlefield in 1919 (discussed in detail in chapter 4); and one erected in Jacksonville's Evergreen Cemetery in 1928 commemorates a unique Civil War naval action.

Jacksonville, Hemming Plaza, 1898

When the Civil War began in 1861, Jacksonville was an important Atlantic Ocean port city that dominated the St. Johns River route into East Florida, a center for commercial lumbering mills, and a vital railroad center. Jacksonville was the terminus of the Florida, Atlantic, and Gulf Central Railroad line, which opened in March 1860 and ran west to Lake City, where it connected to the Pensacola and Georgia line, which was completed in December 1860 and extended to Tallahassee.[56] The Florida, Atlantic, and Gulf Central also crossed the Florida Railroad at Baldwin just west of Jacksonville. The Florida Railroad opened in March 1861 and connected Fernandina on the Atlantic with Cedar Key on the Gulf of Mexico.[57] As such, Jacksonville soon became a focus for Union military activities in the region and was occupied on four separate occasions between 1862 and 1864. The final occupation began in February 1864, when the city was seized for use as a base for a major Union expedition into Florida that culminated in the Battle of Olustee. After their defeat, the Union forces retreated back to Jacksonville, where they fortified the city and remained until the end of the war. During this period, Jacksonville was used as a base for conducting numerous raids along the St. Johns River and into the surrounding areas.[58]

On June 16, 1898, a large and ornate Confederate monument was dedicated in St. James Park in the center of downtown Jacksonville (see figure 29).

Figure 29. Hemming Park and 1898 Confederate monument, Jacksonville, ca. 1910 postcard. Courtesy of William B. Lees.

The monument was a gift to the State of Florida from Charles C. Hemming and his wife, Lucy. Hemming, a Confederate veteran from Jacksonville, had moved to Texas after the war and become a very wealthy banker. Costing $20,000, the monument was designed and manufactured by a Chicago firm owned by George H. Mitchell using granite supplied by the Venable and Collins Granite Company of Atlanta.[59]

The dedication ceremony was preceded by a parade through the city that culminated at the monument site for a program of prayers, music, and speeches. Led by mounted police and a U.S. military drum corps, the parade included U.S. Army troops stationed in Jacksonville training for the invasion of Cuba in the recently declared Spanish-American War, Confederate veterans, and even Union veterans. Among the floats in the parade was one drawn by four horses and containing sixteen girls dressed in the colors of the Confederacy with white dresses and red sashes. Fifteen of the girls represented the Confederate states (eleven seceded states, three border states, and the Indian Territory) while the other represented the entire Confederacy.[60]

The featured speakers included four former Confederate military officers—former Florida governor Francis P. Fleming, former Florida U.S. congressman Robert H. M. Davidson, current Florida governor William D. Bloxham, and Major General Fitzhugh Lee, commander of the U.S. Army

VII Corps training in Jacksonville for duty in the Spanish-American War. Although much of the oratory was devoted to the valor of the Confederate soldiers and the southern women on the home front, the speakers also addressed the postwar reunification of the country, particularly in light of the new war with Spain. In his remarks, Davidson noted that "the thousands of men from the North and the South, in the uniform of American soldiers [to fight the Spanish], all, all, tell us that we are not a divided people, and that the Union has been, and is forever restored." Governor Bloxham stated that northerners and southerners now "stand as one people, with one hope, one flag, and one destiny." In a similar vein, Major General Lee stated that the country was now united "under one flag, for a common cause, the only rivalry being as to which shall carry the flag further for freedom."[61]

Sixty-two feet tall, the monument is topped with an eight-and-one-half-foot-tall bronze Confederate soldier set on a highly ornate cornice. Standing at parade rest with both hands on his musket, the soldier is dressed in a winter uniform with a greatcoat with cape and is equipped with a cartridge box and a scabbard with a bayonet. On his head he wears a kepi with the initials "J. L. I.," which stands for Jacksonville Light Infantry, the unit Hemming joined when he entered Confederate service. Below the cornice is a seventeen-and-one-half-foot-tall round-column shaft made of one solid piece of granite on top of an ornate pedestal with pediments and a base on a three-stepped foundation. All four pedestal faces contain bronze plaques, and the pediments above them are decorated with bas-relief symbols.

The front, or south, pedestal face contains a bas-relief bust of Captain J. J. Dickison, the Florida Confederate officer known as the "Swamp Fox of the Confederacy" for his skill in defending the interior of Florida from Union raids and attacks, with the words "TRIED AND TRUE" above and "J. J. DICKINSON [*sic*]" below. On the pediment above are two crossed swords in their scabbards from which a bugle hangs on cords. The north pedestal face contains a bas-relief bust of General Edmund Kirby Smith, the highest-ranking Floridian in Confederate military service during the war, with the words "A CHRISTIAN SOLDIER" above and "E. KIRBY SMITH" below. Smith led the vast Trans-Mississippi Department for most of the war, and his command was the last major Confederate army to surrender at war's end. On the pediment above are two crossed rifles resting on laurel leaves. The west pedestal face contains an elaborate bas-relief image of Generals Robert E. Lee and Stonewall Jackson on horseback in the midst of Confederate soldiers with a forest in the background. Above them are the words "OUR HEROES," while the pedestal base is inscribed with "GOD BLESS OUR COUNTRY. 1898." The pediment above this is decorated with two crossed cannons in front of stacked rows of cannonballs.

The plaque on the east pedestal face contains a dedicatory verse: "TO THE SOLDIERS OF FLORIDA. THIS SHAFT IS BY A COMRADE RAISED IN TESTIMONY OF HIS LOVE, RECALLING DEEDS IMMORTAL, HEROISM UNSURPASSED. WITH RANKS UNBROKEN, RAGGED, STARVED AND DECIMATED, THE SOUTHERN SOLDIER, FOR DUTY'S SAKE, UNDAUNTED STOOD TO THE FRONT OF BATTLE UNTIL NO LIGHT REMAINED TO ILLUMINATE THE FIELD OF CARNAGE, SAVE THE LUSTRE OF HIS CHIVALRY AND COURAGE." This is followed by a quotation from the 1847 poem "The Bivouac of the Dead" by Theodore O'Hara: "NOR SHALL YOUR GLORY BE FORGOT WHILE FAME HER RECORD KEEPS, OR HONOR POINTS THE HALLOWED SPOT WHERE VALOR PROUDLY SLEEPS." On the pediment above the plaque is an anchor over two crossed oars, and the pedestal base is inscribed with "CONFEDERATE MEMORIAL. 1861–1865."

To honor Hemming for his donation of the monument, the City of Jacksonville changed the name of the monument site from St. James Park to Hemming Park in 1899. On May 3, 1901, only three years after its dedication, a fire began in Jacksonville, that before the end of the day, burned 146 city blocks and 2,638 buildings, including most of downtown. The Hemming Park monument was one of the few landmarks in Jacksonville that survived. As historian T. Frederick Davis described it, "The monument in Hemming Park, although centered in the hottest part of the fire, went through it all unscathed. . . . [O]nly the cement at the base of the monument showed a reddened glow. The bronze soldier at the top stood firm amidst the withering torrent of fire about him."[62] A photograph taken after the fire shows the monument surrounded by grass and walkways (see figure 30).[63] A postcard with a 1907 cancellation date shows the monument surrounded by a square grass apron bounded by a low retaining wall and a wide walkway.[64] By about 1920 the grass apron and retaining wall remained, but a large area of the surrounding park had been paved.[65] In 1977 the City of Jacksonville renamed the park Hemming Plaza and began a series of major renovations.[66] Today the monument is surrounded by a reflecting/wading pool, and its three-stepped foundation is now tile-covered (see figure 31).

The monument erected in Jacksonville through the Hemmings' generosity is perhaps the most handsome of all the monuments erected in the state. Today it stands as a rare survivor of the 1901 Jacksonville fire and as a centerpiece of a park that is a focal point of a rebuilt downtown. The monument is rich in

Above: Figure 30. Hemming Park and 1898 Confederate monument in the aftermath of Jacksonville's Great Fire of 1901. Florida Photographic Collection, State Archives of Florida, image no. N032735.

Left: Figure 31. 1898 Confederate monument in Jacksonville's Hemming Plaza in 2008. Photograph by William B. Lees.

symbolism and pays tribute to some of the state's most prominent Confederate soldiers as well as two heroes of the Confederacy. It is at the same time somewhat modest in that it honors the soldiers and sailors for their heroism and courage more than it honors the cause for which they fought. Contrast this to the message on the equally grand Pensacola monument erected only a few years earlier, where the cause is at the forefront. It is likely that this focus on the individual rather than the cause is at least partly due to the fact that this monument was a private gift rather than a project of a movement.

Although the Jacksonville monument was not intended as a reconciliatory monument, its less adversarial message probably facilitated the dedication's becoming an act of reconciliation. Whether or not Mr. and Mrs. Hemming, neither of whom attended the dedication, had any role in the tenor of the day is unclear. Regardless, the fact that the dedication was staged shortly after the United States entered the war with Spain in 1898, the sizable attendance, and the day's speeches made by former Confederate officers show the power of a national emergency as an engine of reconciliation. This pull toward national unity would be felt again with the onset of World War I and World War II.

St. Petersburg, Greenwood Cemetery, 1900

In what appears to have been an overt effort at reconciliation, Union and Confederate monuments were erected side by side in Greenwood Cemetery in St. Petersburg and dedicated on the same day in 1900 (see figure 32). On February 22 of that year, the anniversary of George Washington's birth, "a large crowd" attended the dedication of the two monuments. For the ceremony, a temporary wooden bandstand and speaker's platform was constructed between the monuments. A parade through St. Petersburg featuring the city's brass band and "over two hundred school children" carrying flags preceded the dedication ceremony. Featured speakers included Congressman Stephen M. Sparkman of Tampa, Union veteran J. F. Chase, and Confederate veteran Thomas Givens. "Elegant refreshments in great abundance were served" following the ceremony to those in attendance.[67]

Both monuments were designed and built by Zephaniah Phillips, a Union veteran of both the army and the navy. Although Phillips appears to have paid for and been the driving force behind these monuments, at least nominally the Union monument was sponsored by the Kit Carson Post of the GAR, while the Confederate monument was sponsored by "Confederate veterans and friends." An early settler in Pinellas County after the Civil War, Phillips

Figure 32. Dedication of Union and Confederate monuments in Greenwood Cemetery, St. Petersburg, in 1900. St. Petersburg Museum of History, Historic Photo Archives.

served as commander of the GAR's Kit Carson Post. After his death in 1903 he was buried in Greenwood Cemetery north of the Union monument.[68]

The two monuments are identical in design and are located on either side of a central flagpole within an oval drive at the center of the cemetery. As shown in a historic photo of the dedication ceremony, the flagpole was a part of the monuments' original design. Each monument consists of an approximately six-foot-high rectangular pedestal made of stucco-covered masonry topped with an identical Civil War–era mortar donated by the U.S. government (see figure 33). Unlike the mortar on the Union monument, the mortar on the Confederate monument currently has a cannonball in its tube, although this does not appear in the photo of the 1900 dedication ceremony. Both monuments have marble plaques inserted into the front side of the pedestal. The Union monument plaque reads "IN MEMORY OF UNION DEAD. ERECTED BY KIT CARSON POST G.A.R. 1900," while the Confederate monument plaque reads "IN MEMORY OF CONFEDERATE DEAD. ERECTED BY CONFEDERATE VETERANS AND FRIENDS. 1900." The dedication ceremony photo shows that both pediments originally had stacks of cannonballs, also donated

Figure 33. 1900 Confederate monument in St. Petersburg's Greenwood Cemetery. Photograph by William B. Lees, 2011.

by the U.S. government, on each corner surrounding the mortars and at least one additional cannonball on the base of the Confederate monument, but these are no longer present. The historic photo also clearly shows the mortars mounted on original carriages, which were replaced at an unknown time by simple iron supports.[69]

The St. Petersburg monuments are simple and understated not only in design but also in message, being dedicated simply to the soldier dead. What is remarkable about these twin monuments is that they were erected as an offer of reconciliation, symbolized by their twin design and their dedication in a single ceremony. That this happened through the efforts of a private individual, rather than an organization, is not at all surprising given the tension that had developed in the preceding decades between Civil War heritage groups seeking to memorialize what had become differing Union and Confederate memories.

Jacksonville, Evergreen Cemetery, 1928

During the Union blockade of Charleston, South Carolina, the Confederate military employed several innovative naval weapons in their attempts to break the Union navy's stranglehold on the city's seaborne commerce. Charleston Harbor was the site of the first successful submarine attack in history on February 17, 1864, when the *H. L. Hunley* attacked and sank a Union warship, the *Housatonic,* although the *Hunley* also sank during or shortly after the attack. The Confederates also used semi-submersible torpedo boats armed, like the *Hunley,* with a spar torpedo attached to the vessel. When water was taken into its ballast tanks, a torpedo boat operated very low in the water, with only the open-top conning tower and the boiler's smokestack visible above the surface.

On October 5, 1863, the Confederate torpedo boat *David* attacked the Union warship *New Ironsides* off Charleston. Although the Union vessel was damaged, it did not sink. Among the four crewmen on the *David* was its

Figure 34. 1928 monument to the crew of the CSS *David* in Jacksonville's Evergreen Cemetery. Photograph by William B. Lees, 2013.

engineer, James Hamilton Tomb. After water thrown up by the explosion extinguished the *David*'s boiler fires, three of the crewmen, including Tomb, abandoned the boat. However, Tomb returned to the vessel a short time later and was able to relight the fires. He and the ship's pilot, who had stayed aboard because he could not swim, were able to return the boat to Charleston, while the other two crewmen were captured by the Union navy. Following the war, Tomb served as an officer in the Brazilian navy and eventually settled in Jacksonville, where he had lived as a young boy.[70]

In 1928 Tomb had a monument erected at his family plot in Evergreen Cemetery in honor of his shipmates on the *David* (see figure 34).[71] The ten-foot-high granite monument consists of an obelisk shaft partially covered in a tasseled shroud with a pedestal and base on a one-stepped foundation. The front base is inscribed with "TOMB." The right side pedestal contains the inscription "IN MEMORY OF MY SHIPMATES OF THE CONFEDERATE TORPEDO BOAT DAVID CHARLESTON S.C. OCT. 5, 1863" followed by the names of the four crewmen, including "CHIEF ENGINEER JAMES HAMILTON TOMB, C.S.N." The opposite pedestal face contains an engraved dedication to a family member, James Harvey Tomb Jr., with the date of May 5, 1905. James Hamilton Tomb died in 1929 and is buried in a marked grave next to the obelisk monument.

UNITED DAUGHTERS OF THE CONFEDERACY COMMUNITY MONUMENTS

The UDC saw the erection of Confederate monuments as a key component of their program to vindicate the South. Although the influence of the emerging Lost Cause narrative that was championed by the UDC can certainly be seen in monuments erected in Florida by LMAs during the nineteenth century, it was less evident in monuments erected by private individuals at the turn of the century. Although the UDC was established in 1894, it did not erect its first monument in Florida until 1901. This monument was placed in the Confederate plot containing dead from the Battle of Olustee in the Oaklawn Cemetery at Lake City (discussed in detail in chapter 4).

In her book on the UDC, historian Karen L. Cox observes that most Confederate monuments date after 1895 and that the number exploded between the turn of the twentieth century and World War I. Cox argues that this was due to the dramatic increase in influence of the Daughters during this period.[72] For reasons related to World War I and a feeling within the organization that its goal of vindicating the Confederacy had been achieved, Cox concludes that 1918 for all practical purposes marks the end of the era of the promotion of the Lost Cause through education and construction of monuments and was, in fact, the start of a general decline of the organization.

In his recent master's thesis, Barrett Codieck argues that this does not hold true for Florida and that the work of the UDC in the state continued in earnest through the 1920s.[73] Codieck does not provide a comprehensive analysis of UDC monuments but instead focuses on other significant work conducted by that organization. Our research on Florida monuments supports Codieck's assertion. Although some of the monuments erected in Florida in the 1920s certainly had their genesis years before, the fact remains that this decade saw the placement of the highest number of UDC monuments. Although monument construction declined drastically after 1930, the UDC continued to erect monuments in Florida at a steady pace through the Civil War Centennial of 1961–65.

In addition to the sheer number of monuments erected in Florida communities during the 1910s and 1920s, the Daughters also achieved some profound successes in marking Florida Civil War battlefields during that period. A massive monument co-sponsored by the UDC and the State of Florida was dedicated on the Olustee Battlefield in October 1912. In November 1921 a monument co-sponsored by the UDC and the State of Florida was dedicated in commemoration of the Battle of Marianna. On Confederate Memorial Day in April 1922, an impressive monument co-sponsored by the UDC and the State of Florida was dedicated on the Natural Bridge Battlefield.

The UDC monuments at the Lake City cemetery, Olustee, Marianna, and at Natural Bridge, as well as the Benjamin Confederate Memorial at Ellenton, commemorate places where major events occurred in Florida during the Civil War and are discussed in chapter 4 because of that connection. Other UDC monuments discussed in that chapter are the 1936 Colquitt and 1951 Finegan monuments at the Olustee Battlefield, the 1942 monument to the escape of Judah P. Benjamin in Sarasota, and the 1951 monument at Yellow Bluff Fort in Jacksonville. Although the UDC used all of these monuments to advance their general mission of vindication, their location at a place of conflict sets them apart from others that do not have this association.

In this section we consider what we call community monuments. These are monuments placed by the UDC in their local communities and erected to provide a permanent addition to the landscape that would carry the message of Confederate vindication into the future. These were not erected because of any particular event during the Civil War, but were seen by the Daughters as a crucial part of their program to instill the message of the Lost Cause within their community as an adjunct to their school education programs. Their goal was to place monuments in public places that children and adults would be certain to encounter during their daily activities, thereby serving as a constant reminder of the "true story" of the Confederacy.

Gainesville, 1904

By the time of the Civil War, Gainesville was an important stop on the Florida Railroad, which ran from Fernandina on the Atlantic coast to Cedar Keys on the Gulf coast and had opened in March 1861 just prior to the outbreak of hostilities.[74] Cotton and foodstuffs from the region's rich agricultural lands and cattle from South Florida were shipped from Gainesville to ports on the Atlantic and the Gulf of Mexico. The town was also a center for commercial lumber mills. During the Civil War it gained added importance as a supply depot for the Confederacy.[75]

Gainesville was the scene of two military engagements during the war. In February 1864 a Union force of fifty men entered Gainesville in an attempt to capture or destroy railroad trains that they believed to be there. They occupied the community for more than two days and skirmished with a small Confederate force before returning north to their base at Sanderson after they had destroyed what Confederate supplies they could locate. In August 1864 a larger Union force of 340 men under the command of Colonel Andrew Harris reoccupied Gainesville. Here, they were attacked by a Confederate force of 175 men commanded by Captain J. J. Dickison of the Second Florida Cavalry. In the ensuing battle, the Union force was completely routed with two hundred casualties, most of whom were captured, while the Confederate force suffered less than ten killed or wounded.[76]

On January 19, 1904, the anniversary of Robert E. Lee's birth, the Kirby Smith Chapter of the Florida Division of the UDC dedicated a monument costing $1,000 on the grounds of the 1886 Alachua County Courthouse in Gainesville (see figure 35). According to a UDC report of the period, the monument was erected at "the spot where Lt. Worthington fell at the [February 1864] Battle of Gainesville," although this is not commemorated on the monument itself.[77]

The monument was designed and constructed by the George N. Clark Company of Jacksonville.[78] It is topped with a statue of a Confederate soldier imprinted with a foundry mark below the soldier's right foot stating that it was "Manufactured by W. H. MULLINS. Salem, Ohio. J. SEGESMAN

Figure 35. 1904 Confederate monument in front of the 1886 Alachua County Courthouse in Gainesville, 1919 photograph. Florida Photographic Collection, State Archives of Florida, image no. RC03412.

Sculptor." The W. H. Mullins Company featured the monument in a 1913 promotional booklet along with some forty-five other Union, Confederate, and Revolutionary War monuments it had produced.[79] According to this booklet, "Sheet metal is now a standard material for the expression and execution of the sculptor's art, the same as stone and cast metals. . . . Sheet copper and sheet bronze statuary being much lighter than cast bronze and the process being comparatively simple, we are enabled to produce artistic results far more economically than by other processes. . . . Our statues are executed in sheet bronze and copper only."[80]

Also believed to be the sculptor of the Union soldier statue on the 1921 monument at Lynn Haven, Florida (see chapter 3), Segesman was born in

Figure 36. 1904 Gainesville Confederate monument as it appeared in 2011. Photograph by William B. Lees.

Switzerland and joined the Mullins Company as a modeler in 1896. He went on to become their lead sculptor in 1899 and worked for the company for twenty-five years.[81] Prior to the monument's unveiling, lists of the members of the UDC's Kirby Smith Chapter, members of the local UCV chapter, and the more than four hundred people who contributed to the monument's construction were placed in "a basin, or pocket between the first and second stones at the base of the monument."[82]

An estimated two thousand people attended the dedication ceremonies, and Gainesville businesses were closed during the program, which included music, prayers, and speeches. Featured speakers included Judge Horatio Davis, a Confederate veteran and later mayor of Gainesville; Willis Lucullis

Palmer, son of a Confederate veteran and former mayor of Orlando; and Confederate brigadier general Robert Bullock of Ocala, who for a time commanded the Florida Brigade in the Army of Tennessee. After the unveiling, "the cadets from East Florida Seminary [present-day University of Florida] fired a salute of three guns [cannons]" causing "$45 worth of glass to tumble from the windows of the court house nearby," which the UDC later paid to replace. Following the ceremonies, a "grand barbeque and fish chowder" meal was served to the attendees.[83]

Eighteen feet tall in total, the Gainesville monument features at its top a six-foot-tall sheet bronze/copper Confederate soldier holding his musket at parade rest (see figure 36). The musket originally had a bayonet affixed to it, but the bayonet was broken off sometime after 1971. Standing with his left foot on a knapsack with a rolled blanket strapped to the top, the soldier is wearing a wide-brimmed hat, an empty Enfield bayonet scabbard, a cartridge box, a haversack, and a percussion cap box on his belt. The statue stands on a Georgia granite pedestal, which is topped with an ornate pediment in the form of a crenellated castle turret, and a four-stepped base. The statue itself is made of sheets of copper or bronze visibly fastened together with rivets.[84]

The front, or north, face of the pedestal is inscribed with "IN MEMORY OF THE CONFEDERATE DEAD 1861 1865" with an engraved image of a Confederate First National Flag between the dates. The south pedestal face contains the inscription "ERECTED BY KIRBY SMITH CHAPTER NO. 202 U.D.C. A.D. 1904." Engraved on the pedestal's west face are the following lines from the poem "March of the Deathless Dead" by Father Abram J. Ryan: "THEY FELL FOR US, AND FOR THEM SHOULD FALL THE TEARS OF A NATION'S GRIEF." The east pedestal face is engraved with "THEY COUNTED THE COST AND IN DEFENCE OF RIGHT THEY PAID THE MARTYR'S PRICE."

In 1905 a low masonry wall was added around the monument by the Kirby Smith Chapter at a cost of $100, but this feature is no longer present. The adjacent 1886 Alachua County Courthouse was demolished and replaced by a new courthouse in 1958. That building, enlarged in 1962, now serves as the Alachua County Administration Building. A bronze plaque on this building, which may have also been on the 1886 courthouse, lists the roster of the "Stonewall Camp No. 1438" of the UCV. The monument's statue has undergone several restorations since its original erection. In 1965 it had to be repaired after "vandals smashed the face of the Confederate soldier." In 1993 it was taken down from the monument and given a thorough cleaning and sealing before being reinstalled.[85]

Ocala, 1908

When the war began in 1861, Ocala was an important commercial center for the rich agricultural lands of Central Florida. During the war, several units were raised from the region for service in the Confederate military, and a number of area residents distinguished themselves. The most prominent of these was Captain J. J. Dickison of the Second Florida Cavalry, a local plantation owner who became known as the "Swamp Fox of the Confederacy" for his skill in defending the interior of Florida from Union raids and attacks.

After several years of fund-raising, which included a $500 contribution from Marion County, the Dickison Chapter of the Florida Division of the UDC had, by 1908, raised the $1,500 necessary for the erection of a large Confederate monument in Ocala. They ordered a monument from the McNeel Marble Company of Marietta, Georgia, which they planned to dedicate in January 1908 in honor of the anniversary of Robert E. Lee's birth. However, "on account of the impossibility of the manufacturers to complete the monument by the time fixed for the unveiling," the ceremony was postponed to April 25, 1908. April 26 was Confederate Memorial Day, but since that date fell on a Sunday in 1908, the chapter decided to dedicate it on the preceding day to avoid interfering with church activities (see figure 37). By early April 1908 the monument was in place on the southwest corner of the grounds of the 1906 Marion County Courthouse—facing southwest—in the downtown Ocala Public Square.[86]

A parade through the city with the city band, the local Florida National Guard unit, Ocala High School teachers and students, UDC members, Confederate veterans, and Ocala citizens preceded the dedication. The ceremony, which was "largely attended," included musical selections, prayers, poetry, and several "addresses." Speakers included Frank Harris, editor of the *Ocala Banner;* Dr. G. A. Nunnally, a Confederate veteran and president of Columbia College in Lake City; and Colonel John M. Martin, a Confederate veteran of the Ninth Florida Infantry who had also served as a Confederate congressman. As was common to many dedication ceremonies of the era, the band played "Dixie" while thirteen girls in white dresses with sashes representing the states of the Confederacy (eleven seceded states and two border states) decorated the monument.[87]

In addition to praising the righteousness of "our southern cause" and the courage of Confederate soldiers and women, many of the speakers devoted their remarks to the legacy of the Civil War in the South. Harris stated that,

Figure 37. Dedication of Confederate monument on grounds of the Marion County Courthouse in Ocala in 1908. Florida Photographic Collection, State Archives of Florida, image no. RC03941.

as a result of the war, "those of us now living enjoy a larger measure of freedom and a greater tolerance of opinion than that possessed by any other nation at any other time in the world's history, and these truths tell us that the war drums of 1860 did not beat in vain." Dr. Nunnally noted that the war's aftermath produced "a wonder without precedence—how a nation so defeated could so soon be brought back into harmony and fellowship, and today, as recent events [the Spanish-American War] disclose, no part of this country is more loyal in its allegiance to the stars and stripes than that represented in the Confederate states." Colonel Martin stated that the ceremony was "an occasion for sorrow, as well as rejoicing. For sorrow because memory recalls the friends of our younger years, who are now gone. For rejoicing because they have left behind them a heritage to their country and children that must and ever will be cherished."[88]

The ornate monument is twenty-four and one-half feet tall and topped with a statue of a Confederate soldier made of Italian marble. Standing at parade rest with both hands on his musket, the soldier wears a wide-brimmed hat and is equipped with a blanket roll across his torso, a scabbard with a bayonet, and a canteen. Braced against a tree stump, he stands on a granite shaft topped with a castle-like turret pediment. This pediment is reminiscent of that on the Gainesville monument, erected only four years prior, and which may have served as an inspiration, although Gothic Revival architecture for churches and public buildings still held favor at this time. Below the shaft is a Georgia granite pedestal and plinth which currently rest upon a three-stepped granite foundation.[89]

The front face of the monument is the most elaborate. The pedestal contains the dedicatory verse "THE SOUTH REVERES HER WASHINGTON, JEFFERSON, MADISON, MONROE, ANDREW JACKSON, AND OTHERS, WHO LAID THE FOUNDATIONS OF OUR GRAND REPUBLIC. SHE HONORS HER LEE, STONEWALL JACKSON, STUART, JOHNS[T]ON, FOR[R]EST, AND EVERY BRAVE SON WHO FOUGHT TO PRESERVE OUR LIBERTIES, GUARANTEED BY THE FATHERS, UNDER THE CONSTITUTION." At the top of the pedestal are the dates "1861–1865," while the pedestal base contains the word "CONFEDERATE." The plinth facade contains a marble plaque with the inscription "ERECTED A.D. 1908 BY DICKISON CHAPTER NO. 56, U.D.C. IN HONOR OF THE HEROES OF THE CONFEDERACY."

The other three pedestal sides are decorated with bas-relief symbols. One side contains a partially furled Confederate battle flag with "CSA" above and, below, the following lines from the poem "The Conquered Banner" by Father Abram J. Ryan, the "Poet-Priest of the South": "ITS FAME ON BRIGHTEST PAGES, PENNED BY POETS AND BY SAGES, SHALL GO SOUNDING DOWN THE AGES." Another side contains crossed flags with "1861–1865" above, while the other side has crossed rifles below "CSA."

There have been several locations for this monument since it was first erected in 1908. In 1965 the 1906 Marion County Courthouse was demolished, and a new one was built several blocks to the northwest. After considerable community debate and controversy over its appropriate location, including a suggestion to place it on the Central Florida Junior College (now the College of Central Florida) campus just west of Ocala, the monument was moved to the new courthouse's northeast corner. In 1987 the monument was removed and stored during a courthouse expansion project, and in 1991 it was reinstalled on the southeast corner of the now-renamed Marion County Judicial Center. The 1991 reinstallment was also controversial, as leaders in the local African American community protested its being located in front of a county building. In 2007 an expansion of the Marion County Judicial Center resulted in the monument's relocation to a nook on the building's south side,

Figure 38. 1908 Ocala Confederate monument at its new location in Veterans Memorial Park in 2011. Photograph by William B. Lees.

where its prominence and visibility were compromised. After considerable community debate between those who raised concerns about its visibility at its new site and those who felt it should not be located at a county building at all, it was moved again in 2010 with private funding to a new location in the Ocala–Marion County Veterans Memorial Park about two miles east of downtown Ocala. Known locally as the "Johnny Reb" monument, it was rededicated at its current location on April 16, 2011 (see figure 38).[90]

The Ocala monument stands out as significant among Florida Confederate monuments because of the inscribed dedicatory verse, which is the most profound expression of the Lost Cause narrative in Florida and probably on par with any throughout the South. By invoking Washington, Jefferson, Madison, and Monroe as founders of the country and framers of the Constitution, and by also invoking Andrew Jackson, whose imprint on Florida was large and whose philosophy on national governance fit well with the Lost Cause narrative, the inscription on this monument sets the stage for the just cause of the Confederacy. But to make things clear, the inscription goes on to designate Robert E. Lee, Stonewall Jackson, Jeb Stuart, Joseph E. John-

Figure 39. Confederate veterans and members of the United Daughters of the Confederacy at the 1909 Confederate monument in Madison's city park, early 1900s photograph. Florida Photographic Collection, State Archives of Florida, image no. MA0273.

ston, and Nathan Bedford Forrest as champions of constitutional liberties for which, in the Lost Cause narrative, the South had gone to war. The inclusion of Forrest in this list also probably raises additional symbolism. As one of the founders of the original Ku Klux Klan in Tennessee, Forrest embodied a plank of the narrative that involved preservation of white privilege in the post-emancipation South.[91]

Madison, 1909

During the war, Madison was an important stop on the Pensacola and Georgia Railroad route for the transportation of Confederate soldiers and war materials, as well as cotton and foodstuffs from Middle Florida's rich agricultural lands. Several Confederate camps for the mustering and training of soldiers were located in the Madison area. In 1852 the Madison Shoe Factory was constructed ten miles west of town. It was the state's largest leather factory and annually produced eleven thousand pairs of shoes, as well as wagon harnesses and other leather goods, for the Confederate government.[92]

On June 23, 1909, a "great crowd" attended the dedication of the Confederate monument erected by the Elizabeth Harris Chapter of the Florida Division of the UDC in the center of Madison's downtown city park (see figure 39). The monument was designed and manufactured by the McNeel Marble Company of Marietta, Georgia, at a cost of $1,250. "To the strains of martial music" provided by the city band, the ceremony began with a procession of UDC members, Confederate veterans, and city children from the Madison County Courthouse across the street to the monument site where a crowd had assembled. There, the program consisted of music, prayer, and speeches. Speakers included a UDC representative, a UCV representative, Mayor Randell Rowe, and Confederate colonel James Knox Livingston of Bennettsville, South Carolina, a former resident of Madison. A band played "Dixie" as the monument was unveiled. After the ceremony, Confederate veterans were invited "to a nearby soda fountain where the Daughters had provided ice cream and cold drinks for their refreshment."[93]

Twenty-three feet tall, the monument is topped with an Italian marble statue of a Confederate soldier at parade rest holding his musket with both hands and braced against a tree stump (see figure 40). The soldier is wearing a wide-brimmed hat, a blanket roll across his torso, a percussion cap box, and a canteen. The statue stands on a marble shaft, below which is a marble pedestal and plinth resting on a marble three-stepped foundation. Marble cannonballs that once rested on corners of the pedestal base, as shown in historic photographs, are no longer present.[94]

All four pedestal faces are decorated with bas-relief symbols. The front, or west, face of the pedestal is decorated with an image of a Confederate battle flag on a broken staff with the date "1861" above and "1865" below. The north pedestal face has a wheeled artillery piece, while the east pedestal face contains a Southern Cross of Honor inscribed with "UNITED DAUGHTERS CONFEDERACY TO THE U.C.V." The south pedestal face contains an image of two crossed swords attached to sword belts with trees in the background. The plinth facade below it contains the words "OUR CONFEDERATE SOLDIERS" in bas-relief. Topped with a slightly different soldier statue and bearing different inscriptions, the shaft and base of this monument are identical to that erected a year later in Lakeland, also by the McNeel Marble Company (described later in this chapter).

Located in the center of the city park, a raised grass apron enclosed by a square masonry retaining wall encircled the monument as early as 1911.[95] Sometime later, the grass apron was replaced by bushes and the retaining wall

Figure 40. 1909 Confederate monument in Madison's city park in 2011. Photograph by William B. Lees.

was ringed by paved surrounding and feeder walkways.[96] Recently, the concrete around the retaining wall was replaced with a wide brick pavement. In 2003 a bronze plaque was added below the front pedestal of the monument by the Sons of Confederate Veterans (SCV) with "LEST WE FORGET" at its top. The plaque lists the names of approximately three hundred Confederate soldiers from units formed in Madison County who were "KILLED IN ACTION" or "DIED IN SERVICE."

Erected only a year after the Ocala monument, which profoundly invokes the Lost Cause, this monument is remarkably focused simply on commemorating the soldiers of the Confederacy. Unusual, and important, is the dedication wording on this monument contained within the Southern Cross of

Honor, which documents that this monument is a gift from the UDC to the UCV. By this period, the national UDC was focused on vindication of the Confederacy, of course embodied by the Confederate veteran himself, but this direct connection between the Daughters and the UCV on a monument itself is rare and perhaps more locally relevant than the national cause of vindication.

Lakeland, 1910

Munn Park, in the middle of downtown Lakeland, was the scene of a Confederate monument dedication on June 3, 1910, the anniversary of Jefferson Davis's birth (see figure 41). The monument was sponsored by the Lakeland Chapter of the Florida Division of the UDC, which, since 1905, had been raising funds for its purchase. Fund-raising activities conducted before and after the monument's erection included benefit baseball games, a minstrel show and play, donations from Lakeland merchants, a "tag day" sale and bazaar, and sales of cake, cookies, ice cream, and lemonade. In 1908 the UDC and the Lakeland City Council agreed to erect the monument in the center of Munn Park. By 1910 the UDC chapter, with the assistance of a $200 contribution from the Lakeland City Council, had raised enough funds to order a large monument from the McNeel Marble Company of Marietta, Georgia. Erected that spring, the monument cost $1,750. The UDC paid the remaining balance due on the monument by 1912, two years after its placement.[97]

The June 3, 1910, dedication ceremony was attended by, as one newspaper described it, "probably the largest crowd in her [Lakeland's] history," with roughly a thousand out-of-town visitors, including some three hundred Confederate veterans, joining the local citizenry at the event. The dedication was preceded by music in Munn Park performed by the Tampa Municipal Band, lunch in the park for the veterans, and a procession of UDC members and veterans to the monument site. The featured speaker was Florida attorney general and future governor Park Trammell of Lakeland. In his remarks, Trammell paid considerable homage to the service of southern women on the home front during the war and to the preservation of this spirit by the UDC. The monument, he stated, was evidence that "the patriotic love and devotion of the women of the South of those days has been transplanted into the minds and hearts of the present generation." Other speakers included Confederate major general Evander M. Law, UDC Florida Division president Sister Esther Carlotta, and Lakeland mayor W. K. Jackson. Common to many dedications of the period, the monument was unveiled by thirteen girls

Figure 41. Members of the United Daughters of the Confederacy at the 1910 Confederate monument in Lakeland's Munn Park, 1915 photograph. Florida Photographic Collection, State Archives of Florida, image no. N033917.

in white dresses with red sashes representing the states of the Confederacy (eleven seceded states and two border states).[98]

Topped by an Italian marble statue of a Confederate soldier standing at parade rest, the monument stands some twenty-six feet in height. With both hands on his musket, the soldier is wearing a wide-brimmed hat and is braced against a stump (see figure 42). He is equipped with a haversack, a scabbard with bayonet, and a cartridge box. Below the statue are a long shaft, a pedestal and plinth, and a three-stepped foundation, all made of Georgia marble. A

Figure 42. 1910 Confederate monument in Lakeland's Munn Park in 2009. Photograph by William B. Lees.

bas-relief image of two crossed Confederate battle flags with the date "1861" above and "1865" below decorates the front, or southeast, face of the pedestal. The plinth facade on this side contains "CONFEDERATE DEAD" in bas-relief and an engraved "CSA" on the shaft above. Inscribed on the northeast pedestal face is "THIS MONUMENT WAS ERECTED BY THE LAKELAND CHAPTER, UNITED DAUGHTERS OF THE CONFEDERACY IN MEMORY OF THE NOBLE SONS OF THE SOUTH. A.D. 1910."

A poem is inscribed on the southwest pedestal face: "IN MEMORY OF THAT NOBLE BAND, WHO HAVE CROSSED THE MYSTIC STREAM, AND ARE RESTING NOW IN THAT HAPPY LAND, WHERE PEACE AND PLEASURE REIGN SUPREME. THE HEROIC DEEDS WILL NEVER FADE, FROM MEMORY'S BRIGHTEST PAGE, AND THEIR BRAVE DEFENSE OF COUNTRY AND HOME, IS LEFT AS A GLORIOUS HERITAGE." Historic photographs show that the monument originally had four marble cannonballs on the top of the pedestal base, one in each corner. These are no longer present, but indentations on the monument where they were located are still visible.[99]

A 1915 photograph of the monument surrounded by members of the UDC shows the monument situated in the middle of Munn Park surrounded by nothing more than bare earth.[100] A wrought-iron fence was later added around the monument, as can be seen in a 1936 photograph, but it was apparently removed in the 1980s due to deterioration.[101] Today the monument remains the centerpiece of the park and is complemented by lighting, a circular brick path and feeder walks, and plantings.

Tampa, 1911

One of the most striking Confederate monuments in Florida was erected in Tampa in 1911. During the war Tampa was an active area for Confederate blockade-running and salt production, and it was blockaded by Union vessels throughout the war. A number of military actions took place there, including the shelling of the city and adjacent Fort Brooke in 1862 and 1863 and several Union raids on Tampa Bay–area saltworks. A Union raid on Tampa in 1863 resulted in the destruction of three blockade runners and a sharp skirmish with a Confederate force at Ballast Point. For two days in May 1864, a Union force temporarily occupied the city and destroyed the battery at Fort Brooke.[102]

In 1903 the Tampa Chapter of the Florida Division of the UDC began an effort to erect a Confederate monument in Tampa. For the next eight years the chapter conducted a series of fund-raising activities, including bake sales and selling dolls at Christmas. At one point the chapter sponsored a spelling bee, a popular activity in that era, at the city's opera house with an admission charge of twenty-five cents, which drew a full house. The effort came to fruition in 1911.[103]

Erected on the grounds of the 1891 Hillsborough County Courthouse on a plot at the southwest corner of Franklin Street and Lafayette Street (now Kennedy Boulevard), the Tampa Confederate monument was dedicated on February 8, 1911 (see figure 43). It was originally scheduled to be dedicated on January 19 of that year, on the anniversary of Robert E. Lee's birth, but funds "were still being raised and groundbreaking did not occur until January 21, 1911," causing the date to be pushed forward. The McNeel Marble Company of Marietta, Georgia, designed and manufactured the monument at a cost of $3,000, which included a $500 contribution from the City of Tampa.[104]

The dedication ceremonies began with a program of music, prayer, and speeches at the nearby Greeson Theater. Speakers included Tampa mayor Donald B. McKay, UDC Florida Division president Sister Esther Carlotta, prominent local businessman William G. Brorein, and prominent Tampa attorney Herbert S. Phillips, who was the featured speaker. In his remarks, Phillips stated that the monument symbolized not only "the heroism and courage of those who wore the gray" but also "their fortitude under defeat, their manly acceptance of the result, [and] their entire post bellum record as patriotic and upright citizens." Continuing this conciliatory theme, he noted that the monument stood "in honor of the men and women who gave us the Old South and out of the ashes of war have given us the New South, which is the best part of the Union, as the Union is the best part of the world." At the conclusion of the program, a procession of the program audience led by mounted police and the Tampa Municipal Band marched to the monument site, where an estimated five thousand people witnessed the unveiling to the singing of "Dixie." The size of the crowd was bolstered by students and teachers from Tampa who were able to attend because the school board had authorized the closure of schools for the afternoon.[105]

Standing approximately fifty feet tall, the monument consists of a tall marble obelisk shaft, pedestal, and base on a four-stepped foundation. Approximately halfway up the shaft, the dates "1861" and "1865" are wrapped in a band around the obelisk, and the front of the shaft contains a bas-relief Confederate battle flag. Unique to this monument are two marble statues of Confederate soldiers fabricated in Italy that flank the pedestal on separate ornate columns (see figure 44). On the north side is a young Confederate sol-

Figure 43. 1911 Confederate monument on the grounds of the 1891 Hillsborough County Courthouse in Tampa; photograph taken prior to its 1953 relocation. Florida Photographic Collection, State Archives of Florida, image no. RC11760.

Figure 44. Detail of 1911 Tampa Confederate monument *Memoria in Aeterna* showing paired soldier statues. Photograph by William B. Lees, 2009.

dier who is well equipped and marching proudly off to war. Wearing a wide-brimmed hat cocked to one side and a new uniform, he carries a musket on his shoulder and is equipped with a blanket roll across his torso, a scabbard with bayonet, a cartridge box, and a canteen. The upper part of his musket is now missing. On the column below this statue are the words "UNITED IN THE PAST; ONE IN THE FUTURE." On the south side is a Confederate soldier returning home from war. With his head bandaged and his uniform in tatters, he carries his hat in one hand and uses his musket as a walking stick or cane with the other, and is without a blanket roll. As with the other statue, the upper part of his musket is now also missing. On the column below this soldier are the words "LEST WE FORGET."[106]

The west pedestal face contains the following in raised letters: "TO THE HONOR AND COURAGE OF THE PATRIOTS OF THE CONFEDERATE STATES OF AMERICA, THIS MONUMENT IS DEDICATED BY TAMPA CHAPTER, NO. 113, U.D.C., AND THE CITIZENS OF TAMPA. JANUARY 1911." On the base below are the words "MEMORIA IN AETERNA" (Latin for "In eternal remembrance"). Etched into the east pedestal face is a poem by Sister Esther Carlotta: "NOT THEIRS THE RUSH OF MADDENED WRATH THAT RECKLESS SUNDERED TIES OF BLOOD, BUT HONOR'S BEACON SHOWED THE PATH WHERE DAUNTLESS DUTY STOOD. THROUGH FAMINE YEARS THEY FOLLOWED FAR WHERE HER UNSWERVING BANNERS LED—BEYOND HER GLORY'S FLAME-TIPPED STAR—BEHIND HER—HONOR'S DEAD. THE YEARS THEIR SLOW PROCESSION KEEP, THE BANNER BARRED WITH RED IS FURLED—BUT NOW ITS GRAY CLAD SOLDIERS SLEEP THE HEROES OF A WORLD. SR. E. C." Sister Carlotta, an Episcopal nun, served as president of the UDC's Florida Division from 1909 to 1916.

In August 1911 the UDC had one of the soldier statues replaced, as the original figure "did not meet with the specifications."[107] In October 1946 a U.S. Navy sailor who was "frolicking" on the courthouse grounds with other sailors in celebration of Navy Day climbed onto the monument and "accidentally" caused the statue of the soldier marching off to war to fall, breaking it into three pieces. A photograph of the courthouse taken in the late 1940s clearly shows the monument without this statue. The sailor was charged with destroying property and fined $300. The UDC presented a bill to the Navy Department of $1,100 to pay for its replacement. Sculpted in Italy, the replacement statue was dedicated in a ceremony on June 3, 1949, the anniversary of Jefferson Davis's birth, with Florida congressman James Hardin Peterson as the featured speaker.[108]

In 1952 a new Hillsborough County Courthouse was constructed several blocks to the east of the old (1891) building that was demolished in 1953. At this time the monument was moved to its current location at the new courthouse, and its orientation was slightly changed in the process. The monument now is parallel with the city grid, facing west-southwest. In 1996, Hillsborough County, in collaboration with the national "Save Outdoor Sculpture" program sponsored by the nonprofit organization Heritage Preservation, oversaw a condition assessment, thorough cleaning, and conservation treatment of the monument. "In order to maintain the original integrity" of the monument, the broken muskets were not repaired. In 1999 vandals severed the hand of one of the Confederate soldiers, but Hillsborough County paid for its repair and the fabrication of a new hand. In 2000 the UDC and the SCV undertook a thorough hand-sanding, cleaning, repair, and sealing of the monument.[109]

The oratory of the 1911 dedication of this monument is clear in defining the Confederate soldier as a national patriot and identifying the New South (formed by the former Confederate states) as the best part of the nation, all in keeping with the Lost Cause narrative. The symbolism on the monument—in particular, the twin statues of the soldiers going to war and returning home—provides a profound statement of the effect of the war on the soldier-veterans themselves, if not on the home front, following the cessation of hostilities. "United in the past, one in the future" signifies the eternal bond between these heroes of the South, whose defeat in war the UDC had accepted as its duty to vindicate and transform into victory.

Orlando, 1911

On June 3, 1911, the anniversary of Jefferson Davis's birth, a Confederate monument was dedicated at the intersection of Central Boulevard and Main Street (now Magnolia Avenue) in Orlando (see figure 45). After several years of fund-raising activities, which included bake sales, strawberry and ice cream festivals, and the solicitation of donations from Orlando residents and winter visitors, the Annie Coleman Chapter of the Florida Division of the UDC had raised $2,500 to purchase a large monument from the McNeel Marble Company of Marietta, Georgia.[110]

The featured speaker at the dedication ceremony was Florida attorney general Park Trammell, who had also been the featured speaker for the 1910 dedication of the Confederate monument in Lakeland. Trammell would later be elected governor of Florida and a U.S. senator. Others in attendance included Orlando mayor William Hayden Reynolds and former mayor William H. Jewell, a Confederate veteran. Similar to other monument dedications of the period, thirteen girls representing the states of the Confederacy (eleven seceded states and two border states) participated in its unveiling.[111]

The monument is twenty-eight feet tall and consists of a Georgia marble shaft, pedestal, and base on a two-stepped foundation, surmounted by a marble statue of a marching Confederate soldier braced against a marble stump. Wearing a wide-brimmed hat, the soldier carries his musket on his shoulder and is equipped with a blanket roll across his torso, a canteen, and a cartridge box. All four sides of the monument are decorated with bas-relief symbols and raised inscriptions.[112]

The front, or east, pedestal face contains two crossed Confederate battle flags with the date "1861" above and "1865" below. On the base below is a quote from the poem "The Conquered Banner" by the "Poet-Priest of the South," Father Abram J. Ryan: "TIS WREATHED AROUND WITH GLORY AND 'TWILL LIVE IN SONG AND STORY, THOUGH ITS FOLDS ARE IN THE DUST." On the shaft just above the pedestal there is an ornate raised "CSA."

The north pedestal face contains sponsorship information, "ERECTED BY ANNIE COLEMAN CHAPTER NO. 225, UNITED DAUGHTERS OF THE CONFEDERACY, OF ORLANDO, FLORIDA. A.D. 1911," while the base contains a bas-relief of two crossed rifles with a forest in the background. The south pedestal face contains "TO THE HONORED MEMORY OF THE SOLDIERS, THE SAILORS, THE STATESMEN OF THE CONFEDERATE STATES OF AMERICA" followed by lines from the 1814 Lord Byron (1788–1824) poem "On the Death of Sir Peter Parker": "TIME CANNOT TEACH FORGETFULNESS WHEN GRIEF'S FULL HEART IS FED BY FAME." The base on this side contains a bas-relief of two crossed swords in their scabbards with a forest in the background.

The west pedestal face contains a quotation from the "In Memory" epitaph written by John Dimitry for Confederate general Albert Sidney John-

Figure 45. 1911 Confederate monument at the intersection in front of the 1892 Orange County Courthouse in Orlando. Postcard ca. 1915. Florida Photographic Collection, State Archives of Florida, image no. PC2516.

Figure 46. 1911 Orlando Confederate monument at its original location centered in a city intersection. Postcard ca. 1915. Courtesy of William B. Lees.

ston, who was killed at the 1862 Battle of Shiloh, Tennessee: "THE CAUSE FOR WHICH HE SUFFERED WAS LOST; THE PEOPLE FOR WHOM HE FOUGHT WERE CRUSHED; THE HOPES IN WHICH HE TRUSTED WERE SHATTERED; BUT HIS FAME, CONSIGNED TO THE KEEPING OF TIME, WHICH HAPPILY, IS NOT SO MUCH THE TOMB OF VIRTUE AS ITS SHRINE, SHALL, IN THE YEARS TO COME, FIRE MODEST WORTH TO NOBLE ENDS."[113] On the base below is a dedicatory statement: "THIS MONUMENT SHALL STAND THROUGH THE YEARS TO COME AS OUR LOVING TRIBUTE TO THE CONFEDERATE SOLDIER AND AS A MEMORIAL OF HIS HEROIC COURAGE, HIS UNPARALLELED DEVOTION AND HIS UNSELFISH PATRIOTISM."

Originally erected in the middle of the intersection of Central Boulevard and Magnolia Avenue at the location of the 1892 Orange County Courthouse, the monument was soon deemed a traffic hazard as both Orlando's population and the use of the automobile grew. While at that location, it was guarded by a two-rail pipe fence (see figure 46).[114] In 1917 it was moved to

Figure 47. 1911 Orlando Confederate monument in its current location overlooking Lake Eola and the modern cityscape in 2009. Photograph by William B. Lees.

its present location in Lake Eola Park, with the City of Orlando paying one-half of its relocation cost. When moved to the east end of Lake Eola Park the monument was surrounded by grass, but it was eventually incorporated into a wide landscaped concrete walkway system that today serves as a major entrance to the park (see figure 47). In 1965 the soldier's musket was broken into pieces, presumably in an act of vandalism. The musket was repaired at no cost by the renowned sculptor Albin Polasek of nearby Winter Park.[115]

The original placement of this monument within the intersection of city streets in Orlando is a perfect reflection of the program of monument building promoted by the national UDC. This program sought to place monuments in prominent public places, where those passing by, especially children, would see the monument on a daily basis and absorb the message the monument was designed to convey. This message was, of course, the narrative of the Lost Cause, which is overtly contained in the engravings on the Orlando monument through, among other things, reference to the soldier's heroic courage, devotion, and patriotism.

Miami, 1914

In 1910 the Southern Cross Chapter of the Florida Division of the UDC established a fund for the erection of a Confederate monument in Miami, and by the fall of 1913 sufficient funds had been raised for that purpose. Prior to the monument's erection, the chapter debated whether the monument should be placed on the grounds of the 1904 Dade County Courthouse or in the Confederate plot at the Miami City Cemetery. In August 1913 the chapter decided that the monument should be placed in the cemetery. Then, in September 1913, city leaders persuaded the chapter to erect it on the southeast corner of the courthouse grounds instead. Work on the monument commenced that month.[116]

The monument was constructed by the Clark Monument and Stone Company of Jacksonville at a cost of $885. The dedication was originally scheduled for September 27, 1913, Marianna Day, the anniversary of the Battle of Marianna, but was postponed until June 3, 1914, the anniversary of Jefferson Davis's birth (see figure 48). Some two thousand people attended the dedication ceremony, which included prayers, music by Miami's Stanage Orchestra, and speeches. The speakers, who included Confederate veteran C. M. Brown, Judge R. B. Gautier, and community leader James F. Jaudon, paid tribute to

Figure 48. 1913 Confederate monument on the grounds of the Dade County Courthouse in Miami. Postcard postmarked 1922. Florida Photographic Collection, State Archives of Florida, image no. PC2108.

Figure 49. 1913 Miami Confederate monument as it appeared in 2009, minus the obelisk and reassembled in Confederate Circle in the Miami City Cemetery. Photograph by William B. Lees.

the Confederate dead and to the UDC for raising the funds for the monument. As the orchestra played "Florida, My Florida," the monument was unveiled by eleven girls representing the seceded Confederate states in white dresses with red sashes.[117]

The original monument stood twenty-five feet high and consisted of an obelisk, pedestal, and three-stepped base. Contemporary newspaper accounts state that the obelisk was made of marble, while the rest of the monument is granite.[118] The front face was originally decorated with an intertwined bas-relief "CSA" on the cornice, a bas-relief image of a Confederate battle flag on a staff, "1861–1865" in large raised numbers on the uppermost base step, and "OUR HEROES" on the base step below. The opposite-side pedestal contains the inscription "ERECTED 1913" in raised letters surrounded by a bas-relief laurel wreath and ribbon on the pedestal and the engraved inscription "ERECTED BY THE SOUTHERN CROSS CHAPTER UNITED DAUGHTERS OF THE CONFEDERACY TO ALL WHO WORE THE GREY" on the topmost base step. On the base step below is a quotation from Jefferson Davis: "IT IS A DUTY WE OWE TO POSTERITY TO SEE THAT OUR CHILDREN SHALL KNOW THE VIRTUES AND BECOME WORTHY OF THEIR SIRES." The quotation is from a speech Davis gave on April 25, 1882, in New Orleans, and is found on several Confederate monuments throughout the South.

In 1926, during the construction of the new and larger Dade County Courthouse, the monument was reported as having been disassembled in sections and placed in storage in a construction shed. Although the plan was to reassemble the monument on the grounds of the new courthouse after its completion in 1928, it was ultimately moved to the Miami City Cemetery (see figure 49). The obelisk shaft was snapped off during a hurricane, most likely in 1935, and was never replaced; it is missing in a 1941 newspaper photograph of the monument. Also, at some point, either when the monument was moved or when it was repaired after the hurricane, it was incorrectly reassembled. As a result, the bas-relief Confederate flag is now on the back of the monument, while the laurel wreath and date of erection are on the front below the bas-relief "CSA."[119]

The remaining portion of the monument is approximately seven feet tall and rests on a masonry pad in the middle of Confederate Circle in Miami City Cemetery surrounded by nineteen marked graves of Confederate veterans. The headstones are laid flat on the ground rather than being erect, including one very large one at the base of the monument's front. This plot was given by the City Cemetery Board to the UCV and the UDC for their use in 1905.[120]

In 2002, improvements were made to Confederate Circle, including the planting of fourteen palm trees and the replacement of curbing. In 2004, two small granite benches were added to the east side of Confederate Circle adjacent to the monument in honor of the one hundredth anniversary of the Southern Cross Chapter of the UDC. The base of each bench is inscribed with "UDC #796," the chapter number of the Southern Cross Chapter. The seat of the northernmost bench is inscribed with "HUSBAND FATHER AND

BROTHER," while the southernmost bench seat is inscribed with a biblical verse.[121]

Brooksville, 1916

At the time of the war, Brooksville was a commercial center for the farms and plantations of west-central Florida. In July 1864 the "Brooksville Raid" was launched by a Union force of 240 men who landed near Bayport on the coast and advanced inland toward Brooksville to destroy Confederate supplies. For a week the Federals raided and destroyed plantations in the area surrounding Brooksville, although they never entered the city itself. After skirmishing with Confederate Home Guard troops on several occasions, the Union force fell back to the coast and returned to their post at Fort Myers with several Confederate prisoners, contraband slaves, and captured cotton and livestock.[122]

The dedication of the Confederate monument on the grounds of the 1913 Hernando County Courthouse in Brooksville occurred on June 3, 1916, the anniversary of Jefferson Davis's birth (see figure 50). The ceremony was preceded by a parade, including the Tampa Military Band and automobiles decorated in Confederate colors and flags carrying Confederate veterans and members of the UDC, which proceeded from the railroad station to the monument site. Some five thousand people attended the ceremony, which featured a program of music, prayers, and speeches. Speakers consisted of local community leaders, UDC officials, Brooksville mayor W. R. Chalker, and former Florida Supreme Court justice Charles B. Parkhill of Tampa, the son of a Florida Confederate soldier killed in the war. As the band played "Dixie," the monument was unveiled, and following the ceremony a barbecue picnic dinner was served to the attendees.[123]

Sponsored by the Brooksville Chapter of the Florida Division of the UDC, the monument was designed and manufactured by the McNeel Marble Company of Marietta, Georgia.[124] Approximately twenty feet tall, the monument consists of an Italian marble statue of a Confederate soldier on a pedestal and base resting on a granite three-stepped foundation (see figure 51). Standing at parade rest with both hands on his musket and braced against a stump, the soldier wears a wide-brimmed hat and is equipped with a blanket roll across his torso, a scabbard with a bayonet, a cartridge box, and a canteen.

The front, or southeast, pedestal face contains a bas-relief Confederate battle flag with the dates "1861" above and "1865" below. Below this is an inscription in raised letters, "ERECTED BY BROOKSVILLE CHAPTER NO. 71.

Above: Figure 50. 1916 Confederate monument in front of the Hernando County Courthouse in Brooksville, 1926 photograph. Florida Photographic Collection, State Archives of Florida, image no. RC03417.

Left: Figure 51. 1916 Confederate monument on the grounds of the historic Hernando County Courthouse in Brooksville in 2008. Photograph by William B. Lees.

UNITED DAUGHTERS OF THE CONFEDERACY JUNE 3, 1916," and the historical UDC motto, "LOVE MAKES MEMORY ETERNAL." On the cornice above the pedestal is "CSA" in raised letters, and on the base below is "CONFEDERATE SOLDIERS" in raised letters.

The northwest pedestal face contains a dedicatory inscription with lines from the poem "March of the Deathless Dead" by Father Abram J. Ryan, the "Poet-Priest of the South," inserted in the middle of the verse: "THIS MONUMENT PERPETUATES THE MEMORY OF OUR FALLEN HEROES,—'WE CARE NOT WHENCE THEY CAME; WHETHER UNKNOWN OR KNOWN TO FAME THEIR CAUSE AND COUNTRY STILL THE SAME, THEY DIED AND WORE THE GRAY,'—LEAVING TO POSTERITY, A GLORIOUS HERITAGE—AN IMPERISHABLE RECORD OF DAUNTLESS VALOR."

St. Augustine, William Wing Loring, 1920

On December 30, 1920, the Anna Dummett Chapter of the Florida Division of the UDC dedicated a monument to Major General William Wing Loring on the Government House grounds in St. Augustine (see figure 52). A "large number of people" attended the ceremony, held on the thirty-fourth anniversary of Loring's death, which began in the Jefferson Theatre with a program of prayer, music, and speeches. Featured speakers included St. Augustine city attorney Edward N. Calhoun, St. Augustine mayor Peter R. Perry, and Loring's niece Mrs. William Loring Spencer. Following the ceremony in the theater, the audience moved across the street, where the monument was unveiled followed by the singing of "The Star-Spangled Banner." Most downtown businesses closed during the dedication "as a mark of respect for the dead hero, and in deference to the many who desired to attend the unveiling ceremonies."[125]

Born in 1818, Loring was raised in St. Augustine after his family moved there from North Carolina when he was four. A career soldier, he served in the Second Seminole War, the Texas War for Independence, and the Mexican-American War, where he was badly wounded and his left arm had to be amputated. He then served for many years with the U.S. Army on the western frontier, rising to the rank of colonel. When the Civil War began in 1861, Loring resigned his commission to join the Confederate army. He was commissioned a brigadier general in 1861 and a major general in 1862. Loring served in both the eastern and western theaters of the war as a division commander. In the postwar period he served as an officer in the Egyptian army for ten years before finally returning to the United States in 1879. Loring died

Figure 52. 1920 William Wing Loring monument on the grounds of Government House in St. Augustine in 2008. Photograph by William B. Lees.

in New York City in 1886 and the following year was reburied in an elaborate funeral at Evergreen Cemetery in St. Augustine.

Loring's gravesite at Evergreen Cemetery was maintained by the Anna Dummett Chapter while they raised funds to erect a monument to him within the city. In 1919 Loring's niece and namesake, Mrs. William Loring Spencer, returned to St. Augustine after the death of her husband in Nevada. She joined in the effort by the Anna Dummett Chapter to raise funds for a Loring memorial in an unusual manner, giving "reading[s] of head, face and hands" in a tent by the post office. The chapter was quick to deny that this was "fake fortune telling," rather describing it as "scientific psychlogic [*sic*] readings" by "the gifted niece of a distinguished uncle."[126]

On July 3, 1920, a fifteen-square-foot site on the Government House grounds (then known as the Federal Building Park or Postoffice [*sic*] Park) was granted to the Anna Dummett Chapter by the U.S. Treasury Department for the Loring monument. With the consent of his family, Loring's remains were reinterred on this site in a small copper case on July 6, 1920, and on July 13 an obelisk monument was erected over his remains. After its dedication in December 1920, the 1921 Florida Legislature appropriated $2,000 to be paid to the Anna Dummett Chapter to add to the $1,225 raised by the chapter. The state funds were designated for "making the final payment for the Loring Memorial" and for "properly completing the curbing, railing and concrete work" on the monument.[127]

The McNeel Marble Company of Marietta, Georgia, constructed the twenty-five-foot-tall monument, which consists of an obelisk shaft on a pedestal and a two-stepped base that rests on a foundation of poured concrete made with coquina shells.[128] A panel on the south pedestal face is engraved with "IN MEMORY OF A DISTINGUISHED AMERICAN SOLDIER, CITIZEN OF ST. AUGUSTINE, FLA. BORN DECEMBER 4, 1818. DIED DECEMBER 30, 1886. HIS COURAGE IN BATTLE WAS CONSPICUOUS; HIS DEVOTION TO DUTY UNFAILING; HIS ABILITY RECOGNIZED BY THREE GOVERNMENTS. HE COMMANDED THE FIRST TRANS-CONTINENTAL MARCH; CONVOYING TO CALIFORNIA, IN SAFETY AN EMIGRANT TRAIN OF THREE HUNDRED WAGONS, THROUGH PATHLESS AND HOSTILE TERRITORY; AN UNSURPASSED RECORD. THIS MEMORIAL IS ERECTED BY ANNA DUMMETT CHAPTER DAUGHTERS OF THE CONFEDERACY, AND FRIENDS, THAT THE RECORD OF HIS LIFE MAY BE AN INSPIRATION TO AMERICAN YOUTH. 1920." Below this on the uppermost base step is "WILLIAM WING LORING" in large raised letters.

The north pedestal face contains a panel engraved with "THE LORING ME-

MORIAL" and a chronology of the events and dates regarding the monument's erection. Below this is a bas-relief image of the Egyptian flag, and a history of Loring's service with the Egyptian army is engraved on the topmost base step. In front of the monument on this side is a large bronze plaque set in a granite block with a detailed history of Loring's life and military service. This plaque was placed at Loring's gravesite by the State Museum, University of Florida, in May 1920 and was moved to its present location after Loring's remains were reinterred at the monument site in July 1920.

The west pedestal face contains a panel with a bas-relief image of the Confederate battle flag with "CONFEDERATE STATES ARMY 1861–1865. BRIGADIER GENERAL MAY 1861. MAJOR GENERAL FEBRUARY 1862" engraved below. On the east pedestal face is a panel with a bas-relief image of the American flag with "FLORIDA TROOPS 1832–1838: 'THE BOY SOLDIER.' UNITED STATES ARMY 1846–1861: CAPTAIN, MAJOR, COLONEL" engraved below.

The Loring monument was erected following the United States' involvement in World War I. According to historian Karen Cox, the South's patriotic response in terms of soldier volunteers and public and UDC assistance to the war effort represented the final proof of vindication for the South and its soldiers. While this monument did not itself promote the Lost Cause narrative, the project is interesting as an example of the UDC's memorialization of the Confederate service of a man who also had a very long and distinguished career in service to the United States.

Key West, 1924

The city of Key West with its massive brick fortification, Fort Zachary Taylor, remained in Union possession throughout the war and served as an important supply base and military headquarters for the Union army and navy. However, many of its citizens harbored sympathies for the South, and a number of them fled Union-held Key West to form a military company known as the Key West Avengers. The unit first served in the Confederate Coast Guard at Tampa and later in the Seventh Florida Infantry Regiment, which fought in the western theater.

As early as 1915, the Stephen R. Mallory Chapter of the Florida Division of the UDC began to raise funds for the erection of a monument to these Confederate troops. The chapter's namesake, Mallory, had served as Confederate secretary of the navy and prior to the Civil War had made Key West his home. After several years of fund-raising, the monument was erected at the entrance of Key West's Bayview Park, which then had an unobstructed view

Figure 53. 1924 Confederate monument in Bayview Park in Key West, ca. 1930s postcard. Courtesy of William B. Lees.

of the bay. The monument was erected immediately east of, and in harmony with, Bayview Park's historic bandstand (see figure 53). The dedication took place on January 19, 1924, the anniversary of Robert E. Lee's birth, with a program of prayers, music, and speeches. A "large crowd" attended the ceremony, which featured the unveiling of the monument by four granddaughters of Confederate veterans as the band played "Dixie" as well as the laying of bouquets at the monument base by seventeen great-granddaughters of Confederate veterans. Mayor F. H. Ladd accepted the monument on behalf of the City of Key West. The featured speaker was Key West attorney Jeptha Vining Davis, son of a Confederate veteran of the same name who had moved to Key West from Mississippi after the Civil War. The program ended with the singing of the "Star-Spangled Banner" and a benediction.[129]

Designed by Clinton G. Bailey of Key West, a civil engineer by trade, this distinctive monument consists of four connected pergola-type archways. Constructed of stucco-covered masonry, the monument is thirteen and three-quarters feet tall, while the rectangular base measures twenty-three feet by fourteen and one-half feet. The monument is supported by two columns set on pedestals at all four corners and is open-aired on the sides and top. On the front, or northeast, pedestals are two marble plaques. The southern pedestal plaque is inscribed with "TO THE SOLDIERS AND SAILORS OF THE CONFEDERACY," and the northern pedestal plaque is inscribed with "ERECTED BY STEPHEN R. MALLORY CHAPTER NO. 1562 U.D.C. JANUARY 19, 1924."[130]

The monument appears to have undergone some major changes over time (see figure 54). UDC correspondence from 1924 states that the monument had "a flat roof . . . in the center of which is placed an arc light" for night illumination, but these features are no longer present. A circa 1930s postcard also shows the roof and an inscription above the columns on the roof structure facing the street which reads "1861 IN MEMORIAM 1865." This inscription is also not present today. The original monument plan included placement of bronze tablets with the names of Key West's Confederate dead, which, if ever installed, are no longer present.[131]

The Confederate monument in Bayview Park is located further south than the 1866 Union monument in Clinton Square (see chapter 1) and the New York Union monument, also in Bayview Park (see chapter 4). This Confederate monument therefore appears to be the southernmost Civil War monument in the United States.

Figure 54. 1924 Confederate monument in Key West's Bayview Park as it appeared in 2012. Photograph by William B. Lees.

Bradenton, 1924

In the years leading up to the war, the Manatee River area was a major sugar production region with large sugarcane plantations located near the Village of Manatee (now known as Bradenton), which became the target of Union raiders during the war. During one such attack, in early August 1864, a Union naval force raided the village where they destroyed a large saw and grist mill before proceeding to the Gamble Plantation at nearby Ellenton where they destroyed its sugar mill. Later that month, Union soldiers landed at the Village of Manatee and occupied the community for several weeks before departing.[132]

In the 1920s the Judah P. Benjamin Chapter of the Florida Division of the UDC undertook fund-raising activities to purchase the Gamble Plantation, which had fallen into a state of disrepair, and to erect a Confederate monu-

Figure 55. Red-sashed girls who had just participated in the 1924 unveiling of the Confederate monument at the Manatee County Courthouse in Bradenton. Manatee County Public Library, Historical Image Digital Collection, image no. M01-03356-A.

ment on the Manatee County Courthouse grounds in Bradenton. By March 1924 the chapter raised over $1,300 for the monument and then, "feeling assured that the remaining funds necessary will be subscribed," proceeded to place an order with the McNeel Marble Company of Marietta, Georgia.[133]

As indicated by the date on the monument, the chapter had apparently planned to dedicate the monument on June 3, 1924, the anniversary of Jefferson Davis's birth. It was not, however, until shortly after that date that the local contracting company of Shirley and Mattison completed the concrete base and the McNeel Marble Company shipped the monument. The dedication was held on June 22, 1924 (see figure 55).[134]

Attended by "more than a thousand people," the dedication ceremony included a program of prayer, music, and speeches. Captain William W. Carnes, a Confederate veteran from Tennessee who moved to Florida after the war, served as master of ceremonies, and the monument was unveiled by four girls in white dresses with red sashes as the orchestra played "Dixie." Featured speakers included Bradenton mayor Whitney Curry, prominent Bradenton attorney and later Florida state senator Dewey Dye, and former Florida Supreme Court justice Judge Charles B. Parkhill of Tampa, whose father, a Confederate officer from Florida, had been killed in the Civil War. In his remarks, Parkhill lauded the courage of the Confederate leaders and soldiers but concluded that "it was well . . . that the result [of the Civil War] was as it was, so that this country could go on one and indivisible and as the greatest single force in the world." The ceremony ended with the singing of "The Star-Spangled Banner."[135]

Approximately twenty feet high and made of white granite, the monument consists of an obelisk shaft with a flared base set on a concrete foundation (see figure 56). The front, or north, base of the shaft contains a bas-relief image of a Confederate battle flag on a staff with the words "IN MEMORY OF OUR CONFEDERATE SOLDIERS" inscribed below. The west shaft base contains the inscription "ERECTED BY JUDAH P. BENJAMIN CHAPTER UNITED DAUGHTERS OF THE CONFEDERACY JUNE 3, 1924" with "STONEWALL JACKSON" inscribed below.

The south shaft base is decorated with a bas-relief image of an elaborate, interwoven "CSA" surrounded by a laurel wreath with streamers and the inscription "1861 1865 LEST WE FORGET." Below this is inscribed "JEFFERSON DAVIS." The east shaft base is inscribed with "CALM AND NOBLE IN PEACE. COURAGEOUS AND CHIVALROUS IN WAR. TRUE TO THE BEST TRADITIONS OF THE SOUTH. THE CONFEDERATE SOLDIER LIVES ENSHRINED IN THE

Figure 56. 1924 Bradenton Confederate monument in front of the historic Manatee County Courthouse in 2009. Photograph by William B. Lees.

HEARTS OF HIS GRATEFUL COUNTRYMEN." Below this is inscribed "ROBERT E. LEE."

The reason why only four girls were used in the ceremony, rather than the traditional eleven or thirteen, is left to speculation. The dedication remarks, which acknowledged not only the courage of the Confederate soldier but also the importance of the reunified country as a world power, appear to reflect on the extraordinary effort of the United States in the recent World War I. Nonetheless, the monument invokes the honor of the Confederate soldier, the importance of his values to later generations, and the role of Jackson, Davis, and Lee as heroes and patriots.

In 2003, construction of a new Manatee County Judicial Center adjacent to the courthouse spurred considerable community debate as to whether the monument should be removed from the courthouse grounds. Some advocated its relocation to the antebellum Gamble Plantation purchased by the Judah P. Benjamin Chapter in 1925 and donated to the State of Florida the following year (see a more complete discussion of Gamble Plantation in chapter 4). Despite opposition to the monument remaining on the grounds of a public building, particularly from leaders in the local African American community, it was not relocated. In 2013, as part of courthouse grounds renovation, the county announced plans to move the monument about twenty feet from the front of the building to its west side to make way for the construction of a gazebo. The monument remains in its previous orientation at its new location with its front facing north.[136]

Palatka, 1924

During the war, several Confederate military camps were located in the Palatka area, but after Union gunboats gained control of the St. Johns River in 1862, most residents abandoned the city and resettled in Confederate-held interior areas. Union gunboats landing at the city found it mostly deserted, but in March 1863 an attempted landing at Palatka was repulsed by Confederate troops. However, a stronger Union force returned in March 1864 and occupied the community until April. In July 1864, Palatka was again occupied by a strong Union force, which remained until August when they abandoned the city for the duration of the war. During both 1864 occupations, Union pickets fought several skirmishes with Confederate troops in the area.[137]

On April 26, 1924, Confederate Memorial Day, a ceremony was held for the laying of the cornerstone for a Confederate monument in Palatka on the grounds of the 1909 Putnam County Courthouse. The event was sponsored by the Patton Anderson Chapter of the Florida Division of the UDC. Activities that day included a parade, music from the Palatka Band, and speeches, with Judge A. V. Long of Palatka as the featured speaker.[138]

On November 11, 1924, a dedication ceremony was held for the completed monument in conjunction with Armistice Day, now known as Veterans Day, activities (see figure 57).[139] Armistice Day celebrated the signing of the armistice that brought an end to World War I. Selection of that day to dedicate a Confederate Civil War monument is not surprising given the importance

Above: Figure 57. 1924 Confederate monument on the grounds of the Putnam County Courthouse in Palatka, 1925 photograph. Florida Photographic Collection, State Archives of Florida, image no. RC03413.

Left: Figure 58. 1924 Palatka Confederate monument on the grounds of the Putnam County Courthouse in 2008. Photograph by William B. Lees.

of World War I for sectional reconciliation. The UDC's national organization had very vocally expressed the opinion that sectional reconciliation had finally been achieved as a result of World War I, and it is likely this sentiment was also held by local chapters such as the one in Palatka.

Activities that day included a band concert at the courthouse, a parade of decorated automobiles and floats, and a speech by U.S. senator Park Trammell, followed by a second parade from the St. Johns River to the monument site for the dedication. Parade participants included police and fire departments, bands, Boy and Girl Scouts, UCV members, other veterans' organizations, UDC members, and local civic organizations and dignitaries.[140]

The dedication ceremony included music by the Palatka Band, prayers, and speeches. The featured speaker was former Florida Supreme Court justice Charles B. Parkhill of Tampa, who had also been the featured speaker at earlier Confederate monument dedications in Monticello in 1899, Brooksville in 1916, and Bradenton in 1924. A crowd "estimated at over 14,000 persons—the largest crowd ever assembled in Palatka"—attended the ceremony. Following the ceremony, other activities included a football game between Putnam High School and the University of Florida "Rats" (as their freshman team was known) and a dance at the Casino on the St. Johns River.[141]

Constructed by the Clark Monument and Stone Company of Jacksonville, the monument consists of a granite pedestal and base on a one-stepped foundation topped with a sheet bronze/copper statue of a Confederate soldier (see figure 58). Based on a comparison with statues from their 1913 catalog, the soldier was probably manufactured by the W. H. Mullins Company of Salem, Ohio.[142] Standing at parade rest with both hands on his musket, the soldier is equipped with a wide-brimmed hat, a bedroll across his torso, a percussion cap box, a bayonet in its scabbard, a cartridge box, and a canteen. In 1986 the monument was vandalized and the musket was damaged.[143]

The front, or south, pedestal face is decorated with a bas-relief image of three crossed Confederate flags—the First National flag with seven stars, the Confederate battle flag, and the Third National flag. Below the flags is engraved "ALTHOUGH THE FLAG THEY DIED TO SAVE FLOATS NOT O'ER ANY LAND OR SEA THROUGHOUT ETERNAL YEARS SHALL WAVE THE BANNER OF THEIR CHIVALRY." On the pedestal base below is "1861—OUR CONFEDERATE HEROES—1865" in large raised letters and numbers.

The north pedestal face is engraved with "ERECTED A.D. 1924 BY PATTON ANDERSON CHAPTER UNITED DAUGHTERS OF THE CONFEDERACY WITH THE ASSISTANCE OF WILLIAM IVERS, C.S.A. AND OTHER FRIENDS AS A ME-

MORIAL TO THE HEROISM, FORTITUDE AND GLORY OF THE MEN WHO WORE THE GRAY IN THE SIXTIES. WITH THE HOPE THAT THEIR LOVE OF COUNTRY, DEVOTION TO PRINCIPLE, AND FIDELITY TO THE CAUSE THEY BELIEVED WAS RIGHT, MAY BE AN INSPIRATION TO PEOPLE OF EVERY AGE." William Ivers of Palatka served in the Second Florida Infantry Regiment as a private and fought with the Florida Brigade in the Army of Northern Virginia. After the war he returned to Palatka, where he made his fortune in real estate.

The east pedestal face is engraved with a quotation from the 1847 poem "The Bivouac of the Dead" by Theodore O'Hara: "NOR SHALL YOUR GLORY BE FORGOT WHILE FAME HER RECORDS KEEP." The west pedestal face is engraved with "THE PRINCIPLES FOR WHICH THEY FOUGHT WILL LIVE ETERNALLY."

At the corners of the statue foundation are four artillery projectiles, each on its own small concrete base—two iron conical shells, one iron cannonball, and one concrete faux cannonball. The iron artillery projectiles were reportedly recovered from Civil War engagements in the Palatka area and appear to be original to the monument, as they are present in a photograph taken in 1925.[144]

Dixie Highway—Bradfordville, 1927, and Nassau County, 1928

In the 1920s the UDC began a campaign to erect monuments containing bronze plaques to mark the route of the Dixie Highway and to honor Robert E. Lee. The monument plaques generally followed a uniform design and inscription developed by Mrs. James Madison Gudger Jr. of the North Carolina Division of the UDC.[145] Between 1926 and 1935 at least eleven such monuments were erected, with seven in North Carolina, one in Ohio, one in South Carolina, and two in Florida.

The Dixie Highway was not a single route but rather a series of interconnecting segments that provided alternate routes between the Great Lakes region and Florida. In Florida, the Eastern Division of the Dixie Highway provided two routes from Macon and Savannah, Georgia, to Jacksonville and then south to Miami, while the Western Division ran from Macon through Tallahassee south to Orlando and then Naples. Several options to cross over between the Eastern and Western Divisions ran from Jacksonville to Tallahassee, from West Palm Beach to Arcadia, and from Miami to Naples.[146]

On September 30, 1927, about a thousand people attended a dedication ceremony for a Dixie Highway/Robert E. Lee monument north of Tallahassee near Bradfordville (see figure 59). The ceremony included prayers, music

Figure 59. Dedication of Robert E. Lee/Dixie Highway monument in 1927 at Bradfordville, Leon County. Florida Photographic Collection, State Archives of Florida, image no. N046318.

from the Tallahassee Junior Band and a quartet of Tallahassee male singers, and speeches. Speakers included Dr. Sumter L. Lowry of Tampa, the commander in chief of the SCV; Thomas J. Appleyard of Tallahassee, a Confederate veteran and prominent journalist and printer; Mrs. Franklin L. Ezell of Leesburg, president of the Florida Division of the UDC; and Fons A. Hathaway of Tallahassee, chairman of the Florida State Road Board. Also on the dais were three Union veterans from Ohio who had traveled to Florida to return a Confederate battle flag captured during the Civil War. The event was filmed by Paramount News.[147]

The land for the monument site was deeded to the Anna Jackson Chapter of the Florida Division of the UDC by one of its members, Mrs. Nicholas Ware Eppes (Susan Bradford Eppes). As shown on the illustration of the original monument plaque on the dedication ceremony program and as stated by the chapter president in 1964, the monument was erected in 1926 but not dedicated until the following year. A photograph of the dedication ceremony shows that the monument was originally situated in an open, grassy plain and was surrounded by a rectangular concrete pad that extended three to four feet from the base. The Anna Jackson Chapter made improvements to the site over the years so that it eventually included a small garden, was surrounded by a low masonry wall, and was reached by a set of stairs from U.S. Highway 319 (also known as Thomasville Road).[148]

Since its dedication in 1927, the monument has been relocated twice, the first time after having apparently been vandalized. In November 1941 and September 1946 the monument's plaque was reported missing by the Anna Jackson Chapter. In 1964 the chapter president reported that the "oval bronze inset of Gen. Lee and his horse Traveller was missing" and that the bronze plaque "had been removed and tossed to the side." The Leon County Commission contributed $50 for cleaning the monument and "restoring the bronze inset," and state agencies assisted in cleaning up the monument site. That same year, the chapter proposed deeding the monument property to the state, but the Florida Board of Parks and Historic Memorials rejected the offer due to a "lack of funds with which to maintain this property." Soon thereafter, in an apparent effort to prevent further vandalism, arrangements were made to have the monument moved by the State Road Department to a new and more publicly visible location on Thomasville Road across from the entrance to Maclay Gardens State Park, about five miles south of its original location. The monument, "which had been defaced," was subsequently "restored and moved." On January 19, 1966, the anniversary of Robert E. Lee's birth, a rededication ceremony was held for the monument at its new location. The featured speaker was Mallory Horne, former Florida House Speaker and later president of the Florida Senate, and a descendant of Confederate secretary of the navy Stephen R. Mallory.[149]

In the late 1990s the monument was removed during a widening of Thomasville Road and placed in storage at the Maclay Gardens State Park. The original Bradfordville monument site with its wall and steps was destroyed during this road-widening project. Following its storage at Maclay Gardens, the deteriorated monument was repaired and refurbished, and in 2003 it was erected at its present location on the west side of Thomasville Road in a turnoff about one mile south of the Florida/Georgia state line. A rededication ceremony was held on January 19, 2009, by the Anna Jackson Chapter.[150]

Approximately five feet high, the monument consists of a bronze plaque on a white marble slab resting on a one-stepped foundation pad (see figure 60). On the plaque is an oval inset with a bas-relief image of General Lee

Figure 60. 1927 Robert E. Lee/Dixie Highway monument as it appeared in 2010 in its current location. Photograph by William B. Lees.

on horseback with two laurel branches in the background. Below the oval inset, the plaque is inscribed in raised letters with "ERECTED AND DEDICATED BY THE UNITED DAUGHTERS OF THE CONFEDERACY AND FRIENDS IN LOVING MEMORY OF ROBERT E. LEE AND TO MARK THE ROUTE OF THE DIXIE HIGHWAY[.] 'THE SHAFT MEMORIAL AND HIGHWAY STRAIGHT ATTEST HIS WORTH—HE COMETH TO HIS OWN'—LITTLEFIELD—ERECTED 1927." The quotation is by poet and author A. W. Littlefield of Massachusetts from his poem "A Highway Memorial," published in the 1925 *Minutes of the Thirty-Second Annual Convention of the United Daughters of the Confederacy* and on the cover of the January 1926 issue of the *Confederate Veteran* magazine.[151]

The design and inscription on this monument, including the Littlefield verse, is identical to the seven 1926–28 North Carolina monuments and the

1927 Ohio monument. The 1935 South Carolina monument contains the same design but different wording, including a verse from a different author. The image of Lee on the Bradfordville monument shows, however, that the oval inset is not the original. This monument's image of Lee is unique because, although, like the others, it depicts Lee on horseback, all of the other monument insets have a fence in the background rather than laurel branches. Further, comparison of the current plaque with that shown in a photograph of the monument taken during its 1927 dedication and with the illustration on the dedication ceremony program clearly shows that they are not the same. A new Lee oval inset with a different design was apparently crafted in the mid-1960s to replace the missing original. At some point, perhaps around the same time, the entire bronze plaque was also apparently replaced, as it now states "Erected 1927" instead of the original "Erected 1926" as shown on the dedication ceremony program.[152]

A second Florida Lee/Dixie Highway monument was dedicated by the Florida Division of the UDC on October 10, 1928, in Nassau County on U.S. Highway 1 just south of the St. Marys River, which forms the Florida/Georgia state line. The monument is described as "a beautiful rough granite boulder with a bronze tablet such as is being used on all Lee Markers." Dedication speakers included representatives of the UDC, the UCV, the SCV, and the State Road Department, several of whom had also spoken at the Bradfordville monument dedication. Music was provided by the Jacksonville Police Band and a quartet of singers from Jacksonville. The monument was unveiled by the honorary president of the Florida Division of the UDC, Mrs. Francis P. Fleming Sr., the widow of a Confederate officer and former governor of Florida. Photographs show that the monument was still standing until at least 1953.[153]

Our visits to the area in December 2012 and January 2013 failed to locate this monument. Subsequent communications with the West Nassau Historical Society indicate that the monument was eventually taken down and laid at the side of the road, possibly in conjunction with the construction of a new U.S. Highway 1 bridge across the St. Marys River in 1956 just west of the old bridge. At some point around 2008 the monument was reportedly given by a local landowner to a Civil War heritage group in Georgia, and the West Nassau Historical Society is undertaking efforts to locate it and return it to Florida.[154]

Bartow, Major General Evander M. Law, 1932

On January 20, 1932, a monument to Major General Evander McIver Law was dedicated on the lawn of the Bartow Women's Club by the Father Ryan Chapter of the UDC's Florida Division (see figure 61). The monument unveiling was preceded by a program in the Women's Club building, which was Law's former home. The featured speaker was Captain T. W. Gary, an instructor at the South Florida Military Institute in Bartow, which Law had founded in 1894. Following the program, a granddaughter and grandson of Law unveiled the monument.[155]

A native of South Carolina, Evander McIver Law was in Alabama at the outbreak of the Civil War and served as a captain with the Alabama state troops that assisted in the seizure of the Pensacola Navy Yard and adjacent forts in early 1861. Following this he went to Virginia as a captain with the Alabama troops and was wounded at the Battle of First Manassas (Bull Run) in July 1861. After his recovery, Law continued to rise in the ranks of the

Figure 61. 1932 monument to Major General Evander M. Law, lower left corner, beside his former home in Bartow, ca. 1930s photograph. Florida Photograph Collection, State Archives of Florida, image no. FR0478.

Figure 62. 1932 Monument to Major General Evander M. Law at its current location in 2013. Photograph by William B. Lees.

Confederate army and by 1865 had been promoted to major general. Law commanded Confederate troops in the major battles of the war in the eastern theater, including the Seven Days Battles, Second Manassas (Bull Run), Antietam, Gettysburg, and the Overland Campaign, where he was severely wounded. He also commanded troops in the western theater for periods, including the Battles of Chickamauga, Georgia, and Chattanooga, Tennessee, in 1863, and in the Carolinas in 1865.[156]

Following the war, Law eventually moved to Bartow in 1893, where he established the South Florida Military Institute the following year. While in

Bartow he was active in the Florida Division of the UCV and served on both the Olustee Monument Commission and the Florida Chickamauga Monument Commission (see chapter 4). Law was a featured speaker at the 1910 dedication of the Lakeland Confederate monument, the 1912 dedication of the Olustee monument, and the 1913 dedication of the Florida Chickamauga monument. Law died in Bartow in 1920. Hundreds of mourners attended his funeral procession to Bartow's Oak Hill Cemetery on November 2, 1920, and all Polk County businesses and schools closed early that day in observance of the occasion.[157]

The monument consists of an approximately four-foot-high rustic granite boulder with a bronze plaque on its front (see figure 62). The plaque is inscribed in raised lettering with "THIS MEMORIAL MARKS THE HOME FROM 1904 UNTIL HIS DEATH 1920 OF MAJ. GEN. E. M. LAW. C.S.A." A historic photograph of the Bartow Women's Club shows the monument on what appears to be a large concrete pad between the building and the sidewalk. Although still on the site of the Law home, the monument has been moved from its original location and its large pad has been removed. It is currently located on a small concrete footing between the sidewalk and the curb on West Summerlin Street near its intersection with South Broadway Avenue.[158]

After Law's death, his home was purchased in 1924 by the Bartow Women's Club and used as its clubhouse for about forty years. The property was then sold to a church and then a bank, and the house was subsequently demolished. A bank building now stands on the property. On January 19, 1990, the Law monument was rededicated by the Francis S. Bartow Chapter of the Florida Society of the Military Order of the Stars and Bars.[159]

Leesburg, 1935

On April 26, 1935, Confederate Memorial Day, the Confederate Gray Chapter of the Florida Division of the UDC dedicated a memorial fountain with an "impressive ceremony" in Leesburg's Lone Oak Cemetery (see figure 63). The ceremony was conducted in cooperation with the Lone Oak Cemetery Association, which had co-funded construction of the fountain. Although the UDC had provided the fountain's memorial plaque and assisted in funding the fountain material, it was dedicated not solely to Confederate veterans but rather to all veterans buried in that cemetery. At the time of its dedication at least eighty-five Civil War veterans—sixty-nine Confederate and sixteen Union—were buried there, as well as veterans from the Spanish-American War and World War I.[160]

Figure 63. 1935 United Daughters of the Confederacy fountain in the Lone Oak Cemetery in Leesburg in 2013. Photograph by William B. Lees.

The memorial consists of a circular fishpond twelve feet across with an approximately two-foot-high wall made of rustic limestone rocks. A more recent concrete apron around the pond extends three feet beyond the rock wall. At the center of the pond is an approximately three-foot-high pedestal on a circular base four feet across, both also made of rustic limestone. On top of the limestone rock pedestal is a decorative birdbath bowl with a flowered pedestal in its center topped with two doves, all made of concrete and painted white. The fountain aspect of the memorial is no longer operational. A horizontal bronze plaque attached to the front of the pond wall is inscribed in raised letters with "MEMORIAL FOUNTAIN DEDICATED IN HONOR OF THE SOLDIERS OF ALL WARS SLEEPING IN LONE OAK CEMETERY ERECTED BY LONE OAK CEMETERY INC. AND CONFEDERATE GRAY CHAPTER NO. 641 UNITED DAUGHTERS OF THE CONFEDERACY 1935."

On April 26, 2005, Confederate Memorial Day, the Confederate Gray Chapter dedicated a twenty-foot flagpole adjacent to the memorial which flies the American flag year-round and the Confederate First National flag below it in April. A granite block with a polished surface at the base of the flagpole is inscribed with "IN MEMORY OF THE SEVENTY NINE KNOWN CIVIL WAR VETERANS BURIED IN LONE OAK U.D.C. CHAPTER 641 2005."[161]

Gamble Plantation, 1937

In 1844, Major Robert Gamble began the development of a thirty-five-hundred-acre sugar plantation at Ellenton near the Manatee River. Here he constructed the Gamble Plantation mansion and a sugar mill of brick and tabby between 1845 and 1856. The Gamble family sold the plantation in 1858, and in the spring of 1862 the Confederate government expropriated the plantation from its new Louisiana-based owners. Blockade runner Captain Archibald McNeill became the caretaker of the plantation and lived in the mansion until 1873. In August 1864 a Union navy raiding force destroyed the plantation's sugar mill but left the mansion untouched.[162]

With the collapse of the Confederacy, Secretary of State Judah P. Benjamin fled to Manatee County in May 1865 during his eventual escape to

Figure 64. 1937 Confederate monument as it appeared in 2011 on the grounds of the Gamble Plantation Historic State Park and Judah P. Benjamin Memorial. Photograph by William B. Lees.

England. Captain McNeill assisted Benjamin in eluding the Union troops searching for him, and Benjamin was hidden briefly at the Gamble Mansion before escaping Florida by boat from neighboring present-day Sarasota County.[163]

On October 10, 1937, a small Confederate monument was dedicated on the grounds of the Gamble Plantation by the UDC, which had purchased the mansion in 1925 (see figure 64).[164] The monument consists of a granite slab on a masonry foundation. A Confederate battle flag on a staff is engraved in the top of the monument face. Below this is engraved "THIS MEMORIAL DEDICATED TO CONFEDERATE VETERANS 1861–1865 MEMORIA IN AETERNA" ("Memoria in aeterna" is Latin for "In eternal remembrance") followed by "ERECTED OCTOBER 10, 1937" and the names of the three members of "THE STATE COMMISSION" of the UDC.

On the same day, adjacent to the Confederate monument, the UDC dedicated a monument identical in form and size but engraved with an American flag in honor of Florida's World War I veterans. The erection of a World War I monument by the Daughters is not at all surprising given the organization's commitment to the war effort, including funding of five wards at the American Hospital Number One in Neuilly, France.[165]

Stonewall Jackson Highway, St. Petersburg, 1940, and Jefferson County, 1950

By 1940, U.S. Highway 19 extended from Erie, Pennsylvania, through Clarksburg, West Virginia (the birthplace of General Stonewall Jackson), to a southern terminus in St. Petersburg, Florida. In January 1940, Florida governor Fred P. Cone issued a proclamation designating the portion of U.S. Highway 19 in his state as the Stonewall Jackson Memorial Highway. Other states along the route had already done so, and most had already placed markers along the route.[166]

On January 22, 1940, a dedication ceremony was held in St. Petersburg for a Florida Stonewall Jackson Memorial Highway monument erected by the Dixie Chapter of the Florida Division of the UDC (see figure 65). The ceremony was preceded by a luncheon at the St. Petersburg Shrine Club attended by about 150 people. Luncheon speakers included Governor Cone's representative Judge H. P. Baya of Tampa, St. Petersburg mayor Ian V. Boyer, UDC officials, and representatives of local civic groups.[167]

Costing "over $100.00," the approximately three-and-one-half-foot-high monument consists of a large bronze plaque attached to a travertine rock

Figure 65. 1940 southern terminal monument of the Stonewall Jackson Memorial Highway in St. Petersburg in 2012. Photograph by William B. Lees.

boulder donated by the L. F. Fernald Stone Company from its quarry near New Port Richey, Florida.[168] The inscription on the plaque reads "THIS MARKS THE TERMINAL OF THE STONEWALL JACKSON MEMORIAL HIGHWAY ERECTED BY DIXIE CHAPTER UNITED DAUGHTERS OF THE CONFEDERACY ST. PETERSBURG, FLA. JANUARY 22, 1939" followed by the UDC symbol of a Confederate First National flag surrounded by a laurel wreath. The year of erection listed on this monument appears to be an error, as the month and day correspond exactly with the dedication date in 1940. Also, the minutes of the October 1939 UDC Florida Division annual convention state that the monument would "be placed there January 22nd, 1940," and the Dixie Chapter report at the 1940 annual convention states that it was erected during that year.[169]

According to 1963 and 1964 newspaper accounts, the first monument boulder of travertine was donated by a quarry at Oneco, near Bradenton, but the

Figure 66. 1950 monument in Jefferson County honoring General Thomas Jonathan "Stonewall" Jackson as it appeared in 2013. Photograph by Frederick P. Gaske.

truck carrying the stone "broke through a frail bridge and dumped the stone forever into a deep stream." A second stone was then obtained from the Fernald quarry at New Port Richey shortly before the dedication date.[170]

In 1954, U.S. Highway 19 was extended southward across the new Sunshine Skyway Bridge to north of Palmetto in Manatee County, but the Jackson Highway "southern terminus" monument remained in place at the east end of Central Avenue in St. Petersburg. In 1963 the monument was removed during construction associated with the redesign of area streets. It was reinstalled in 1964 on the east side of Bayshore Drive slightly east of its previous location.[171]

As part of the commemoration of the Stonewall Jackson Memorial Highway in Florida, the Florida Division of the UDC erected cast-iron markers along U.S. Highway 19. By 1941, fourteen such markers had been erected from the Florida/Georgia state line to St. Petersburg. Manufactured by the Maddox Foundry Works of Archer, Florida, these markers measured twenty-two and one-half inches by twenty-four and one-half inches and were mounted on a cast-iron post with a concrete foundation. Typical of these markers is the one at Capps in Jefferson County, which is inscribed in raised letters with "STONEWALL JACKSON MEMORIAL HIGHWAY ERECTED BY UNITED DAUGHTERS OF THE CONFEDERACY 1940." This particular marker was rededicated by the UDC in 1993 after it had been found "in the underbrush" by a Florida Department of Transportation maintenance engineer, refurbished by a Tallahassee metalsmith, and reinstalled on a metal post.[172]

On February 26, 1950, the Florida Division of the UDC dedicated a second Stonewall Jackson monument on U.S. Highway 19, just south of the Florida/Georgia state line in Jefferson County (see figure 66). About one hundred people attended the dedication ceremony, which featured prayers, music from the Monticello High School Band, and speeches by UDC officials, including UDC president general Mrs. William Haggard, and by Dr. Charles S. Davis, professor of history at Florida State University.[173]

The monument consists of an upright rustic granite slab, approximately four feet high, on a granite base with a bronze plaque fastened to its front. The plaque is inscribed in raised letters with "TO HONOR GENERAL THOMAS JONATHAN JACKSON 1824–1863 ACKNOWLEDGED BY ALL TO BE ONE OF THE WORLD'S GREATEST MILITARY GENIUSES; AND WHOSE SPOTLESS CHARACTER STANDS AS AN EXAMPLE TO ALL WHO TRAVEL THIS ROAD[.] ERECTED AND DEDICATED FEBRUARY 26TH, 1950 BY THE FLORIDA DIVISION OF THE UNITED DAUGHTERS OF THE CONFEDERACY."

West Palm Beach, 1941

Planning for a Confederate monument in West Palm Beach began as early as 1935, and fund-raising began in earnest in 1936. However, it was not until 1941 that the monument was erected in Woodlawn Cemetery by the Thomas Benton Ellis Chapter of the Florida Division of the UDC. Costing "over $1,100.00," the monument was dedicated on April 26, 1941, Confederate Memorial Day, "with befitting services."[174]

This approximately ten-foot-tall granite monument consists of an upright rectangular monolith with a truncated top that sits on a base and a one-stepped six-foot-by-four-foot foundation (see figure 67). The front, or east, side is engraved at its top with a Confederate battle flag on a staff.

Figure 67. 1941 Confederate monument in Woodlawn Cemetery in West Palm Beach in 2012. Photograph by William B. Lees.

Below this are engraved several lines adapted by an Ellis Chapter member from a 1923 poem by Lucian Lamar Knight, the state historian of Georgia: "FOREVER NOW, AMONG THE IMMORTAL DEAD, WHOSE DUST BELONGS TO GLORY'S DREAMLAND, SLEEPS THE FAIR CONFEDERACY. RIGHT PRINCIPLES CAN NEVER DIE, NO CAUSE FOR WHICH THE BRAVE HAVE BLED IN VIRTUE'S NAME, FOR WHICH THE TRUE HAVE KEPT THE FAITH, FOR WHICH THE DEAD HAVE DIED IN HOLY MARTYRDOM, WAS EVER LOST!" Knight's 1923 book-length poem, titled *Stone Mountain, or The Lay of the Gray Minstrel:*

An Epic Poem in Twenty Four Parts, was an ode to the Confederacy inspired by the ongoing work to carve a massive Confederate memorial onto Stone Mountain in Georgia. Below the quotations from the poem is engraved "IN MEMORY OF OUR CONFEDERATE SOLDIERS ERECTED BY UNITED DAUGHTERS OF THE CONFEDERACY A.D. 1941."[175]

The reverse, or west, side is also engraved with a Confederate battle flag on a staff at its top. Below this is engraved an adaptation of a quotation from Knight's 1923 poem: "FURLED IS OUR CONQUERED BANNER BUT ITS FOLDS, RICH IN IMMORTAL MEMORIES, BORE NO STAIN SAVE THE BLOOD OF HER MATCHLESS HEROES."[176] The Great Seal of the Confederate States of America with "1861–1865" engraved below decorate the two narrower monument sides on the north and south. The circular seal contains a bas-relief image of George Washington on horseback at its center surrounded by a wreath of southern agricultural products such as cotton, tobacco, rice, sugarcane, corn, and wheat. The outer circle of the design is engraved with "THE CONFEDERATE STATES OF AMERICA 22 FEBRUARY 1862 DEO VINDICE." February 22, 1862, is the date of Jefferson Davis's inauguration as the first (and only) president of the Confederate States of America, after having served as provisional president. He had been selected as the provisional president in February 1861 and was then elected without opposition to a six-year term as president in November 1861. The Latin phrase "Deo Vindice" was the national motto of the Confederacy and is generally translated as "Under God, Our Vindicator." The Confederacy appropriated Virginia native son George Washington, hero of the American Revolution and first president of the United States, as symbolic of the revolutionary Confederate States of America.

DeLand, 1959

On November 22, 1959, the Stonewall Jackson Chapter of the Florida Division of the UDC dedicated a monument at Oakdale Cemetery in DeLand in honor of the Confederate veterans buried there (see figure 68).[177] The veterans so honored served in units from throughout the Confederacy, including the states of Florida, North Carolina, Virginia, Tennessee, Alabama, and Georgia.

The monument consists of an approximately three-and-one-half-foot upright granite slab with two bronze plaques fastened to its front. The top of the upper plaque contains a dedicatory statement: "IN LOVING TRIBUTE TO THE MEMORY OF OUR CONFEDERATE VETERAN DEAD IN OAKDALE CEMETERY DELAND, FLORIDA." Below this are the names with units of eleven Confeder-

Figure 68. 1959 monument in Oakdale Cemetery in DeLand as it appeared in 2011, honoring the Confederate veterans buried there. Photograph by Gregg G. Harding.

ate veterans followed by "DEDICATED SEPTEMBER 27, 1958 BY STONEWALL JACKSON CHAPTER NO. 1981 FLORIDA DIVISION UNITED DAUGHTERS OF THE CONFEDERACY." Below this plaque is a smaller one with the name and unit of an additional Confederate veteran apparently added to correct an omission. The monument is located in a seven-foot-square brick plaza surrounded by four posts linked with a heavy chain.

Although the monument plaque states that the dedication was on September 27, 1958, contemporary newspaper accounts report that the formal ceremony was held on November 22, 1959.[178] The 1958 date appears to have been the date of the monument's erection.

Daytona Beach, 1961

On April 26, 1961, Confederate Memorial Day, the Daytona Beach Chapter of the Florida Division of the UDC dedicated a monument to the Confederate dead in Riverfront Park (renamed the J. Saxton Lloyd Riverfront Park in 1991 in honor of a local civic leader). Attending the ceremony were members of the UDC, the American Legion, Veterans of Foreign Wars, local religious, civic, and business leaders, and four daughters and one son of Confederate veterans. The featured speaker was Henry Coleman, president of the Florida Chamber of Commerce.[179]

The monument was designed by Mrs. Lionel J. Martoccia of the Daytona Beach Chapter and was constructed by a local monument firm. When first constructed, the approximately five-and-one-half-foot-high pink marble monument consisted of a column and base topped with an equatorial sundial and was inscribed with "TIME FADES ALL BUT MEMORIES." The sundial was decorated with signs from the zodiac and a highly ornate gnomon (the part on the sundial that casts the shadow). The column was engraved with three vertical lines and a vertical decorative swirl motif above them. A bronze plaque is attached to the base with the inscription "GIVEN IN LOVING MEMORY OF OUR CONFEDERATE DEAD BY THE SOUTHERN CITIZENS OF DAYTONA BEACH SPONSORED BY THE UNITED DAUGHTERS OF THE CONFEDERACY CHAPTER 1955." Below this on the plaque are the dates "1861" and "1961" on either side of the UDC logo.[180]

This monument has undergone considerable change over time. A 1982 photograph shows that, although the column remained, the elaborate sundial gnomon on top was no longer present. Currently, all that remains of the monument is the marble base with its attached plaque. It appears that the monument may have been relocated one block north of its original location, perhaps when the Veterans Memorial Plaza was built in 2003. Newspaper and UDC magazine articles from 1961 state that it was located "just north of Magnolia Avenue," but it is now adjacent to the Veterans Memorial Plaza north of International Speedway Boulevard.[181]

Fort Myers, 1966

Lee County in southwest Florida was named in honor of Robert E. Lee when the county was created in 1887 from a portion of Monroe County. In addition to his service to the Confederacy, Lee visited Florida in 1849 as a U.S. Army engineer. He helped compile a report on the military and economic resources of the west and east coasts of the state from Pensacola to Fernandina, including the coast of what would become Lee County.[182]

In January 1864, Union troops reoccupied the former U.S. Army post at Fort Myers, which had been abandoned in 1858 with the end of the Third Seminole War. It became a base of operations for Union raids into the interior to disrupt Confederate cattle supplies and provided a refuge for escaped slaves, Confederate deserters, and Unionist refugees. In February 1865 the post was attacked by a force of Confederate "Cow Cavalry," but the attack was

Figure 69. 1966 Robert E. Lee monument in downtown Fort Myers as it appeared in 2011. Photograph by William B. Lees.

repulsed with light casualties on both sides. Despite the Confederate failure to capture the post, the Federals evacuated Fort Myers in March 1865.[183]

Fund-raising for a monument to General Lee in Fort Myers was begun in 1915 by the Laetitia Ashmore Nutt Chapter of the Florida Division of the UDC. By 1917, "$700 and more" had been contributed to the monument fund. However, with America's entry into World War I in 1917, "the National UDC voted to side-track all collections for monuments" in order to concentrate on the war effort and "the Chapter gave all the money collected to the [Lee] County Hospital, with the proviso that the name be changed from Lee County Poor Farm to the Robert E. Lee Memorial Hospital."[184]

In the early 1940s, the funds raised from a subsequent effort to erect the monument were again donated to the Lee Memorial Hospital to assist them in furnishing their nursery. After a new fund-raising campaign, the UDC finally completed the project in 1966 when the monument was dedicated on January 19 of that year, the anniversary of Lee's birth (see figure 69). "Several score spectators" observed the ceremony, which featured an American Legion "firing squad," the Lee Junior High School Band, the Edison Junior College Choral Group, and speeches by local civic leaders and the chairman of the county commission.[185]

Costing $6,000, a one-and-a-half-times-life-size bronze bust of Lee fabricated by Italian sculptor Aldo Pero tops the ten-and-one-half-foot-high monument. It sits on a pedestal made of gray Georgia granite with a two-stepped base manufactured by the Crone Monument Company of Memphis, Tennessee. The front, or south, face of the pedestal is inscribed with "ROBERT E. LEE 1807–1870." The north pedestal face is inscribed with "THE ERECTION OF THIS MONUMENT WAS SPONSORED BY THE UNITED DAUGHTERS OF THE CONFEDERACY, FORT MYERS CHAPTER, AND COMPLETED IN 1966 A.D. WITH THE ASSISTANCE OF THE CITIZENS OF LEE COUNTY IN HONOR OF THE MAN FOR WHOM THIS COUNTY WAS NAMED." The upper and lower sections of the pedestal are decorated with a row of incised stars. The monument rests on a concrete foundation in which are entombed twelve Civil War relics donated by a collector, such as bullets and shells from Gettysburg, Harpers Ferry, Fredericksburg, Spotsylvania, and other Virginia battlefields.[186]

Since its erection, the monument has been refurbished several times, including in 2003, 2007, and 2012. This work included removing the bronze bust and replacing it after cleaning and coating with lacquer, and permanently engraving the inscription on the front pedestal face.[187]

UNITED CONFEDERATE VETERANS MONUMENTS

A major project of the UCV in Florida was the construction and operation of the Old Soldiers and Sailors Home in Jacksonville. This project also enjoyed the cooperation of the SCV and the UDC during its operations between 1893 and 1938. Although the erection of monuments was mainly the work of the women of the South through LMAs and the UDC, several monuments were erected in Florida by the UCV. The first extant monument to be erected by the UCV honored Captain J. J. Dickison, also known as the "Swamp Fox of the Confederacy." Another was dedicated to the women of the South, and one marks a veterans plot. Photographs also record a temporary monument that served as a prop for one of numerous UCV reunions held in the state; others like it may very well have existed.

The UCV held their twenty-fourth national reunion in Jacksonville in 1914 and their thirty-seventh in Tampa in 1927. Although a comprehensive listing is not available, state and local UCV reunions and other informal gatherings were very common in Florida. Examples of such events include the Orange County Camp reunion in Orlando in 1894, and reunions remembered by photographs taken in Franklin County (ca. 1900), Tallahassee (ca. 1902), Crawfordville (1904), Lakeland (1914), Madison (1917), Marianna (1927), and at unknown dates in Monticello, Forty Oaks, and Wakulla County.[188]

Live Oak, 1909

On October 20 and 21, 1909, the Florida Division of the UCV held their nineteenth annual reunion in the community of Live Oak in Suwannee County. For the occasion, Winder J. Hillman paid for construction of a monument in the middle of the intersection of Howard Street and Ohio Avenue in downtown Live Oak (see figure 70). Hillman was a wealthy businessman and local political leader in Live Oak.[189]

Built of wood and plaster, the monument was approximately fifteen feet tall. It consisted of an obelisk shaft on a pedestal with a one-stepped base. Historic photographs show three sides of the pedestal, all of which carried inscriptions. It can be surmised that the fourth pedestal face was also inscribed. One pedestal face is inscribed with "THE CONFEDERATE STATES OF AMERICA 1861–1865," above which was hung a portrait of Robert E. Lee on the obelisk. Another pedestal face is inscribed with "IN HONOR OF THE CONFEDERATE SOLDIER DEAD AND LIVING," and another is inscribed with "TO DIE FOR ONE'S COUNTRY IS GLORIOUS."[190]

The fragile nature of the monument's construction material and its location in the middle of the city's main intersection ensured that the monument was a temporary structure constructed for the reunion, and not meant to last. Other monuments, permanent in nature, were placed in intersections (see, for example, the 1911 monument in Orlando discussed earlier), and an inspection of the historic photographs did not immediately reveal that this monument was temporary. When a visit to Live Oak turned up no sign of a monument, additional research was conducted that verified its temporary construction. Other historic photographs of UCV reunions in Florida also show elaborate temporary structural features. Photographs of the 1914 state UCV reunion at Lakeland show, for example, a large archway over a street under which the accompanying parade progressed.[191]

Figure 70. Confederate veterans in front of the temporary Confederate monument in Live Oak in 1909. Florida Photograph Collection, State Archives of Florida, image no. RC05119.

Jacksonville, Evergreen Cemetery, 1910

Captain John Jackson "J. J." Dickison, known as the "Swamp Fox of the Confederacy," died in Ocala on August 23, 1902, and was buried in his Confederate uniform in Jacksonville's Woodlawn section of Evergreen Cemetery. At the fourteenth annual reunion of the Florida Division of the UCV, held in Ocala in November 1904, "Comrade Boyleston presented resolutions relative to the lot on which Gen. J. J. Dickison is buried, asking a contribution to purchase the remaining half of the lot and to erect a monument over his grave, which was adopted without reference."[192] The rough-hewn granite monument was

Figure 71. 1910 monument to General J. J. Dickison in Jacksonville's Evergreen Cemetery in 2013. Photograph by William B. Lees.

placed in 1910, with the monument itself furnished by the Reed E. LaMance Company, which also later produced the monument erected at the Olustee Battlefield in 1912.[193]

The monument measures approximately seven feet in height and consists of a pedestal and base on a one-stepped foundation (see figure 71). The top portion of the pedestal face is adorned with a bas-relief Confederate battle flag on a staff. Below this, a smoothed circular portion of the pedestal contains the following information in raised lettering: "GEN. J. J. DICKISON CAPT. CO. H. 2ND. FLA. CAV. FLORIDA'S GREAT PARTISAN LEADER." The smoothed upper portion of the base contains his birth and death dates in raised letters and numbers, "MAR. 27, 1816, AUG. 23, 1902." The rough-hewn lower base portion is inscribed with "ERECTED BY FLA. DIVISION UCV." Although Dickison never attained the rank of general during the Civil War, he served as Florida's adjutant general from 1876 to 1880 and as major general and commander of the Florida Division of the UCV after its formation in 1891.[194]

Tampa, Woodlawn Cemetery, 1913

In 1912, the W. W. Loring Camp of the Florida Division of the UCV appointed a committee of its members to raise funds for the erection of a Confederate monument in Tampa's Woodlawn Cemetery. It would cost "about $800," and fund-raising activities for the monument, including a $100 contribution from the City of Tampa, continued into the following year. The committee also requested a contribution from Hillsborough County. By the spring of 1913, enough funds had been raised to order the monument.[195]

On May 18, 1913, about fifty Confederate veterans and "a large assemblage of ladies" attended the monument's dedication ceremony, which included a program of prayer, music, and speeches. The featured speaker was George P. Raney of Apalachicola, a Confederate veteran who served as Florida attorney general and chief justice of the Florida Supreme Court in the postwar period.[196]

Constructed of Georgia marble, the approximately twelve-foot-high monument consists of an obelisk finial on a pedestal and base that rests on a one-stepped foundation (see figure 72). Each of the pedestal's four corners is decorated with a carving of an upright cannon topped by a cannonball. The front, or southeast, face of the monument is the most elaborate with a pediment above the pedestal containing an elaborate, interwoven "CSA." The pedestal face contains an elaborate bas-relief image of two crossed swords in their scabbards and a revolver over a Confederate battle flag on a staff that

Figure 72. 1913 monument for Confederate veterans in Tampa's Woodlawn Cemetery in 2009. Photograph by William B. Lees.

drapes over the swords. Below this image in raised letters is "ERECTED BY LORING CAMP U.C.V. 1913." The pedestal base contains "CONFEDERATE DEAD" in large, raised letters. The northeast, northwest, and southwest pedestal faces have inscribed on them the names of thirty (including one "Unknown") Confederate veterans and their grave plot numbers. The monument was originally topped with cannonballs and bronze stacked rifles on the pedestal, the stocks of which can be seen in a 1929 newspaper photo, but these are no longer present. The monument now has a pointed stone pediment that does not appear in the 1929 photo. We believe this was placed on the monument when the bronze stacked arms and cannonballs were removed.[197]

The monument is located in the center of a Confederate plot at the cemetery with thirty graves of veterans, some with markers bearing their name and unit, surrounded by a low masonry wall and a marble threshold in the entrance inscribed with "CONFEDERATE VETERANS." Adjacent to it is a Union plot of similar size that contains a monument dedicated in 1924 by the Woman's Relief Corps and which is also surrounded by a low masonry wall (see chapter 3). A grass walkway separates the two plots.

After the monument was erected, the Loring Camp still owed "nearly a hundred dollars" for the monument. They continued their fund-raising activities in the summer of 1913, which included a benefit by the Peruchi-Gypzene Company, a nationally known theatrical company, at the Greeson Theater in Tampa.[198]

The temporary monument erected in Live Oak and the Tampa monument are interesting when compared to other Confederate monuments in Florida at the time. Although the Live Oak monument that proclaims "to die for one's country is glorious" can be seen to be influenced by the Lost Cause narrative, it is less eloquent a statement than would have been found on a monument erected by the UDC at the same time. The permanent monument in the Tampa cemetery does nothing to invoke the Lost Cause and very simply and with dignity honors the Confederate dead.

Jacksonville, Confederate Park, 1915

Despite the rarity of monument projects by the UCV, they did embark on a mission to honor the women of the South for their contribution to the home front during the Civil War. In 1881, Jefferson Davis dedicated his book *The Rise and Fall of the Confederate Government* to the women of the Confederacy, and did so in quite eloquent terms. Certainly fueled to some degree by Davis's position on the importance of southern women to the Lost Cause, discussions began soon after the formation of the UCV on how best to commemorate this contribution. Despite some women's opposition to a monument—ironically including the Daughters, who saw monuments as central to their program—in favor of things such as a scholarship program for young ladies of the South, the UCV settled on a plan that proposed identical monuments be erected on the grounds of the capitol of each of the former Confederate states.[199]

Although the UCV followed through with designing a standard sculpture to be used on monuments in each state, the plan fell through in practice. Only Mississippi (dedicated in 1917) and Tennessee (dedicated in 1926) used this sculpture, whereas committees in South Carolina (1912), Arkansas (1913), North Carolina (1914), Florida (1915), and Maryland (1918) erected monuments of their own design. Monuments were not erected in the other states of the former Confederacy.[200]

After several years of discussion regarding the need for a monument "to the memory of the women of Florida who wrought so loyally for the Southern Confederacy during the war," the Florida Division of the UCV, at its 1910 annual reunion in Bartow, appointed a three-member "board of trustees" to coordinate statewide fund-raising activities. In 1911 they successfully lobbied the Florida Legislature to appropriate $5,000 for the construction of the monument, provided the UCV also raise $5,000 for the project. The legislation established a board of trustees consisting of the governor, the comptroller, the attorney general, and three UCV Florida Division representatives to oversee the expenditure of the funds. The legislation also stated that the monument was to be located in Tallahassee unless the UCV Florida Division voted "by a not less than two-thirds vote" that the monument "be located elsewhere" in the state.[201]

During this period, the state legislature met every other year. At its next session, in 1913, the legislature increased the appropriation to $12,000, provided the UCV raised the same amount. This legislation also provided that the location of the monument be changed to Dignan Park in Jacksonville, a change that ended the last hope for a prominent statewide monument in the Florida capital. By 1915 the UCV had raised $10,387 for the monument. Of the 1913 appropriation of $12,000, the three state members of the board of trustees eventually authorized the payment of only $10,757 based on their interpretation of the legislation "and the inability" of the UCV Florida Division "to raise in full" their $12,000 share of the cost. Legislators also raised concerns about the alleged attempt of a UCV Florida Division member to obtain a $2,000 "commission on the work" from the monument contractors. This situation was rectified by the legislature in 1915 when it approved the expenditure of nearly $3,900 "or so much thereof as may be necessary" in state funds to finish payment on the monument.[202]

In February 1912 the UCV awarded the contract for the design and installation of a monument that "will cost $25,000" to the McNeel Marble Company of Marietta, Georgia. The McNeel Company commissioned New York sculptor Allen G. Newman (1875–1940) to create two bronze statues that were to be placed inside and on top of the monument's granite structure. One of the leading American sculptors of his day, Newman created numerous works found on monuments throughout the country, including the Henry Hudson monument in New York City; the General Philip Sheridan monument in Scranton, Pennsylvania; the Joel Chandler Harris Monument in Atlanta; the *Triumph of Peace* monument in Atlanta; and the General Sterling Price monument in Keytesville, Missouri. He is perhaps best known for his statues of a Spanish-American War soldier, *The Hiker*, and a World War I soldier, *The Doughboy*, casts of which were placed in several cities.[203]

The Jno. Williams Inc. Bronze Foundry of New York produced the sculptures for Newman. Founded in 1875 by John Williams, this foundry was responsible for many art bronzes, including numerous sculptures on Union and Confederate Civil War monuments throughout the country. In addition to the Florida monument, the foundry also cast the statue for the North Carolina women's monument.[204]

By May 1913 the monument's foundation was nearly complete, and it was the intention of the Florida Division to have the monument ready for unveiling during the UCV's twenty-fourth national reunion scheduled for May 1914 in Jacksonville. Although the monument could not be completed in time for the event, the UCV reunion drew an estimated seventy thousand visitors to Jacksonville, including some eight thousand veterans, many of whom camped in tents in Dignan Park. To commemorate the event, the City of Jacksonville changed the park name to Confederate Park in October 1914. In April 1915 the two bronze Newman statues were placed in and on the monument and veiled in preparation for the dedication ceremony.[205]

The completed monument was dedicated on October 26, 1915, with "between 5,000 and 7,000 persons," including Florida governor Park Trammell, in attendance (see figure 73). Jacksonville mayor J. E. T. Bowden declared a half-day holiday so that city employees could attend the afternoon dedication and asked that "all business houses be closed during the ceremonies" so that their employees might also be able to attend. The ceremony was preceded by a parade through Jacksonville that included a police squad, a band, local National Guard units, and "hundreds of automobiles" carrying Confederate

Figure 73. Circa 1930s postcard view of 1915 Florida Confederate women's monument in Confederate Park, Jacksonville. Courtesy of William B. Lees.

veterans, UDC members, and citizens. The parade began at Hemming Park, the site of the 1898 Confederate monument, and ended at the new monument site in Confederate Park for a program of prayers, music, and speeches.[206]

Speakers included Mayor Bowden, Florida state legislator Theodore T. Turnbull of Monticello, and U.S. senator Duncan U. Fletcher. In their remarks they paid tribute to the role of Florida's women during the Civil War, who, noted Senator Fletcher, "endured suffering, heart-breaking partings, cruel sacrifices, with inspiring fortitude and infinite patience." In his speech, Turnbull asserted that it was the women on the home front who "bore the brunt of the blow" and suffered the most during the war. As the band played "Dixie," the monument, which had been "encased in four mammoth Confederate flags," was unveiled when the daughter of a Confederate veteran "pulled the cord and the flag veils dropped to the ground revealing the monument."[207]

Approximately forty-seven feet tall, this impressive monument is in the form of a granite open-air canopy, or "temple," structure (figure 74). It is very similar in appearance to the 1913 Florida monument at the Chickamauga Battlefield in Georgia, also designed by the McNeel Marble Company (discussed in detail in chapter 4). This similarity was noted by at least one trade journal of the period. The twenty-eight-foot-square monument base sits on an earthen mound surrounded by a low concrete wall and landscaping. The canopy roof is capped with a dome, on top of which is a thirteen-and-one-half-foot-high bronze statue of a robed standing female holding a half-furled

Confederate battle flag on a staff in her right hand. The statue stands on a small tiered base or plinth. At the base of the dome are eight decorated pediments that circle the structure.[208]

The front face of the canopy roof contains a panel with "A TRIBUTE TO THE WOMEN OF THE SOUTHERN CONFEDERACY" in large raised letters. The panel is flanked by "1861" on one side and "1865" on the other. The canopy roof is supported by three Ionic columns on a pedestal at each corner. Attached to the left front column pedestal facing west is a bronze plaque with "ERECTED BY THE MCNEEL MARBLE COMPANY MARIETTA, GA. COMPLETED APRIL 1, A.D. 1915" followed by the six names of the monument "TRUSTEES" from the "FLORIDA DIVISION U.C.V." and the "STATE OF FLORIDA."

At the center of the canopy is an approximately five-and-one-half-foot-tall bronze statue of a seated woman reading to two children and teaching them "the true story of the Civil War" (see figure 75).[209] On one side of the statue base is inscribed the name of the foundry where it was produced, "JNO. WILLIAMS INC. N.Y." The statue rests on an approximately seven-foot-tall

Figure 74. 1915 Florida Confederate women's monument as it appeared in 2009 in Confederate Park, Jacksonville. Photograph by William B. Lees.

Figure 75. April 1915 cover of *Confederate Veteran* magazine, featuring the sculpture for the Florida Confederate women's monument at Jacksonville. Courtesy of William B. Lees.

tiered pedestal decorated with bas-relief wooden stick bundles or fasces. The front of this pedestal contains a bronze plaque inscribed with "IN MEMORY OF THE WOMEN OF OUR SOUTHLAND 1861–1865 LET THIS MUTE BUT ELOQUENT STRUCTURE SPEAK TO GENERATIONS TO COME, OF A GENERATION OF THE PAST. LET IT REPEAT PERPETUALLY THE IMPERISHABLE STORY OF OUR WOMEN OF THE 60S. THOSE NOBLE WOMEN WHO SACRIFICED THEIR ALL UPON THEIR COUNTRY'S ALTAR. UNTO THEIR MEMORY THE FLORIDA DIVISION OF UNITED CONFEDERATE VETERANS AFFECTIONATELY DEDICATE THIS MONUMENT." The placement of the central sculpture within this "architectural setting was meant to enshrine it, as the Greeks honored their gods by placing them in temples."[210] The underside of the canopy roof has four marble panels with a decorative bronze medallion in the center. The original plans had called for a "great electric globe" where the bronze medallion is located.[211] Granite steps lead into the canopy on the south side.

Restoration work was conducted on the monument in 2007 with funds raised by the Springfield Improvement Association and Woman's Club. The statues were cleaned under the supervision of sculptor Joe Segal of St. Augustine. Necessary granite and marble restoration work was undertaken by Pedroni's Cast Stone company of Jacksonville.[212]

As is true of many of the monuments discussed in this book, the story behind this monument is every bit as insightful and important as the message conveyed. That the Florida women's monument had its genesis in a nationwide project by the UCV intended to result in the erection of identical monuments in each of the former Confederate states is little known because it did not come to pass. The resistance of the UDC, who will ever be known as prime movers in the erection of Civil War monuments, to this project to honor the women of the South in favor of a project with more tangible benefits for the young women of the present is also little known. However, it is certainly understandable for the times. This was, after all, a period when women were fighting for equal voting rights and opportunities. This monument itself is profound; its sculpture shows a woman instructing the future generations, which is itself a mission that the UDC had embraced by way of instructing the youth of the South about the true history of the Civil War.

A second ornate monument to the women of the Confederacy was planned at about the same time for erection in Jacksonville, this time at Riverside

Figure 76. Circa 1915 postcard view of the design for an alternate Confederate women's memorial, with the inscription, as if it had been built, "THE CONFEDERATE WOMEN'S MEMORIAL MONUMENT, RIVERSIDE PARK, JACKSONVILLE, FLA." Courtesy of William B. Lees.

Park, by the R. E. Lee Camp of the Florida Division of the UCV, as shown on a circa 1915 postcard (see figure 76). In 1912 the Lee Camp received an appropriation of $1,200 from the Jacksonville City Council for "building the base" of this monument "which is to cost $21,000."[213] However, this second monument was apparently never erected.

MONUMENT RAISED BY CRESTVIEW LIONS CLUB, 1958

On January 19, 1958, the Crestview Lions Club dedicated a small monument and a flagpole in Crestview in honor of William "Uncle Bill" Lundy and all Florida Confederate soldiers. The ceremony was attended by "a large number of residents," including six of Lundy's sons. The principal speaker was state senator Newman Brackin, with Thomas Beasley, the speaker-elect of the Florida House of Representatives, serving as the master of ceremonies. A band from nearby Eglin Air Force Base played "Dixie" as the Confederate flag was raised on the flagpole.[214]

William A. Lundy was said to be the last surviving Civil War veteran pensioner in Florida when he died in 1957, bringing to an end seventy-two years of state pension benefits to Confederate veterans in Florida. Born in Alabama, Lundy moved to Florida after the Civil War and filed for a Confederate pension from the State of Florida in 1931. He claimed service with the Alabama Home Guard during the war and, during the last years of his life, reached celebrity status as one of the last surviving Confederate veterans. However, recent historical research raises strong doubt about Lundy's Civil War service claim and his alleged date of birth on the pension application.[215]

The monument consists of a sloped granite block on a one-stepped base with a bronze plaque on it with the inscription in raised letters "CONFEDERATE PARK DEDICATED TO UNCLE BILL LUNDY FLORIDA'S LAST CONFEDERATE VETERAN 1848–1957 AND ALL CONFEDERATE SOLDIERS OF FLORIDA[.] DEDICATED BY CRESTVIEW LIONS CLUB 1958" (see figure 77). Behind the monument stands a tall flagpole on which the American flag, Crestview banner, and Confederate battle flag are flown.

The monument was originally erected in a downtown city park in Crestview at the intersection of State Road 85 and U.S. Highway 90. When a Florida Highway Patrol building was constructed on the property, the monument was moved several yards in the park. Some years later, in order to resolve a traffic hazard issue, the monument was relocated about one-third of a mile northeast to its current location in a small triangular median park owned by the City of Crestview at the intersection of State Road 85 and East First Avenue.[216]

In recent years the presence of a Confederate battle flag on the flagpole behind the monument in the public park has generated opposition from leaders of the local African American community. In 1996 the Crestview City Council in a three-to-two decision voted to allow the flag to keep flying. Despite boycott threats, the city council voted again in 2002, this time unanimously, to keep the flag in the park. In 2013 the issue came before the city council again and a special council meeting was held on November 14 to receive pub-

Figure 77. 1958 monument to alleged oldest Florida Confederate veteran, Bill Lundy, in Crestview in 2011. Photograph by William B. Lees.

lic input. However, "after an hour and a half of often impassioned addresses," the city council adjourned without taking any action on the issue.[217]

* * *

The Confederate community monuments discussed in this chapter are the most common of all Civil War monuments within Florida. They continue a narrative begun with the Confederate monuments erected during Reconstruction in Walton County and St. Augustine. Erected by Ladies' Memorial Associations prior to 1900 and by the UDC afterward, with a few significant contributions by the UCV and private individuals, these monuments mirror national patterns in the increasing use of the Lost Cause narrative through World War I. Perhaps in contradiction to national patterns, the Florida UDC continued to include monument construction as an important part of their program between World War I and the Civil War Centennial. After World War I, however, the narrative on the monuments became more muted, apparently a reflection of satisfaction with achievement of at least some level of sectional reconciliation based on recognition of Confederate values and worth.

The number of Confederate monuments erected in Florida from the close of Reconstruction through the end of the Civil War Centennial is not large compared with many other states of the former Confederacy. We believe this is a simple result of Civil War–era demographics. Florida gave relatively few soldiers to the Confederacy—some 15,000 of a total white population of almost 78,000 (South Carolina had the next-smallest white population, 291,300, but Georgia and Alabama each exceeded half a million). Although available records make it difficult to make comparisons, the percentage of Florida's white population serving the Confederacy (roughly 19 percent) was certainly at least as high as for any other Confederate state. Most of Florida's small population was concentrated in the northern half of the state, which raised most of Florida's troops. Many of the antebellum communities from which many a Confederate regiment marched are today graced with monuments to their memory. In the postwar period, the state's population expanded southward into areas sparsely settled during the Civil War. Many of those who initially moved to those parts of the state brought their memories of the "Old South" with them and erected monuments reflecting that heritage. From this perspective, Florida's community monuments are a reflection of the importance of the Confederate memory in a state that had once joined ten others in seceding from the Union.

3 REMEMBERING THE UNION SOLDIER AND SAILOR

> We should guard their graves with sacred vigilance. All that the consecrated wealth and taste of the nation can add to their adornment and security is but a fitting tribute to the memory of her slain defenders. Let no wanton foot tread rudely on such hallowed grounds. Let pleasant paths invite the coming and going of reverent visitors and fond mourners. Let no vandalism of avarice or neglect, no ravages of time, testify to the present or to the coming generations that we have forgotten as a people the cost of a free and undivided republic.
>
> **Grand Army of the Republic General Orders No. 11, May 5, 1868**

Compared to monuments that memorialize the Confederate experience, those dedicated to the Union are rare in Florida. Four of these mark places of conflict and are discussed in chapters 1 and 4. Of these the earliest was the wooden monument erected in 1866 to mark the common grave of Union dead at the Olustee Battlefield. Although a granite representation of this monument was placed on the battlefield in 1991, the original had disappeared by 1873. Another monument, also no longer extant, was erected in a cemetery near Green Cove Springs where Union dead from the garrison at Magnolia were buried. Two other monuments in Key West remember the presence and sacrifice of Union soldiers at Key West, including members of New York regiments who died of yellow fever during the war. The remaining Union monuments in Florida are community monuments associated with the Grand Army of the Republic and its auxiliary, the Woman's Relief Corps, although one was erected largely through the efforts of a private citizen.

Societies of Union officers came into existence even as the war raged on. In 1862, for example, the Third Army Corps Union was established to raise money to ensure that officers who paid the ultimate price would be embalmed and sent home for proper burial.[1] After the end of the war, Union officer organizations such as the Society of the Army of the Tennessee, the Society of the Army of the Cumberland, the Society of the Army of the James, the Society of the Army of the Potomac, and the Military Order of the Loyal Legion of the United States were formed (the Military Order remains a viable organization to this day).[2] The purpose of these organizations varied slightly, but at some level they sought to preserve the collegiality enjoyed by the officers during the Civil War.

Also at the end of the war, organizations formed with the intention of advocating for the needs of veterans, initially focusing on the need for assistance for disabled veterans and for the families of soldiers who had died during the conflict. In August 1865 the United States Soldiers and Sailors Protective Society formed to urge attention be paid to the claims for assistance being made by veterans.[3] In September 1865 the Soldiers' and Sailors' National Union League and the United Service Society formed, also to advance the interests of veterans.[4]

Established in Decatur, Illinois, in April 1866, the Grand Army of the Republic was a fraternal organization composed of Union veterans focused on advocating issues they believed to be of importance. Historian Mary Dearing has argued that the first iteration of the GAR focused on the job of getting politicians elected to office rather than pressing a veterans agenda with politicians seated in office. This, and an overly hierarchical organizational structure, led to the eventual reform of the organization by about 1880.[5] Afterward, the GAR focused on "charity, patriotism, and good fellowship among veterans of all political stripes."[6] The focus of the GAR was on benefits for Union veterans, especially pensions for all who served, although they were also quick to protect the status of the Union and the Union veteran as the victor in the Civil War. When it came to the expenditure of the federal treasure, the GAR was steadfast that it should not be utilized to care for or commemorate Confederate soldier dead or care for Confederate veterans, widows, or orphans.

Historian Barbara A. Gannon makes a compelling argument that the GAR was also an exceptional organization of the late nineteenth century because it accepted both black and white veterans to equal membership and near equal participation. "The GAR was an interracial social organization because its members, both black and white, thought it should be," writes Gannon. "Since black and white soldiers had served together in the Civil War, African American veterans joined this organization, and they were able to do so because most white veterans believed that their organization should include these men."[7] This is not to say that all levels of the GAR were interracial, since all-white and all-black posts existed. However, even if it was not always so at the local level, interaction between blacks and whites did occur at the departmental and national levels of the organization.

The organizational structure of the GAR relied on a central political gathering, with memorial, social, and historical functions as well, in the form of the national encampment. Between 1866 and 1949, annual GAR national encampments were almost exclusively held in the loyal northern states from which most of the Union soldiers had served. Several encampments were held in border states: Baltimore, Maryland, in 1882; St. Louis, Missouri, in 1887; Louisville, Kentucky, in 1895; and Kansas City, Missouri, in 1916. Only once was the national encampment held in a former Confederate state, that being in Chattanooga, Tennessee, in September 1913. It is interesting that the twenty-third annual reunion of the United Confederate Veterans was also held in Chattanooga just a few months earlier, in May 1913.[8] The year 1913 of course marked the fiftieth anniversary of significant battles waged for control of this vital town.

Assisting the GAR in its mission were auxiliaries in the form of the Ladies of the Grand Army of the Republic (LGAR), which required a blood relationship to a Union veteran for membership, and the Woman's Relief Corps (WRC), which was open to all who supported its mission. The former was first established as the Loyal Ladies League in 1881 but changed its name to the Ladies of the Grand Army of the Republic in 1886. By 1910 the LGAR had circles (chapters) in twenty-nine states and more than sixty thousand members. The WRC, which erected two Union monuments in Florida, was organized in 1882 and by 1896 had 140,305 members. An additional auxiliary, which was to become the designated heir to the GAR itself, was first formed in 1881 as the Sons of Veterans in Pennsylvania and changed its name to Sons of Veterans of the United States of America in 1882. Composed of male descendants of Union veterans, the organization was renamed the Sons of Union Veterans of the Civil War in 1925. Female descendants formed the National Alliance of the Daughters of Veterans of the United States of America in 1885 and changed their name to Daughters of Union Veterans of the Civil War in 1925.[9]

UNION VETERANS MOVE TO FLORIDA

At the end of the Civil War the economy of southern states was in disarray, and Florida, along with other southern states, knew that attracting immigrants was one key to economic recovery. Perhaps the first unintended inducement to immigrants had been the experiences of the Union soldiers and sailors who were stationed in Florida during the war. Although some certainly encountered unpleasant experiences, such as New York regiments who were decimated by disease during their year at Key West, many were favorably impressed. In addition to those from New York, regiments from Connecticut, Maine, Massachusetts, New Hampshire, Ohio, Pennsylvania, Rhode Island, and Vermont spent time in Florida.[10] It was also, somewhat ironically, individuals from these loyal northern states that Florida businessmen and politicians hoped would move to and invest in the state.

As early as 1868, the new Florida Constitution, which had been required for readmission of the state to full status within the Union, provided for a commissioner of immigration. Soon thereafter the state embarked on a campaign to promote Florida in the North through the development and distribution of promotional pamphlets and books and by sponsoring journalists to tour the state and write about its merits in northern papers and magazines. The success of these promotional efforts created demand, which attracted the attention of railroad developers such as Henry Plant and Henry Flagler. By the 1880s railroads were increasingly making Florida accessible for both visitors and new residents, with rail reaching as far as Key West by 1912. The success of these efforts did result in a substantial growth in the population of Florida, which increased from 187,748 in 1870 to 528,542 in 1900.[11] With the immigrants from northern states came, of course, Union veterans of the Civil War, first seeking new economic opportunities and later a destination for retirement.[12]

As Union veterans from northern states moved to Florida, they joined the native Florida veterans who had served with the Union army or navy during the conflict, including many African American veterans who had been recruited and served in Florida with units such as the Second United States Colored Troops. These native and immigrant veterans formed posts of the GAR throughout the state. Despite the lack of a central state or national archive, Florida GAR researcher Roger Heiple has compiled a list of forty-five posts around the state.[13] Many communities had more than one post, and at least six were African American posts.[14] Although no national GAR encampments were held in the state, the Department of Florida held annual encampments from its first in Pensacola in 1884 until the final encampment in 1944.[15] The 1939 encampment in Miami is the only one that seems to have been associated with the dedication of a Union monument.

In the 1890s, as the numbers of surviving Union veterans began to dwindle rapidly, interest of the veterans and of the GAR began to focus increasingly on veteran care in old age. Out of this, although not necessarily for reasons that were totally benevolent, arose interest in developing retirement communities in the Deep South where Union veterans could make a good investment in real estate and enjoy their final years in a more hospitable climate. Although these communities offered an attractive climate and investment opportunities for the veteran, they were also a profit-driven venture for the principals of the companies formed to facilitate their development.[16] The first of these developments occurred in Georgia and resulted in the establishment of the town of Fitzgerald, but three others followed in Florida and provided the genesis of the communities of Zephyrhills, St. Cloud, and Lynn Haven.

Building on an idea floated in 1890 in his newspaper, the *American Tribune*, Indiana publisher Philander H. Fitzgerald partnered with former Georgia governor William J. Northern in 1894 to purchase land in south Georgia on which a veterans colony could be developed.[17] In 1882 Fitzgerald had purchased the *Veteran Review* newspaper and renamed it the *American Tribune*. It was one of several newspapers focused on topics of interest and concern to Union veterans of the Civil War, and it attained a circulation of about twenty-five thousand per week.[18]

In 1895 Fitzgerald formed the American Tribune Soldiers Colony Company, which he promoted through his paper. Although in theory the community was open to all, it was promoted heavily to Union veterans from the midwestern states from Nebraska to Ohio. It is reported that some twenty-seven hundred Union veterans purchased land in the development, along with an unknown number of Confederate veterans, and some one thousand buildings were constructed by the time the City of Fitzgerald was incorporated on December 2, 1896.[19]

Possibly inspired by the success of the American Tribune Soldiers Colony Company in Georgia, three veterans colonies were established in Florida at roughly the same time. Early in 1909, Pennsylvania Civil War veteran Captain Howard B. Jeffries traveled to Florida to find land for a veterans colony. He soon located suitable property in Pasco County north of Tampa, which was purchased in August 1909 and included the area known as Abbott. The

Figure 78. Dedication of Grand Army of the Republic meeting hall in St. Cloud, 1914. Florida Photographic Collection, State Archives of Florida, image no. N039840.

Zephyrhills Colony Company was soon thereafter incorporated in the State of Delaware by Jeffries and other investors from New York and New Jersey, and in May 1910 Abbott was renamed Zephyrhills.[20] On February 18, 1911, the Florida secretary of state issued the Zephyrhills Colony Company a permit to operate within the state.[21] Within a few years, the population of Zephyrhills had reached several thousand, and in 1912 the GAR post erected a meeting hall, which after one hundred years still stands in this community. Zephyrhills hosted the Department of Florida GAR encampments in 1912, 1923, 1931, and 1937.[22]

Also in 1909, at the behest of John McElroy, New York capitalist Raymond Moore and Zephyrhills founder Howard Jeffries identified thirty-five thousand acres in the Kissimmee River valley suitable for yet another soldiers colony. McElroy was editor of the *National Tribune*, a Union veterans paper that was a rival to Fitzgerald's *American Tribune* and the unofficial organ of the national GAR. The Seminole Land and Investment Company, of which

Moore was a principal, subsequently purchased this land, which became the St. Cloud community. The *National Tribune* promoted St. Cloud, which in its first year enjoyed remarkable growth with some four hundred buildings and one thousand residents.[23] Lured by the favorable climate, GAR members purchased lots measuring 25 by 150 feet for $50, sight unseen, and slept on cots in old army tents while they built their homes. The community had a population of more than two thousand within a few years, and in 1911 the Florida Legislature granted a charter of incorporation.[24] Initial town development included a veterans park and a wood-framed meeting hall for GAR members. This original frame meeting hall was replaced with an impressive two-story brick "memorial hall" in 1914 that remains part of the St. Cloud landscape and is considered today one of the best remaining examples of GAR halls in the country (figure 78). Department of Florida GAR encampments were held at St. Cloud in 1914, 1920, 1925, 1933, 1936, and 1940.[25]

Although close on the heels of both Zephyrhills and St. Cloud, Lynn Haven was the last of the veterans colonies established in Florida. In the spring of 1910, apparently at the invitation of Panama City entrepreneurs, a land deal on St. Andrews Bay associated with this new colony had been pitched to Union veteran W. H. Lynn of New York City. Lynn arrived in Florida accompanied by other potential investors from New York and New Jersey in June 1910, and an article in the *National Tribune* announced that another veterans colony would soon open in Florida.[26]

The St. Andrews Bay Development Company established the new colony, which was formed following Lynn's St. Andrews Bay visit. This company eventually aggregated more than forty thousand acres, but the focal point was the community of Lynn Haven, whose location was announced to curious local residents and investor-veterans in December 1910. Platting of town lots began in early 1911, followed by construction of homes, businesses, and churches.[27]

When the city was surveyed in 1911, a city block was given to the local Stanton Post of the GAR for their use and for the use of their Ladies Auxiliary Circle. Construction of a two-story frame GAR hall was completed on this block by the end of 1911, although this building no longer stands (see figure 79). Interest in erecting a monument to the Union in Lynn Haven dates to 1913, and an impressive monument was erected on the block north of the GAR hall in 1920 and dedicated the following year.[28] Surprisingly, there is no record of Lynn Haven ever having hosted a Department of Florida GAR encampment.[29]

Figure 79. 1911 Grand Army of the Republic meeting hall and 1921 Union monument, Lynn Haven, ca. 1922 photograph. Bay County Public Library, Local History Collection, image no. 76-2-1.

Development of GAR retirement communities in the South corresponded with the aging of the veteran population, and each of these communities struggled to remain viable with the passing of the people they had recruited to be their first generation of residents. Of course, these veterans in the GAR communities joined scores of other Union veterans who had moved to Florida starting in the late nineteenth century and who lived immersed in other communities in the state, such as Pensacola, Tallahassee, Jacksonville, Tampa, and Miami. With the aging of these veterans, the influence of the GAR and their female auxiliaries dwindled, and the torch of memory bearer passed to descendant organizations such as the Sons and Daughters of Union Veterans of the Civil War.

UNION COMMUNITY MONUMENTS IN FLORIDA

Although the first Civil War monuments erected in Florida were Union, at the Olustee Battlefield and in Key West (both in 1866), others would not be erected until the end of the nineteenth century. This timing correlates with the increase in migration to the state from the North, which by the 1880s had given the GAR hope that Florida could become a fertile ground for recruitment of members.[30] Even though the GAR did become well established throughout the state, and despite three successful veterans communities in Florida, only a few monuments were erected.

Jacksonville, 1891

On May 30, 1891, Decoration Day (now known as Memorial Day), the O. M. Mitchel Post of the GAR dedicated an ornate monument to Union soldiers and sailors in Evergreen Cemetery, which had been established in 1881 in north Jacksonville. "Costing with the lot nearly $1,000," the monument was manufactured by the Monumental Bronze Company of Bridgeport, Connecticut, and includes a large statue of a Union soldier. The monument is at the center of a relatively small plot that contains only twelve Union veteran headstones. After his death in 1902, Captain J. J. Dickison, "The Swamp Fox of the Confederacy," was buried not far west of this Union monument in the Woodlawn section of Evergreen Cemetery.[31]

Among those who were instrumental in procuring funding for the Union monument was the Reverend Samuel D. Paine, a veteran of the British army during the Crimean War and the Army of the Potomac during the Civil War. During the 1862 Battle of Fredericksburg in Virginia, Paine, who served as first lieutenant of the Twenty-Fourth Maine Battery, reportedly had three horses shot out from under him. After moving to Florida around 1880 he served as commander of the Mitchel Post, chaplain of the GAR Department of Florida, and chaplain in chief of the GAR. In 1889 he traveled to New York City to raise funds from Union veterans for the construction of the monument in Evergreen Cemetery.[32]

The uniqueness of having a Union monument erected in Florida at this time is evidenced by remarks made by the keynote speaker at the dedication of the Pensacola Confederate monument the following month (see chapter 2). In his speech, Confederate veteran Robert W. Davis noted, "In Jacksonville, in this state!—mind you in Florida—a similar ceremony to this took place within a month past, but it was not the unveiling of a Confederate monument, it was the ceremony of unveiling a monument to the Federal dead." Davis went on to state that, although he was not present at the Union monument dedication, he "was pleased, too, that the sentiments expressed on that occasion were so manly and loyal and at the same time the merits of the Southern soldier were so fully recognized."[33]

Approximately eighteen feet tall, the monument is topped by a statue of

Figure 80. 1891 Union monument in Jacksonville's Evergreen Cemetery showing backward leaning soldier statue as it appeared in 2010. Photograph by William B. Lees.

a Union soldier made of what is referred to as white bronze, "the trade name given to refined and purified zinc, the surface finished with the sand blast, and used for making monuments, statuary, and other works of art."[34] The detailed sculpture depicts a soldier standing at parade rest with his hands on what appears to be an 1860s-era Springfield musket (see figure 80). He wears a forage cap, a knee-length greatcoat with the right part of the cape flung over his shoulder, and a U.S. pattern cartridge box at his back. The statue sits atop an ornately designed pedestal and base of white-bronze-covered masonry. It is sand-cast zinc sandblasted at the foundry and meant to imitate stone—a process unique to the Monumental Bronze Company. A faux granite foundation, also of white bronze, supports the pedestal and base, and this in turn sits on a true masonry foundation.

The monument contains bas-reliefs of popular emblems of the period on each of the pedestal faces and bas-reliefs of traditional epitaphs and phrases associated with the Civil War on each base. The pedestal front, or west, face contains an eagle, shield, and crossed flags motif at its base with the words "IN MEMORY OF OUR COMRADES WHO DEFENDED THE FLAG OF THE UNION, ON LAND AND SEA, 1861–1865." On the south face is a detailed depiction of a mounted cavalry trooper with the GAR's motto "FRATERNITY, CHARITY AND LOYALTY" below, while the east face contains a ship's anchor with chain and a quotation from President Lincoln's 1865 second inaugural address, "WITH MALICE TOWARD NONE, WITH CHARITY FOR ALL," below. The north face is decorated with a GAR medal and ribbon pin with the words "ERECTED BY O. M. MITCHEL POST, NO. 4, DEPARTMENT OF FLORIDA, G.A.R., MAY 30, 1891" below.

The Monumental Bronze Company was established in 1879 and ceased production of monuments and statuary in 1914. The company's "American Soldier" statue, which adorns this monument, was its most popular zinc (white bronze) soldier. The pedestal is also a Monumental Bronze Company standard design (Number 557), as are the bas-relief emblems that adorn the faces of the pedestal. The "American Soldier" was probably the most-produced zinc statue of all, and at least eighty-six copies are known. In many examples of the white bronze "American Soldier" monuments, "uneven distribution of the statue's weight relative to its center of gravity has led to a slight backward tilt toward the figure's right heel." This is even more so the case with the Evergreen Cemetery monument, where the soldier statue is leaning backward at a prominent angle. The monument displays separation of the metal on the top of the soldier's cap and on the monument's pedestal base where the masonry interior is exposed. Water intrusion at the separations threatens the monument's stability, and cracking is apparent below the statue's right heel. This deterioration presents a severe threat to the monument.[35]

St. Petersburg, 1900

Greenwood Cemetery in St. Petersburg was first platted in 1897 through the efforts of Henry Peter Bussey. A Civil War veteran from Nashville, Bussey had moved to St. Petersburg in 1892 and started a funeral home in 1895. He subsequently purchased five acres for use as a cemetery. The cemetery is said to have been referred to as Veterans Cemetery due to the large number of Civil War veterans interred there, both Union and Confederate. The veterans' graves are located throughout the cemetery rather than being in designated veterans' plots.[36]

As introduced in the previous chapter, the twin Union and Confederate monuments dedicated in 1900 in Greenwood Cemetery in St. Petersburg represent an apparently deliberate act of reconciliation. This is demonstrated by the fact that the monuments are identical and exist in the landscaped center of the cemetery balanced on either side of a central flagpole, as well as by their joint dedication with speakers including both Union and Confederate veterans (see figure 32 in chapter 2). It is perhaps very symbolically important that they were dedicated on February 22, the anniversary of George Washington's birth. Confederate monuments were typically dedicated on Jefferson Davis's birthday, Robert E. Lee's birthday, the date of the death of Stonewall Jackson, or the date of the surrender of Joseph E. Johnston (Confederate Memorial Day in Florida), whereas Abraham Lincoln's birthday or Decoration Day (Memorial Day) was favored for Union monuments. Using Washington's birthday clearly avoided these sectionally important dates, but it may also be important that Washington was an icon of both the North and the South. Washington's importance to the United States is obvious; his importance to the Confederacy is clear by the use of an image of Washington on the official Confederate Seal and to Florida by the inclusion of his name on the Confederate monument erected in 1908 in Ocala.[37]

Although it appears that both of the Greenwood Cemetery monuments were designed and funded by Union Civil War veteran Zephaniah Phillips, the Union monument is marked as at least nominally being sponsored by the Kit Carson Post while "Confederate veterans and friends" sponsored the Confederate monument. Phillips served as commander of the Kit Carson Post of the GAR and, after his death in 1903, was buried in Greenwood Cemetery in sight of his monument project. His grave is marked simply with "CAPT. Z. PHILLIPS[,] CO. F 120, ILL. VOL. MAR. 2, 1837[,] JAN. 21, 1903."[38]

Located on either side of a central flagpole within an oval drive at the

Figure 81. 1900 Union monument in St. Petersburg's Greenwood Cemetery in 2011. Photograph by William B. Lees.

center of the cemetery, the two monuments are identical in design (see figure 81). The flagpole, as shown in a historic photo of the dedication ceremony, was a part of the monuments' original design. Each monument consists of an approximately six-foot-high rectangular pedestal made of stucco-covered masonry topped with identical Civil War–era mortars that were donated by the U.S. government. Both monuments have marble plaques inserted into the front side of the pedestal. The Union monument plaque reads "IN MEMORY OF UNION DEAD. ERECTED BY KIT CARSON POST G.A.R. 1900."[39]

Orlando, 1910

On November 20, 1910, the U. S. Grant Post of the GAR dedicated a monument in Orlando's Greenwood Cemetery to the unknown Union dead. The featured speaker was William H. Mock, the GAR's former department commander of Washington State and Alaska, who had moved to Orlando earlier that year.[40]

The monument consists of a granite obelisk shaft on a three-stepped base set atop a large two-stepped masonry foundation and is topped with an iron cannonball pediment (see figure 82). The front face of the shaft is engraved with "IN MEMORY OF THE ARMY AND NAVY 1861–65," and the upper base step is engraved with "G.A.R." The upper section on the front of the shaft also contains a band of decorative engravings. On the foundation a bronze plaque

Figure 82. 1910 Grand Army of the Republic monument in Orlando's Greenwood Cemetery in 2011. Photograph by William B. Lees.

reads "TO OUR UNKNOWN SOLDIER DEAD." A GAR grave marker is attached to another side of the foundation and may have been added at a later date.

Greenwood Cemetery was established in 1880 as the Orlando City Cemetery. It was purchased by the City of Orlando in 1892 and renamed as Greenwood Cemetery in 1915.[41] The cemetery contains the remains of some two hundred Union and Confederate veterans. The Union monument is located within a "pie-shaped" wedge plot surrounded by a low masonry wall and a masonry entry threshold to which are attached the brass letters "G.A.R." The

Union plot also contains two ground-level stone markers of recent origin erected by Union heritage groups. One of unknown date is engraved with "IN MEMORY OF DAUGHTERS OF UNION VETERANS CIVIL WAR 1861–1865." The second is engraved with the date 2007 followed by the initials of five Union heritage groups and "FRIENDS." To the east is a Confederate veterans plot, also in a mirror-image pie-shaped configuration. The Confederate section contains a ground-level stone marker of unknown date engraved with "OUR CONFEDERATE DEAD." The Confederate plot does not contain any other general monument.

St. Cloud, 1915

The history of the community of St. Cloud is linked closely with the GAR and was reviewed in the introduction to this chapter. Although Veterans Park and a park on Ohio Avenue were located within the confines of the community, and although photographs dating from the 1910s and 1920s document large patriotic gatherings in the parks, neither was graced with a Civil War monument until the twenty-first century, when two were erected in Veter-

Figure 83. 1915 Union monument erected by the Woman's Relief Corps in St. Cloud's Mt. Peace Cemetery. Photograph by William B. Lees, 2012.

ans Park (see chapter 5). At some point, however, a temporary monument was erected in the park on Ohio Avenue. In 1917, the Memorial Day ceremony was conducted at "the park on Ohio Avenue, where the exercises were held . . . [and] the procession gathered around the monument in the park erected as a tablet on its base explained 'To the Memory of the Unknown Dead.' It was very realistic, even if it was a temporary monument."[42] This temporary monument was apparently still standing on Memorial Day in 1919.[43]

The only permanent, historic Union monument in the highly successful GAR veterans colony of St. Cloud was not in a downtown park but in the town cemetery on its outskirts. Very little historical documentation exists on this important Union monument, and it almost escaped our attention. The Mt. Peace Cemetery was established in 1911 and contains the graves of over 370 Civil War veterans (including at least two Confederate veterans) and a large number of veterans from the Spanish-American War.

In 1915 the L. L. Mitchell Corps of the WRC undertook the construction of a monument at Mt. Peace Cemetery dedicated "To Our Unknown" (see figure 83). Among those who constructed the monument was William J. Mallett of St. Cloud, a cement and concrete contractor. Approximately nine feet tall, the masonry monument consists of an obelisk shaft on a pedestal and base that rests on a two-stepped foundation. The monument is painted white, and the front pedestal is inset with the dedication "TO OUR UNKNOWN 1861 1865." As part of St. Cloud's centennial celebrations in 2009, the city constructed an inscribed brick walkway around the monument.[44]

Lynn Haven, 1921

The history of Lynn Haven—as explained at the outset of this chapter—is also linked closely with the GAR. In 1913, Union veterans of Lynn Haven's Stanton Post of the GAR began planning a memorial to their fellow soldiers in the form of a monument. Dr. William W. Krape, a Union veteran and later mayor of Lynn Haven, was a leader in this effort. Many of the contributions came from the GAR post members, who donated small portions of their monthly pension checks to the project, and from members of the Ladies Auxiliary, who raised funds for this purpose. By 1920 enough money had been raised to construct in a small memorial park an impressive monument topped by a statue of a Union soldier. The W. H. Mullins Company of Salem, Ohio, was contracted to construct the monument's statue, which was most likely designed by John G. Segesman of that company. The Swiss-born Segesman joined the Mullins Company as a modeler in 1896 and became

Figure 84. Union veterans from the Lynn Haven Grand Army of the Republic post in front of the 1921 Union monument in 1928. Bay County Public Library, Local History Collection, image no. 6590.

their lead sculptor in 1899, ultimately working for the company for twenty-five years. Segesman was also the sculptor for the Confederate monument in Gainesville dedicated in 1904 (see chapter 2).[45]

Erected in 1920, the finished monument was dedicated on February 12, 1921, the anniversary of Abraham Lincoln's birth. The dedication address was held in the GAR hall, located immediately south of the new monument and featured "exceedingly interesting" remarks by the Reverend Harry G. Vandervoort (see figure 84). In an article on the dedication, one contemporary newspaper proclaimed, "Lynn Haven is full of Northern tourists every winter, and among them are hundreds of old veterans who are also 100 per cent Americans who, with their money, liberally assisted in the completion of this glorious patriotic effort, liberal contribution also having been received

Figure 85. 1921 Grand Army of the Republic monument in Lynn Haven as it appeared in 2012. Photograph by William B. Lees.

from almost every State in the Union. There it will stand, silently preaching 100 per cent Americanism to those now living and to generations unborn for many years to come."[46]

A bronze statue of a Union soldier facing north who is wearing a forage cap and uniform frock coat tops the monument (see figure 85). He is standing at parade rest with hands placed on a prewar musket (possibly modeled after a U.S. Springfield Model 1842) and is equipped with a U.S. model cartridge box with U.S. box plate, a knapsack with a rolled blanket on top, and a canteen. The statue sits atop a shaft and pedestal resting on a three-stepped foundation, all made of masonry.

Including the statue, the monument is about twenty-six and one-half feet in height. There were originally bronze plaques on all four faces of the pedestal base. The front, or north side, bronze plaque reads "MONUMENT IN MEMORY OF THE UNION SOLDIERS OF THE CIVIL WAR 1861–1865 1920." On the west face the plaque reads "GRAND ARMY OF THE REPUBLIC," while the east plaque contains the wording of "THE AMERICAN'S CREED" followed by "ERECTED A.D. 1920." The south face plaque reportedly contained information about a "patriotic organization" in the Midwest, the area from which many of Lynn Haven's settlers had come. This plaque was stolen sometime during the 1940s, and the remaining plaques were removed for safekeeping. Photographs of the monument printed in newspapers in 1959 and 1962 show that the three removed plaques were still absent, but by 1972 they had been reinstalled. Holes from the bolts that held the stolen plaque are still visible on the monument.[47]

The monument was featured in a "Ripley's Believe It Or Not" newspaper panel as "The Only Monument to a Union Soldier in the South—Erected with Funds Raised in the North."[48] Although the monument was paid for in part with funds raised in northern states, the rest of this claim, while not accurate, may be traced to an article in the February 17, 1921, issue of the *Panama City Pilot*, which reported that the monument "is unique in probably being the first monument of the kind erected in Florida, or the lower south."[49] The *Bay County Beacon-Tribune* of April 12, 1921, repeated and actually strengthened this claim by saying the monument was "the first of the kind in this far Southland."[50] As late as 1962, a newspaper article proclaimed that the monument "is probably the site of the only monument in Florida to Union veterans of the Civil War."[51] While these claims are not accurate, it is the only privately funded Union monument in Florida not located in a cemetery[52] and is certainly one of the few such monuments in the South.[53]

A number of newspaper articles about the monument indicate it was the target of vandalism through the years, some of it based on slow-healing sectional wounds from the Civil War. A telling photograph of the overgrown city park with the graffiti-covered monument including a large "R. E. Lee" painted on its base was carried in a newspaper article published in 1959.[54] On November 10, 1956, the monument was rededicated in "a quiet ceremony" to U.S. veterans of all wars.[55]

Tampa, 1924

In 1922 the WRC requested that the Tampa City Commission permit them to erect a monument to the GAR in a city park or other city property. In response, Mayor Charles H. Brown appointed a committee of the four other city commissioners to consider the request. On May 16, 1922, the committee reported "that they did not deem it advisable to permit such a monument to be erected in public parks, but recommended that the WRC be granted permission to erect it on their property" in Woodlawn Cemetery. The committee's recommendation was "generously" adopted by the city commission, "provided the design, plans, specifications, etc., of the proposed monument" be submitted to the commission for their approval.[56]

On February 12, 1924, the anniversary of Abraham Lincoln's birth, the completed monument was dedicated in front of "a large gathering" of GAR

Figure 86. 1924 Union monument and veterans plot in Tampa's Woodlawn Cemetery in 2009. Photograph by William B. Lees.

and WRC members at Woodlawn Cemetery. The featured speaker was the Reverend Charles DeWolfe Brower, pastor of the First Congregational Church. In his speech on "The Meaning of This Monument," he spoke of the "evil" of slavery and Lincoln's efforts "to lead a great people into a new place of freedom and justice." In a somewhat conciliatory gesture, Brower went on to discuss "the long and terrible Civil War" by noting that the monument "recalls the devotion of men and women who were in combat with a sincere, self-sacrificing American foe—brother against brother, with a culmination which insured the destruction of slavery and the life of the nation." Following his speech, the American flag draped over the monument was lifted and the crowd sang "The Star-Spangled Banner."[57]

The approximately eleven-foot-high monument consists of a gray marble obelisk shaft and pedestal set on a two-stepped foundation (see figure 86). On the front side of the pedestal is a bas-relief dedication that reads "IN MEMORY OF OUR UNION VETERANS 1861–1865" with a decorative scroll above it that continues around the entire pedestal. On the foundation step directly below is "ERECTED BY W.R.C." in bas-relief. The front shaft face has a large "G.A.R." in bas-relief with a decorative scroll above it that encircles the shaft.

The monument is located in the center of a Union plot at the cemetery with twenty-one marked graves of veterans surrounded by a low masonry wall and a masonry threshold in the entrance inscribed with "G.A.R." Adjacent to it is a Confederate plot of similar size that contains a monument dedicated in 1913 by the United Confederate Veterans (described in chapter 2). That monument is also surrounded by a low masonry wall. A grass walkway separates the two plots.

Miami, 1939

What we believe to be the southernmost Union monument erected by the GAR is located in the Woodlawn Park Cemetery in Miami, which was established in 1913 (see figure 87). Dedicated in 1939, seventy-four years after the end of the Civil War, it was certainly one of the last monuments erected by the GAR, whose numbers at that time were greatly diminished. One of the Union veterans who led the effort to erect the monument was Charles J. Rose, an Ohio native who settled in what is today Homestead, Florida, in 1891 and organized the GAR's Henry Clay Roome Post in Miami. At the time of the monument dedication, Rose was ninety-five years old and served as the commander of the GAR's Department of Florida. Rose himself put on his

Union uniform and posed for sculptor Porter V. Skinner for the creation of the statue that was to grace the monument.[58]

A fund-raising medal for this monument shows an illustration of the proposed monument with an inscription "MONUMENT TO BE ERECTED ON BISCAYNE DRIVE, MIAMI, FLORIDA" on one side and "HENRY CLAY ROOME POST G.A.R. NO. 42 MIAMI FLORIDA" on the other (see figure 88). These circular medals were manufactured by the Green Duck Metal Stamping Company, which was located in Chicago from 1906 until 1962, at which time it relocated to Hernando, Mississippi, where it went out of business in 2004. The final version of the monument is different from the one depicted on the medal, and its final location was in Woodlawn Park Cemetery.

Figure 87. Captain C. J. Rose of the Grand Army of the Republic dedicating the 1939 Miami Union monument that bears his likeness. Photo from 1939 dedication brochure. Courtesy of Frederick P. Gaske.

Figure 88. Fund-raising medal, one inch in diameter, for Miami Grand Army of the Republic monument, 1930s. Photograph by Ray Stanyard, Courtesy of Frederick P. Gaske.

The monument dedication ceremony was held on April 12, 1939, in conjunction with the fifty-sixth encampment of the GAR's Department of Florida, which was held at the Everglades Hotel in downtown Miami (demolished in 2005). The Dunn Bus Company provided transportation as a courtesy for the convention attendees from the hotel to Woodlawn Park Cemetery, where the University of Miami Band played patriotic songs as the crowd assembled. Speakers included representatives of the GAR and the WRC, with the principal address being made by Samuel S. McCahill, past commander of the Miami American Legion Post. The ceremony ended with a benediction and the playing of "Taps."[59]

The approximately fifteen-foot-high monument consists of a hexagonal pedestal and foundation made of cut limestone topped by the cast stone soldier statue for which Charles Rose had posed (see figure 89). The seven-foot-high statue is of a soldier in a Union uniform with a sidearm holstered on his waist belt fastened with a "US" belt buckle. Wearing a kepi hat with "GAR" on the front, the soldier stands at attention as he holds at his side a cast stone American flag on a metal pole topped by a metal finial. He wears a corporal's chevrons on his sleeves. At the base of the statue is engraved the name of the sculptor, "Porter V. Skinner 38," followed by a Y in a circle symbol. The "38" apparently refers to the year, 1938, in which the statue was created.

Figure 89. 1939 Grand Army of the Republic monument in Miami's Woodlawn Park Cemetery in 2012. Photograph by William B. Lees.

The six-sided pedestal, which rests on a one-stepped foundation, has bronze plaques or decorative items attached on all sides. The largest plaque is on the front of the monument. Decorated with an eagle motif, the plaque reads "HENRY CLAY ROOME POST NO. 42, GRAND ARMY OF THE REPUBLIC, MIAMI, FLORIDA" on top and "G.A.R. MEMORIAL DEDICATED APRIL 12, 1939" below. In between are the names of ninety-two Union veterans of the Roome

Post. Below this is another small plaque, which reads "CAPTAIN C. J. ROSE BY PORTER V. SKINNER, SCULPTOR."

Another side contains a "MEMORIAL DAY ORDER" plaque with the wording of "GENERAL ORDERS NO. 11" issued by the GAR's commander in chief, John Logan, on May 5, 1868, regarding the decoration of Union graves. The other four sides are decorated with bronze medal and ribbon pins of the monument's sponsoring organizations: the GAR, the WRC, the Sons of Union Veterans, and the Daughters of Union Veterans. A dedication ceremony brochure includes a photograph that appears to show the monument to have been painted white.[60] Today, much of the monument is gray with the patina of age.

* * *

In the years prior to the Civil War Centennial in the 1960s, only eleven Union monuments were erected in Florida. One of these was a short-lived wooden monument marking Union graves at the Olustee Battlefield (see chapter 1). Another was erected in the Magnolia Springs Cemetery at Green Cove Springs at an unknown date following the Civil War but was heavily damaged; it had disappeared by the 1970s (see chapter 4). Two others are in Key West and were erected with public funds, one through the sale of government property (see chapter 1) and the other through an appropriation of the New York State Assembly (see chapter 4). The seven remaining monuments were erected with private funds, and all are associated with the GAR or its auxiliaries. They span a period of roughly fifty years between 1891 and 1939.

The fact that only one of the privately funded monuments was placed outside a cemetery is noteworthy. Although Florida had successfully recruited individuals from northern states to move to the state after the Civil War, and although many native Floridians had remained loyal to the Union during that conflict, Florida was a southern state whose population was galvanized by the rhetoric of the Lost Cause. That Union monuments were not generally welcome in public spaces is clearly evident by the example of the WRC's 1922 petition to the Tampa City Commission to place a monument in a city park or other city property. Although the commission denied the WRC's request despite the erection in 1911 of a large monument to the Confederacy on the grounds of the Hillsborough County Courthouse in downtown Tampa, they did approve placement of a monument, of approved design, on the WRC's own property in Woodlawn Cemetery. In 1939 the Miami GAR erected their monument in Woodlawn Park Cemetery despite original plans to place it on Biscayne Drive, which is a public thoroughfare.[61] Only in Lynn Haven, a community of Union veterans, was such a monument erected in a city park.

Of all the monuments erected by the GAR or any of its posts, the 1939 monument in Miami appears to be the one furthest south. Due to its late date, it is certainly also one of the last erected. The final annual national encampment of the GAR was held in 1949, and the last member of the organization died in 1956.

The message on Union monuments in Florida might appear to be somewhat muted compared to the Lost Cause message carried on contemporary Confederate monuments, but it is consistent with the message found on Union monuments elsewhere in the South and in the loyal northern states. This message is one that seeks to remember the unknown dead, the soldiers and sailors who fought during the Civil War, and the veterans. This simple message, contrasted with the more purpose-driven message of Confederate monuments, is a physical reminder of the status of the North as victor in the Civil War and the struggle of the South to vindicate its defeat in the conflict.

4 REMEMBERING HALLOWED GROUND

But, in a larger sense, we can not dedicate—we can not consecrate—we can not hallow—this ground. The brave men living and dead who struggled here, have consecrated it far above our poor power to add or detract.

Abraham Lincoln, Gettysburg Address, engraved on Lincoln Memorial

Civil War soldiers spent far more time in camp than on the battlefield. Camps were spread throughout the theaters of conflict and came and went with the movement of the troops. Some, such as the sprawling winter camps of the Union Army of the Potomac and the Confederate Army of Northern Virginia, were larger than most towns in 1860s America. These camps housed tens of thousands of soldiers and the accompanying wagon trains, field hospitals, sutlers, horses, artillery, and quartermaster stores. Early in the war these winter camps in northern Virginia were a sea of well-ordered canvas tents, but as the war progressed, log huts and dugouts became more common as the soldiers sought to endure the long, cold months waiting for warm weather and new campaigns and battles. Cold weather and poor sanitary conditions caused soldiers to die in droves of disease, of which chronic diarrhea was among the most common.

Further south, the tropical climate created problems of its own. Lucky were Union troops of the Seventh Regiment of Vermont Volunteer Infantry who occupied Pensacola in November 1862. An officer of that regiment, Colonel William C. Holbrook, remarked after the war that the climate was better than during their previous stay in New Orleans: "The climate we found equable and generally pleasant. The air was pure and, in our [debilitated] condition, highly invigorating. The effects of this change from the malarious banks of the Mississippi were decidedly favorable upon the health and spirits of our men, and were perceptible at once."[1] In Key West, which is today a highly desired tourist destination, troops of the Ninetieth and Ninety-First New York Regiments were less than enamored with their location and lost scores of their own to yellow fever—a loss so profound that in the 1920s the New York State Assembly appropriated funds for a monument to commemorate the suffering of its native sons.

These and other camps and garrisons are largely forgotten, their locations known mainly by those who, with metal detector and shovel, disturb the remains of the huts and campfires for curiosity or profit.[2] Despite the importance of camps as part of the Civil War landscape, it has been the places of conflict that early on became a focus of commemoration of the Civil War. In August 1890 Congress authorized the establishment of the Chickamauga and Chattanooga National Military Park, the first of what are now an impressive number of national battlefields. A few days later, Congress approved acquisition of part of the Antietam Battlefield, followed by Shiloh in 1894, Gettysburg in 1895, and Vicksburg in 1899.[3] But long before these important events, commemoration of the fields of conflict of the Civil War had begun. In the introduction we mentioned the erection of a carved limestone monument commemorating the dead of the Thirty-Second Indiana Volunteer Infantry shortly after the December 17, 1861, Battle of Rowlett's Station, Kentucky, and the 1865 Union monuments that still stand on the Manassas National Battlefield Park. These and the hundreds that followed mark hallowed ground, as if to say for the veterans when they are no longer able, "This is where we were on that day, when we stood side by side, to face a worthy foe, and where we conducted ourselves with a valor worthy of our cause."

The erection of these monuments on fields of conflict preceded large-scale actions to preserve the actual battlefields, but it certainly aided the eventual state and national movements to protect these grounds by bringing them into public ownership. In addition to the battlefields themselves, which naturally became the focus of much of the Civil War narrative in the years following the war, monuments were also erected on places beyond the battlefield that became hallowed in their own right.

With conflict came casualty. Men who died on the battlefield, or later in nearby field hospitals, were often buried very close to where they died, in graves that were often shallow and at best poorly marked, if at all. Sometimes their names were unknown to those who buried them, who were often the enemy victors of the battle. In other cases, names listed on temporary grave markers were lost to time.

Sometimes, battle casualties were quickly buried in nearby cemeteries, such as in Florida at Madison's Oak Ridge Cemetery. Here, Confederate soldiers were buried after dying in a field hospital where they had been taken after the Battle of Olustee. In other cases, soldiers were gathered and buried in common cemeteries on the battlefield soon after the end of fighting. Most famous of these is the U.S. Cemetery at Gettysburg, dedicated by President Lincoln in November 1863. The cemetery at Gettysburg was one of the thirteen cemeteries established between 1862 and 1863 by the U.S. War Department that marked the genesis of the nation's system of national cemeteries.[4]

An unknowable number of soldiers whose names are now lost to history remain in hastily dug individual or mass graves. For some these burial locations are known, such as several trench graves of Confederates at the Shiloh National Military Park. For others, such as the mass grave of Union dead at the Olustee Battlefield, the locations are unknown today.[5]

After the war, the care of the graves of soldier dead was a matter of profound concern throughout the reunited country. The federal government went to great effort to establish a system of national cemeteries, many located near major battlefields and fortifications, and to collect the Union dead from temporary graves on battlefields, near field hospitals, and at campsites and former military installations. In the late 1860s contracts were let by the Quartermaster Department for the identification and removal of U.S. soldier dead extending from the east coast to the far west and to their reinterment in national cemeteries.[6] Most of those so removed are marked "unknown." Excluded by policy, Confederate dead were only rarely buried in these national cemeteries. Noteworthy exceptions are Confederate dead buried in the nation's premier national cemetery, Arlington, where Rebel graves are graced with a magnificent monument, and at the Barrancas National Cemetery in Pensacola. At Barrancas, these burials occurred when the fort was in Confederate possession. After the Union reoccupied the fort in 1862, Union soldier dead surrounded these graves. At Arlington, Confederates who died during the battles in the vicinity of Washington, D.C., were reinterred in a dedicated plot within the cemetery in 1900 after years of urging by the United Daughters of the Confederacy.[7]

When it became clear that the federal government would not provide for the care of Confederates' graves, local efforts were organized, often by Ladies' Memorial Associations. This involved burial of battlefield dead in dedicated sections of nearby cemeteries, such as the plot for Confederate dead from the Battle of Olustee at the Oaklawn Cemetery in Lake City. New cemeteries were also established to serve as the final resting places for Confederate dead from a nearby battle or as a place to gather the dead from several nearby battles, hospitals, and camps in a fashion following the model of the U.S. national cemeteries. These typically were private, such as the McGavock Confederate Cemetery in Franklin, Tennessee.

Some of these new plots and cemeteries housing Confederate dead were deemed fitting places for monuments to commemorate the collective sacrifice of soldiers in battle, camp, or hospital. One step removed from where soldiers fought and died, these cemeteries are no less hallowed grounds forever linked to the conflict that necessitated their very existence.

FLORIDA PLACES

If one looks at a map of all the battlefields and skirmishes of the Civil War, it can be concluded that most of the fighting and dying was happening somewhere besides Florida. But just as "all politics are local," what constitutes hallowed ground worthy of commemoration is a very personal determination. Within its borders Florida has a number of places where the sacrifice of soldiers and sailors was significant and where this sacrifice has been memorialized through the erection of monuments. The first such monuments were erected at and near the site of Florida's largest battle.

Battle of Olustee, 1866 (1991), 1901, 1912, 1928, 1936, 1951

At the Battle of Olustee (also known as the Battle of Ocean Pond), on February 20, 1864, Confederate forces repulsed an attempted Union thrust through Florida in the state's largest Civil War engagement. Brigadier General Truman Seymour and his force of approximately five thousand Union soldiers, including a large number of U.S. Colored Troops, moved west from Jacksonville in mid-February with the aim of disrupting lines of supply from Florida to the rest of the Confederacy and returning Florida to the Union in time for the 1864 presidential election. East of Lake City, near Olustee and Ocean Pond, the Federals met a Confederate force of similar size led by Brigadier General Joseph Finegan, which included reinforcements sent from Georgia. The ensuing engagement, which resulted in more than twenty-eight hundred casualties, was a clear Confederate victory, and Union soldiers retreated to Jacksonville. The Battle of Olustee is commemorated by several monuments located on the battlefield and by two in nearby Lake City.[8]

Olustee Battlefield, Union, 1866 (1991)

The first monument at the Olustee Battlefield was erected in honor of Union casualties. In 1866 a detachment of U.S. Army soldiers erected a twelve-foot-high wooden monument at the location of a mass grave of Union soldiers killed during the battle (described in detail in chapter 1). By 1873 the wooden monument was no longer standing, and in the ensuing years the precise location of the Union mass grave was lost. In May 1991 a granite representation of the original wooden monument was erected by a Civil War reenactment organization, the Union Army District of Florida (UADF), at a location thought to be close to the original (see figure 90).

The 1866 U.S. Army report regarding the reburial of the Union dead at

Figure 90. Union reenactors in 2011 at the annual memorial service at the 1991 Union monument, Olustee Battlefield State Historic Site. Photograph by William B. Lees.

Olustee did not specify the monument's design. The UADF chose a cross for the replacement monument, reasoning that it would have been the most likely design for the army detail to have constructed in the field considering the time constraints they would have been under and the limited tools that would have been available to them. The UADF reasoned that a wooden obelisk design would not have been likely under the circumstances. Following a two-year fund-raising effort, the new monument was constructed by a monument company in nearby Starke, Florida, at a cost of $4,000.[9]

The front base of this monument below the cross is engraved with an inscription from the original monument: "TO THE MEMORY OF THE OFFICERS AND SOLDIERS OF THE UNITED STATES ARMY WHO FELL IN THE BATTLE OF OLUSTEE FEBRUARY 20, 1864." Below this on the foundation is engraved "THIS MEMORIAL REPLACES THE ORIGINAL WOODEN ONE ERECTED ON THIS SITE MAY 1866." The other three sides of the base are also engraved with the original monument's inscriptions: "UNITY AND PEACE," "OUR COUNTRY," and "MAY THE LIVING PROFIT BY THE EXAMPLE OF THE DEAD." Two of the foundation sides below these are inscribed with the names of Union army "PARTICIPATING UNITS" from the battle, while the third is inscribed with "ERECTED BY UNION ARMY DISTRICT OF FLA. MAY 1991."

Olustee Confederate Dead, Oaklawn Cemetery, Lake City, 1901

Oaklawn Cemetery in Lake City contains 155 graves of Confederate soldiers, mostly unknown by name, who were casualties from the nearby Battle of Olustee. The cemetery contains soldiers killed in battle and brought here for final burial as well as wounded soldiers who later died in nearby hospitals such as that established at the Cathey House Hotel in Lake City (no longer standing).[10] As such, this is one of those places hallowed as the final resting place of Confederate soldiers killed in a specific battle.

The monument erected within the cemetery, dedicated on January 4, 1901, commemorates the importance of this place as hallowed ground (see figure 91). Sponsored at a cost of $500 by the Stonewall Chapter of the Florida Division of the UDC, this is the oldest extant UDC monument in Florida. Prior to the dedication ceremony, civic, military, and educational groups from Lake City and Columbia County, as well as Confederate veterans and UDC members, paraded from downtown Lake City to the cemetery. Among those marching in the parade were faculty and students of Florida Agricultural College in Lake City, which in 1905 merged with three other educational institutions and relocated to Gainesville to form the University of Florida.

Figure 91. 1901 United Daughters of the Confederacy monument in the Confederate soldier plot in Lake City's Oaklawn Cemetery. Photograph by William B. Lees, 2008.

Speakers at the dedication ceremony included the chairman of the Columbia County Board of County Commissioners, the mayor of Lake City, and two Confederate veterans.[11]

Designed and constructed by the Artope and Whitt Company of Macon, Georgia,[12] the monument consists of a marble obelisk shaft and pedestal on a three-stepped marble base set on a granite block that rests on a brick masonry foundation. The front, or north, face of the lowest marble step contains the words "OUR CONFEDERATE DEAD" in bas-relief. On the pedestal above this is engraved "TO THESE SLEEPING HEROES OF OUR FAIR SOUTHLAND THIS HUMBLE SHAFT IS ERECTED. THEY FELL AT THE BATTLE OF OLUSTEE." The east pedestal face is engraved with "THEIR NAMES ARE UNKNOWN. BUT THEIR UNWAVERING VALOR IS WRITTEN IN EVERY SOUTHERN HEART." The west pedestal face is engraved with "LOVINGLY DEDICATED TO THEIR

MEMORY BY STONEWALL CHAPTER NO. 47, LAKE CITY[,] FLA." An elaborate, interwoven "CSA" found on many Confederate monuments of this era is engraved on the obelisk itself.

This monument sits on a slightly raised mound of earth in the middle of a field of small unmarked marble stones with rounded tops marking the individual graves. In the earthen mound in front of the monument is a ground-level granite block engraved with "ERECTED JANUARY 4, 1901 BY THE STONEWALL CHAPTER # 47 REDEDICATED FEBRUARY 16, 1996 BY THE OLUSTEE CHAPTER # 2488 FLORIDA DIVISION UNITED DAUGHTERS OF THE CONFEDERACY." In a corner of this plot is a standard Confederate grave marker with a peaked top on which is engraved the Southern Cross of Honor (first authorized in 1930 by the U.S. War Department for government-issued Confederate gravestones) and the inscription "IN THIS AREA ARE BURIED 155 UNKNOWN CONFEDERATE SOLDIERS KILLED IN BATTLE OF OLUSTEE OR DIED IN CONF HOSPITAL 1864–1865."[13]

Olustee Battlefield, Confederate, 1912

In 1897 the Florida Division of the UDC began raising funds for the erection of a monument at the Olustee Battlefield. In 1899, at the urging of the UDC, the Florida Legislature passed a bill that authorized the governor to appoint a five-person commission to oversee the construction of a Battle of Olustee monument and appropriated $2,500 for its erection. However, the bill's original language to honor only the Confederate soldiers of Olustee had been changed by the legislature so that the monument was to be dedicated to both "the Federal and Confederate officers and soldiers who participated in said battle."[14]

Inclusion of a dedication to the Union participants on the proposed monument in the 1899 legislation was controversial. Reflecting social attitudes present in the nation at the time, the UDC adopted a resolution calling for the repeal of the bill, as "they did not care to divide honors intended for the confederate dead with negro dead of the union army." As one UDC representative stated, "If the union dead had been white men it is possible that we would have remembered them in the bill, but as they were negroes, and we ignored them in the bill, we consider the change made by the legislature as worthy of our highest indignation."[15]

Although the written record appears to indicate that the rationale behind the UDC's desire not to honor Union participants at Olustee was racially motivated, other factors were also at play. Starting with the general exclusion of federal attention to Confederate dead, including exclusion of Confederates from national cemeteries and continuing with limiting federal pension rights to Union soldiers, the GAR and the UDC had been at war over commemoration of the Civil War and over federal care of soldier dead and veterans. The GAR had been very effective in ensuring that the federal treasure was in general not used to honor the Confederacy or its soldiers or to care for Confederate dead or veterans. Although perhaps unstated, this was certainly at play in the UDC's decision to insist that funds from the former Confederate state of Florida honor only its native sons and other loyal Confederates who fought at Olustee.

The Olustee monument became an issue in at least one 1900 Florida congressional election race. The Democratic primary in northeast Florida's Second Congressional District pitted Frank Clark, who, as a member of the state legislature, had voted for the change to the Olustee monument bill, against incumbent congressman Robert W. Davis. Clark stated that he believed "that the dead negroes at Olustee were just as deserving of a monument . . . as were the confederates." Davis, a Confederate veteran, expressed his "hearty sympathy with the Daughters of the Confederacy" and regarded "their position as a most laudable one." With the support of the UDC, Davis was reelected to the U.S. Congress.[16]

During this period, the Florida Legislature met every other year. At its next session, in 1901, it amended the 1899 bill to delete the reference to Union participants so that the monument would be dedicated solely to "Confederate officers and soldiers." With this issue settled, the UDC turned their attention to raising funds for the monument, but donations were slow in coming. In 1906 the Olustee Monument Commission issued an "urgent appeal" for contributions so that they could "reach a decision on the character and size of the monument as soon as possible and to have it erected without further delay."[17]

The commission had been created by the 1899 monument legislation and included members of the UDC, the United Confederate Veterans, and the Sons of Confederate Veterans. Among the noted members of the commission over time were Confederate veteran Captain Francis P. Fleming, who was Florida's governor from 1889 to 1893; Confederate veteran Major General Evander M. Law; and Duncan U. Fletcher, who was the longest-serving U.S. senator from Florida from 1909 to 1936.[18]

In 1907 the City of Lake City offered to donate $1,000 and a site in their downtown city park toward the monument's construction at that location. Commission chairman Law and the UDC recommended that this offer to

Figure 92. Confederate veterans of the Battle of Olustee at the dedication of the battlefield monument in 1912. Florida Photographic Collection, State Archives of Florida, image no. RC11560.

put the monument in Lake City be accepted and that the battlefield itself be marked with a granite boulder. This issue was heavily debated in Florida newspapers and in the legislature. In 1908 the UDC "reversed itself and withdrew all objections to locating the monument on the field of battle."[19]

In 1909, landowners Austin B. Fletcher and John and Eliza Brown donated three acres of the Olustee Battlefield to the State of Florida,[20] and the decision was made to place the monument on the battlefield rather than in Lake City. The unveiling of the monument on the battlefield was originally scheduled for February 20, 1912, the forty-eighth anniversary of the battle. However, the monument commission decided to postpone the ceremony until the Florida Division of the UCV held their annual state reunion in nearby Lake City in October of that year. Arrangements were made for a special train to run from Lake City to Olustee for the dedication ceremony, and other arrangements were made to stop regular trains between Jacksonville and Lake City at the monument site.[21]

On October 23, 1912, a crowd of some four thousand, including Florida governor Albert W. Gilchrist, gathered on the Olustee Battlefield to dedicate a grand monument with a program of prayers, music, and speeches (see figures 92 and 93). Confederate veterans were present in large numbers for the ceremonies, presided over by former Confederate major general Evander Law, chairman of the Olustee Monument Commission. Senator Duncan U. Fletcher, who delivered the keynote address, praised the erection of a monument "built of granite" on the field where occurred "true and rare heroism, extraordinary endurance and valor, by men whose conduct, deeds and daring covered them with glory eternal." He stated that, in the postwar period, "a new era is dawning" in which "order has been wrought out of chaos and victory out of defeat" as the South now "takes position at the head" of a reunited country. Following "an intermission of two hours" after Fletcher's speech, during which lunch was served to the attendees, the program resumed with the presentation of the monument by representatives of the UDC to Governor Gilchrist, who accepted it on behalf of the State of Florida.[22]

Figure 93. Battle of Olustee monument during its dedication in 1912. Florida Photographic Collection, State Archives of Florida, image no. RC11559.

Figure 94. 1912 Confederate monument on the Olustee Battlefield in 2005. Photograph by William B. Lees.

The monument is a spectacular "gothic castle" structure on a three-stepped foundation made of Georgia granite blocks covering an area fifteen feet square with a tower rising forty feet above the ground (see figure 94). Constructed by the Reed E. LaMance Company of Jacksonville, Florida, the monument cost $5,000, with half paid by the State of Florida and half raised by the UDC and the UCV.[23]

The front, or south, side of the monument's base has a marble panel engraved with "THE BATTLE OF OLUSTEE WAS FOUGHT ON THIS GROUND FEBRUARY 20TH 1864. BETWEEN 5,000 CONFEDERATE TROOPS COMMANDED BY GENERAL JOSEPH E. FINEGAN AND 6,000 FEDERAL TROOPS UNDER GEN-

ERAL TRUMAN SEYMOUR. THE FEDERALS WERE DEFEATED WITH A LOSS OF 2,000 MEN. THE CONFEDERATE LOSS WAS LESS THAN 1,000." There is also a marble panel on the reverse side of the monument, engraved with "TO THE MEN WHO FOUGHT AND TRIUMPHED HERE IN DEFENCE OF THEIR HOMES AND FIRESIDES THIS MONUMENT IS ERECTED BY THE UNITED DAUGHTERS OF THE CONFEDERACY AIDED BY THE STATE OF FLORIDA IN COMMEMORATION OF THEIR DEVOTION TO THE CAUSE OF LIBERTY AND STATE SOVEREIGNTY. MCMXII." On three sides of the monument's tower is an inset panel of marble with a bas-relief image of a Confederate battle flag.

In 1915 the Florida Legislature appropriated funds to the UDC "not to exceed five hundred dollars for the first year, nor to exceed one hundred dollars for any succeeding year" for "maintaining in proper condition, the grounds belonging to Olustee Monument." Using these state funds, a fence consisting of faux stone concrete blocks with a smooth capstone on the property's south side and heavy wire fencing with stone posts on the other sides was installed around the three state-owned acres in 1916. This work also included installation of auto and pedestrian entrances with wrought-iron gates on the park's south side. The faux stone pillars surrounding the entrance gates were originally topped with large urns, but these are no longer present (see figure 95). On the center entry gate pillar, "OLUSTEE BATTLE FIELD" is inscribed in large letters.[24]

Figure 95. Olustee Battlefield gate pillar showing the now-missing urn and the 1912 monument in the background, 1920s photograph. Florida Photographic Collection, State Archives of Florida, image no. PR10766.

In 1994 a granite band with inscriptions was installed in a concrete pad surrounding the monument. Sponsored by the Andrew Jackson Padgett Chapter of the Florida Division of the UDC and the Olustee Battlefield Citizens Support Organization, work also included stabilization of the monument base. The south side of the band is inscribed with "THIS MONUMENT AT OCEAN POND IS REDEDICATED TO THESE SOUTHERN UNITS THAT FOUGHT HERE ON FEBRUARY 20, 1864. DONE THIS FEBRUARY 20, 1994 THE 130TH ANNIVERSARY OF THE BATTLE." Names of Confederate units that participated in the battle are inscribed on the other three sides. The dedication ceremony on February 20, 1994, was attended by "several thousand visitors, most of them in period dress."[25]

Olustee Confederate Dead, Lake City, 1928

During the war, Lake City served as an important Confederate transportation and supply depot center. The community was the eastern terminus of the railroad from Tallahassee and the western terminus of the line from Jacksonville. After the Battle of Olustee on February 20, 1864, thirteen miles to the east, scores of the more severely wounded, both Confederate and Union, were treated in Lake City hospitals and private dwellings. Union prisoners were also kept there before being sent to other locations and eventually to the prison camp at Andersonville, Georgia.[26]

Twenty years after first envisioned, the Florida Legislature in 1927 appropriated $5,000 for the erection of a monument at Lake City to the Confederate soldiers killed at the Battle of Olustee and buried in that community. This legislation also authorized Governor John W. Martin to appoint "a commission of three members of the Legislature" to oversee its construction. In June 1927, Governor Martin appointed state senator William C. Hodges of Tallahassee, state senator William W. Phillips of Lake City, and state representative R. W. Farnell, also of Lake City, to the commission, which became known as the Confederate Monument Commission.[27]

Erected in Lake City's downtown Olustee Park in front of the 1902 Columbia County Courthouse, the monument was dedicated on January 18, 1928, with a ceremony attended by some seventy-five hundred people (see figure 96). The featured speakers were Governor Martin and Major General Charles P. Summerall, the U.S. Army chief of staff, who had been born in Columbia County. Both were descendants of Confederate soldiers who had fought in the battle, and their remarks paid "due honors to the dead Confederate soldiers, buried in beautiful Oaklawn cemetery." Summerall also noted

Figure 96. *Left to right*: Colonel Thomas Jefferson Appleyard of the United Confederate Veterans, Major General Charles P. Summerall, Florida governor John Martin, and Florida senator William W. Phillips at dedication of Lake City monument to the Battle of Olustee in 1928. Florida Photographic Collection, State Archives of Florida, image no. N046311.

that it was "an evidence of the greatness of our country . . . that the son of a Confederate veteran is now chief of staff of the American army." The ceremony ended with the University of Florida band "of fifty pieces" playing "The Star-Spangled Banner." After the ceremony, a barbeque luncheon was served to the attendees. This was followed by an afternoon reception, an evening banquet at the Blanche Hotel, and a fireworks display that night.[28]

Figure 97. 1928 Battle of Olustee monument in downtown Lake City in 2008. Photograph by William B. Lees.

The tall granite monument consists of an obelisk shaft on a pedestal and base that sits on a one-stepped foundation (see figure 97). The front, or west, face of the obelisk is decorated with an elaborately intertwined bas-relief "CSA" on the shaft and a bas-relief image of two crossed swords in their scabbards on the obelisk base. Below this on the pedestal are engraved the names of the Florida "OFFICERS COMMANDING" at the Battle of Olustee, including

"BRIGADIER-GENERAL JOSEPH FINNEGAN [*sic*]" and four lieutenant colonels who commanded Florida battalions. The pedestal base contains a granite plaque upon which is engraved "THIS MONUMENT ERECTED TO PERPETUATE IN LOVING MEMORY THE 151 SOLDIERS OF THE CONFEDERATE ARMY WHO LOST THEIR LIVES IN THE BATTLE AT OLUSTEE AND WHO NOW LIE BURIED IN OAKLAWN CEMETERY, LAKE CITY, FLORIDA." On the foundation below is engraved "FEBRUARY 20TH—OLUSTEE BATTLE—1864."

A flat granite block adjacent to the west foundation is engraved with "BODIES LIE TEN BLOCKS NORTHWEST FROM THE MONUMENT IN OAKLAWN CEMETERY" and may have been added after the construction of the monument. On the east face of the pedestal are engraved the names of twenty-nine Florida soldiers killed at the Battle of Olustee. The majority of the 151 soldiers cited on the monument as being buried at Oaklawn Cemetery are unknown by name. As noted in a 1928 newspaper account and shown in a 1928 photograph of the dedication ceremony, the monument originally had four granite cannonballs on the top of the pedestal, one in each corner. The cannonballs were still there as late as 1960 but are no longer present.[29]

Olustee Battlefield, Colquitt, 1936

In addition to the 1912 main monument, two other Confederate monuments are located on the Olustee Battlefield, both located on the state-owned parcel. These monuments were placed forward of and to either side of the 1912 monument, and both are upright granite boulders on a one-stepped foundation.

On April 20, 1936, the Alfred Holt Colquitt Chapter of the Georgia Division of the UDC erected the first of these in memory of the chapter's namesake, Brigadier General Alfred H. Colquitt of Georgia, the field commander during the Confederate attack at the Battle of Olustee (see figure 98). In the postwar period Colquitt served as governor of Georgia and as a U.S. senator. He is buried in Rose Hill Cemetery in Macon, Georgia. Erected on the anniversary of his birth, the monument was dedicated the following month in a ceremony attended by Colquitt's son and daughter and more than twenty of his grandchildren and great-grandchildren.[30]

Four feet high, the monument consists of a rough-hewn granite boulder and foundation with an inset flat surface on which is engraved "HERE WAS FOUGHT ON FEBRUARY 20, 1864 THE BATTLE OF OCEAN POND UNDER THE IMMEDIATE COMMAND OF GENERAL ALFRED HOLT COLQUITT 'HERO OF OLUSTEE' THIS DECISIVE ENGAGEMENT PREVENTED A SHERMAN-LIKE

Figure 98. 1936 General Alfred Holt Colquitt monument at Olustee Battlefield as it appeared in 2005. Photograph by William B. Lees.

INVASION OF GEORGIA FROM THE SOUTH. ERECTED APRIL 20, 1936 BY THE ALFRED HOLT COLQUITT CHAPTER UNITED DAUGHTERS OF THE CONFEDERACY GA. DIV."

Olustee Battlefield, Finegan, 1951

More recent is a monument to the Confederate commander at the Battle of Olustee, Brigadier General Joseph Finegan of Florida, dedicated on March 5, 1951 (see figure 99). Erected by the Florida Division of the UDC in 1950, this monument faces the Colquitt monument. The dedication ceremony included music from a local high school band and chorus and speeches by UDC representatives, state representative B. Robert Burnsed, Park Committee chairman C. C. Fraser, and historian Dena Snodgrass of Jacksonville.[31]

The monument is four and one-half feet high and consists of a rough-hewn granite boulder and foundation with a large inset marble plaque on which is engraved "PLACED BY THE UNITED DAUGHTERS OF THE CONFED-

ERACY FLORIDA DIVISION IN MEMORY OF BRIG. GEN. JOSEPH FINEGAN COMMANDER OF DISTRICT OF MIDDLE AND EAST FLORIDA 'SO WELL DID HE PERFORM HIS PART THAT A SIGNAL VICTORY OVER THE FEDERALS WAS WON IN THE BATTLE OF OLUSTEE FEB. 20, 1864.'" Following his victory at Olustee, Finegan went on to command the Florida Brigade in the Army of Northern Virginia from May 1864 to March 1865, and after the war he was elected to the Florida Legislature. Born in Ireland, Finegan died in 1885 and is buried in Jacksonville's Old City Cemetery.

Figure 99. 1951 dedication of Brigadier General Joseph Finegan monument at the Olustee Battlefield. Florida Photographic Collection, State Archives of Florida, image no. N042029.

Olustee Battlefield Historic State Park

From its dedication in 1912 until 1949, the Olustee Battlefield Memorial and the three acres on which it sits were managed and maintained by the Florida Division of the UDC with the assistance of small appropriations from the state legislature. In 1949 the Florida Board of Parks and Historic Memorials, the forerunner of today's Florida Park Service, assumed responsibility for this site. Since this site came under state ownership in 1909, Olustee became the oldest unit in what is today the Florida State Parks system. Today the Olustee Battlefield Historic State Park consists of the original plot on which the 1912 monument is located and, through a cooperative agreement, an additional 688 acres of Olustee Battlefield land owned by the U.S. Forest Service. The annual reenactment of the Battle of Olustee, the largest Civil War reenactment in the state, is held during the second weekend of February at the park.[32]

Battle of Marianna, 1921

In September 1864, Brigadier General Alexander Asboth, commander of Union forces at Pensacola and of the District of West Florida, undertook a campaign to disrupt Confederate facilities at Marianna after receiving reports that it was being fortified and that Union prisoners were being held there. He led a force of some seven hundred mounted troops to Marianna and on September 27 engaged its approximately three hundred defenders, consisting of some Confederate cavalry and troops home on leave but made up mostly of reserves and local Home Guard militia. After an initial success at stopping the Union advance at the community's edge, many of the Confederates retreated further into town, with some militia taking cover in the Episcopal church and surrounding houses. The fighting reached a climax in and around the church cemetery and ended when Asboth's troops set fire to the church. Several Confederate defenders who refused to surrender perished in the fire. After occupying Marianna and pillaging its buildings, the raiders withdrew the next day back to Pensacola.[33]

Well into the early twentieth century, many Florida communities observed Marianna Day on September 27 with activities usually organized by local chapters of the UDC. Beginning in 1920, the Florida Division of the UDC made the erection of a monument to the Battle of Marianna a priority. Each Florida UDC member was asked to contribute twenty-five cents to the division's Marianna Monument Fund, and a Marianna Day booklet compiled by the William Henry Milton Chapter in Marianna was offered for sale. In May 1921 the state division reported that it had raised over $1,000 for the monument. That same year, the Florida Legislature appropriated $5,000 for the project, directing that the funds "be expended under the direction and supervision of William Henry Milton Chapter, Daughters of the Confederacy and the State Chairman of Monument Fund, Daughters of the Confederacy." On November 2, 1921, with some four thousand people in attendance, a monument to the Confederate defenders in the battle was dedicated in a park in downtown Marianna (see figure 100).[34]

A parade through town preceded the dedication ceremony and featured decorated cars, floats, a U.S. Navy band from Pensacola, Florida National Guard units, Boy Scouts, UDC members, Confederate veterans, and other state and local groups. Speakers included Marianna mayor N. A. Baltzell; Dr. Theophilus West of Marianna, who was an assistant surgeon with the Eighth Florida Infantry during the Civil War; and Florida governor Cary A. Hardee. Two young girls unveiled the monument. One was the great-granddaughter of John Milton, governor of Florida for most of the Civil War, and granddaughter of the Confederate veteran for whom the Marianna UDC

Figure 100. 1921 monument to the Battle of Marianna, 1920s photograph. Florida Photographic Collection, State Archives of Florida, image no. RC03331.

Figure 101. 1921 monument commemorating the Battle of Marianna as it appeared in 2008. Photograph by William B. Lees.

chapter was named. The other was the granddaughter of a Confederate veteran who fought in the Battle of Marianna and the grandniece of Brigadier General William Miller, the Confederate field commander at the Battle of Natural Bridge.[35]

Made of Georgia granite, the monument was manufactured by the McNeel Marble Company of Marietta, Georgia.[36] It stands thirty-six feet in height and consists of an obelisk shaft on a pedestal and base resting on a two-stepped foundation. On the pedestal cornice are four cannonballs, one at each corner (see figure 101). The obelisk on the front, or west side, is decorated with an interwoven "CSA," and the obelisk base contains a bas-relief image of two crossed swords in their scabbards. The pedestal face below contains an inscription in raised letters: "BATTLE OF MARIANNA SEPT. 27, 1864 WHERE OVERWHELMING FEDERAL FORCES WERE STUBBORNLY RESISTED BY A HOME GUARD OF OLD MEN AND BOYS AND A FEW SICK AND WOUNDED CONFEDERATES AT HOME ON FURLOUGH." The pedestal base contains the dates "1861–1865" in large raised numbers, and the top foundation step carries the inscription "CONFEDERATE HEROES" in large raised letters.

The east pedestal face is inscribed with "ERECTED BY FLORIDA DIVISION UNITED DAUGHTERS OF THE CONFEDERACY, WILLIAM HENRY MILTON CHAPTER AND CITIZENS A.D. 1921" in raised letters. The south pedestal face contains "LIVE FOREVER, IMMORTAL HEROES, DEFENDERS OF HOME AND LIBERTY" in raised letters, and the north pedestal face has in raised letters "THE HEROISM OF THOSE WHO FOUGHT FOR HOME AND HONOR IS A PRICELESS HERITAGE OF A LOYAL PEOPLE."

The original Marianna battlefield was the town itself, which is in the downtown core of the now larger city of Marianna. Although the monument erected to commemorate this battle does not appear to be placed in a battlefield setting as do the monuments at the Olustee and Natural Bridge Battlefields, which are located in rural landscapes, it is in fact placed directly on the battlefield along the main road through Civil War Marianna where this battle raged for a day in September 1864.

Battle of Natural Bridge, 1922

The Battle of Natural Bridge was fought on March 6, 1865, about ten miles south of Tallahassee during a combined Union army and navy campaign launched from Key West. The immediate objective of the campaign was the capture of the blockade-running port of St. Marks guarded by Confederate Fort Ward. Though unclear from Union reports, it is conventionally held, and residents of Tallahassee were convinced, that another objective was to capture Florida's capital city, and possibly Thomasville, Georgia, where it was reported that Union prisoners were being held. Landing from the fleet anchored offshore, the Federals came ashore by the St. Marks Lighthouse and intended to proceed up the east side of the St. Marks River, cross over the bridge at Newport, and attack St. Marks and Fort Ward from the rear. However, their attempt to cross the river at Newport was repulsed, so they proceeded along the St. Marks River to attempt a crossing at Natural Bridge. There they were soundly repulsed again and withdrew back to their fleet in

Figure 102. 1919 Natural Bridge Battlefield pillar monument erected by J. B. Fletcher before being covered with mortar, ca. 1919 photograph. Florida Photographic Collection, State Archives of Florida, image no. PR10757.

the Gulf of Mexico. This battle was held in Confederate lore following the war for having saved Tallahassee from capture, making it the only Confederate state capital other than Austin, Texas, to have avoided that fate.[37]

Natural Bridge is just that—a place where the St. Marks River goes underground. Because of this, at the time of the Civil War there was a road that passed across the St. Marks on the Natural Bridge and along which the battle was fought. This road has remained in service ever since, and today it is called Natural Bridge Road (County Road 2192). Following the 1912 Olustee monument by a decade, commemoration of the battle that saved Tallahassee took a slightly different path but ultimately resulted in the construction of a striking monument that stands today as the centerpiece of Natural Bridge Battlefield Historic State Park.

In 1911, while plans were being solidified for the Olustee monument, the Anna Jackson Chapter of the Florida Division of the UDC in Tallahassee established a committee to acquire a portion of the Natural Bridge Battlefield.

After commissioning a land survey, approximately two acres of the battlefield were offered as a donation to the UDC by owners James R. and Mary A. French in 1911 and eventually deeded to the Anna Jackson Chapter in March 1922. George W. Rhodes donated another four acres to the chapter in 1921.[38]

The first monuments erected at the battlefield were not, however, the work of the UDC but rather were constructed by John B. Fletcher of River Junction (a Gadsden County community near Chattahoochee), a Confederate veteran of the battle. With the assistance of family members and local brick mason Lee Pritchard, Fletcher erected two matching pillars on either side of Natural Bridge Road where it crossed earthworks used by Confederate defenders during the battle (see figures 102 and 103). The three-stepped pillars consisted of a base, pedestal, and shaft that ranged between ten and fifteen feet in height. Photographs in the Florida State Archives taken during and following construction show that they were built of brick and covered with stucco and were painted white. At least one of the monuments was topped by a cannonball reportedly from the battlefield, but this was stolen shortly after its placement. Engraved marble plaques commemorating the Battle of Natural Bridge and some of the Confederate units engaged in the battle were

Figure 103. Pillar monuments erected in 1919 by J. B. Fletcher at the Natural Bridge Battlefield, 1958 photograph. Florida Photographic Collection, State Archives of Florida, image no. FPS00873.

inserted into the bases of the monuments. One of the marble plaques stated that the first pillar was erected on May 9, 1919, and another that the second was erected on September 9, 1919.[39]

A dedication of the first Fletcher monument was held on July 4, 1919, with "over a thousand people in attendance." Speakers included John Fletcher, other Confederate veterans, and Florida secretary of state Henry Clay Crawford. Fletcher noted that he desired "to build a duplicate on the opposite side of the road, and connect same with a beautiful arch." Following the ceremony, a dinner was served to the attendees "which could not have been excelled in excellence and abundance."[40]

The dedication for the second Fletcher monument was held on March 10, 1920, and was "largely attended," including twelve veterans of the battle. Speakers included Fletcher, Secretary of State Crawford, Florida Supreme Court justice William H. Ellis, and UCV officials. A picnic dinner was served to the attendees following the conclusion of the ceremony. In 1921 the UDC agreed to place a plaque in the center of the arch "if the arch between the pillars is completed." However, the connecting arch remained a plan and was never built.[41]

In 1921 the Florida Legislature appropriated $5,000 for "erecting a monument and memorial at the scene of the Battle of Natural Bridge in Leon County." The funds were to "be expended under the direction and supervision of Anna Jackson Chapter, United Daughters of the Confederacy." The legislation also authorized the president of the Anna Jackson Chapter "to appoint a committee of five persons, including herself as the Chairman," to oversee the erection of the monument. John B. Fletcher was among those appointed to the committee.[42]

April 26, 1922, Confederate Memorial Day, saw between two and three thousand in the audience for the dedication of a grand monument honoring the Confederate defenders of Natural Bridge (see figure 104). The program consisted of hymn-singing, prayer, and speeches, with Jacksonville mayor and later governor of Florida John W. Martin being the featured speaker. In his remarks, Martin stated that the South had emerged "from the awful effects" of the Civil War "into a splendor that was the marvel of the ages." The monument was then unveiled by two young girls, one of whom was the grandniece of Brigadier General William Miller, the Confederate field commander at the Battle of Natural Bridge, while the other was the granddaughter of two Confederate veterans who had also fought in the battle. After the ceremony,

Figure 104. Dedication of the Natural Bridge monument in 1922. Florida Photographic Collection, State Archives of Florida, image no. PR10756.

Figure 105. 1922 monument to the Battle of Natural Bridge flanked by 1960s slab monuments as they appeared in 2008. Photograph by William B. Lees.

a fish fry and barbeque was served to the attendees by the citizens of nearby Woodville.[43]

Manufactured by the Clark Monument and Stone Company of Jacksonville,[44] this monument remains the centerpiece of the Natural Bridge Battlefield Historic State Park (see figure 105). The approximately twenty-foot-high granite monument consists of a pedestal and base on a three-stepped platform. The monument's cornice and a short column atop the pedestal are draped with a bas-relief Confederate battle flag on which originally rested an eagle with spread wings made of sheet copper. In 2011 the Florida Park Service permanently removed the eagle for conservation and museum display, and it is scheduled to be replaced with an exact replica.[45] The front, or south, side of the monument is the most elaborate. The pedestal face contains a bas-relief image of two crossed muskets with their bayonets affixed. Above the muskets in raised letters is "IN LOVING MEMORY" and below "DEFENDERS OF NATURAL BRIDGE," with the dates "1861" and "1865" engraved on either side. The base contains a bas-relief image of the Florida State Seal surrounded by a laurel wreath with ribbons on top of a palm frond. Below this in large raised letters is "LEST WE FORGET."

On the east pedestal face is engraved "THIS MONUMENT ERECTED UNDER AUTHORITY OF AN ACT OF THE LEGISLATURE OF FLORIDA OF 1921 AS A JUST TRIBUTE OF THE PEOPLE OF FLORIDA TO COMMEMORATE THE VICTORY OF THE BATTLE OF NATURAL BRIDGE, MARCH 6, 1865, AND TO KEEP IN CHERISHED MEMORY THOSE BRAVE MEN AND BOYS WHO, IN THE HOUR OF SUDDEN DANGER, RUSHED FROM HOME, DESK AND FIELD AND FROM THE WEST FLORIDA SEMINARY AND JOINING A FEW DISCIPLINED TROOPS BY THEIR UNITED VALOR AND PATRIOTISM SAVED THEIR CAPITAL FROM THE INVADERS. TALLAHASSEE BEING THE ONLY CAPITAL OF THE SOUTH NOT CAPTURED BY THE ENEMY DURING THE WAR BETWEEN THE STATES." Although Tallahassee was the only southern state capital east of the Mississippi not captured by the Union during the war, the capital of Texas (Austin) likewise never surrendered. The north pedestal face lists the names of the five members of the monument committee, and the west pedestal face lists the Confederate battle units under "COMMANDS TAKING PART IN THE BATTLE OF NATURAL BRIDGE."

At some point, apparently in the mid-1960s, the two Fletcher pillar monuments were dismantled, perhaps due to their deterioration or improvements to Natural Bridge Road. A 1959 photograph shows both still standing, and a 1964 newspaper article notes that at least one of them was still standing, although it is described as "being weathered away." Although the pillars were taken down, their marble plaques were saved and are currently being stored by the Florida Park Service, with plans to eventually display them.[46]

At approximately the same time in the mid-1960s, two low granite blocks were erected in front and to either side of the 1922 monument. Replicas of the six Fletcher monument plaques were set into the blocks. The granite block on the right, when facing the 1922 monument, contains the duplicate plaque in honor of "COL. GEORGE W. SCOTT AND HIS GALLANT MEN" sponsored by the Anna Jackson Chapter of the UDC; one "IN HONOR OF THE WEST FLORIDA CADETS"; and one stating that J. B. Fletcher had erected a monument (the first pillar) on May 9, 1919. The other granite block has the replica plaque in honor of the "GADSDEN COUNTY GRAYS" unit sponsored "by the Ladies of Quincy, Fla."; another honors "Col. J. J. Daniels Regiment of 1st Fla. Reserves, and Col. Geo. W. Scott 5th Fla. Battalion of Cavalry" sponsored "by J. B. Fletcher and Comrades"; and the third states that J. B. Fletcher had erected a monument (the second pillar) on September 9, 1919.[47]

The 1922 monument was separated from Natural Bridge Road by an iron fence that was present as late as 1965, but it was subsequently removed and replaced with a wooden railing fence. On March 5, 2000, the Florida Department of Environmental Protection's Division of Recreation and Parks, the Natural Bridge Historical Society, the UDC, and the SCV dedicated a new low rectangular granite monument at the base of the north side of the 1922 monument. This new monument honors both the Union and Confederate soldiers who were killed at the Battle of Natural Bridge or who later died of their wounds and lists their names.[48]

The six-acre Natural Bridge Battlefield tract owned by the UDC was managed by that organization until 1950, when it was donated to the State of Florida and became the Natural Bridge Battlefield Historic State Park. An additional three battlefield acres were acquired by the state in 1970, fifty-five more acres in 2009, and then an additional fifty-five acres in 2011. A reenactment of the Battle of Natural Bridge is held annually at the park in early March.[49]

Gamble Plantation, 1925

The Gamble Plantation was introduced in chapter 2 as the location of a Confederate monument erected by the UDC in 1937. The mansion itself has become consecrated as Confederate hallowed ground by the Daughters because of its association with the flight of Secretary of State Judah P. Benjamin at the close of the Civil War.

Following the war, the plantation went through a number of owners, and the property was divided. The mansion was in poor condition by the 1890s, and in 1920 three acres containing the plantation home were sold to the Armour Fertilizer Works. This company apparently utilized the house to store raw manure during composting, which would have accelerated deterioration. In 1925 the Judah P. Benjamin Chapter of the Florida Division of the UDC purchased the mansion in order to develop it as a Confederate memorial honoring its association with Secretary of State Benjamin. On June 18, 1926, the UDC gifted the mansion to the State of Florida, and it became the Judah P. Benjamin Confederate Memorial at Gamble Plantation Historic State Park. Through this action, the UDC saved what is now the only surviving antebellum-period mansion in south Florida. The UDC continued to operate the memorial until 1949, when it turned over management to the state. By agreement with the state, the UDC continues to maintain a role at the site although it is operated by the Florida Park Service.[50]

Figure 106. Confederate veterans at the Gamble Plantation in the 1920s after its purchase by the United Daughters of the Confederacy. Florida Photographic Collection, State Archives of Florida, image no. PR10555.

During the early years of state ownership, the mansion was restored and furnished with assistance from the UDC, and self-guided tours were offered.[51] Prior to World War II, and continuing in some fashion to this day, Gamble Plantation has served as a memorial in every sense of the word. It was a reunion and gathering place for Confederate veterans and the UDC, where the focus was the Confederacy and antebellum social life (see figure 106). Although not a constructed monument such as that placed on the grounds by the UDC in 1937 (see chapter 2), Gamble Mansion was purposefully preserved through the actions of the UDC and then entrusted to the state as a symbol that specifically recalls it as a place of Confederate importance in helping a member of Jefferson Davis's cabinet escape to freedom.

Key West, New York Regimental Monument, 1930

Following the Civil War, many states, both Confederate and Union, erected monuments on distant battlefields and other locations to honor the valor and suffering of their regiments. One such state-commissioned regimental monument exists in Florida. Known locally as the "Yellow Fever Monument," it honors the sacrifices of the Ninetieth and Ninety-First New York Infantry Regiments while in service at Key West.

Organized in New York City and Albany, respectively, the Ninetieth and Ninety-First Regiments were stationed in Key West for much of 1862 before being transferred to other theaters of the war. The Ninetieth Regiment returned to Key West for a short period in 1863. During their stays at Key West, these regiments lost 117 men to disease, mostly yellow fever. These soldiers did not die on the battlefield, but their ultimate sacrifice was not forgotten by New York State. A major proponent of the monument was Alfred A. Lord, commander of the GAR post in Binghamton, New York, who was stationed in Key West with the Ninetieth Regiment. Lord had contracted yellow fever while there, but he weathered the disease.[52]

As early as 1921, legislation for funding the monument was introduced in the New York State Assembly by Lord's nephew, Assemblyman Bert Lord. In 1927 the assembly appropriated $12,000 for the monument, but this item was vetoed by Governor Al Smith. In 1928 the state assembly again appropriated $12,000 for the monument, and this time it did not receive Governor Smith's veto. The appropriation called for the erection at Key West of "a monument, suitably inscribed, in memory of the civil war veterans from this state who are buried in that city."[53]

In February 1929 the chairman of the New York Monuments Commission, Charles A. Shaw, traveled to Key West to select a site for the monument. Accompanying Shaw was noted architect Edward Pearce Casey (1864–1940), who would design the monument. Casey had already designed the New York Monument at Antietam Battlefield (1919), the elaborate Ulysses S. Grant Memorial in Washington, D.C. (1922), and the New York Auxiliary Monument at Gettysburg Battlefield (1925). Key West's Bayview Park was selected as the memorial site, and in May 1929 the Charles F. Parson Company of New York City was awarded the contract to fabricate the monument and ship it to Key West. The site for the New York monument was within view of the Confederate arch erected by the UDC in Bayview Park in 1924 (see chapter 2). The monument was installed at Bayview Park in July 1929 by Charles

Kappes, a masonry contractor from Gettysburg, Pennsylvania, and two helpers. Construction and installation costs totaled $9,270, and the remainder of the $12,000 appropriation was set aside to assist in sending a delegation from New York to the dedication ceremony.[54]

Dedication of the monument took place the following year in conjunction with Armistice Day (now Veterans Day) activities on November 11, 1930. The ceremony was preceded by a parade through Key West organized by the American Legion that ended at Bayview Park. Parade participants included military units, veterans, drum and bugle corps, Boy and Girl Scouts, decorated cars, and floats. Business was "practically suspended for the day" for the festivities, with stores closing at noon and some government departments closed the entire day.[55]

An "immense throng" of some five thousand people attended the dedication, including a delegation of eighteen dignitaries from New York that had traveled by train to attend the ceremony. The delegation included two Union Civil War veterans, sons of Union Civil War veterans, New York State assemblymen and senators, representatives of veterans organizations, and delegation family members. The dedication ceremony consisted of prayer, music, and speeches. Speakers included Key West mayor Leslie A. Curry, New York senator William T. Byrne, and Charles A. Shaw, chairman of the New York Monuments Commission, himself a Union Civil War veteran. The speakers extolled the New York soldiers who died in Key West as "unsung heroes" of the Civil War, with Byrne noting that their courage was "as lofty as that of those who died on the field of battle." The ceremony concluded with the singing of "The Star-Spangled Banner."[56]

Made of Indiana limestone, the monument is twenty feet in height and rests on a twelve-and-one-half-foot-square concrete foundation (see figure 107). The monument is topped with a funerary urn decorated with ornamental bas-relief depicting the Seal of the State of New York at its front on a background of entwined olive leaves that encircle the entire urn. The names of the 117 men of the two regiments who perished while on duty in Key West are engraved on the front, or north, face of the monument pedestal. Engraved above the names is "THE STATE OF NEW YORK IN MEMORY OF THE MEN OF THE NINETIETH AND NINETY-FIRST NY VOL REGS OF INFANTRY WHO PERISHED HERE MAINLY OF YELLOW FEVER IN 1862." The top of the pedestal has a band of bas-relief decoration, while the pedestal base has a different decorative band. On the east side of the pedestal base is engraved the name of the monument's designer, "Edward Pearce Casey Architect."

Figure 107. 1930 monument to yellow fever victims of the Ninetieth and Ninety-First New York Infantry in Key West. Monroe County Public Florida History Department Images.

The remains of the soldiers honored by this monument had been moved to the Barrancas National Cemetery at Pensacola after the U.S. military closed the Key West Post Cemetery in 1927. Regardless, the State of New York decided to place the monument in the place where their 117 soldiers suffered and died and where they were initially buried, so far from their homes.[57]

Union Dead, Magnolia Springs Cemetery, Green Cove Springs, pre-1939

In 1864, Union forces established a garrison at the community of Magnolia on the west bank of the St. Johns River in Clay County near the present-day community of Green Cove Springs. From this strongpoint, Union raiding parties ranged into the surrounding countryside. One of these raids was on nearby Middleburg in October 1864 and involved a substantial skirmish that resulted in some forty Union dead, wounded, or captured. Casualties from this skirmish and other Union soldier dead who were stationed at the garrison were buried in the Magnolia Springs Cemetery.[58]

At an unspecified date following the Civil War, a stone obelisk shaft monument was erected in the cemetery. This monument, which stood about three feet in height, was inscribed with "MEMORIAL TO UNION SOLDIERS OF 1864." The monument was reported as being present in the "abandoned cemetery" in 1939, and a 1958 photograph shows it was still standing at that time, but in 1973 it was reported as being "th[r]own down in a pile." It disappeared completely sometime after 1973 along with the headstones that once marked individual graves.[59]

In 2011 a dedication ceremony was held for a larger representation of the original monument erected by the Clay County Historical Commission at the cemetery (see chapter 5). The new seven-foot granite obelisk monument is dedicated to both Union and Confederate soldiers.

Sarasota, Judah P. Benjamin Escape Monument, 1942

After hiding out in several locations in Florida, including the Gamble Mansion at Ellenton, Confederate secretary of state Judah P. Benjamin left the state by boat at Sarasota Bay in June 1865 and escaped to the Bahamas and eventually England. On January 22, 1942, a monument was dedicated in Sarasota near the location where Benjamin is believed to have made his escape. Sponsored by the John A. Fite Chapter of the Florida Division of the UDC, the monument was designed by Asa L. Wooten of the U.S. Marble and Granite Company of Oneco, Florida. The dedication took place shortly after the American entry into World War II, which gave it added significance. Newspaper editorials and dedication ceremony speeches noted that Benjamin was Jewish and that this monument represented "the south's personal challenge to Nazism and hate."[60]

Dedication ceremony activities began with a luncheon at the John Ringling Hotel (razed in 1998), which was followed by a parade down Main Street

Figure 108. Governor and Mrs. Spessard Holland at the unveiling of the Judah P. Benjamin monument in Sarasota on January 22, 1942. Sarasota County Department of Historical Resources, Sarasota History Center.

to the municipal auditorium for a program of patriotic music, prayers, and speeches. Parade participants included the American Legion, the Sarasota High School Band, and nearly one thousand George Washington Juniors, a patriotic organization of schoolchildren. Program speakers included UDC officers, local dignitaries, Sarasota mayor E. A. Smith, Florida congressman J. Hardin Peterson, and Florida governor Spessard Holland. In his remarks, Governor Holland referred to Benjamin as "a great American" who was "not a member of the dominant faith of our nation, but a Jew . . . of whom both the north and south can be proud." In a similar vein, Mayor Smith remarked that "it doesn't make any difference if you are a good Jew, Catholic, Protestant, Unionist or Confederate as long as you are a great American."[61]

The sentiments expressed at the dedication were of sectional reconciliation fueled by a national crisis in the form of World War II. The Spanish-American War and World War I had inspired similar reconciliation; in fact, the UDC believed that World War I had served as the final vindication of the South. There is ample evidence, however, that World War II was equally important in uniting the country against a common enemy and healing the deep wounds of the Civil War. It was not, for example, until after World War II, when national hero General Dwight D. Eisenhower visited the city in 1947, that Vicksburg citizens celebrated Independence Day for the first time since it was surrendered on July 4, 1863.

Following the program at the municipal auditorium, the "large audience which filled the auditorium" marched to the monument site, led by the Sarasota High School band. There they observed the unveiling of the monument by Governor and Mrs. Holland and the laying of a wreath by a representative of the Jewish War Veterans of the United States (see figure 108). Margaret Mitchell, author of *Gone with the Wind*, had been invited to the ceremony, but she could not attend and sent a congratulatory message. Other congratulatory messages were sent by British prime minister Winston Churchill and movie star Mary Pickford.[62]

The five-foot-high monument consists of a pink Georgia marble block on a one-stepped foundation topped by a bronze sundial. The bird-figurine gnomon (the part on the sundial that casts the shadow) is no longer present (see figure 109). Engraved on the front of the monument are two crossed flags

Figure 109. 1942 Judah P. Benjamin monument as it appeared in 2011. Photograph by William B. Lees.

below which is engraved "NEAR THIS SPOT ON JUNE 23, 1865 JUDAH P. BENJAMIN SECRETARY OF STATE FOR THE CONFEDERACY SET SAIL FOR A FOREIGN LAND." The interior of the flag on the left currently shows no engraving or other clue as to what it was to represent. The Florida State Seal is engraved in the center of the flag on the right. A newspaper photograph printed a few days prior to the dedication shows the flag on the left to be the Confederate battle flag and that on the right to be the Florida State Flag as adopted in 1900, when diagonal red bars on the white background were added.[63] The details on these flags may have originally been stained or painted, as no evidence of any engraving other than the outlines of the flags and the state seal are visible.

Two pink granite benches are located in front and to either side of the monument. One is engraved with "U. S. MARBLE & GRANITE CO.[,] ONECO, FLORIDA" and the other with "DESIGNED BY ASA L. WOOTEN." A historical marker erected by the Sarasota County Historical Commission in 1999 is located adjacent to the monument and provides information on Benjamin's escape.

In 1955 a second dedication ceremony was held at the monument for an "eternal light" project in the form of two spotlights that would flood the monument in red and white light (official colors of the Confederacy as adopted by the UDC). The lights are apparently no longer in service. In 1957, Mary Brownell, a Sarasota UDC member who had spearheaded the original monument, proposed a second monument to Benjamin in the form of a buoy to be placed in Sarasota Bay. She claimed to have the support of the Sarasota city manager and some county commissioners, but the buoy monument was apparently not constructed.[64]

Yellow Bluff Fort, 1951

Construction of a Confederate earthwork fortification at Yellow Bluff on the north side of the St. Johns River near Jacksonville began in the summer of 1862. In October 1862 the Confederates evacuated Yellow Bluff Fort as a large Union expedition approached. Over the remainder of the war, as Union troops occupied and then evacuated Jacksonville on four occasions, the fort changed hands several times. During the last Union occupation of Jacksonville, beginning in February 1864 and lasting until the end of the war, Yellow Bluff Fort was the site of a Union signal tower and was garrisoned by various regiments of U.S. Colored Troops.[65]

In 1950 the North Shore Corporation donated a little more than an acre of

Figure 110. 1951 Confederate monument at the Yellow Bluff Fort State Historic Site in 2008. Photograph by William B. Lees.

the fort site to the State of Florida for use as the Yellow Bluff Fort Historic State Park. After state acquisition of the property, six Florida chapters of the UDC purchased a monument for the site "at the cost of $442.90." The monument was dedicated on March 4, 1951, the park's official opening day. The dedication ceremony consisted of prayers, music from the Jacksonville Bolles Military School Band and Children of the Confederacy chapters, and speeches by representatives of the UDC and the Florida Board of Parks and Historic Memorials. The UDC also arranged for the donation and installation of five "naval brass cannons" that had been recovered during a dredging operation in the St. Johns River. The cannons were installed in 1953. Only two cannons remain on-site, and these are both iron and in extremely corroded conditions. In 1955 a half-acre plot previously owned by Duval County was added to the park.[66]

Made of granite and standing about five feet in height, the monument consists of an upright shaft on a two-stepped base, topped with a large iron cannonball (see figure 110). Attached to the front, or north, face of the shaft is a copper-colored metal plate with a raised-letter inscription, "DEDICATED TO THE MEMORY OF THE CONFEDERATE SOLDIERS WHO DEFENDED JACKSONVILLE, 1861–1865 YELLOW BLUFF FORT A CONFEDERATE EARTHWORKS DESIGNED AND LOCATED BY GENERAL ROBERT E. LEE AS ONE OF A SERIES OF FORTS FOR THE DEFENSE OF THE SAINT JOHNS RIVER. THIS FORT WAS OCCUPIED BY BOTH CONFEDERATE AND UNION FORCES DURING THE COURSE OF THE WAR AND IS TODAY IN ITS ORIGINAL STATE. ERECTED BY THE UNITED DAUGHTERS OF THE CONFEDERACY." The plaque then lists the names of the six Florida UDC chapters who erected the monument and "SITE DONATED BY THE NORTH SHORE CORPORATION 1950."[67]

Due to its isolated location, the Yellow Bluff Fort monument and park have been subjected to vandalism over the years. The monument has been knocked over at least once, and the metal plaque on it contains several bullet holes.[68]

* * *

The monuments associated with places of conflict within the state of Florida are diverse in terms of design and message. Collectively, but without grand design, these monuments reveal the places and the events that the generations who lived between the Civil War and its centennial believed to be worthy of memorialization. In a former Confederate state where most battles of note were victories for the South, it is not at all surprising that only three monuments dedicated solely to the Union were erected to commemorate hallowed ground.

Despite an influx of Union veterans into the state in the postwar period, at least two of these Union monuments dedicated to hallowed ground were not, in fact, the work of a Union veteran or descent group.[69] One of these, the 1866 monument marking a common grave of Union soldier dead at Olustee, was erected by the U.S. Army and is no longer extant. The other is a regimental monument to the Ninetieth and Ninety-First New York Regiments that the State of New York erected in Key West. We were unable to identify the sponsor of the missing monument to the Union dead at Magnolia Springs Cemetery. Equally noteworthy is that an attempt to commemorate the participation and sacrifice of Union soldiers at Olustee by the Florida Legislature in 1899 was quickly abandoned. Although there is certainly no lack of places that were worthy of commemoration—such as Fort Pickens for never surrendering, the Union victory at Marianna, or the honor-worthy performance of U.S. Colored Troops at Olustee and Natural Bridge—in Florida, this was not to be.

The short-lived wooden Union monument at Olustee was erected in 1866 by a reburial detail to mark the mass grave of Union dead. If not for the messages carved in the base of this monument, this might be construed as a grave marker, albeit a large one, rather than a Civil War monument. Those who constructed it, however, sought to convey a message that went beyond simply marking the grave of fallen comrades. The same could be said for the Magnolia Springs Cemetery Union monument. The other Union monument, erected by the State of New York in Key West, is one of the few regimental monuments in Florida, the only one erected prior to the Civil War Centennial, and the only one sponsored by a state. Although regimental monuments are rare in Florida, they are common elsewhere, such as at Gettysburg, Chickamauga, Shiloh, and Vicksburg. But rather than being just another regimental monument, New York's "Yellow Fever" monument is exceptional in that it commemorates soldiers who died in garrison of disease and extols that their loss was equal to those on the battlefield. In fact, most Civil War soldiers died in the manner of those in Key West, of disease and not battlefield wound, and it is striking, though maybe not surprising, that monuments to them are not more plentiful on the landscape.

Monuments commemorating Confederate hallowed ground in Florida are more plentiful and exist, by and large, through the efforts of the UDC. Except for the Colquitt monument at Olustee, which was sponsored by a UDC chapter from Georgia, all of the other UDC monuments were sponsored by Florida chapters. The Florida Legislature funded the Lake City Olustee monument entirely and provided the bulk of funding for the monuments on the Olustee, Marianna, and Natural Bridge Battlefields. The original Natural Bridge monuments, erected in 1919 and no longer extant, were sponsored by a private individual. The UDC was clearly a force in Florida, and the state would probably not have benefited from the commemoration and preservation of significant places such as Olustee, Natural Bridge, and Gamble Plantation without their efforts. There is also no question but that preservation was a happy by-product of their main goal, which was to make certain a correct and "usable" history of the Civil War was told.

The Confederate monuments focus on what to this day are seen as the most important Civil War battles in the state: Olustee, Natural Bridge, and Marianna. To what degree these monuments have influenced this perception of importance is not addressed here, but it is certainly a matter of useful speculation. The Battle of Olustee has received the most substantial commemoration through monument building. This is easily justified from a historical perspective, as the defeat of the Union force at Olustee was a significant blow militarily and politically if for no other reason than its relation to the U.S. presidential election of 1864.

The 1866 Union monument aside, Olustee Battlefield itself has had three Confederate monuments and one memorial fence erected; there is a monument to the battle and Confederate dead in downtown Lake City; and there is a monument to the Confederate dead in Lake City's Oaklawn Cemetery. These monuments are certainly fitting given the loss of life at Olustee, but the story behind the 1912 monument on the battlefield is the most telling of the sentiment in Florida and in the South as a whole at the end of the nineteenth century, wherein lies the genesis of the monument. The controversy over whether to also honor the Union soldiers on this monument could be interpreted on the one hand as an expected position by the UDC in response to decades of work by the GAR to prevent or minimize use of federal funds to care for Confederate dead, to commemorate Confederate sacrifice or valor, or to care for Confederate veterans. But the record is clear that even if this was a factor, it was issues of race that were in the forefront and that to recognize or honor the Union at Olustee would be to recognize or honor several regiments of U.S. Colored Troops. This narrative is important to understand, but it is one that you do not see simply by reading the words engraved on this monument. In fact, despite the valor of the African American troops at Olustee, the only monument in the state to recognize U.S. Colored Troops was constructed only recently in Fort Myers (see chapter 5).

The other two battles that are commemorated were relatively small affairs in the larger scheme of things and had little consequence on the outcome of the Civil War even in Florida. Although Marianna was a Confederate loss and Natural Bridge a victory, they are similar in a way that may have been the inspiration of their popularity with the UDC. At Marianna, a superior and victorious Union force from Pensacola was, as the 1921 monument says, "stubbornly resisted by a home guard of old men and boys and a few sick and wounded Confederates at home on furlough." At Natural Bridge, a strong

Union force was defeated by, as the monument declares, "those brave men and boys who, in the hour of sudden danger, rushed from home, desk and field and from the West Florida Seminary and joining a few disciplined troops by their united valor and patriotism saved their capital from the invaders." Given the late date of this battle, few would argue that the outcome changed much of anything. What is clear, however, is that both events were used as a means to vindicate the men of the South by showcasing contests pitting southern men, including civilians young and old, against overwhelming odds from superior numbers of well-trained and well-equipped Union soldiers.

Equally remarkable is the purchase for preservation of the Gamble Plantation house by the UDC in 1925. The story here, however, is not the preservation of the plantation house but rather the Daughters' attempt to transform it into a Confederate memorial honoring an association with the fugitive Confederate secretary of state, Judah P. Benjamin. During the time the Daughters operated the plantation house, the site's narrative was one of upper-class antebellum life and the honor of the Confederacy as represented by Secretary Benjamin. Gamble Plantation became the focal point of Confederate commemoration and ceremony in southern Florida prior to the Civil War Centennial, and although the Florida Park Service has broadened the narrative, it remains the Judah P. Benjamin Confederate Memorial at Gamble Plantation Historic State Park.

Related, of course, is the monument in Sarasota erected by the Daughters in 1942 to mark the spot where Benjamin made his way shipboard for his successful escape from the United States. This monument is important not so much for the engraved words it carries as for the story of its dedication during the early months of World War II. The dedication focused on reconciliation of North and South and condemnation of Nazi Germany through the honoring of an American Jew who was a member of Jefferson Davis's cabinet and was, ironically, fleeing the country to escape imprisonment for treason.

The monument that the UDC erected at Yellow Bluff Fort after World War II is important for its reconciliatory tone. Although it honors the Confederate defenders of Jacksonville, it also acknowledges that both Confederate and Union soldiers served at this fortification. After World War II the country had come a long way in healing the wounds of the Civil War; shortly before erection of the monument at Yellow Bluff Fort, Vicksburg had even begun celebrating U.S. Independence Day again.

Florida raised some fifteen thousand troops for the Confederacy out of a total white population of approximately seventy-eight thousand.[70] Very early in the war, needs in the eastern and western theaters resulted in most of these troops being reassigned outside the state. One result was an increasing occupation and control of Florida's coast by Union troops and by the South Atlantic, East Gulf, and West Gulf Blockading Squadrons. Another was the participation of Florida troops in significant military campaigns in the western and eastern theaters, including many battles that are seen as pivotal to the outcome of the Civil War itself.

The primary assignments of Florida troops outside the state were in the western theater with the Army of Tennessee and in the eastern theater with General Robert E. Lee's Army of Northern Virginia. With the Army of Northern Virginia, Florida regiments served in the 1862 Peninsula Campaign, where the Second Florida Infantry saw its first action at Williamsburg, Virginia. Joined by the Fifth and Eighth Florida Infantry after the Peninsula Campaign, the Florida Brigade saw significant action in most of the major battles in which the Army of Northern Virginia was engaged. They suffered significant losses in the September 1862 Battle of Antietam, or Sharpsburg as it was called in the South, and in the July 1863 Battle of Gettysburg. In 1864 they were joined by the Ninth, Tenth, and Eleventh Florida Infantry and fought bravely at the June 1864 Battle of Cold Harbor, Virginia. For the remainder of 1864 and early 1865 they suffered in the siege lines around Petersburg, Virginia. What remained of the Florida Brigade was surrendered by General Lee at Appomattox Court House, Virginia, on April 9, 1865.[71]

In the west, the Army of Tennessee fought throughout Kentucky, Tennessee, Mississippi, Alabama, and Georgia before ending the war in North Carolina in 1865. The Floridians were heavily engaged at places such as Shiloh, Tennessee, in April 1862; Perryville, Kentucky, in October 1862; Stones River, Tennessee, in December 1862 and January 1863; in the defense of Jackson, Mississippi, in July 1863; and at Chickamauga, Georgia, in September 1863. After their various units were merged into a single Florida Brigade, they participated in the Battles of Missionary Ridge, Tennessee, in November 1863; the Atlanta Campaign in 1864; Franklin and Nashville, Tennessee, in November and December 1864; and Bentonville, North Carolina, in March 1865. The Florida Brigade of the Army of Tennessee was surrendered on April 26, 1865, by General Joseph E. Johnston at Bennitt Farm, North Carolina.[72]

As a result of the service of Florida troops in other states, commemorative monuments have been placed on several battlefields and their associated cemeteries. In the western theater are monuments at the Chickamauga and Vicksburg battlefields and at the McGavock Confederate Cemetery, where Florida casualties of fighting at the Battle of Franklin, Tennessee, are buried. A recent monument to Florida dead is located in the Confederate cemetery at Tullahoma, Tennessee (see chapter 5). In the eastern theater are a monument at the Gettysburg Battlefield and a monument at the Stonewall Confederate Cemetery in Winchester, Virginia, where Florida casualties of the Battle of Antietam are laid to rest. Florida shafts are also located in the Groveton Cemetery at the Manassas Battlefield, Virginia, and in the Blandford Cemetery at Petersburg, Virginia, where Florida dead from the siege of Petersburg are interred.

McGavock Confederate Cemetery, Franklin, Tennessee, 1890

At the Battle of Franklin, Tennessee, on November 30, 1864, the Florida Brigade of some 700 men, temporarily commanded by Colonel Robert Bullock, participated in the Army of Tennessee's bloody and unsuccessful assaults against strongly fortified Union positions. The Florida Brigade participated in the general frontal assault against General John Schofield's well-entrenched Federals as dusk fell across the landscape. After advancing into heavy fire from the protected Union soldiers, the Floridians were forced to lie down on the battlefield and did not withdraw until around 11 P.M. The Florida Brigade suffered significant losses (between 50 and 100 men), and the Confederate army in total had nearly 7,500 casualties, including some 1,750 who perished. In the early morning of December 1, Schofield moved his army to Nashville, leaving the battlefield to the Confederacy but taking with him a decisive victory.[73]

In 1866 the McGavock family donated two acres of their property near Franklin to be used as a permanent burial ground for Confederate casualties from the battle. The remains of nearly 1,500 Confederate soldiers were exhumed from the battlefield area and reburied in sections organized by state. Each grave was marked with a cedar headboard bearing the name and unit of the soldier, when known. However, after a number of years the wooden headboards suffered deterioration and needed to be replaced.[74]

In 1890 the John L. McEwen Bivouac of the Tennessee Division of the Association of Confederate Soldiers undertook the task of replacing the wooden headboards with limestone headstones. They also erected a monu-

Figure 111. 1890 Florida monument in the McGavock Confederate Cemetery in Franklin, Tennessee, in 2013. Photograph by Emily C. Lees.

ment for each state engraved with the number of soldiers from that state buried there. Formed in 1887, the Association of Confederate Soldiers became affiliated with the UCV after the latter organization's formation in 1889.[75]

The Florida monument, made of limestone, is approximately five feet tall and consists of a shaft and base on a one-stepped foundation (see figure 111). On the face of the shaft is a bas-relief intertwined "CSA" with "4 KILLED AT FRANKLIN" engraved below it. On the base is "FLORIDA" in large raised letters. As indicated on the monument, the gravesites of four Confederate soldiers with markers are located in the Florida section. Other Florida soldiers who died at Franklin are buried in this cemetery in unmarked graves or still remain on the battlefield.

In 1911 the cemetery property was deeded to a newly chartered corporation, the McGavock Confederate Cemetery, whose trustees were Confederate veterans. Beginning in 1926, members of the Franklin Chapter of the UDC were authorized to serve as trustees. As the veterans passed away, the UDC took over care and maintenance of the cemetery, a responsibility they continue to the present day. The McGavock Confederate Cemetery is believed to be the largest privately held Confederate cemetery in the United States.[76]

Stonewall Confederate Cemetery, Winchester, Virginia, 1902

Three Florida Infantry regiments were initially sent to serve with the Army of Northern Virginia. Formed in the spring of 1861, the Second Regiment of Florida Infantry, after spending some time in the defense of Yorktown, Virginia, saw its first action at the Battle of Williamsburg during the 1862 Peninsula Campaign. In August, after the Union army had retreated from Virginia, the Second was joined by the Fifth Regiment of Florida Infantry, formed in the spring of 1862, and the Eighth Regiment of Florida Infantry, formed in the summer of 1862. In the reorganization of the Army of Northern Virginia these regiments were brigaded together within Major General James Longstreet's First Corps.[77]

The Florida regiments were present at the August 1862 Battle of Second Manassas but were held in reserve and saw limited action. They were heavily engaged during Lee's invasion of Maryland at the Battle of Antietam (Sharpsburg) in September 1862, where all three took heavy losses in the fighting at Sunken Road or Bloody Lane. After Antietam, Lee retreated back into Virginia, and the Confederate First Corps, including the Florida Brigade, went into camp at Culpepper and the Second Corps went into camp at Winchester. While in camp at Culpepper the Florida regiments were organized as the Florida Brigade; they would go on to claim distinction at places such as the July 1863 Battle of Gettysburg, where they suffered heavy losses. Winchester, Virginia, was closer to Antietam than Culpepper, and although the Florida Brigade went to Culpepper, apparently many of the wounded of the Second, Fifth, and Eighth Florida Regiments were transported to hospitals in Winchester or its vicinity.[78]

On October 25, 1866, the five-and-one-half-acre Stonewall Confederate Cemetery, now part of the Mount Hebron Cemetery in Winchester, Virginia, was dedicated by the Ladies' Stonewall Memorial Association. The association raised $14,000 to purchase the cemetery land and to have the remains of Confederate soldiers from surrounding battlefields and private cemeteries exhumed and reburied there. This cemetery contains the graves of 2,575 soldiers who died on battlefields in this vicinity, including at the Battles of Winchester, Cool Spring, Kernstown, and Cedar Creek, and in local hospitals.[79]

At the center of the Stonewall Confederate Cemetery is a forty-nine-foot-high monument dedicated to the unknown dead from the aforementioned battles who are buried in four plots around the monument. Topped with an Italian marble statue of a Confederate soldier, this monument was dedicated in 1879 and probably marks some unknown dead from Florida. It was manufactured by the Thomas Delahunty Marble and Granite Works of Philadelphia, which later produced the 1881 Confederate monument in Tallahassee (see chapter 2). Around the monument are plots for soldier dead from the individual states of Alabama, Arkansas, Florida, Georgia, Kentucky, Louisiana, Maryland, Mississippi, North Carolina, South Carolina, Tennessee, Texas, and Virginia. Originally, each state section was marked with "a wooden shaft, appropriately inscribed to the fallen heroes of that particular State." In 1879 the Ladies' Stonewall Memorial Association dedicated a marble obelisk monument to the Virginia dead and encouraged the other states to also erect monuments of granite or marble to replace the wooden shafts. Many states did, including Florida.[80]

On June 6, 1902, observed as Confederate Memorial Day in the lower Shenandoah Valley, a joint dedication ceremony was held for the Florida and Tennessee monuments, which were unveiled simultaneously. The Florida Division of the UDC sponsored the Florida monument, which was designed and constructed by T. J. Orndorff of Winchester at a cost of $500 (see figure 112). Half of the cost was paid by Charles B. Rouss, a Confederate veteran from Winchester who moved to New York City after the war and became a wealthy businessman. Rouss also contributed to several other Confederate monuments at the cemetery.[81]

A crowd of twelve thousand people, "the largest throng ever seen on the streets of Winchester," attended the joint dedication ceremony. The ceremony was preceded by a parade of Confederate veterans, UDC and SCV members, bands, firemen, and schoolchildren. The featured speakers were Confederate veterans Major Albert Akers, from Tennessee, and Major Samuel J. C. Moore, from Virginia.[82]

Figure 112. 1902 monument in the Florida section of the Stonewall Confederate Cemetery in Winchester, Virginia, in 2011. Photograph by William B. Lees.

Approximately fifteen feet in height, the Florida monument consists of a granite obelisk and pedestal on a one-stepped foundation that sits on a slight mound of earth. On the front, or west, face of the obelisk is a bas-relief intertwined "CSA," and the pedestal is engraved with "1861–1865." On the base of the pedestal is "FLORIDA" in large raised letters. The north pedestal face is engraved with "FLORIDA'S DAUGHTERS TO HER BRAVE SONS," and the south pedestal face is engraved with "THEIR NAMES SHALL NE'ER FORGOTTEN BE WHILE HONOR CALLS THE ROLL." Behind the monument are the graves of thirty-eight Florida Confederate soldiers marked with headstones.

Given the history of this cemetery, one's first impression would be that the Florida soldiers buried here were engaged in the many significant battles fought in the Winchester vicinity commemorated on the central monument honoring the unknown dead. Although the thirty-eight headstones surrounding the Florida monument are much eroded with time, each is marked with a name (in one case only with initials), and most are marked with company and regimental affiliation and date of death. The reliably discernible regiments represented in the Florida section include one member of the Second, five of the Eighth, and twenty-two of the Fifth. Dates of death are from September through December 1862. The fact that the names, company and regiment, and dates of death of these individuals are marked on the headstones suggests they died in hospital, and the dates of death fall after the Battle of Antietam. Because the Second, Fifth, and Eighth Regiments retreated to Culpeper following Antietam, these death dates indicate that these were wounded from the fighting at Sunken Road at Antietam who were transported to hospitals in Winchester or the vicinity and who subsequently died.

Groveton Cemetery, Manassas Battlefield, Virginia, 1904

Groveton Cemetery in the Manassas National Battlefield Park contains the remains of some five hundred Confederate dead who fell mostly in the Battle of Second Manassas (also known as Second Bull Run) in August 1862, but it may also contain some casualties from the Battle of First Manassas (First Bull Run) in July 1861. The vast majority are unknown, with only two identified by grave markers. Florida troops did not participate in First Manassas as they had just arrived in Virginia on the day of the battle. Present at Second Manassas but held in reserve, the Second, Fifth, and Eighth Florida Infantry Regiments did receive casualties, some mortal, from artillery fire on their position. Some of these casualties may be among the many unknown Confederate soldiers buried in Groveton Cemetery.[83]

As with the Stonewall Confederate Cemetery in Winchester and others throughout the South, the Groveton Confederate Cemetery was established by local women. Formed in 1867, the Groveton and Bull Run Memorial Association secured the land, oversaw the reinterment of the remains from the surrounding countryside, and maintained the cemetery until they were no longer capable of that responsibility and it was taken over by the Bull Run Chapter of the Virginia Division of the UDC around the turn of the century. On August 30, 1904, this chapter dedicated a sixteen-foot-tall granite-and-marble obelisk monument to the Confederate dead at the cemetery.[84]

Fourteen evenly spaced white marble shafts surround and face the main monument, each engraved with the name of one of the Confederate states (eleven seceded and three border states) (see figure 113). As with the other state shafts, Florida's measures approximately one foot across and one foot

Figure 113. 1904 Confederate monument surrounded by state shafts at the Groveton Confederate Cemetery on the Manassas Battlefield in Virginia; the 1904 Florida shaft is on the circle left of the entrance walkway. Photograph by William B. Lees, 2013.

high and is bevel-cut toward the main monument so that the back is slightly higher than the front. Its beveled front face is inscribed with "FLORIDA." These state shafts were erected in 1904 at the same time as the main monument.[85]

Chickamauga Battlefield, Georgia, 1913

Perhaps the most impressive out-of-state monument to Florida troops in the Civil War is located at the Chickamauga and Chattanooga National Military Park. It honors the participation of Florida units in the September 19–20, 1863, Battle of Chickamauga in northwest Georgia. This was one of the bloodiest battles of the Civil War, with nearly thirty-five thousand Union and Confederate casualties, and was a major Confederate victory.

The Battle of Chickamauga was the result of a struggle between the armies of Union major general William S. Rosecrans and Confederate general Braxton Bragg that began in middle Tennessee. Bragg had retreated to and fortified Chattanooga, which was a critical city for the Confederacy. When Rosecrans moved his army to the south of Chattanooga, Bragg also moved south and on September 18 posted his troops on the west bank of the Chickamauga Creek. The next day the two armies clashed with no clear advantage, but on the afternoon of September 20 the Confederates were able to rout the Federals, who withdrew to and occupied the defenses of Chattanooga that night. Despite the loss of Chattanooga, the Battle of Chickamauga was a substantial Confederate victory. It was followed in November, however, by the defeat of Bragg's army at the Battle of Chattanooga.[86]

Seven Florida units participated, suffering over 550 casualties. These units were the First and Third Florida Infantry (consolidated) and the Fourth Florida Infantry in Stovall's Brigade of Breckinridge's Division; the Sixth and Seventh Florida Infantry and the First Florida Cavalry (dismounted) in Trigg's Brigade of Preston's Division; and the Marion Artillery in Williams's Artillery Battalion. The Florida units in Trigg's Brigade saw significant action in the southern part of the battlefield on September 19. At midday Preston's Division advanced toward General Jefferson C. Davis's Federals. Trigg's Brigade advanced toward the Viniard House as part of this attack. The Sixth Florida became separated from the brigade when other units moved to the right to support General Jerome Robertson's Texas Brigade and, coming under Union artillery fire, took heavy casualties. Floridians in Stovall's Brigade were lightly engaged that day.[87]

On the morning of September 20, Stovall's Brigade was part of Breckinridge's morning attack on the Union line along LaFayette Road. After easily pushing the Federals, Stovall's Brigade turned to attack the Union flank. Although they encountered stiff resistance from entrenched Federals and eventually had to withdraw with heavy losses, the action by Stovall's Brigade contributed materially to Confederate success that day. Although fighting for Stovall's Brigade was over by midday, fighting continued and Trigg's Brigade was pressed into action at Horseshoe Ridge, which lasted until sundown. As one of the last actions of the battle, the Sixth Florida pressed the Union flank while the Seventh advanced toward their front.[88]

In 1907 the Florida Legislature appropriated $15,000 "for the erection of a suitable monument on the battlefield of Chickamauga in memory of the soldiers of Florida who took part in that battle." The legislation also established "a committee of five suitable persons" to be appointed by the governor "to carry out the purposes of this act." The Chickamauga Monument Commission, as it became known, directed the site selection, design, and construction of the monument. The five members appointed to the commission were all Confederate veterans—Evander M. Law of Bartow (Alabama Brigade), Fred L. Robertson of Tallahassee (Second South Carolina Infantry), Pulaski Broward of Jacksonville (Marion Light Artillery), Martin I. Coxe of Palatka (First

Figure 114. Florida officers at the 1913 Florida monument at the Chickamauga Battlefield, Georgia, 1930s photograph. Florida Photographic Collection, State Archives of Florida, image no. N029068.

Florida Cavalry), and Samuel Pasco of Monticello (Third Florida Infantry). Two of the members died before the monument was erected, Robertson in 1908 and Coxe in 1912. Newspaper and U.S. War Department reports in 1912 and 1913 also list another Confederate veteran, Francis C. Brent of Pensacola (Sixty-Second Alabama Infantry), as a commission member, although he is not listed in the state's biennial reports of boards and commissions.[89]

The release of state funds for the monument was delayed by the national financial crisis sparked by the Panic of 1907. Finally, in 1911, the Florida Legislature passed legislation "to make available" the $15,000 appropriation, which "has been delayed because of the condition of the State Treasury," and to release the funds "upon the requisition of the committee."[90]

In 1912 the McNeel Marble Company of Marietta, Georgia, was selected to design and install the monument. Sculptor Louis Milione was commissioned to create the bronze statue to be placed inside the monument's granite canopy structure. Construction was completed in 1913 at a cost of $13,500 (see figure 114). The dedication of the Florida monument, as well as that of the

Figure 115. 1913 Florida monument on the Chickamauga National Battlefield in Georgia in 2012. Photograph by William B. Lees.

Alabama monument an hour later, was held on May 28, 1913, in conjunction with the twenty-third national UCV reunion being held at nearby Chattanooga. Special trains from Chattanooga brought "throngs of visitors" to the dedication. Speakers included two of the Florida Monument Commission members who had fought at the Battle of Chickamauga, Evander Law and Samuel Pasco.[91]

The monument is eighteen feet square at the base, stands twenty-four feet in height, and is built of granite from Mount Airy, North Carolina. It is in the form of an open-air canopy, or "temple," design with a dome atop the canopy roof (see figure 115). The dome is topped with a sphere on an ornately decorated base or plinth. On each corner at the base of the dome is a decorated pediment. The canopy is supported by three Doric columns at each corner on a pedestal. The underside of the canopy roof is decorated with an ornate floral-design bronze medallion in its center. Granite steps on each side provide access to the interior, which contains a six-foot-tall bronze statue of a soldier on an approximately four-foot-high pedestal.

The soldier is standing at parade rest holding a musket with both hands placed around the barrel. The musket appears to be a Model 1842 Springfield, yet it is fitted with a Manyard tape primer found on the Model 1855 Springfield. The soldier is wearing a wide-brimmed hat and is equipped with a blanket roll across his torso, a canteen, a percussion cap box, a cartridge box, and a rectangular CSA belt plate. He is wearing brogans, and his socks are bloused over his pants. Inscribed on the right side of the base of the soldier sculpture is "L. Milione Sculptor." A renowned sculptor of the period, Louis Milione was born in Italy but later immigrated to Philadelphia.[92]

A bronze plaque mounted on a pediment at the base of the dome contains the Florida State Seal. Below this, on the front face of the canopy roof, is engraved "FLORIDA" in large letters with "1861" on one side of it and "1865" on the other. The front face of the statue's pedestal contains a bronze plaque declaring "THIS MONUMENT HAS BEEN ERECTED IN MEMORY OF THE SOLDIERS OF THE STATE OF FLORIDA WHO TOOK PART IN THE BATTLE FOUGHT HERE SEPTEMBER 19–20, 1863 WHETHER THEY FELL IN BATTLE OR LIVED TO RENDER FURTHER SERVICES TO THEIR STATE AND COUNTRY." On the back side of the pedestal is a bronze plaque with "FLORIDA TROOPS ENGAGED IN THE BATTLE OF CHICKAMAUGA SEPTEMBER 19–20, 1863" on top followed by a list of Florida units involved in the battle.

The Florida monument at Chickamauga is very similar in appearance to that of the later monument to the women of the Confederacy in Jacksonville's Confederate Park, which was dedicated in 1915 (discussed in detail in chapter 2). That monument was also designed by the McNeel Marble Company. This similarity was noted by at least one trade journal of the period.[93]

Blandford Cemetery, 1917–1919, and Blandford Church, 1912, Petersburg, Virginia

Used as a burial ground since the early 1700s, the Blandford Cemetery contains the largest mass Confederate gravesite in Virginia, with some thirty thousand Confederate troops, most of whom are unknown by name, buried in the cemetery. Many of these men died during the siege of Petersburg from June 1864 to April 1865, but others may have died in hospital after receiving wounds at places such as the Wilderness and Cold Harbor leading up to the siege.[94]

General Lee rushed troops to defend Petersburg after he realized that General Grant had silently withdrawn from the Cold Harbor battlefield in order to attack and capture that vital transportation and supply center, which was key to Richmond itself. Florida troops, heavily engaged at Cold Harbor, arrived in Petersburg on June 19 as part of Major General William Mahone's Division. Floridians in this division helped repulse Union attempts to destroy the Weldon railroad on June 21 and participated in the Confederate victory at the First Battle of Ream's Station on June 29, but afterward they settled into defensive positions in the trenches surrounding Petersburg. On August 20, Floridians under Mahone took part in the Battle of Globe Tavern, which was a Confederate defeat and in which some one hundred Florida soldiers were casualties. For the remainder of 1864 and the first part of 1865, Florida troops suffered as conditions in the besieged town deteriorated. In February 1865 they participated in the Battle of Hatcher's Run, which was yet another Confederate defeat despite excellent performance by Florida troops. On April 3, Florida troops withdrew as the Army of Northern Virginia evacuated Petersburg. Florida soldiers who died during or from wounds in these engagements at Petersburg or from sickness while in the defenses of this town are among those buried in Blandford Cemetery.[95]

The Ladies' Memorial Association of Petersburg, organized in 1866, was granted a section of the Blandford Cemetery, now known as Memorial Hill, by the City of Petersburg. The association coordinated the removal and reburying of the remains of Confederate soldiers from area battlefields, military hospitals, and other sites to the cemetery. Sections of varying size for each of the Confederate states were laid out and separated by curving paths and circular flowerbeds. In 1884 a Gothic-style iron arch was erected at the entrance to the Confederate section but was subsequently destroyed by a storm. It was replaced in 1914 by a large stone arch with an automobile passageway through its center and a pedestrian entryway on each side.

In 1890 the association erected a Confederate monument at the crest of Memorial Hill dedicated to the "UNKNOWN." The monument consists of a thirty-foot granite column topped with a six-foot statue of a Confederate soldier in white zinc manufactured by the Monumental Bronze Company of Bridgeport, Connecticut. The statue sits on a pediment engraved with "GLORIA VICTIS" ("Glory to the vanquished"), which can be interpreted as referring to a glorious or worthy life. On the base is the Virginia State Seal with the state motto, "SIC SEMPER TYRANNIS" ("Thus always to tyrants"), below which is engraved "Plant the fair column o'er the vacant grave[,] A hero's honors let a hero have." Among the inscriptions on the monument column are the names of thirteen Confederate states (eleven seceded and two border states), including Florida. In 1909 the association constructed a memorial gazebo

Figure 116. Florida shaft erected between 1917 and 1919 in the Confederate section of the Blandford Cemetery at Petersburg, Virginia, as it appeared in 2013. The 1890 central Confederate monument stands in the background. Photograph by William B. Lees.

near the monument. Its dedication on July 30 of that year was to the memory of Petersburg soldiers killed in battle.[96]

Between 1917 and 1919 the Burns and Campbell Granite and Marble Works of Petersburg installed individual Confederate state shafts made of rough-hewn granite in the Memorial Hill section of the cemetery. The two-and-one-half-foot-tall Florida shaft is located south of Arch Avenue near the center of the state's section (see figure 116). Approximately one foot wide, it is inscribed on its polished top surface with "FLORIDA 1861–65." Blandford Church records identify ten Florida soldiers by name; the others are unknown.[97]

Adjacent to the Blandford Cemetery is the Blandford Church, built in 1735 as an Anglican house of worship. The building was abandoned by 1803, after a new church was constructed in downtown Petersburg, and in 1819 it was donated to the city. The building was left largely unattended and suffered deterioration until 1901, when the Ladies' Memorial Association of Petersburg was delegated authority by the City of Petersburg to restore it as a mortuary chapel and Confederate memorial. As part of the restoration project, the association commissioned the renowned Tiffany Studios of New York City to produce fifteen stained-glass windows for the building. To pay for the windows, the association solicited contributions from individuals and associations in the former Confederate states to sponsor a state memorial window at a cost of $385. Between 1904 and 1912, windows were dedicated for thirteen Confederate states (eleven seceded and two border states), including Florida. Another window was dedicated to the Ladies' Memorial Association of Petersburg, and the Tiffany Studios donated an additional decorative window.[98]

The Florida window was dedicated on June 24, 1912. The featured speaker at the ceremony was State Attorney Emmett Wilson of Pensacola, the grandson of a Florida senator in the Confederate Congress, Augustus Emmett Maxwell. The large Florida window contains the state seal at its top, an image of St. Matthew in the center, and an inscription at the bottom that reads "FLORIDA DEDICATES THIS WINDOW TO THE GLORY OF GOD AND IN SACRED MEMORY OF HER CONFEDERATE DEAD[,] TO THEM WHICH SAT IN THE REGION AND SHADOW OF DEATH LIGHT IS SPRUNG UP." The last portion of the inscription is from Matthew 4:16.[99]

Vicksburg Battlefield, Mississippi, 1954

During the Union siege of Vicksburg, Mississippi, in 1863, the First, Third, and Fourth Florida Infantry Regiments served in General Joseph E. Johnston's Army of Relief during its unsuccessful attempt to break the siege. After gathering in Jackson, the Mississippi capital, Johnston advanced on Vicksburg only days before Lieutenant General John C. Pemberton surrendered his garrison and the city, and did not arrive near the town until July 5. Unaware that Vicksburg had surrendered the day before, Johnston determined that the Union rearguard, commanded by Major General William T. Sherman, was too strong to attack and on July 6 countermarched to Jackson. Sherman followed, and between July 10 and 16 the two armies fought for control

Figure 117. 1954 Florida monument erected on Florida Circle in Vicksburg as it appeared in 2012. Photograph by William B. Lees.

of the capital. On July 16, Johnston abandoned Jackson. Although engaged at Jackson, none of the Florida regiments saw action in front of Vicksburg.[100]

As early as 1923, efforts were initiated to raise funds for the erection of a monument to these Florida troops. It was not until 1954, however, that these efforts were successful, and on April 17 of that year the Florida monument located in Florida Circle on Confederate Avenue was dedicated in front of an audience of approximately one hundred people. Sponsored by the Florida Division of the UDC, the monument was designed and erected by Atlantic Memorials Inc. of Jacksonville at a cost of $5,000 (see figure 117). The dedication ceremony included prayer, music by Vicksburg's Carr Central High School band, and speeches from Vicksburg mayor Pat Kelly and representatives of the UDC, the SCV, the Mississippi Department of Archives and History, the Florida Board of Parks and Historic Memorials, and the Vicksburg Chamber of Commerce. The monument was presented to the Vicksburg National Military Park by Mrs. Murray Forbes Wittichen, president of the Florida Division of the UDC, and was accepted by Superintendent James R. McConagie. In his remarks, McConagie commended the UDC for their efforts to commemorate Florida at the park, adding, "When all States that had sons in this memorable action have thus memorialized them the park may be considered as nearing completion."[101]

The monument is a four-foot-high polished-surface monolith made of gray granite from Elberton, Georgia, on a half-foot-high one-stepped foundation. The polished surface portion is two and two-thirds feet wide along its front and back and one foot along its sides. The Florida State Seal is engraved on the front, or south, face of the stone, below which is "IN TRIBUTE TO THE 1ST AND 3RD FLORIDA INFANTRY REGIMENTS COMMANDED BY COL. W. S. DILWORTH AND THE 4TH INFANTRY REGIMENT COMMANDED BY LT. COL. E. D. BADGER, WHO PARTICIPATED IN MISSISSIPPI DURING THE WAR BETWEEN THE STATES AS A PART OF STOVALL'S BRIGADE, OF BRECKINRIDGE'S DIVISION OF GENERAL JOHNSTON'S ARMY IN 1863. ERECTED BY FLORIDA DIVISION UNITED DAUGHTERS OF THE CONFEDERACY 1954." The reverse, or north, side of the stone carries the inscription "WHETHER SLEEPING IN DISTANT PLACES, OR GRAVELESS, THIS MONUMENT HAS BEEN ERECTED TO THE MEMORY OF THE MEN WHO SERVED THE CONFEDERATE STATES OF AMERICA."

Florida's Vicksburg monument was erected on lands originally included within the Vicksburg National Military Park. The placement of the monument at the south end of the park related to the fact that Florida troops did not actually participate in the siege of Vicksburg. Superintendent McConaghie explained this to his regional director in a memorandum about the dedication: "The Florida Division of the United Daughters of the Confederacy instigated a movement to have a monument placed in the Vicksburg National Military Park as a memorial to the Florida troops who served with Johnson's [*sic*] Army. In the past other organizations have placed small memorials in the southern section of the park to their troops even though they may not have served at Vicksburg." Because this land was less heavily engaged than the northern sections in the siege, it was subsequently deeded to the City of Vicksburg in the late 1950s in a land exchange between the federal government and the city related to closing city streets through the main part of the park and the pending nearby construction of U.S. Interstate Highway 20.[102]

Gettysburg Battlefield, Pennsylvania, 1963, 1965

At the Battle of Gettysburg, the Florida Brigade, also known as Perry's Brigade in honor of its commander and comprising the Second, Fifth, and Eighth Florida Infantry Regiments under the command of Colonel David Lang, participated in the heaviest fighting of July 2 and 3, 1863. Lang had assumed command of the Florida Brigade when its commander, Brigadier General Edward Perry, was sidelined by illness. Remaining in reserve on the first day of the battle, the Florida Brigade was heavily involved on July 2 in a massed assault from Spangler's Wood to attack the exposed line of the Union Third Corps along Emmitsburg Road. The assault succeeded in pushing the Federals back toward Cemetery Ridge, but the lack of reinforcements caused the Floridians and others involved in this assault to fall back to their original position by nightfall. Although the Union Third Corps was devastated by this attack, the Florida Brigade also took significant losses.[103]

Day three of the battle saw the Floridians covering some of the same ground as the day before, in support of the ill-fated Pickett's Charge. The Florida Brigade was ordered forward after the first wave of the charge had been repulsed and, along with troops from Alabama, headed for Emmitsburg Road. After coming under heavy musket and artillery fire, the Floridians and Alabamians veered right. Alabama troops retired from the field, but the Florida Brigade sought refuge in woods along Plum Run, where they were routed and many captured by Union soldiers from Vermont. At the end of the day the tally of casualties for the Florida Brigade at Gettysburg had, by some accounts, surpassed by percentage that of any other Confederate brigade present at Gettysburg.[104]

In 1895 the Florida Legislature enacted legislation in response to a request from the Gettysburg National Military Park Commission to assist them in accurately locating "the positions and movements of . . . the Florida troops in order that they be marked by permanent memorial tablets." The legislation directed Governor Henry L. Mitchell "to appoint three commissioners who shall be ex-Confederate soldiers who took an active part in the battle of Gettysburg" and authorized an appropriation of $300 to cover their expenses. Two of the appointees, Walter R. Moore and William Duncan Ballantine, were officers in the Second Florida Infantry who had been wounded and captured at the battle. The third was Colonel David Lang, who had commanded

Figure 118. Members of the Florida commission at Devil's Den, Gettysburg Battlefield, in 1895. Florida Photographic Collection, State Archives of Florida, image no. PR15185.

Figure 119. One of the two Florida Brigade markers placed with the help of the Florida commission as it appeared on the 150th anniversary of that battle in 2013. Erected in 1908. Photograph by William B. Lees.

the Florida Brigade during the battle. In the summer of 1895 the three men returned to the Gettysburg Battlefield to assist the park commission with marker placements (see figure 118). In 1902 an iron marker with information on the Florida (Perry's) Brigade at the battle was erected on West Confederate Avenue by the Gettysburg National Military Park Commission. This marker was replaced with a larger bronze marker on a granite pedestal in 1910. The commission erected a second Florida (Perry's) Brigade iron marker on Emmitsburg Road in 1908 (see figure 119).[105]

However, it was not until 1963, on the one hundredth anniversary of the battle, that the State of Florida erected a monument to the participating Florida regiments on the Gettysburg Battlefield. In 1963 the Florida Legislature appropriated $20,000 for a Florida monument at Gettysburg and authorized Governor Farris Bryant to "appoint five (5) suitable persons . . . to do and perform all acts necessary to carry out the purposes of the act." Apparently the short period between passage of the legislation and approval by the governor in May 1963 and the proposed monument dedication date of July 1963 allowed for only three members to be appointed to what became known as the Gettysburg Memorial Commission. The commission consisted of chairman Adam G. Adams, Mrs. Wilson L. Baker, president of the Florida Division of the UDC, and Paul W. Danahy Jr.[106]

The work of the commission resulted in the erection of the Florida monument at Gettysburg that was dedicated on July 3, 1963, on the one hundredth anniversary of the Florida Brigade's assault to assist Pickett's Charge (see figure 120). The featured speaker was Florida U.S. congressman Sam M. Gibbons of Tampa. In his remarks, Gibbons addressed the civil rights struggle of the period by noting that "those that died here will have died in vain . . . if America becomes a land in which freedom, equality and opportunity are only for the white man."[107]

Constructed of "select southern granite," the monument was designed by J. B. Hill of Tate, Georgia, who was the principal designer for the Georgia Marble Company from 1927 to 1962, and was constructed and erected by the Bruns Monumental Company of Columbia, South Carolina. Hill and the Bruns Monumental Company also designed and constructed the South Carolina monument, which was dedicated at Gettysburg on July 2, 1963.[108]

The Florida monument consists of two upright tablets, the larger of which reaches a height of about fourteen feet (see figure 121). Attached to the south side of the larger tablet is a short shaft decorated with a band of laurel leaves at its top. The larger tablet is engraved with "FLORIDA" and the state seal on front and back. The smaller tablet is located north of, and slightly in front of, the larger one. It is engraved on the front with a row of three stars at its top, representing the three Florida regiments who fought at Gettysburg. Below this is engraved "FLORIDIANS OF PERRY'S BRIGADE" followed by a description of the action and losses of Florida troops at this epic battle. Below this in turn is engraved "LIKE ALL FLORIDIANS WHO PARTICIPATED IN THE CIVIL WAR, THEY FOUGHT WITH COURAGE AND DEVOTION FOR THE IDEALS IN WHICH THEY BELIEVED. BY THEIR NOBLE EXAMPLE OF BRAVERY AND ENDURANCE, THEY ENABLE US TO MEET WITH CONFIDENCE ANY SACRIFICE WHICH CONFRONTS US AS AMERICANS." The reverse of this smaller tablet is engraved with the names of the three members of Florida's Gettysburg Memorial Commission and Governor Farris Bryant. The entire monument is mounted on a three-stepped base that measures eleven and two-thirds feet by four and one-half feet.

Figure 120. Dedication of the Florida monument at the Gettysburg Battlefield in 1963. Courtesy of William B. Lees.

Figure 121. 1963 Florida monument on the Gettysburg Battlefield in 2012. Photograph by William B. Lees.

The smaller monument tablet states that of the 700 men in the Florida Brigade, 445 were killed, wounded, or captured (a loss of 65 percent). A 2005 study concluded that the Florida Brigade started with 739 men and suffered 343 casualties (46 percent).[109] A 2010 study determined that the Florida Brigade began the battle with 742 men and suffered 461 casualties (62 percent).[110] By any calculation, the Florida Brigade suffered among the highest percentage of casualties of any Confederate brigade at the Battle of Gettysburg.

In 1965 the monument was partially dismantled and resealed to prevent water intrusion. In 1988 the Tallahassee Historical Society raised $800 and sent the monument to the Gettysburg National Military Park where it was repointed and given a protective coating treatment to maintain it in good condition.[111]

In 1965 the Florida Legislature appropriated $3,000 to "participate with the other Southern states" in erecting a monument on the Gettysburg Battlefield to all Confederate armed forces. Dedicated on August 25, 1965, the approximately nineteen-foot-high monument to "THE SOLDIERS AND SAILORS OF THE CONFEDERACY" is topped with a bronze statue of a charging Confederate flag bearer looking back and urging his fellow troops to follow. The round column pedestal, made of pink granite, lists the names of each state that contributed men to the Confederacy, including Florida. The monument's architect was Henry Dacy, and the bronze statue was created by sculptor Donald DeLue, who also designed and sculpted the elaborate statues on the Louisiana (1971) and Mississippi (1973) monuments on the Gettysburg Battlefield.[112]

Arlington National Cemetery, Virginia, 1914 and others

In addition to the 1965 Gettysburg Battlefield monument, several other monuments of note list Florida on their inscriptions along with the other states of the Confederacy. Several of these monuments are located in Virginia cemeteries where Florida soldiers who died from battle or disease in the eastern theater are buried. These include the 1868 central tapered-block obelisk monument in the Lynchburg Old City Cemetery, the oldest Confederate cemetery monument in the state, where thirty-eight known Florida soldiers are buried, mostly from the Second, Fifth, and Eighth Florida Infantry Regiments. Others include the 1871 obelisk monument in Richmond's Oakwood Cemetery, where some sixteen thousand soldiers from thirteen Confederate states (eleven seceded and two border states) are buried; the 1884 monument in the Fredericksburg Confederate Cemetery, where at least seventeen Florida soldiers are buried; and the 1888 Thornrose Cemetery monument in Staunton, which states on the monument that eight Florida soldiers are buried there. The massive 1907 Jefferson Davis monument in Richmond contains bronze medallions across the arch on the colonnade behind the main central column with the state seals of the Confederate states, including Florida.[113]

On some Confederate cemetery monuments in Virginia, the names of the soldiers buried in the cemetery are listed on the monument. These include the 1893 University of Virginia Cemetery monument in Charlottesville, which lists the names of thirteen Florida soldiers from the Fifth and Eighth Florida Infantry Regiments on a monument plaque; the circa 1900 Emory and Henry Cemetery obelisk monument in Emory, which lists the name of one Florida soldier from the Seventh Florida Infantry on a monument plaque; the 1998

Memorial Wall surrounding the 1877 monument in the Warrenton Cemetery, on which is inscribed the names of five Florida soldiers from the Fifth and Eighth Florida Infantry; and the 1998 triptych monument (three large granite tablets) adjacent to the 1903 monument in Our Soldiers Cemetery in Mount Jackson, which lists the names of five Florida soldiers from the Fifth and Eighth Florida Infantry on its plaques.[114]

Another monument that contains information on the service of Florida troops along with those of other Confederate states is the Confederate Mound at Oak Woods Cemetery in Chicago. Dedicated in 1895, this thirty-foot granite monument topped with a bronze statue of a Confederate soldier was funded through the efforts of the UCV. It marks a mass grave containing the remains of some forty-three hundred Confederate prisoners of war who perished from disease and exposure at the nearby Union prison camp of Camp Douglas. In 1911 the monument was lifted up and placed on a base of granite. Bronze plaques were attached to the base containing the names of Confederate soldiers known to be buried in the mass grave. Among those listed are twenty-five Florida soldiers from the First, Second, Third, Fourth, Sixth, and Seventh Florida Infantry and First Florida Cavalry.[115]

A second monument dedicated to Confederate prisoners of war is located at Johnson's Island near Sandusky, Ohio. The island's Confederate Cemetery contains the remains of 267 Confederate soldiers, mostly officers, who died at the Johnson's Island prison camp. In 1910 the UDC dedicated a nineteen-foot-tall granite monument topped with a bronze statue of a Confederate soldier, titled *The Lookout*, at the cemetery. The monument was designed by Moses Ezekiel, who would later design the Confederate monument at Arlington National Cemetery in Virginia. In 2003, two granite tablet monuments were erected adjacent to the 1910 monument by the UDC and the SCV. These monuments list the names of the Confederate soldiers buried in the cemetery by state. On one of them, the names of six officers from the Second, Fourth, Fifth, and Eighth Florida Infantry are inscribed.[116]

Perhaps the most significant monument that lists Florida with the other southern states was erected through the efforts of the UDC in Arlington National Cemetery in Virginia. The cornerstone to this monument was dedicated in 1912, and the completed monument "TO OUR DEAD HEROES" was dedicated on June 4, 1914 (see figure 122). The genesis of this monument has been attributed to reconciliatory remarks made by President William McKinley in Atlanta in 1898 where he suggested the federal government should help care for Confederate graves. In 1900 Congress enacted legislation allowing Con-

Figure 122. Unveiling of the Confederate monument at Arlington National Cemetery in 1914. Library of Congress, Prints and Photographs Division, image no. LC-DIG-npcc-31774.

federate soldiers buried on northern battlefields, including the Washington, D.C. area, to be buried in Arlington. In 1906, Washington-area Confederate organizations, headed by the local chapter of the UDC, began planning for a monument to be placed in the new Confederate section of Arlington. This planning resulted in the creation of the Arlington Confederate Monument Association (ACMA), which gained permission from Secretary of War William Howard Taft to erect the monument.[117]

In 1910 the renowned sculptor Moses Ezekiel was retained by the ACMA and the UDC to design the monument with a theme of "peace for the living and honor to the dead." The monument was produced by the H. Gladenbeck and Son foundry in Berlin, Germany. It carries the names of each of the Confederate states, including Florida, and is rich in symbolism. Historian Karen L. Cox has put it this way: "Most Confederate monuments are considered symbols of the Lost Cause; the Confederate monument at Arlington is no less than a pro-southern textbook illustrated in bronze. . . . It was a monument of reconciliation, but a reconciliation based on terms that the white South found to be acceptable. As a token given to the nation, it acknowledged military defeat and nothing more."[118] Reflecting the personal importance he placed in this work and in his status as a Confederate veteran, Ezekiel, who died in 1917, is buried at the foot of the monument.[119]

The Arlington monument is at the center of Confederate Circle, which is surrounded by hundreds of headstones of Confederate soldiers. Three of these mark the graves of Florida soldiers from the Second, Eighth, and Eleventh Florida Infantry. These long-dead Florida soldiers bore mute witness to an elaborate dedication ceremony that brought together the UDC, the UCV, and other Confederate organizations with the federal government. That this was a momentous achievement on the part of the UDC and others and bore important national commentary was signified by, among other things, the roles of President William Howard Taft, who had approved the monument as secretary of war, in laying the cornerstone of the monument in 1912, and President Woodrow Wilson, who accepted the monument on behalf of the United States during the 1914 dedication ceremony.[120]

Florida troops fought in nearly all of the major battles of the Civil War in both the eastern and western theaters. Undoubtedly, other Confederate monuments in other states, although not listed here, also acknowledge the contributions made by Florida to the Confederacy during the Civil War.

* * *

Few monuments were erected solely to commemorate Florida soldiers who participated in the western and eastern theaters of war, in the Army of Tennessee and Army of Northern Virginia, respectively. Four of these commemorate soldier dead. The monument in the Stonewall Confederate Cemetery in Winchester, Virginia, commemorates Florida soldiers who apparently were wounded at Antietam and died in hospitals in Winchester or its vicinity. This monument was sponsored by the Florida UDC, but half of the cost was paid by a private individual with no Florida connection. Another is in the McGavock Confederate Cemetery in Franklin, Tennessee, and marks the remains of four Florida soldiers who died at the Battle of Franklin. Monuments were erected for all the states represented in this cemetery by the Association of Confederate Soldiers (later affiliated with the UCV) without any involvement from Florida associations or the state legislature. The Florida shafts in the Groveton Cemetery at the Manassas Battlefield and the Blandford

Cemetery at Petersburg, Virginia, were erected by the local chapters of the UDC and the Ladies' Memorial Association, respectively.

Monuments commemorating the actions of Florida Confederate regiments on significant battlefields are found at Chickamauga, Vicksburg, and Gettysburg. The Chickamauga monument was funded by the Florida Legislature certainly with the blessing if not the insistence of the UDC and UCV. It is a very impressive monument erected during the heyday of monument building on the major battlefields. Florida troops were heavily engaged at this battle and suffered significant casualties, and it is fitting that this participation was commemorated. Surprising is that what is probably an even greater sacrifice by Florida troops at Gettysburg was not commemorated until the Civil War Centennial, in 1963. This late date is even more unexpected given the creation by the Florida Legislature of the Florida commission in 1895. Although the mission of this commission focused on assisting in the proper interpretation of the battlefield with markers, it is surprising that it did not inspire the newly formed Florida UDC to action in erecting a monument to Florida on the Gettysburg Battlefield. Chickamauga was, of course, a Confederate victory perhaps more befitting of southern commemoration.

Surprising in another manner is the 1954 monument to Florida troops at the Vicksburg battlefield. This monument is not unusual because of its equally late erection but rather because Florida troops had little involvement in the siege that is commemorated at the Vicksburg National Military Park. It seems that the Florida UDC was bound and determined that Florida would not be absent on Vicksburg's Confederate Avenue on one of the most monument-covered battlefields in the nation.

5 MONUMENTS ERECTED AFTER THE CIVIL WAR CENTENNIAL

> The Civil War is our only "felt" history—history lived in the national imagination. This is not to say that the War is always, and by all men, felt in the same way. Quite the contrary. But this fact is an index to the very complexity, depth, and fundamental significance of the event. It is an overwhelming and vital image of human, and national, experience.
>
> **Robert Penn Warren,** *The Legacy of the Civil War* **(1963)**

The Civil War Centennial of 1961 to 1965 marked the passing of the generations most closely related to the Civil War and the entrance of the United States into a world increasingly different from that of the 1860s. The centennial did not, however, mark the end to commemoration of the Civil War in Florida through placement of monuments. Although continuities with the pre-centennial "golden era" of Civil War monument construction exist, there are a number of changes as well.

Since the centennial there has been an expansion of the organizations sponsoring monuments. The United Daughters of the Confederacy was a major force prior to the centennial and has remained a frequent sponsor of monuments since that time. Joining the UDC, and replacing the United Confederate Veterans, are the Sons of Confederate Veterans, the Military Order of the Stars and Bars, the Confederate Sons Association of Florida, and the Order of Confederate Rose. Taking the place of the Grand Army of the Republic and the Woman's Relief Corps are the Sons of Union Veterans of the Civil War and the Daughters of Union Veterans of the Civil War, both of which began as Allied Orders of the Grand Army of the Republic. In addition to the descent groups, the City of Fort Myers, the Clay County Historical Commission, and the Alachua Lions Club have also erected monuments.

Originally called the United Sons of Confederate Veterans, the Sons of Confederate Veterans (SCV) was founded by male descendants of Confederate soldiers in 1896 during the national United Confederate Veterans reunion in Richmond, Virginia.[1] The SCV's mission is to serve as "a historical, patriotic, and non-political organization dedicated to insuring that a true history of the 1861–1865 period is preserved." The SCV includes erection of monuments among its current programs.[2]

Seventeen Confederate officers and forty-seven sons and grandsons of Confederate officers formed the Order of the Stars and Bars in 1938 in Columbia, South Carolina. In 1976 the name was changed to the Military Order of the Stars and Bars. They pride themselves on being the only heritage association still in existence actually founded by Confederate veterans. They are dedicated to the preservation of southern history and include erection of monuments among their goals.[3]

Although the SCV and the Military Order of the Stars and Bars are relatively old organizations, other heritage associations that have sponsored Florida monuments following the centennial appear to be very recent in origin. According to their Web site, the Confederate Sons Association of Florida, founded in 2006, "is a fraternal and non-political Southern heritage organization based on patriotic, historical, educational, and benevolent principles and ideals."[4] Established in 1993, the Order of Confederate Rose is an association of independent women's groups that support the SCV and their local camps. The Order of Confederate Rose places a special emphasis on the preservation of Confederate symbols.[5]

One thing that is striking related to the timing of Civil War monument construction in Florida since 1966 is that there was a relatively steady pattern until near the end of the twentieth century. At that time there was a virtual explosion of monument building in Florida. Between 1968 and 1997, at least eleven monuments were erected in Florida. The period between 1998 and 2013 saw nearly twice as many added to the list, with at least six erected in 2007 alone. As the following review of post-centennial monuments will show, there are several trends that explain this recent increase in the placement of monuments in Florida.

STARKE, 1968

On April 28, 1968, the W. T. Weeks Chapter of the Florida Division of the UDC dedicated a monument to the Confederate dead of Bradford County

Figure 123. 1968 Confederate monument erected at Crosby Lake Cemetery near Starke. Photograph by Sarah E. Miller, 2013.

at the entrance to Crosby Lake Cemetery west of Starke (see figure 123). The dedication ceremony included an invocation, music performed by violinist W. B. McKinney, and speeches from UDC representatives, including the Florida Division president. The monument was unveiled by the granddaughter of the Florida Confederate veteran for whom the chapter was named. On May 6, 2012, the Florida Division of the UDC rededicated the monument with the unveiling of a new plaque on the monument.[6]

The approximately nine-foot-high granite monument consists of an obelisk shaft and pedestal on a one-stepped foundation. A bronze plaque on the front pedestal is inscribed in raised letters with "IN MEMORY OF OUR CONFEDERATE DEAD 1861–1865 W. T. WEEKS CHAPTER OF U.D.C. OF BRADFORD COUNTY[,] STARKE, FLORIDA." A plaque on the obelisk shaft above is inscribed with "REDEDICATED BY FLORIDA DIVISION U.D.C. 6 MAY 2012."

JACKSONVILLE EVERGREEN CEMETERY, 1973

In 1973 the Alexander H. Stephens Chapter of the Florida Division of the UDC erected a low granite tablet monument in honor of Confederate veterans interred in Jacksonville's Evergreen Cemetery. The interior section of the monument is inscribed with "DEDICATED TO ALL CONFEDERATE VETERANS" followed by the chapter name and "1861–1973." The monument is located to the rear of a cemetery section containing seventeen marked gravesites of Confederate veterans. In 1986 the Martha Reid Chapter of the UDC dedicated a two-and-one-half-foot-high marble monument at the front of the section noting that their chapter purchased the plots in 1897 for Confederate veterans.[7] A Union monument, erected in 1891, is also located in Evergreen Cemetery (see chapter 3), as is a monument to Confederate captain J. J. Dickison and another to the crew of the CSS *David* (see chapter 2).

TAMPA OAKLAWN CEMETERY, 1975, 1996, AND ONE UNKNOWN DATE

In 1975 a monument was erected "IN HONOR AND MEMORY OF CONFEDERATE STATES SOLDIERS AND SAILORS 1861–1865 INTERRED HERE" in Tampa's Oaklawn Cemetery (see figure 124). Hillsborough County established the cemetery in 1850 as a public burial ground for both whites and blacks. It was transferred to the City of Tampa in 1855.[8] It contains the remains of over sixty Confederate veterans. This Confederate monument is a low granite tablet

Figure 124. 1975 Confederate monument in Tampa's Oaklawn Cemetery. Photograph by William B. Lees, 2010.

Figure 125. Union monument in Tampa's Oaklawn Cemetery, placed at an unknown date, as it appeared in 2010. Photograph by William B. Lees.

Figure 126. 1996 monument commemorating Union attack on Tampa in Oaklawn Cemetery. Photograph by William B. Lees, 2010.

sponsored by the Heights Garden Circle, the UDC, and the John T. Lesley Camp of the Florida Division of the SCV.

Two other Civil War–related monuments are also located in Oaklawn Cemetery. One of these is a small rustic boulder placed "IN MEMORY OF OUR FATHERS" by the Daughters of Union Veterans of the Civil War (see figure 125). Although we are uncertain as to the date of its erection, we believe it dates from after the centennial. The other is a small granite monument that commemorates the cemetery as a place of conflict due to the shelling of Tampa by a Union gunboat (see figure 126). Erected by the Tampa Historical Society and dedicated on April 14, 1996, the monument is inscribed with "DURING THE CIVIL WAR THE USS SAGAMORE ON JUNE 30–JULY 1, 1862 BOMBARDED TAMPA. AN 8 INCH SHELL LANDED IN THE CEMETERY."[9] The shelling of Tampa followed refusal of the Confederate garrison to surrender and was answered by guns of the Rebel battery at Fort Brooke.

BARTOW, 1982

On July 3, 1982, a monument honoring Company E of the Seventh Florida Infantry Regiment (the "South Florida Bulldogs") was dedicated on the grounds of the 1909 Old Polk County Courthouse in Bartow (see figure 127).[10] This is an impressive upright four-foot-high granite slab sitting on a rough-hewn granite base. Engraved with the company designation and nickname on the front, it is dedicated "IN MEMORY OF THE 79 MILITIA MEN UNDER COMMAND OF CPT NATHAN S. BLOUNT WHO MARCHED FROM THIS SITE TO GAINESVILLE TO MUSTER INTO THE CS ARMY RENDERING GALLANT SERVICE FROM APRIL 10, 1862–APRIL 26, 1865." On the back is engraved a list of the nineteen battles in which this company participated while serving with the Army of Tennessee in Kentucky, Georgia, Tennessee, and North Carolina. General Joseph E. Johnston surrendered the company as part of the Army of Tennessee on April 26, 1865, in North Carolina.

The General Evander M. Law Camp of the Florida Division of the SCV sponsored the monument. It is one of only two Confederate unit monuments in Florida, with the other erected in Plant City by the UDC in 2007 to the First Florida Battalion of Special Cavalry (discussed later in this chapter). Two Union regimental monuments are also located in Florida—the monument to the Ninetieth and Ninety-First New York Infantry dedicated in 1930 in Key West by the State of New York (see chapter 4) and the monument to

Figure 127. 1982 monument to "South Florida Bulldogs" erected in Bartow. Photograph by William B. Lees, 2009.

the Second U.S. Colored Troops erected in 1998 by the City of Fort Myers (discussed later in this chapter).

FORT MEADE, 1983

An upright granite slab monument on a rough-hewn granite base "IN MEMORY OF LT. GEN. THOMAS J. 'STONEWALL' JACKSON" was dedicated in Fort Meade on July 4, 1983. Sponsored by the General Evander M. Law Camp of the Florida Division of the SCV, the approximately six-foot-tall monument contains biographical information on Jackson, including his service as a first lieutenant in the U.S. Army at Fort Meade in 1850–51 and as a Confederate general during the Civil War.[11] The top of the monument contains an ornate silhouette carving of Jackson on horseback. The community of Fort Meade itself is named for Lieutenant George Meade, who surveyed the area for a military road and post in 1849. Meade was promoted to general during the Civil War and commanded the Union army at the Battle of Gettysburg in 1863.

CRAWFORDVILLE, 1987

On May 17, 1987, an approximately seven-foot-tall granite obelisk monument with a three-stepped base was dedicated at Hudson Memorial Park in Crawfordville with a program of prayers, music, and speeches (see figure 128). The featured speaker was Judge B. K. Roberts, chief justice of the Florida Su-

Figure 128. 1987 Crawfordville monument dedicated to the service of Confederates from Wakulla County. Photograph by Barbara A. Hines, 2012.

preme Court, who was also the grandson of two Confederate veterans and the great-grandson of another. The R. Don McLeod Chapter of the Florida Division of the UDC sponsored the monument. Engraved on the front of the obelisk is "1861–1865 IN LOVING MEMORY OF THOSE FROM WAKULLA COUNTY WHO SERVED THE CONFEDERACY DURING THE WAR BETWEEN THE STATES." Above this is engraved the First National Flag of the Confederacy with seven stars, and below is engraved "ERECTED BY R. DON MCLEOD CHAPTER 2469 UNITED DAUGHTERS OF THE CONFEDERACY MAY 17, 1987."[12]

OLUSTEE BATTLEFIELD, 1991

We have discussed previously the monument erected on the Olustee Battlefield in 1991 as a representation of the original one placed in 1866 to mark the common grave of Union casualties of the battle (see chapters 1 and 4; see figure 90). The monument is a rustic granite cross on a granite base and one-stepped foundation on which the inscriptions of the original wooden monument are replicated and modern dedicatory information is added. The Union Army District of Florida, a Civil War reenactment association, placed the monument, which is the scene of a memorial service by Union and Confederate reenactors during the annual Battle of Olustee reenactment.

CLEARWATER, 1993

The Mary Custis Lee Chapter of the Florida Division of the UDC dedicated an upright granite slab monument with a two-stepped base on April 26, 1993, Confederate Memorial Day, at their UDC Memorial Building in Clearwater.[13] The approximately seven-foot-tall monument is inscribed with "IN MEMORY OF THE MEN, WOMEN AND CHILDREN WHO SERVED THE SOUTH 1861 1865 THE WAR BETWEEN THE STATES."

CHATTAHOOCHEE, 1994

On May, 27, 1994, the William Anderson Sanders Chapter of the Florida Division of the UDC dedicated a monument costing "approximately $3,000" in Chattahoochee to commemorate the sailors who died on the Confederate gunboat *Chattahoochee* during the Civil War (see figure 129). Approximately two hundred people attended the ceremony. Dedication speakers included UDC officials, historians, the director of the Confederate Naval Museum in

Figure 129. 1994 Confederate monument erected in Chattahoochee to commemorate those lost in the explosion of the *Chattahoochee*. Photograph by William B. Lees, 2012.

Columbus, Georgia, and a descendant of the ship's commander. Attendees included descendants of sailors who died on the ship, and the Sneads High School ensemble provided the music.[14]

On May 27, 1863, the boilers of the *Chattahoochee* exploded while the vessel was near Blountstown on the Apalachicola River, killing seventeen sailors. This represented the greatest loss of Confederate combatants along the Apalachicola River during the war. The sailor dead were brought to Chattahoochee for burial in a grave that is no longer marked and whose location is in the approximate area where the monument was erected.

The upright granite slab is engraved with a likeness of the *Chattahoochee* and is dedicated "TO HONOR THE MEMORY OF THOSE KILLED IN THE EXPLOSION OF THE CSS CHATTAHOOCHEE MAY 27, 1863." The monument, dedicated on the 131st anniversary of this naval disaster, lists by name those killed and "BURIED NEAR THIS SITE MAY 28, 1863." The *Chattahoochee* returned to service but later was scuttled by Confederate forces in April 1865 at Columbus,

Georgia, as Union forces approached the city. A thirty-foot section of the vessel and the steam engines were recovered in the 1960s and are now on display at the National Civil War Naval Museum in Columbus.[15]

MADISON, 1996

In 1996 a monument was erected in the downtown park in Madison that is not a Civil War monument per se but is worthy of mention (see figure 130). This monument, which is a granite obelisk sitting on an engraved shaft and a two-stepped base, also of granite, is dedicated to former slaves: "THIS

Figure 130. 1996 monument to former slaves of Madison County. Photograph by William B. Lees, 2012.

MONUMENT IS DEDICATED TO THE FORMER SLAVES OF MADISON COUNTY, THEIR SUPPORTERS AND THE UNSUNG HEROES WHO GAVE THEIR PRAYERS, BLOOD, SWEAT, AND TEARS TO HELP MAKE OUR COMMUNITY WHAT IT IS TODAY." Dedication of the monument was on May 20, 1996, which is the anniversary of the announcement of the Emancipation Proclamation in Florida by Union brigadier general Edward M. McCook on May 20, 1865. Located at the northwest corner of the park, it is within sight of the 1909 Confederate monument at the park's center (see chapter 2) and opposite the Four Freedoms Monument dedicated in 1944, which honors World War II hero and Madison native Captain Colin P. Kelly.

FORT MYERS, 1998

In 1998 a significant monument to the Second Regiment, U.S. Colored Troops (USCT), was erected in Fort Myers's Centennial Park (see figure 131). This is one of only four regimental monuments in Florida, and it is the only monument in the state dedicated to the commemoration of the service of African American troops during the Civil War. Organized at Arlington, Virginia, in 1863, the Second USCT was assigned to the Department of the Gulf following training, where it served until the end of the Civil War. Companies of this unit saw service from New Orleans to Key West, including the defense

Figure 131. Monument to the Second Regiment U.S. Colored Troops, erected in 1998 by the City of Fort Myers. Photograph by William B. Lees, 2011.

of Fort Myers against a Confederate attack in February 1865. The Union force engaged at the Battle of Natural Bridge in March 1865 was composed largely of members of this regiment and the Ninety-Ninth USCT. While in Florida the Second USCT continued recruiting members, including escaped slaves who had taken refuge in Union-occupied areas.

The City of Fort Myers erected the monument at a cost of $48,000 and dedicated it on November 11, 1998, Veterans Day. The monument consists of two ornamental walls and a stepped platform on which a well-executed and detailed sculpture of a sergeant of the USCT stands. This figure is known locally as "Sergeant Clayton," allegedly because the sculptor, D. J. Wilkins, required a "ton of clay" to sculpt the bronze figure. The statue depicts a well-equipped African American sergeant standing at parade rest and holding his musket. He wears a forage cap, belt with U.S. belt buckle, fatigue blouse (sack coat), cartridge box, cap box, canteen, and what appears to be an Enfield-pattern bayonet scabbard. The statue stands on a three-stepped masonry-and-tile platform and in front of two masonry walls to its left and right, which bear a number of dedicatory plaques. On the end of the left wall a bronze plaque identifies this as a project of the City of Fort Myers and lists the names of the mayor and city council members. At the end of the right wall a bronze plaque acknowledges the local American Legion post for its role in the project, followed by a listing of post officials, historical adviser, sculptor, model, and others involved in the monument design. An inset granite plaque on the front face of the left wall provides information on the history of the Second USCT at Fort Myers, and on the right wall an identical granite plaque carries a poem, "In Freedom Cover Me," attributed to "Clayton."[16]

HAVANA, 1999

In the late 1990s the Florida Division of the SCV began a project they called "Flags across Florida" to erect memorials with monuments and large flagpoles flying the Confederate flag at sites along heavily traveled highways in the state. The SCV dedicated the first such monument and flagpole on December 11, 1999, on U.S. Highway 27 about four miles north of Havana in Gadsden County near the Florida/Georgia state line. Costing "about $10,000," it consists of a four-foot-high black granite slab monument inscribed with a detailed dedication to Confederate "Soldiers, Sailors & Marines of Florida" at the base of a sixty-foot-tall flagpole.[17] By 2008, two more "Flags across Florida" memorials had been erected by the SCV (discussed later in this chapter).

On November 11, 2000, Veterans Day, the City of St. Cloud and the Lucius L. Mitchell Camp of the Sons of Union Veterans of the Civil War dedicated a monument in St. Cloud's Veterans Park, "In memory of THE GRAND ARMY OF THE REPUBLIC and those UNION VETERANS who in 1909 settled the 'WONDER CITY' of ST. CLOUD, FLORIDA" (see figure 132).[18] This monument is striking because the 1915 GAR monument that stands in St. Cloud's Mt. Peace Cemetery was obviously its model (see chapter 3). Although not an exact copy, it is faithful to the original. It is also of masonry construction,

Figure 132. Grand Army of the Republic monument placed in 2000 in St. Cloud's Veterans Park. Photograph by William B. Lees, 2011.

but unlike the 1915 monument, all of the dedicatory verbiage is contained on a large bronze plaque on the monument's pedestal. The Beers Construction Company's assistance in the construction of the monument is acknowledged on a separate small bronze plaque on the monument.

JACKSONVILLE, 2001

In western Jacksonville, not far from Interstate 10, is a small cemetery acquired in 1976 by the Dr. Thomas M. Palmer Chapter of the Florida Division of the UDC, who named it the Camp Captain Mooney Cemetery. Also known as the Ellis Road Cemetery, this family cemetery of about one and one-half acres contains the remains of some thirty Confederate veterans. After the Dr. Thomas M. Palmer Chapter disbanded, the Florida Division of the UDC accepted ownership of the cemetery in 1997. On September 8, 2001, the Florida Division dedicated a monument at the cemetery to the Confederate soldiers who were killed during a March 1, 1864, battle referred to in the official records as "Skirmishes at Cedar and McGirt's Creeks" (see figure 133). During this running battle fought in the vicinity of the cemetery, one Union

Figure 133. 2001 Jacksonville monument commemorating Confederate losses in the skirmishes at Cedar and McGirt's Creeks, Jacksonville. Photograph by William B. Lees, 2011.

and seven Confederate soldiers died in the bloodiest one-day action in Duval County during the war. The Fraser Funeral Home in Jacksonville donated the upright granite slab monument dedicated to "THE BRAVERY OF THOSE MEN WHO FELL IN THAT LONG AGO BATTLE."[19]

In the cemetery are five handmade concrete posts marking unknown Confederate graves as well as a handmade grave marker inscribed with "5 UNKNOWN SOLDIER CONFEDERATE STATES ARMY KILLED IN ACTION MAR 1ST 1864 BATTLE OF MCGIRTS CREEK AT CAMP CAPT. MOONEY." In addition, there is a flagpole with a granite slab at its base within a Confederate veterans plot. The slab is engraved with "THIS FLAG FLIES IN HONOR OF ALL THOSE WHO FOUGHT, SERVING OUR COUNTRY, TO KEEP IT FLYING." When we visited the site in May 2011, the flag flying was the Confederate First National Flag.

WHITE SPRINGS, 2002

In 2002 the second of three "Flags across Florida" monuments featuring a huge Confederate flag was constructed on the east side of Interstate 75 about thirty miles south of the Florida/Georgia state line near the community of White Springs (see figure 134). The flag flying over the monument is clearly

Figure 134. Monument plaza of a Confederate "Flags across Florida" monument, erected in 2002 near White Springs, as it appeared in 2011. Photograph by William B. Lees.

visible from the highway, but the monument itself is accessible only by going through the county farmers market and through parking lots of warehouses behind the market. The monument consists of a tiled plaza surrounded by a post-and-chain fence, within which is the one-hundred-foot flagpole, a granite shaft monument, and three upright tablet monuments. The Florida Division of the SCV dedicated the plaza on February 15, 2002.[20]

The central dedicatory monument bears an engraved SCV logo and dedicates the plaza to "THE LIVING MEMORY OF OUR ANCESTORS," to all soldiers, sailors, and marines who served the Confederacy, and to the farmers and ranchers of Florida who helped supply the Confederacy "DURING THE WAR FOR SOUTHERN INDEPENDENCE." The tablet on the left is devoted to sponsors, the one on the right to Confederate ancestors, and the granite shaft in front to ancestors and to the SCV brigade commander and his wife for their service to the organization.

KISSIMMEE, 2002

On April 27, 2002, a granite obelisk monument was dedicated in Rose Hill Cemetery in Kissimmee by the Jacob Summerlin Camp of the Florida Division of the SCV. The monument, which is approximately six-and-one-half-feet in height, was erected as a memorial to Confederate veterans buried in Osceola County, whose names are listed on the faces of the obelisk. Inscriptions on the monument base include the SCV logo with the Summerlin Camp's name and dedication date, the Confederate national motto, and the last words spoken by Generals Robert E. Lee ("Strike the tent") and Stonewall Jackson ("Let us pass over the river and rest under the shade of the trees"). The monument sits in the center of a rectangular red-and-gray brick pavement decorated with a Southern Cross of Honor symbol. Despite some concerns from the African American community about erecting a Confederate memorial on city-owned property, the Kissimmee City Commission had unanimously approved the project in September 2001.[21] The Summerlin Camp erected a nearly identical monument in St. Cloud in 2006 (discussed later in this chapter).

ALACHUA, 2002

On December 8, 2002, the SCV dedicated a monument provided by the Alachua Lions Club in the Newnansville Cemetery, which is located northeast of

Alachua. The monument is a granite obelisk shaft on a two-stepped granite base. The front of the obelisk shaft is engraved "IN HONOR OF OUR CONFEDERATE VETERANS," below which is engraved the Great Seal of the Confederate States of America. On the front of the base is engraved "ALACHUA LIONS CLUB 2002." The back of the obelisk shaft is engraved with the names of twenty-three Confederate veterans who are buried in the cemetery. These veterans are not casualties of the war but rather are veterans who died after the war and were buried in their local cemetery.[22]

SEBASTIAN, 2004

A small Civil War monument was dedicated in the Sebastian City Cemetery on April 24, 2004, by the SCV's Florida Cow Cavalry Camp and the UDC's Governor John Milton Chapter (see figure 135). The beveled front face of the approximately three-and-one-half-foot stucco-over-masonry base has a large bronze plaque attached to it that contains the following dedication statement: "In Memory of the brave Southern soldiers Who fought for their Country In the War Between the States During the terrible years of 1861–1865." The plaque also lists the names of thirteen Confederate veterans "Who are buried here in Indian River County, Florida," including one that appears to have been added at a later date. The monument is unusual in that it also lists the names of two Union veterans and includes "GAR" at the top of the plaque next to "CSA."[23]

DADE CITY, 2006

Mount Zion Cemetery in Dade City is like many other historic cemeteries in Florida in that it contains the graves of veterans of the Civil War. Generally, these are graves of Confederate and Union veterans who died long after the end of hostilities. These are often recognized because they are marked with standard Confederate and Union headstones and are generally marked only with the name of the individual and the regiment and state of service. Mount Zion Cemetery contains the marked graves of seventeen Confederate veterans who served in units from Alabama, Florida, and Georgia.

On April 22, 2006, the Augusta Jane Evans Wilson Chapter of the Florida Division of the UDC and the General Jubal A. Early Camp of the Florida Division of the SCV dedicated a monument to commemorate these Confederate veterans. The monument is a rough-hewn Florida coral rock with a

Figure 135. 2004 monument to Confederate and Union veterans buried in the Sebastian City Cemetery as it appeared in 2013. Photograph by William B. Lees.

polished black granite tablet attached to it that is engraved with "DEDICATED TO THE MEMORY OF THE PASCO COUNTY PIONEERS WHO SACRIFICED FOR THE CAUSE OF THE CONFEDERATE STATES OF AMERICA." Atop the monument is a metal slab lying horizontal on a short post that is inscribed with a cemetery map showing the location of the seventeen gravesites. The monument is at the back of a brick pavement containing individual pavers with the names of the seventeen veterans buried in the cemetery. Directly behind the monument is a historical marker for the "MOUNT ZION METHODIST CHURCH AND CEMETERY" and a twenty-five-foot flagpole from which flies a Confederate battle flag.[24]

Almost a century after Union veterans settled the new community of St. Cloud, a Confederate monument was erected in Veterans Park near the monument to the GAR's town founders that had been placed in 2000 (discussed earlier in this chapter). Dedicated on April 22, 2006, by the Jacob Summerlin Camp of the Florida Division of the SCV, this is a well-crafted granite shaft sitting on a base and foundation, also of granite (see figure 136). It rests in the center of a circular red-and-gray brick pavement depicting the Southern Cross of Honor. The base of the monument is engraved with dedication information, the last words of General Robert E. Lee and General Stonewall Jackson, and the national motto of the Confederacy, "Deo Vindice" (generally translated as "Under God, Our Vindicator"). On the shaft itself are engraved

Figure 136. 2006 monument to Confederate veterans buried in Osceola County placed in St. Cloud's Veterans Park. Photograph by William B. Lees, 2011.

the names of Confederate veterans buried in Osceola County. This monument is nearly identical to the one erected by the Summerlin Camp in Kissimmee's Rose Hill Cemetery in 2002 (discussed earlier in this chapter).[25]

LAKELAND, 2007

The Annie H. Darracott Chapter of the Florida Division of the UDC dedicated an upright granite slab monument on April 14, 2007, at Roselawn Cemetery in Lakeland in honor of that community's Confederate veterans. The approximately three-foot-high monument is inscribed with "SACRED TO THE MEMORY OF THE CONFEDERATE VETERAN" followed by additional dedicatory language.[26]

OXFORD, 2007

In April 2007, the Maj. Gen. John C. Breckinridge Camp of the Florida Division of the SCV dedicated a monument in Pine Level Cemetery at Oxford in Sumter County. Inscribed with "Oxford Confederate Veterans," the approximately five-foot-tall granite tablet monument contains dedicatory language and the names, ranks, and birth/death years of twenty-seven Confederate veterans buried in that cemetery. These veterans are from six southern states, with the majority having served in Florida units.[27]

PERRY, 2007

A small Confederate memorial plaza is located along U.S. Highway 19 just northwest of Perry at the Taylor County Sports Complex. The centerpiece of the plaza is a monument that consists of an upright granite slab with a partially rough-hewn granite base (see figure 137). The Second Lieutenant Joseph Morgan Camp of the Florida Division of the SCV and the Nancy Hart Chapter of the Order of Confederate Rose sponsored the monument, which was dedicated on August 25, 2007.[28]

The monument, which is engraved with the SCV's Southern Cross of Honor logo and the logo of the Order of Confederate Rose, is "DEDICATED TO THE LIVING MEMORY OF OUR CONFEDERATE ANCESTORS." Below the dedication is a poem by Rosemary Duvall followed by "Lest They Be Forgotten . . ." with an engraving of a Confederate soldier carrying a battle flag. The base of the monument is engraved with "CSA." The logos, the flag in the

Figure 137. 2007 monument to "Our Confederate Ancestors" as it appeared in 2011 along U.S. Highway 19, west of Perry. Photograph by William B. Lees.

hands of the soldier, and the lettering on the base are in color. At the time of our visits, a flagpole behind the monument featured a Confederate battle flag. A border with landscape gravel surrounds the monument.

MARIANNA, 2007

In September 2007 a small granite monument to the Confederate defenders at the Battle of Marianna was dedicated in the city's Riverside Cemetery by the Dr. Theophilus West Camp of the Florida Division of the SCV (see figure 138). The monument is near graves of several Confederate soldiers who were casualties of the battle or who fought in the battle and died in the postwar period. Also in the cemetery is a grave marker for Lieutenant Isaac Adams of the Second Maine Cavalry. Adams and other Union casualties were buried here after the battle, but their remains were relocated to the Barrancas National Cemetery at Pensacola after the war. Although Adams's remains are no longer in this grave, his headstone remains.[29]

Figure 138. 2007 monument in Marianna's Riverside Cemetery at the burial site of casualties of the Battle of Marianna. Photograph by William B. Lees, 2010.

OLD TOWN, 2007

In 2007 the short-lived United Sons of the Confederacy of Dixie County placed a monument "IN MEMORY OF 'ALL AMERICAN VETERANS'" along U.S. Highway 19 west of the small community of Old Town. Although this monument is dedicated to all veterans, it is clear that a major purpose of its placement was to honor Confederate veterans. This is seen in the central granite monument, which carries the Great Seal of the Confederate States of America and the Southern Cross of Honor. In the engraved text, the monument is specifically dedicated to Confederate veterans.

Congressman Allen Boyd was a featured speaker at the dedication on November 10, 2007. The monument consists of an upright granite tablet placed at the back of a large concrete pavement surrounded by landscaping and two flagpoles, which at the time of our visits were flying the U.S. and Third Confederate national flags. The dedication clearly expresses the sentiment that Confederate veterans are indistinguishable from other veterans of the United States and, in the spirit of the Lost Cause, "ALL SHARED A COMMON, UNDENIABLE GOAL—TO VOLUNTARILY PROTECT OUR COUNTRY'S FREEDOM."[30]

The First Battalion of the Confederate Florida Special Cavalry, also known as the Cow Cavalry, was formed in early 1864 to protect the cattle herds of South Florida as they were moved upstate toward destinations in other Confederate states. These herds came under increasing pressure from Union raiding parties, as well as from bands of deserters and others who were taking advantage of a general lack of security in South Florida as the war progressed.[31] The Plant City Chapter of the Florida Division of the UDC sponsored a monument to Company B of the First Battalion, which was raised in the Plant City area (see figure 139). Dedicated on November 17, 2007, it is located on the grounds of the 1914 Plant City High School Community Center.

The monument consists of a large circular bronze plaque mounted on top of a large granite block that slopes toward the monument front and sits

Figure 139. 2007 monument in Plant City commemorating the First Battalion of the Confederate Special Cavalry. Photograph by William B. Lees, 2011.

on a granite platform surrounded by a wide pavement containing sponsors' bricks. The elaborate bronze plaque, sculpted by Mike Bethune, depicts a dismounted member of the Cow Cavalry standing in front of his horse with cattle in the background. The front of the monument is engraved "IN MEMORY COW CAVALRY CO. B 1ST BATTALION FL. SPECIAL CAVALRY C.S.A." below which are engraved sponsorship details and a brief description of the service of Company B. Engraved on the other three sides of the monument are the names and ranks of the men who served with the company.

This monument, which cost $20,000, is important as one of the very few regimental monuments erected in Florida. It stands out in that it does not contain, by design, Confederate symbolism that has become controversial, in particular the Confederate battle flag. The monument did cause some local controversy, because the East Hillsborough Historical Society, the administrators of the city-owned community center, had not requested the city's permission before agreeing to place the UDC's monument on city property and because of the concerns of an African American member of the city commission regarding the placement of a Confederate monument on city property. In December 2007 the city commission passed a resolution prohibiting future permanent monuments or displays on the community center grounds without prior city approval.[32]

TULLAHOMA, TENNESSEE, 2008

Tullahoma, Tennessee, is the site of a Confederate cemetery established in 1862 to bury soldiers who died in the hospitals that had been established in that community. This cemetery contains more than four hundred graves, including fifty-two known soldiers from Florida regiments. Neglected for years, individual grave locations and associated names have been lost, but records of those interred exist. These records show that the Florida soldiers are from the First, Third, and Fourth Florida Infantry Regiments who went into winter camp at Tullahoma with the Army of Tennessee at the end of 1862. The Florida troops camped in tents and reported very difficult conditions marred by poor and muddy camp locations.[33]

On April 5, 2008, the Florida Division of the UDC, with the assistance of the Tullahoma Confederate Association, the Kirby Smith Chapter of the Tennessee Division of the UDC, and the Major General B. F. Cheatham Camp of the Tennessee Division of the SCV, dedicated a small monument honoring Florida soldiers buried at Tullahoma (see figure 140). Because

Figure 140. 2008 monument to Florida soldiers in the Tullahoma Confederate Cemetery as it appeared in 2011. Photograph by William B. Lees.

the exact location of the Florida soldier dead is unknown, the monument is placed in association with the larger monument erected in 1964 to honor all Confederates buried in the cemetery. The Florida monument is a small granite block with beveled face on which is mounted a bronze plaque with the dedication "Sacred to the memory of our Florida Soldiers buried here in Tennessee soil[,] United Daughters of the Confederacy Florida Division April 5, 2008."[34]

TAMPA, 2008

A huge Confederate battle flag was raised for the first time in a small Confederate memorial park near Tampa at the intersection of U.S. Interstate Highways 75 and 4 on June 3, 2008. The project was the third "Flags across Florida" monument featuring a huge Confederate flag along major Florida highways erected by the Florida Division of the SCV and was spearheaded by the local General Jubal Early Camp. Other "Flags across Florida" monuments had been erected near Havana in 1999 and near White Springs in 2002 (described earlier in this chapter). The flagpole is 139 feet in height, and the flag raised in June 2008 measured thirty by fifty feet—"the size of a semitrailer truck," as one newspaper article described it. An even larger flag, measuring thirty by sixty feet, was raised in October 2008.[35]

In addition to the huge flagpole, the memorial park contains a large granite tablet monument at the base of the flagpole dedicated "TO THE SOLDIERS, SAILORS & MARINES OF THE CONFEDERATE STATES OF AMERICA" and several other large granite tablets inscribed with the names of Confederate ancestors and park sponsors. Landscaping consists of a brick border wall, iron fencing, and ornamental plants. Constructed at a cost of about $100,000, the memorial park was dedicated on April 25, 2009, in a ceremony attended by more than one thousand people.[36]

The monument caused considerable controversy and attracted national media coverage because of the different meanings that have become associated with the Confederate battle flag. Members of the Hillsborough County Commission requested that the SCV take the flag down in the interests of racial harmony. The SCV refused, insisting that "the flag is a symbol of Southern heritage and that Confederate veterans should be honored just as other Americans who fought and died in wars." A suggested compromise by several county commissioners that the Confederate flag be flown only on special occasions and the U.S. flag be flown otherwise was also rejected by the SCV.[37]

TRENTON, 2010

Gilchrist County's Veterans Park in downtown Trenton features a plaza around which are situated monuments dedicated to the memory of veterans of World War II, Korea, Vietnam, and Operation Iraqi Freedom. On April 24, 2010, a monument honoring Confederate veterans from what are today Gilchrist, Dixie, and Levy Counties joined the others on the plaza. The

Figure 141. 2010 Confederate monument in the Gilchrist County Veterans Park in Trenton as it appeared in 2011. Photograph by William B. Lees.

monument is a four-sided polished granite shaft on a rough-hewn granite base. The John Hance O'Steen Camp of the Florida Division of the SCV sponsored the monument (see figure 141).[38]

The monument is engraved on all four sides. One side identifies the sponsor, one dedicates the monument to "VETERANS FROM THE WESTERN PART OF ALACHUA COUNTY THAT BECAME GILCRIST COUNTY IN 1925," another to "VETERANS FROM THE SOUTHERN PART OF LAFAYETTE COUNTY THAT BECAME DIXIE COUNTY IN 1921," and the other to "VETERANS FROM LEVY

COUNTY." Although Levy County had been formed out of Alachua County in 1845 prior to the Civil War, neither Gilchrist County nor Dixie County existed during the conflict. In explaining the reason for the monument, the O'Steen Camp commander was quoted as saying, "Alachua County has a Confederate monument outside the courthouse, but Gilchrist, Dixie and Levy counties didn't have one, so we added them to this monument." The referenced Alachua County monument was erected in 1904 in Gainesville and is discussed in chapter 2.[39]

GREEN COVE SPRINGS, 2011

We have discussed previously the monument erected prior to 1939 in the Magnolia Springs Cemetery near Green Grove Springs to mark the gravesites of Union troops buried there (see chapter 4). On February 12, 2011, the Clay County Historical Commission dedicated a larger representation of the now-missing original monument at the cemetery (see figure 142). Placement of the monument followed an extensive research project by the historical commission, sponsor of the monument. The research included a survey of the cemetery with ground-penetrating radar by the Florida Public Archaeology Network. The new monument is seven feet in height and consists of a polished granite obelisk on a square granite base. The obelisk is dedicated to both Union and Confederate soldiers: "In honor and tribute to the soldiers of the Union and Confederacy who served in the War Between the States and the citizens of Clay County herein buried Erected 2011" The base is engraved with "MAGNOLIA SPRINGS CEMETERY Established circa 1860."[40]

ORMOND BEACH, 2011

The Pilgrim's Rest Cemetery was established in Ormond Beach in 1908, when the Pilgrim's Rest Primitive Baptist Church building was moved there from its original location on the Tomoka River. The church building was moved again in 1988 to prevent its demolition when the property was sold for commercial development, but the cemetery remained and is ornamented with two elaborate wrought-iron arched gates. On April 17, 2011, a flagpole and monument "Placed in Honor of Our Heritage" in the cemetery by the J. Franklin Hull Light Artillery Camp of the Confederate Sons Association of Florida were dedicated.[41] During our visit, a Confederate First National

Figure 142. 2011 monument to Union and Confederate soldiers placed in Magnolia Springs Cemetery near Green Cove Springs. Photograph by William B. Lees, 2013.

flag was flying below the United States flag. The flagpole's concrete base has mounted in it a bronze Southern Cross of Honor grave marker. The monument itself is a flat black granite slab engraved with images of Nathan Bedford Forrest and Robert E. Lee, and it is engraved with the above dedication and the names of seven Confederate veterans buried in the cemetery. All of these veterans served in Florida Infantry regiments. The decision to feature Forrest on a Florida monument erected in 2011 is unusual due to the lack of his association with Civil War Florida and his postwar association with the Ku Klux Klan.

* * *

The thirty-three monuments covered in this chapter span the period from 1968 to the present. In general, these monuments continue a trend that started well before the Civil War Centennial toward smaller, less elaborate monuments. As much as anything else, this trend is probably associated with evolving design trends and ultimately with increasing costs of elaborate stone and bronze work. Monuments dedicated to the Union remain a very small minority of those erected during this period.

As was reviewed in the introduction to this chapter, a number of new Confederate heritage associations erected some of the more recent monuments. It is noteworthy, however, that the UDC has continued to sponsor monuments at a fairly constant rate up to the present day. The UDC and the SCV co-sponsored several of these monuments. Unlike the period prior to the Civil War Centennial, the SCV has emerged in the years since as one of the principal sponsors of Civil War monuments in Florida by erecting as many as the Daughters.

Many of these monuments continue the important work of commemorating hallowed ground. These monuments include the monument commemorating the shelling of Tampa in 1862; the monument in Bartow marking the spot where the "South Florida Bulldogs" marched off to war; the monument at the approximate location of the graves of Confederate sailors killed in the explosion of the *Chattahoochee;* the monument to the Second USCT commemorating among other things their participation in the Battle of Fort Myers; the monument at Camp Captain Mooney in Jacksonville commemorating the Confederate soldiers killed in the vicinity in 1864; the monument commemorating the Confederate soldiers who died in the Battle of Marianna; the monument erected in a cemetery at Green Cove Springs that contains the gravesites of Union soldier dead; and a monument commemorating the

Florida soldiers buried in the Confederate cemetery at Tullahoma, Tennessee. While many of these are modest, they are nonetheless important efforts. Perhaps the most elaborate is the sculpture-based monument commemorating the Second USCT erected by the City of Fort Myers.

The monument to Company E of the Seventh Regiment of Florida Infantry erected in Bartow and the monument to the Second USCT in Fort Myers also stand out as important regimental monuments. The monument placed in Plant City to commemorate the First Battalion of the Florida Special Cavalry joined these in 2007. Although somewhat controversial, the latter is a well-conceived and well-crafted Civil War monument. To put these three recent regimental monuments in perspective, only one regimental monument was erected in Florida prior to the end of the Civil War Centennial. This 1930 monument is in Key West and commemorates the Ninetieth and Ninety-First Regiments of New York Infantry (discussed in chapter 4). The Fort Myers monument also stands out as the only monument commemorating the contribution of African American troops in Florida during the Civil War.

A new form of monument appears after the Civil War Centennial, and its recent popularity helps to explain the increase in monument erection in Florida since the turn of the twenty-first century. These are monuments that commemorate Confederate veterans buried in local cemeteries or commemorate all Confederate veterans buried within a county's cemeteries. Those of the first type, erected in 1968, 1973, and 1975, in Starke, Jacksonville, and Tampa, respectively, differ from the recent monuments in that they recognize but do not list the Confederate veterans buried in the cemetery. Monuments erected in Alachua (2002), Dade City (2006), Oxford (2007), and Ormond Beach (2011) cemeteries not only commemorate the Confederate veterans in the cemetery but also list them by name on the monument. Monuments of the second type in Kissimmee (2002), Sebastian (2004), and Veterans Park in St. Cloud (2006) list all Confederate veterans buried in cemeteries within the county. All of these monuments differ from those prior to the Civil War Centennial erected within a dedicated Union or Confederate veterans plot in the cemetery.

The three "Flags across Florida" monuments represent what we believe to be a radicalized extension of the work started by Ladies' Memorial Associations in Florida shortly after the end of the Civil War. In some ways, placing these flags prominently on heavily traveled major highways is a natural extension of the UDC's goal of placing monuments in public places visible on a daily basis. Whether the SCV can convey a clear and meaningful message by the simple display of a really large battle flag is, of course, the question. As mentioned earlier, a number of organizations whose goals differ from the SCV's have appropriated the battle flag; this has given the flag a variety of meanings, some of which are quite objectionable.

Several other recent monuments may have had a clear purpose understood by the sponsors, but the message conveyed by the monument itself is less clear. The monument at Old Town, for example, seems to be intent on establishing soldiers who fought for the Confederacy as American patriots on equal standing with soldiers who fought for the United States in other conflicts. If we are correct in our interpretation, this in some ways becomes an expression of the vindication of the southern soldier following that sought by the UDC during the late nineteenth and early twentieth centuries.

All told, important monuments have been raised in Florida since the Civil War Centennial. New monuments will certainly continue to be erected as well. In April 2013 a groundbreaking ceremony at the Hillsborough County Veterans Park near Tampa was held for a proposed "War between the States Memorial" that will be erected following the conclusion of fund-raising.[42] A monument honoring local African American Union soldiers has also been proposed for erection in Key West.[43]

In August 2011, the Florida Department of the Sons of Union Veterans of the Civil War 1861–1865 (SUVCW) proposed the erection of a new monument at the Olustee Battlefield Historic State Park to commemorate the participation of the Union forces in that battle. The group established an Olustee Monument Commission and a fund-raising account and, in February 2013, submitted a monument proposal to the Florida Division of Recreation and Parks (DRP). In response, the DRP determined that such a Union monument would not conflict with the purposes of the state park and that it should be located in the same general area as the three Confederate monuments. The SCV, however, considered it to be a "special monument to invading Federal forces . . . that will disrupt the hallowed grown [ground] where Southern blood was spilled in defense of Florida." On December 2, 2013, the DRP sponsored a meeting in Lake City to present potential locations for the monument and receive public comment, which was attended by approximately one hundred people.[44]

The majority of the meeting speakers, most of them members of the SCV and the UDC, expressed opposition to the placement of the Union monument on the three state-owned acres of the battlefield. Anti-monument speakers asserted that it would be contrary to the purpose for which the three acres were donated to the state, that one of the inscriptions on the 1912 monument already mentions that "Federal troops" fought in the battle, and that the 1991 monument in the nearby cemetery memorializes the Union forces. Many of them also stated that they were not, however, opposed to the Union monument being placed on the adjacent portion of the battlefield owned by the U.S. Forest Service. SUVCW representatives countered that the 1912 monument is clearly a Confederate monument and that a Union monument should be erected on the state-owned three acres, which is the main visitor area. DRP staff said that all of the public comments would be taken into consideration. A final decision had not been made as this book went to press.[45]

One state representative who attended the meeting stated that he was prepared to introduce legislation that would require approval by the Florida Legislature to erect any new monuments within the state park system. In January 2014 a bill was filed to that effect but was not enacted during the 2014 legislative session.[46] What is clear is that even after the passage of more than one hundred years since legislation for a monument at Olustee was first debated, the topic of memorialization of Union sacrifice at this place still stirs controversy of a sort whose lineage can be easily traced to the Civil War and Reconstruction and the development of the Lost Cause narrative.

CONCLUSION

> The Civil War lives . . . in the many statues and monuments erected across our land. These stone images stand as silent sentries of the cost of what today belongs to all Americans.
>
> **James I. Robertson Jr., *The Civil War* (1963)**

When it seceded from the Union in 1861, Florida was the least-populated state of the Confederacy. By the end of the twentieth century it had become one of the most-populated states of the reconstructed and expanded nation. Today, many of the state's residents are non-natives proudly hailing from cold-climate northern states and other parts of the world, to the point that residents joke that Florida is no longer part of the South. In this context, Florida's handful of Civil War monuments are best seen as part of a relict landscape from a period when "the war" could only mean the Civil War and the demographics were much different than today. This historical landscape is decidedly non-Yankee, with a smattering of Union monuments erected alongside a much greater number of those dedicated to the Confederacy.

The monuments discussed in this book erected in the nineteenth century and first half of the twentieth were placed by individuals and groups whose members had a direct connection with the Civil War. Initially, the monument builders had lived through this horrible conflict and knew directly of its human cost. As time went on they were joined by generations who did not experience the war firsthand but rather through stories told by those who had. They understood the importance of their local monuments in a manner that we simply are incapable of today. They are gone, but the monuments remain. It was their hope that their message, which they can no longer convey themselves, lives on through these monuments: Civil War memory preserved in stone and bronze.

Since the close of the Civil War, the mission of these monument builders has grown more difficult to understand by the day. Although interest in the Civil War has remained amazingly high, few have knowledge of, or interest in, the long period of reconciliation starting with Reconstruction and as yet unfinished. If the Florida monuments simply marked locations of prominent events of the Civil War, this would little matter. As we have established in the pages of this book, however, the monuments are less about the Civil War than they are about its aftermath. This is especially true when the backstory reveals that these monuments carry a message different—sometimes significantly different—from the one overtly conveyed by the monuments themselves.

Complicating this is the fact that people today interpret the inscriptions and symbols on these monuments using a twenty-first-century lexicon. This lexicon includes new meanings associated with Confederate words and symbols that have resulted from appropriation of these words and symbols by groups who use them in defiance or hate. Most notable among these appropriated symbols is, of course, the Confederate battle flag, which is used by many organizations with diverse and contradictory purposes and is seen emblazoned on bumper stickers, Web sites, and clothing in ways that would puzzle those who followed this flag into battle.

The trend of population growth and the migration of northerners to Florida that began immediately after the war and increased dramatically after the turn of the twentieth century adds a further challenge to understanding the builders' purposes in erecting monuments. Fewer and fewer residents have deep roots in Florida, and very few have roots that extend to even the early twentieth century. This affects, of course, not just Civil War monuments but many other remnants of Florida's heritage that are simply culturally "invisible" to a population whose roots are elsewhere.

This is the context in which Civil War monuments exist today, and it is the context those seeking to build new Civil War monuments must confront. Those who designed the monument to the "Cow Cavalry" in Plant City, erected in 2007, were mindful of this context and avoided use of controversial Confederate symbols such as the battle flag. In contrast is the recent project of the Sons of Confederate Veterans to erect huge Confederate battle flags at prominent locations along Florida highways. Viewers, especially visitors to the state—are left to assign whatever meanings they associate with this "monument," regardless of the meaning the SCV may have intended.

* * *

In the pages of this book we have considered one hundred Florida Civil War monuments, including six that are no longer standing. Eight of these are located out of state and bear witness to the participation of Florida Confederate troops in the Army of Tennessee and the Army of Northern Virginia.[1] Of the remaining extant monuments, fifty-four in Florida and seven out of state date from the end of the Civil War through the Civil War Centennial (we include here the 1966 monument to Lee erected in Fort Myers). Although we have focused on these early monuments, we also reviewed thirty-three monuments (including one out of state) dating after the centennial, because we believe some legitimately continue the earlier tradition of Civil War commemoration and are important in understanding the relevance of Civil War monuments for our own lives.

The first monuments erected in Florida honored the Union dead and were erected by the U.S. Army at Olustee in 1866 (a wooden monument no longer standing) and by the Navy Club at Key West, also in 1866. Nine additional Union monuments were erected in the state between 1891 and 1939, all but two of them sponsored by the Grand Army of the Republic or the Woman's Relief Corps. One was sponsored by the State of New York to honor the Ninetieth and Ninety-First Regiments of New York Infantry at Key West, and the sponsor of the monument at Magnolia Springs Cemetery is unknown to the authors. The monument at Yellow Bluff Fort, dedicated in 1951 by the United Daughters of the Confederacy, mentions the service there of both Confederate and Union soldiers.

Given Florida's place in southern history, it is not surprising that a much greater number of the state's monuments are dedicated to the Confederacy. The first of these were erected during Reconstruction by Ladies' Memorial Associations in Walton County and St. Augustine. These early monuments were designed to aid in remembering soldier dead buried far from home. These associations continued to erect monuments through the end of the nineteenth century, but the message gradually evolved, following national trends, to focus less on remembering the dead and more on vindicating the South and its soldiers, both living and dead (the Lost Cause narrative). Although private individuals sponsored a few monuments around the turn of the twentieth century—notably including that erected by Charles and Lucy Hemming in downtown Jacksonville—the newly formed UDC, incorporating many of the Ladies' Memorial Associations, picked up the torch of monument building in Florida after 1900.

The first UDC monument erected in Florida was placed in 1901 in the plot within Lake City's Oaklawn Cemetery containing Confederate soldier dead from the Battle of Olustee. From that date onward UDC monument dedications increased steadily into the early 1920s. Although the number of monuments dedicated dropped precipitously after 1925, a steady rate of dedications occurred up through the Civil War Centennial of the early 1960s. Monuments from this period show that the UDC's work in Florida focused on community monuments, but several important projects to commemorate contested ground occurred between 1912 and 1963. These projects resulted in monuments at the Olustee, Chickamauga, Marianna, Natural Bridge, Vicksburg, and Gettysburg battlefields. During the early part of the century, the United Confederate Veterans, not known for their monument building, erected several in Florida, including the significant monument to Confederate women in Jacksonville in 1915.

By reading the inscriptions on the monuments, the evolution of the message of Confederate monuments in Florida becomes clear. Starting with the simple dedication to native sons buried in distant fields, the monuments increasingly evoke the Lost Cause narrative. Promotion of this narrative was begun prior to the formation of the UDC, as early as 1866 in E. A. Pollard's book by that name, but it immediately became a raison d'être for this organization, which working on several fronts—including monument building—sought vindication for the South.

In Florida the Lost Cause narrative was nowhere more clearly evoked than on the 1908 monument that was originally placed on the county courthouse grounds in Ocala. The inscription on this monument juxtaposes the founders of the United States with the leaders of the Confederacy, as if their causes were one and the same and would be mutually acceptable: "THE SOUTH REVERES HER WASHINGTON, MADISON, MONROE, ANDREW JACKSON, AND OTHERS, WHO LAID THE FOUNDATIONS OF OUR GRAND REPUBLIC. SHE HONORS HER LEE, STONEWALL JACKSON, STUART, JOHNS[T]ON, FOR[R]EST, AND EVERY BRAVE SON WHO FOUGHT TO PRESERVE OUR LIBERTIES, GUARANTEED BY THE FATHERS, UNDER THE CONSTITUTION." Only a few years later, in Tampa, also on the county courthouse grounds, the UDC erected the *Memoria in Aeterna* monument, which bears a poem rife with the Lost Cause:

NOT THEIRS THE RUSH OF MADDENED WRATH
THAT RECKLESS SUNDERED TIES OF BLOOD,
BUT HONOR'S BEACON SHOWED THE PATH
WHERE DAUNTLESS DUTY STOOD
THROUGH FAMINE YEARS THEY FOLLOWED FAR
WHERE HER UNSWERVING BANNERS LED—
BEYOND HER GLORY'S FLAME-TIPPED STAR—
BEHIND HER—HONOR'S DEAD.
THE YEARS THEIR SLOW PROCESSION KEEP,
THE BANNER BARRED WITH RED IS FURLED—
BUT NOW ITS GRAY CLAD SOLDIERS SLEEP
THE HEROES OF A WORLD.

The entry of the United States into the war with Spain in 1898, and the staging of much of the war effort in the South due to its proximity to Cuba, did much to advance regional reconciliation by pitting North and South against a common threat. World War I was even more important in this regard, and as an organization the UDC did much to support the war effort. Many Daughters believed that the coming together of the country to support the Allies signaled the final vindication of the South and its soldiers, in part through the performance of southern soldiers in that war.

From a height perhaps represented by the Ocala and Tampa monuments in 1908 and 1911, respectively, it is possible to see a softening of the Lost Cause rhetoric in monuments erected after World War I. Although some scholars have suggested that World War I effectively ended the period of monument building by the UDC, this is not the case for Florida. As already noted, the UDC erected a large number of Confederate monuments in the state during the early 1920s. Despite a decline by 1930, monument building by the UDC continued on a regular pace up through the Civil War Centennial.

In addition to their memorial purposes, Florida monuments are also important outdoor sculpture that adorn our twenty-first-century landscape. As sculpture, we note some patterns for Florida monuments that also mirror boarder national developments. Early on, the Ladies' Memorial Associations obtained monuments from a variety of artisans. For example, the 1871 Walton County monument was produced by Anthony Barret of New Orleans, the

1881 Leon County monument was provided by Thomas Delahunty of Philadelphia, and the 1872 and 1879 St. Augustine monuments were constructed by local craftsmen. Although small local companies continued to construct monuments in Florida, by the 1880s a number of companies had begun to provide monuments on a large and often national scale. Those that provided Florida monuments include the Monumental Bronze Company of Bridgeport, Connecticut; the James Clark and Company of Louisville; the George N. Clark Company (Clark Monument and Stone Company) of Jacksonville; the W. H. Mullins Company of Salem, Ohio; the Reed E. LaMance Company of Jacksonville; and the McNeel Marble Company of Marietta, Georgia. The Monumental Bronze Company specialized in solid zinc monuments and the W. H. Mullins Company in sheet copper and bronze monuments, especially statues. The McNeel Marble Company produced the largest number of Florida monuments, accounting for at least eleven constructed between 1908 and 1924, including the 1913 Florida monument dedicated at the Chickamauga Battlefield in Georgia.

Incorporated in 1892 by N. L. McNeel, the McNeel Marble Company became a leading national manufacturer of marble stonework, large statuary, and monuments by the early 1900s. The company also became adept at aggressively encouraging the construction of Confederate monuments throughout the South, including Florida. As historian Edward L. Ayers describes it, "While its craftsmanship did not surpass that of its competitors, its sales force did." From its headquarters office and quarry in Marietta, the company sent teams of salesmen across the South to visit UDC and UCV chapters and provide advice on raising funds for the construction of Confederate monuments. Their creative sales tactics included offering cash prizes to chapter presidents who successfully completed a monument that was sculpted and installed by their company. In a full-page advertisement in *Confederate Veteran* magazine in 1910 titled "Phenomenal Record of the McNeel Marble Company," the company congratulated the UDC for erecting more monuments in one year (1909) than in any previous decade and boasted that their company had received "more than 95% of all orders for Confederate Monuments . . . in the South" that year. The company went out of existence in 1960.[2]

In many cases, monument companies used their own workers, designers, and sculptors to quarry, carve, fabricate, and install the finished monument and artwork. For some projects, however, they contracted with an outside sculptor to create the statuary, such as the 1904 Confederate monument in Gainesville where the sheet copper soldier statue was provided by the W.

H. Mullins Company for placement on the granite pedestal and base constructed by the George N. Clark Company. Another excellent example is the 1915 monument to Confederate women in Jacksonville. For this monument the McNeel Marble Company contracted with one of the leading sculptors of the day, Allen G. Newman of New York, to produce the two exceptional bronze statues.

As significant outdoor sculptures and a part of the state's cultural heritage landscape, the physical condition of Florida's Civil War monuments is important to consider. Many of Florida's Civil War monuments, both Union and Confederate, are now quite old and historic in their own right. Many are well-executed and spectacular outdoor sculptures of a type that is no longer being constructed. Stripped of any overt or hidden meaning, they remain striking reminders of Florida's past and constitute an important part of the state's heritage landscape.

In the course of our visits to monuments, we have not thoroughly assessed the condition of the monuments, nor are we qualified to perform such work. In the 1990s a number of Civil War monuments in Florida were included in Save Outdoor Sculpture surveys. Save Outdoor Sculpture was begun in 1989 as a largely volunteer project and continues today as a joint program of Heritage Preservation and the Smithsonian American Art Museum. Since its inception, this program has cataloged and assessed some thirty thousand monuments, of which 54 percent "were determined to be in critical or urgent need of conservation to survive."[3] Although environmental conditions may not be as harsh on outdoor sculpture in Florida as in states further north, a significant number of the state's Civil War monuments, especially those dating from prior to the centennial, also need attention.

We have seen many monuments that will require restoration if they are to remain viable parts of our landscape into the future. Topping the list may be the zinc monuments in Jacksonville's Evergreen Cemetery (1891) and in Marianna (1881). Other examples are monuments with broken or missing elements, such as the broken urn on top of the 1930 "Yellow Fever" monument in Key West, and the 1961 monument in Daytona Beach that is gone except for the base and a bronze plaque. More subtle problems can be seen as well, such as vegetation growing between sections of monuments, such as on the 1939 GAR monument in Miami and on the 1930 Key West "Yellow Fever" monument.

The setting of these monuments is also an important consideration. Some have been moved, such as the 1911 Orlando monument, relocated only six years after its erection, and the 1908 Ocala monument, which was moved in 2010. The surroundings of other monuments have been changed, such as by the erection of modern courthouse buildings in Gainesville, where the 1904 Confederate monument sits, and in Marianna, where an important 1881 zinc monument is located. Despite changes in the appearance of these buildings, these monuments are still at their original locations on the grounds of public buildings.

Landscaping around many monuments has changed drastically as well, such as that around the 1898 monument in Jacksonville's Hemming Plaza and the 1909 monument in Madison's city park. By and large, landscaping changes simply confirm that these monuments are a valued part of the city of which they are a part. There are, however, some monuments whose original landscapes are preserved. One need look only to the 1921 Union monument in Lynn Haven to view landscaping that would be very familiar to those members of the GAR who attended its dedication so long ago.

* * *

After delving into the history behind these monuments, both Union and Confederate, we believe that their stories cannot be understood in isolation; nor can they be understood only by the form of a monument and the inscriptions it bears. Union monuments were most commonly dedicated to the soldier dead or to those who served, a simplicity probably deriving from the status of the Union as victor. That Union monuments were rarely placed in public spaces certainly relates to Florida's status as a former Confederate state. Public opinion may have been considered by the GAR or the Woman's Relief Corps when the placement of Union monuments was contemplated, but in at least one case, a local government denied permission to erect a monument in a public place. This occurred in Tampa in 1922, when the city council denied a petition by the Woman's Relief Corps to erect a Union monument in a city park.

Confederate monuments provide numerous insightful stories of their genesis, a few worthy of review. Both of the Reconstruction-era Confederate monuments have a fascinating history. After a monumental tug-of-war, a dispute over the location of the 1871 Walton County monument ended up in the Florida Supreme Court. This speaks to the passion surrounding this first Confederate monument and the importance that people placed on its location. Surprisingly, perhaps, the state supreme court allowed it to remain on the grounds of the county courthouse, an interesting contrast to the placement of a contemporary monument in St. Augustine.

In 1872 a monument to the Confederate soldier dead was erected on church-owned property in St. Augustine when permission to place it on the publicly owned Plaza de la Constitución was denied by the city council due to opposition from the U.S. military commander in the city. This denial, which was in keeping with practice throughout the South during Reconstruction, reflected the federal government's position that the former Confederate states should not be allowed to honor the cause of the Confederacy or the valor of its soldiers in public places. In 1879, two years after Reconstruction ended, permission to move the monument to the plaza was obtained. The monument was dismantled and materials and plaques reused in a reconfigured monument in the public plaza.

In considering the Walton County and St. Augustine monuments, it is important that the former, allowed on the courthouse square, was simply a symbolic device remembering the soldier dead of the county. In contrast, the St. Augustine monument, while extremely mild in its rhetoric compared to later Confederate monuments in Florida, invoked the name of the Confederacy while honoring the service of the local soldier dead. The role of this not-so-minor difference in decisions on where to place the monuments is a powerful commentary on Civil War memory during Florida Reconstruction.

For a state so proud that its capital was not captured during the Civil War, the small and relatively plain monument to the soldier dead of Leon County that stands on the grounds of the state capitol seems puzzling. One would expect a grand monument dedicated to the entire state—perhaps more like the monument in downtown Jacksonville or in Pensacola. In fact, efforts for a statewide monument in Tallahassee had been contemplated as early as 1866, and efforts to raise funds for its construction continued through the 1880s. Despite having a design for the monument in hand, it was never erected.

Resentment over the local association's unilateral decision in 1881 to place a monument on the capitol grounds only in honor of Leon County's soldier dead was probably instrumental in derailing fund-raising efforts for the larger statewide monument. Funds that had been raised were soon diverted to Pensacola to help fund the impressive monument that was erected in Lee Square in 1891. Had the UDC's statewide organization been in operation earlier, a state monument might have become a reality in Tallahassee. By the time the UDC became an effective voice in Florida, funds raised for Tallahassee had been spent in Pensacola, and the Daughters were kept busy with other statewide projects at the Olustee, Natural Bridge, and Marianna battlefields and at the Gamble Plantation.

The story behind the unusual monument dedicated in 1912 at the Olustee Battlefield is one of the most interesting of any in Florida. Efforts to erect a monument to this Confederate victory began during the late nineteenth century and involved considerable endeavors in terms of selecting a location and obtaining funding. The original legislation for this monument provided that it would honor both Confederate and Union sacrifice in the battle. The UDC was strongly opposed to such a dedication to Union soldiers, and the legislation was revised accordingly. This might seem predictable given the UDC's focus on the vindication of the South, and justified in reaction to the successful work by the older GAR to prevent federal funds from being used for proper burial of Confederate dead or the commemoration of Confederate valor. Historical accounts make clear, however, that while this may have been the backdrop to this situation, the Florida UDC was adamant that the Union sacrifice would not be recognized because to do so would acknowledge the service of the U.S. Colored Troops who fought bravely and with great loss at Olustee.

Years later, shortly after the United States had entered World War II, the Daughters dedicated a monument in Sarasota to Confederate secretary of state Judah P. Benjamin. The monument stands on the edge of the bay at a location thought to be where Benjamin left the United States for the last time and boarded a vessel that eventually made good his escape to England. The inscription on this monument simply states this is where Benjamin set sail—missing are any vestiges of the Lost Cause. Striking, however, is the dedication ceremony, in which the UDC, as well as local and state dignitaries, spoke eloquently about the monument as a symbol of anti-Nazi solidarity through the commemoration of Benjamin as a prominent Jewish American.

Although the Robert E. Lee monument in Fort Myers was dedicated in 1966, after the Civil War Centennial, we included it in our main discussions because the project was begun in 1915. The association of Lee with the Confederacy is downplayed on the monument in favor of claiming Lee as the namesake of Lee County and ultimately with Lee's pre–Civil War visits to the state as a U.S. Army engineer. But the story that explains the fifty-year journey leading to the erection of this monument is one of compassion of the local UDC chapter for other local needs, in particular the Lee County Hospital and support for the U.S. war effort. In 1917 and again in 1940, the UDC gave the funds it had raised for the monument to the Lee County Hospital, indicating that monument building was considered less important than supporting local health care and the war effort.

These stories provide important insights into the physical monuments that remain a part of our twenty-first-century landscape. They are important commentary on the times in which these monuments were conceived, constructed, and dedicated. They are the backstory to the overt, carefully constructed statements embodied by monumental sculpture and the all-important words of dedication inscribed thereon, and are as important for understanding individual monuments and Florida's changing social environment. Food for thought, for example, comes from contrasting the racially laden debate surrounding the 1912 Olustee monument with the anti-Nazi dedication speeches for the 1942 Judah P. Benjamin monument.

These are not stories, however, that anyone will take away after visiting a monument, regardless of how long one might gaze upon the sculpture or mull over the dedication verbiage. Given the passage of 150 years since the height of the Civil War and the passing of everyone with a direct connection to the war, the message and its evolution cannot be understood without first understanding the context of Reconstruction and the ensuing years. Nor can they be understood without also considering the history of the organizations and individuals who were responsible for the placement of Civil War monuments in Florida. Since these stories and the enlightenment they engender are not readily available, the public is too often left to their own devices to explain what these monuments are all about. Because of the effective appropriation of Confederate symbols (especially the Confederate battle flag and perhaps even the Lost Cause narrative) by groups preaching hate and intolerance, the lack of understanding of the history of these monuments poses a threat that affects Confederate monuments disproportionately.

This threat is not imaginary. A prime example is the relocation of the Ocala monument from the courthouse grounds to Veterans Memorial Park on the city's outskirts. Nicknamed "Johnny Reb" locally, the monument was moved several times in the course of building and remodeling the county courthouse, and it was eventually partially hidden on one side of the building. Following increasing pressure from those who believed it was inappropriate to keep this monument on the grounds of a county building, it was relocated with private funding in 2010. Although it is in a nicely landscaped setting, the monument is for the first time in over a century far from the city's center.

Prior to this, in 2003, construction of a new judicial building next to the

Manatee County courthouse in Bradenton ignited a debate on the appropriateness of the 1924 Confederate monument. Despite calls for its removal to another location (to the grounds of the Gamble Plantation State Historic Site), the monument remains on the courthouse grounds. In 2007 a new monument was erected to commemorate the Confederate "Cow Cavalry" on the city-owned grounds of a building administered by the local historical society in Plant City. Controversy ensued because the city commission had not given prior approval to this project, and at least one commissioner objected to placing a monument honoring the Confederacy on city property.

These examples demonstrate a growing sentiment that rejects the narrative of the Lost Cause and sees symbols of the Confederacy—including Confederate monuments—as representing the attempt to uphold a social contract originally based on slavery. This is certainly the result of years of appropriation of Confederate symbols by groups such as the Ku Klux Klan and more recently by groups that are radicalizing these symbols in other ways. Given the original intent of many Confederate monuments to vindicate the South for actions that many segments of our modern society would say cannot be vindicated, it is likely that discontent with the presence of these symbols of the Confederacy will continue to increase and that the legitimacy of Confederate monuments as part of the modern public landscape will continue to be questioned.

While we believe this will be the case, we also believe it would be unfortunate to see monuments relocated, especially those that remain in their original settings. We believe it would be even worse to dismantle monuments for storage or disposal. These are part of the historic landscape of our communities, and while they may become controversial, that controversy can, if approached properly, be turned into the proverbial teachable moment. An example of this is found in the response to the monument to Heyward Shepherd in Harpers Ferry, West Virginia.

Also called the "Faithful Slave Memorial," the Shepherd Monument was controversial when first dedicated and has remained so ever since. Shepherd, a slave, was apparently a collateral casualty of John Brown's 1859 raid on Harpers Ferry, through which Brown had hoped to start a general slave revolt throughout the South. The UDC erected a monument to honor Shepherd in 1931 on which he is exemplified for, among other things, being a "faithful slave." When the ground on which the monument is situated became property of the National Park Service, the controversy did not abate, and eventually the monument was covered with a wooden box. After considerable political pressure, the park service removed the box and allowed the public to view the monument, but it also insisted this not be done without placement of an interpretive wayside marker putting the monument in proper historical context.[4]

While erecting an interpretive wayside marker is not an unusual endeavor in a national historic site such as Harpers Ferry, it is certainly unusual for the grounds of a county courthouse, in a city park, or in a cemetery in Florida. Regardless of how the message might be carried, we believe that if the important Civil War monuments in Florida are to remain a part of the public landscape, an effort needs be made to provide the public the information they need to better understand the historical contexts of these monuments and what meaning these monuments have for us today. A Civil War monument, just like an earthwork on a Civil War battlefield, no longer serves its original function but is an artifact with a lesson for us today. Just as the public needs help in understanding the importance of a long-abandoned earthwork, the public needs help in understanding the continuing importance of our Civil War monuments. This will require, in some cases, providing controversial or unpleasant facts about these monuments in an informed discussion of the present.

Is there a place for additional Civil War monuments in Florida? Although we believe that new monuments commemorating Civil War people and events may be appropriate, it might be more useful to preserve and reinterpret those that already exist. Efforts might also be directed toward helping to preserve important Civil War places in the state and assisting in telling the story of Florida during the Civil War in the state's multitude of heritage sites and museums, many in public ownership.

Do Civil War monuments have a valuable role to play today and in the future? We believe they do, both as wonderful outdoor sculptures within Florida's overall heritage landscape and as important physical remnants of our post–Civil War heritage. Constructed with a lesson in mind, these monuments can themselves be lessons in understanding a very important social process in modern U.S. history—the process of remembering the Civil War and its relationship to our contemporary lives.

NOTES

ABBREVIATIONS

FPC Florida Photographic Collection, Florida State Archives, State Library of Florida, Tallahassee

FSA Florida State Archives, State Library of Florida, Tallahassee

FTU *Florida Times-Union* (Jacksonville)

UDC United Daughters of the Confederacy

INTRODUCTION

1. Faust, *This Republic of Suffering*, 3–31.

2. Giuliano, "Legend of the Field Stones," 11–23.

3. Walters, "Union Colony."

4. We use the phrase "soldier dead" to refer to those from all branches of service, which certainly includes sailors, cavalry, marines, as well as soldiers of the Union or Confederate armies, who died during the conflict.

5. "History of the 32nd Indiana Infantry Monument," U.S. Department of Veterans Affairs, accessed November 24, 2012, http://www.cem.va.gov/CEM/bloedner_monument.asp. When the soldier dead of the Thirty-Second Indiana buried on the battlefield were moved to Cave Hill National Cemetery in 1867, the monument was also moved and a base with a dedication in English was added. To prevent further deterioration from the elements, the monument was relocated in 2010 to the Frazier History Museum in Louisville, Kentucky. In 2011, a replacement monument was installed in the cemetery.

6. Sellars, "Pilgrim Places," 32; Zenzen, *Battling for Manassas*, 2; Sedore, *Virginia's Confederate Monuments*, 106; "First Manassas Monuments," Manassas National Battlefield Park, accessed November 24, 2012, http://www.nps.gov/mana/photosmultimedia/First-Manassas-Monuments.htm#. In 1936 the Works Progress Administration and the Georgia Division of the UDC placed a monument to Bartow on the battlefield; the monument, which remains today, is close to the base of the 1861 monument. It proclaims Bartow as "The first Confederate officer to give his life on the field."

7. "Hazen Brigade Monument," Stones River National Battlefield, accessed November 24, 2012, http://www.nps.gov/stri/planyourvisit/upload/Hazen%20Handout.pdf.

8. "Original Surrender Monument," Vicksburg National Military Park, accessed November 24, 2012, http://www.nps.gov/vick/planyourvisit/surmonument.htm. Due to vandalism and souvenir hunters, the monument was moved to the Vicksburg National Cemetery in 1867, but vandalism and relic hunting continued and the monument was eventually placed in storage until becoming part of the exhibits at the Vicksburg National Military Park Visitor Center.

9. Zenzen, *Battling for Manassas*, 2. Constructed by members of the Fifth Pennsylvania Heavy Artillery, these monuments were similar obelisks made of sandstone and decorated with relic artillery shells from the battlefield. They were dedicated with elaborate ceremony on June 11, 1865.

10. Hacker, "Census-Based Count," 307.

11. Heidler and Heidler, *Encyclopedia of the American Civil War*, 860–61.

12. Warren, *Legacy of the Civil War*, 3–4.

13. See, for example, Neff, *Honoring the Civil War Dead*; K. L. Cox, *Dixie's Daughters*; Faust, *This Republic of Suffering*; Blight, *Race and Reunion*; Fahs and Waugh, *Memory of the Civil War*.

14. Neff, *Honoring the Civil War Dead*, 1–13; Faust, *This Republic of Suffering*.

15. Dearing, *Veterans in Politics*; Sellars, "Pilgrim Places."

16. Janney, *Burying the Dead*, 8.

17. K. L. Cox, *Dixie's Daughters*, 2, 13.

18. Neff, *Honoring the Civil War Dead*, 66–102; K. L. Cox, *Dixie's Daughters*, 12–16.

19. Neff, *Honoring the Civil War Dead*; K. L. Cox, *Dixie's Daughters*.

CHAPTER 1. RECONSTRUCTION AND BEYOND

1. Today this is called the State of the Union.

2. J. D. Richardson, *Messages and Papers of the Presidents*, 243–55.

3. U.S. War Department, *Official Records, Armies*, series 1, vol. 46, part 3, 665–66; Randall and Donald, *Civil War and Reconstruction*, 525–26.

4. Original spelling of this name varies depending on source, but "Bennitt" appears to be the correct historical usage, whereas "Bennett" is the one most often found in the myriad historical sources that discuss this important place-name.

5. U.S. War Department, *Official Records, Armies*, series 1, vol. 47, part 3, 313.

6. "Johnston's Surrender," *New York Times*, April 30, 1865.

7. "Major Surrenders of the American Civil War," Bennett Place State Historic Site, accessed December 26, 2012, http://www.bennettplacehistoricsite.com/history/surrender-negotiations; Josephy, *Civil War in the American West*, 385.

8. Buker, *Blockaders, Refugees, and Contrabands*, 3; Brown, *Tampa in Civil War and Reconstruction*, 41; Schafer, *Thunder on the River*, xi; Wynne and Taylor, *Florida in the Civil War*, 91–93.

9. Nulty, *Confederate Florida*, 124–69; D. Cox, *The Battle of Natural Bridge*.

10. Coles, "Far from Fields of Glory," 378–79.

11. Ibid., 381–86.

12. "Site of the Negotiation for the Civil War's Largest Troop Surrender," Bennett

Place State Historic Site, accessed December 26, 2012, http://www.nchistoricsites.org/bennett/main.htm.

13. Nulty, *Confederate Florida*, 69–75.

14. Coles, "Far from Fields of Glory," 27.

15. Thirteenth Amendment to the U.S. Constitution, Library of Congress Virtual Services, Primary Documents in American History, accessed September 26, 2012, http://www.loc.gov/rr/program/bib/ourdocs/13thamendment.html.

16. Castel, *Andrew Johnson*, 23–24.

17. Milton, *Age of Hate*, 171–72; Randall and Donald, *Civil War and Reconstruction*, 528–29; Grant, *Personal Memoirs*, 514–15.

18. Randall and Donald, *Civil War and Reconstruction*, 528–29.

19. Grant, *Personal Memoirs*, 513–18; Castel, *Andrew Johnson*, 23–24.

20. J. D. Richardson, *Messages and Papers of the Presidents*, 213–15. On December 8, 1863, Lincoln had issued a "Proclamation of Amnesty and Reconstruction" which spelled out what he believed to be acceptable terms of reintegration of the citizens and the states into the Union. In this proclamation he offered to restore to individuals who swore to an oath of allegiance "all rights of property, except as to slaves," with the exception of certain officers and agents of the "so-called Confederate government," officers above the rank of colonel in the army and lieutenant in the navy, and those who had left seats in Congress or resigned commissions in the army or navy to aid the rebellion. For the states in rebellion, a vote of at least 10 percent of the number of individuals voting in the 1860 election who had signed the oath of allegiance would reestablish a Republican form of state government. For former slaves, the states would "recognize and declare their permanent freedom" and provide for their education. Except for the guarantee of freedom of former slaves, these provisions are quite similar to those in the initial agreement of surrender for Johnston's army rejected by Johnson and Stanton.

21. Foner, *Short History of Reconstruction*, 182–84; Castel, *Andrew Johnson*, 28–29.

22. Sefton, *Andrew Johnson*, 108–10. The Thirty-Ninth Congress adjourned on March 4, 1865, several weeks before Lincoln's assassination (April 14) and Johnson's swearing-in as president the following day. Inasmuch as the new Congress did not convene until December 4, 1865, Johnson had a window during which, unchecked by Congress, he was able to use his executive authority to put his own reconstruction policies into action.

23. Ibid., 108.

24. J. D. Richardson, *Messages and Papers of the Presidents*, 310–12; Foner, *Short History of Reconstruction*, 182–85.

25. J. D. Richardson, *Messages and Papers of the Presidents*, 312–14.

26. Castel, *Andrew Johnson*, 44.

27. W. W. Davis, *Civil War and Reconstruction in Florida*, 356–64.

28. Castel, *Andrew Johnson*, 67, 70.

29. Foner, *Short History of Reconstruction*, 228–41; "Andrew Johnson 1865–1869," The White House, accessed December 27, 2012, http://www.whitehouse.gov/about/presidents/andrewjohnson; J. D. Richardson, *Messages and Papers of the Presidents*, 398–413; Fourteenth Amendment to the U.S. Constitution, Library of Congress Virtual Ser-

vices, Primary Documents in American History, accessed December 27, 2012, http://www.loc.gov/rr/program/bib/ourdocs/14thamendment.html; Randall and Donald, *Civil War and Reconstruction*, 596. In the Amnesty Act of 1872, Congress restored the right to hold office to most former Confederates excluded from such by the Fourteenth Amendment.

30. Randall and Donald, *Civil War and Reconstruction*, 592–600, 618–22; Foner, *Short History of Reconstruction*, 217–53.

31. Randall and Donald, *Civil War and Reconstruction*, 638–43.

32. Foner, *Short History of Reconstruction*, 412–563.

33. Randall and Donald, *Civil War and Reconstruction*, 685–701.

34. U.S. War Department, *Official Records, Armies*, series 1, vol. 6, 849.

35. "After the Burning of Bagdad," 5.

36. U.S. War Department, *Official Records, Armies*, series 1, vol. 26, part 1, 834.

37. W. H. Richardson, *How I Reached the Union Lines*, 4–6.

38. Sheppard, *By the Noble Daring of Her Sons*, 98–99.

39. "Historical Information," Barrancas National Cemetery, accessed October 20, 2012, http://www.cem.va.gov/cems/nchp/barrancas.asp#hi; Sammartino, *Barrancas National Cemetery*, 8–7.

40. Schmidt and Schmidt, "Key West Post Cemetery," 1, 14.

41. "Beaufort National Cemetery, Beaufort, South Carolina," National Park Service—National Cemeteries, accessed December 5, 2012, http://www.nps.gov/history/nr/travel/national_cemeteries/South_Carolina/Beaufort_National_Cemetery.html.

42. "Rosters of 3rd USCT Companies A, C, and F and 8th USCT Companies A, C, D, and F," Pennsylvania in the Civil War, accessed July 29, 2013, http://www.pa-roots.com/pacw/usct/usctregs.html; Rogers and Saunders, *Swamp Water and Wiregrass*, 107; *Tallahassee Sentinel*, "Decoration Day in Tallahassee," June 3, 1871.

43. Faust, *This Republic of Suffering*.

44. Ibid.; K. L. Cox, *Dixie's Daughters*.

45. Zipf, "Marking Union Victory," 28–29.

46. Ibid., 27–42.

47. K. L. Cox, *Dixie's Daughters*; Janney, *Burying the Dead*.

48. Langdon, "The Dead of Olustee," 461–63.

49. Penton and Leigh, *Olustee Battlefield*, 24–25.

50. Florida Association of Museums, *Florida Civil War Heritage Trail*, 73.

51. The term "Third System" refers to engineering changes incorporated into the construction of American seacoast defenses which differentiate them from the earlier "First System" (1794–1806) and "Second System" (1807–15) fortifications.

52. *United States Army and Navy Journal, and Gazette of the Regular and Volunteer Forces* 3, no. 5, September 23, 1865, 73.

53. "Scene in Key West," ca. 1870, image no. MM00032458, "Clinton Square and the Civil War Monument, Key West," MM00032431, "Custom House and Clinton Square," ca. 1898, MM00030380, and "Clinton Square, Custom House and Building #1," ca. 1910, MM00001458, all in Florida History Department Images, Monroe County Public Library, Key West.

54. "The First Monument to the Confederate Dead," *Macon (Ga.) Telegraph and Messenger*, September 7, 1871.

55. Although his last name is sometimes spelled "Barrett" in contemporary and modern accounts, "Barret" appears on the monument and in the 1870 U.S. Census.

56. "The First Monument to the Confederate Dead," *Macon (Ga.) Telegraph and Messenger*, September 7, 1871.

57. McKinnon, *History of Walton County*, 374; Moore, "Battle over the Confederate Monument," 49.

58. Gardner, *New Orleans Directory*, 72; Merrill, *German Immigrant Artists*, 8.

59. "Confederate Memorial—DeFuniak Springs," ca. 1960, image no. RC15632, FPC.

60. M. Curenton, "Walton County Confederate Monument," 2. In a series of articles in *Walton Relations* between January and June 2012, Curenton provides information on the Confederate soldiers listed on the monument.

61. D. Cox, *The Battle of Marianna*, 34.

62. "Jennett J. McCullom, in Behalf of Herself and Others, Composing the Walton County Memorial Association vs. John Morrison and Murdock E. Morrison, in Florida Supreme Court," *Reports of Cases Argued*, 414–17; Moore, "Battle over the Confederate Monument," 48–50.

63. M. Curenton, "Walton County Confederate Monument," 2.

64. Florida Legislature, "Act Authorizing the Removal," *Regular Session 1927*.

65. M. Curenton, "Walton County Confederate Monument," 2; Angel McCurdy, "Damaged Confederate Memorial Attracts Little Attention," *Northwest Florida Daily News*, November 13, 2011; Jeffrey Powell, "Walton County Heritage Association Looks to Restore Confederate Monument," *DeFuniak Springs Herald*, August 2, 2012.

66. Florida Association of Museums, *Florida Civil War Heritage Trail*, 50.

67. Mrs. Leo R. Vogel, "Confederate Monument to the Memory of Our Dead Heroes," April 14, 1899, Confederate Monuments and Memorials Collection, Museum of the Confederacy, Richmond; Sister Esther Carlotta, "Florida's First [*sic*] Confederate Monument," May 1910, UDC Scrapbook, carton 12, file folder 33, FSA.

68. Vogel, "Confederate Monument to the Memory of Our Dead Heroes"; Carlotta, "Florida's First Confederate Monument."

69. "Battle, Augustine, &c.," *Florida Review* (Mandarin), February 1880; "Confederate Monument—St. Augustine, Florida," ca. 1875, image nos. RC03055 and SV0950, FPC.

70. The Catholic Church retains ownership of the original site of the 1872 monument, which is part of the Cathedral Parish School campus.

71. Vogel, "Confederate Monument to the Memory of Our Dead Heroes"; Carlotta, "Florida's First Confederate Monument."

72. "From St. Augustine," September 14, 1883, and "Doings in St. Augustine," August 4, 1888, *FTU*.

73. Woolson, "Ancient City," 12–13; Lanier, *Florida*, 45–46.

74. Bloomfield, *Illustrated Historical Guide*, 29–30; McQuade, *Cruise of the Montauk*, 417; Osborne, "The President Is Coming," 22.

75. Emerson, *Historic Southern Monuments*, 73–74.

CHAPTER 2. REMEMBERING CONFEDERATE SACRIFICE AND VALOR AFTER RECONSTRUCTION

1. Blight, *Race and Reunion*, 77–78.

2. Gallagher, "Shaping Public Memory."

3. Codieck, "Keepers of History," 1–3.

4. K. L. Cox, *Dixie's Daughters*, 14–15.

5. Ibid., 17–19.

6. Ibid., 34, 50; Codieck, "Keepers of History," 5.

7. "United Confederate Veterans Association Records," Louisiana State University Libraries, Special Collections, accessed October 20, 2012, http://www.lib.lsu.edu/special/findaid/u1357.html.

8. Florida Association of Museums, *Florida Civil War Heritage Trail*, 29.

9. "Memorial Day," April 26, 1881, "Memorial Day, Dedication of the Monument to the Confederate Dead of Leon County," May 3, 1881, and "Two Noble Souls," May 3, 1881, all in *Weekly Floridian* (Tallahassee); "Florida News," *Columbus (Ga.) Daily Enquirer-Sun*, April 28, 1881; *Historical and Commercial Philadelphia*, 87.

10. "Memorial Day; Dedication of the Monument to the Confederate Dead of Leon County," *Weekly Floridian*, May 3, 1881.

11. Ibid.

12. Long, *Florida Breezes*, 385–88; Eppes, *Through Some Eventful Years*, 324–25, 363–66; "Memorial Address," *Weekly Floridian*, May 6, 1879.

13. Willis, *Southern Prohibition*, 84–86.

14. "Florida's Monument," *Weekly Floridian*, August 12, 1879.

15. Eppes, *Through Some Eventful Years*, 365.

16. UDC, Florida Division, *Minutes of the Forty-Second Annual Convention*, 92.

17. Scott and McLeod, *History of Anna Jackson Chapter*, 83.

18. "Florida's Monument to Her Confederate Dead," October 23, 1883, "Florida's Monument," October 30, 1883, and "The State Monument," May 17, 1888, all in *Weekly Floridian*; Towns, "Honoring the Confederacy," 205–6.

19. "View of the City of Tallahassee, State Capital of Florida, County Seat of Leon County, 1885" (Milwaukee: Norris, Wellge & Co., ca. 1885), Library of Congress, Panoramic Maps Collection, accessed March 6, 2012, http://www.loc.gov/item/75693186; Galbraith and Miller, *1902 Florida Capitol Restoration*, appendix 3; Scott and McLeod, *History of Anna Jackson Chapter*, 81.

20. Florida Association of Museums, *Florida Civil War Heritage Trail*, 17.

21. Shofner, *Jackson County, Florida*, 378.

22. "Speech of Hon. J. J. Finley at the Laying of the Corner Stone of the Monument to the Confederate Dead of Jackson County," *Marianna Courier*, December 4, 1879.

23. "Florida News," March 24, 1880, and "Florida News," September 16, 1881, *Columbus (Ga.) Daily Enquirer-Sun*.

24. LaBree, *Confederate Soldier*, 447.

25. Rotundo, "Monumental Bronze."

26. LaBree, *Confederate Soldier*, 447; "First Brick Courthouse—Marianna, Florida," 1880s, image no. N034614, FPC.

27. LaBree, *Confederate Soldier*, 447.

28. "Storm in Florida," April 28, 1908, *Augusta (Ga.) Chronicle*.

29. Confederate Soldiers of Jackson County, sculpture, ca. 1881, *National Art Inventories*, Smithsonian American Art Museum, accessed March 9, 2012, http://www.siris.si.edu.

30. Florida Association of Museums, *Florida Civil War Heritage Trail*, 26.

31. "A Memorable Day at Quincy," *Weekly Floridian*, May 20, 1884.

32. Confederated Southern Memorial Association, *History of the Confederated Memorial Associations*, 79.

33. "A Memorable Day at Quincy," *Weekly Floridian*, May 20, 1884.

34. "The Monument at Quincy," *Weekly Floridian*, June 3, 1884.

35. Ibid.

36. See the section on the 1941 West Palm Beach Confederate Monument later in this chapter for a description of the Great Seal of the Confederate States of America.

37. "Florida in the Civil War, 1861–1865—Symbols of Florida," Museum of Florida History, accessed October 5, 2012, http://www.flheritage.com/facts/reports/civilwar/07.cfm.

38. Florida Association of Museums, *Florida Civil War Heritage Trail*, 10; Pearce, *Pensacola during the Civil War*, 1–67.

39. Florida Association of Museums, *Florida Civil War Heritage Trail*, 10; Pearce, *Pensacola during the Civil War*, 106–30.

40. Florida Association of Museums, *Florida Civil War Heritage Trail*, 10; Pearce, *Pensacola during the Civil War*, 106–30.

41. Pensacola City Clerk's Office, Records, "Memorandum Concerning Florida Square (R. E. Lee Park) in Pensacola," City Ordinance, June 8, 1887, book A-1, 149; City of Pensacola, *Ordinances*, section 104, R. E. Lee Square.

42. Confederated Southern Memorial Association, *History of the Confederated Memorial Associations*, 71–73; Towns, "Honoring the Confederacy," 205–6.

43. Towns, "Honoring the Confederacy," 206–9; Brundage, "'Woman's Hand and Heart and Deathless Love,'" 64.

44. "The Dedication; Pensacola's Confederate Monument Given to History," *Pensacola Daily News*, June 18, 1891; Towns, "Honoring the Confederacy," 209; Brundage, "'Woman's Hand and Heart and Deathless Love,'" 64–65; "Pensacola's Monument," *Macon (Ga.) Telegraph*, June 18, 1891.

45. Earle Bowden, "New Lee Square Question: 11 or 13 States," *Pensacola News-Journal*, December 13, 1964.

46. City of Pensacola, *Ordinances*, section 104, R. E. Lee Square; Towns, "Honoring the Confederacy," 207–8.

47. Collins, "Pensacola's Confederate Monument," 30.

48. LaBree, *Confederate Soldier*, 448; "Confederate Monument in Lee Square—Pensacola, Florida," ca. 1900, image no. RC00-9, "Confederate Monument, Lee Square and Pensacola High School—Pensacola, Florida," post-1905, image no. PC2812, and "Civil

War Veteran Reunion at Lee Square—Pensacola, Florida," ca. 1910, image no. RC06184, FPC.

49. LaBree, *Confederate Soldier*, 448; "Confederate Monument, Pensacola, Fla.," ca. 1903, image no. LC-D4-16277, and "Confederate Park, Pensacola, Fla.," 1905–1915, image no. LC-D4-71815, Library of Congress, Prints and Photographs Division; "Civil War Veteran Reunion at Lee Square—Pensacola, Florida," ca. 1910, image no. RC06184, FPC; "Lee Square," ca. 1930s–40s postcard, author's collection.

50. Collins, "Pensacola's Confederate Monument," 30; "City Repeals Move for Vote on Lee Square," January 8, 1948, "Lee Square: Tunnel Under or Cut Corners?" March 17, 1964, and "Council Votes 6–3 to End Group's Control of Square," April 24, 1964, all in *Pensacola News*; "Council Blocks Lee Square Cut," May 11, 1956, and "Council Takes Historic Action," March 30, 1964, *Pensacola Journal*; Earle Bowden, "New Lee Square Question: 11 or 13 States," *Pensacola News-Journal*, December 13, 1964.

51. Florida Association of Museums, *Florida Civil War Heritage Trail*, 28.

52. Shofner, *History of Jefferson County*, 436.

53. "Florida," *Columbus Daily Enquirer-Sun*, June 16, 1886.

54. "Monticello," *FTU*, May 16, 1899.

55. "Confederate Monument—Monticello, Florida," early 1900s, image no. N029071, and "Confederate Monument—Monticello, Florida," 1940s, image no. RC11405, FPC; McRory and Barrows, *History of Jefferson County*, 78; UDC, "Division News: Florida," October 1996, 32.

56. G. M. Turner, *Florida Railroad History*, 58–65.

57. Ibid., 78–80.

58. Florida Association of Museums, *Florida Civil War Heritage Trail*, 41.

59. "Fair Florida Is Fortunate" and "A Noble Gift," February 23, 1896, and "The Hemming Monument," February 25, 1896, *FTU*; "Hemming Monument for Florida," *Confederate Veteran* 7, no. 1 (January 1899): 110; *Confederate Memorial 1861–1865* [Jacksonville], sculpture by George H. Mitchell, 1897–1898, *National Art Inventories*, Smithsonian American Art Museum, accessed March 9, 2012, http://www.siris.si.edu.

60. "Monument to the Heroes of the South," June 17, 1898, *Florida Times-Union and Citizen* (Jacksonville); Brock, "Ceremonies Attending Unveiling," 110–12.

61. "Monument to the Heroes of the South," June 17, 1898, *Florida Times-Union and Citizen*; Brock, "Ceremonies Attending Unveiling," 112–28.

62. T. F. Davis, *History of Jacksonville*, 226.

63. "Looting in Hemming Park, as a Result of the Fire of 1901—Jacksonville, Florida," 1901, image no. N032735, FPC.

64. Valentine and Sons Publishing Co., New York, "Hemming Park (Confederate Monument and Windsor Hotel) Jacksonville Fla.," postcard, canceled 1907, author's collection.

65. Duval News Co., Jacksonville, "Skyline and Hemming Park from St. James Bldg., Jacksonville, Fla.," postcard canceled ca. 1925, author's collection.

66. "New Life in Vision for Hemming," *FTU*, May 28, 2007.

67. "St. Petersburg Will Have a Great Day," February 22, 1900, and "Impressive Cer-

emonies Held by Blue and Gray at St. Petersburg," February 23, 1900, *Tampa Morning Tribune*.

68. "Zephaniah Phillips," Anne Healy's Genealogy, accessed March 18, 2012, http://www.annefield.net/zephaniahphillips2.htm; "Historic Greenwood Cemetery," Greenwood Cemetery, St. Petersburg, accessed October 29, 2012, http://www.historicgreenwood.com/pages/exhibit.html.

69. Woman's Relief Corps, *Journal of the Twentieth National Convention*, 202; "Greenwood Cemetery—Dedication of a Civil War Memorial," 1900, St. Petersburg Museum of History, Historic Photo Archives.

70. U.S. War Department, *Official Records, Navies*, series 1, vol. 15, 20–21; Leni Bessette and Louis Stanton Warren, "Monument Memorializes Crew Manning Confederate Boat," *FTU*, April 10, 2004.

71. James H. Tomb to Thomas P. Stoney, October 14, 1928, Thomas P. Stoney Correspondence, South Carolina Historical Society Archives, Charleston; "Survivor of Crew of First Submarine Raises Memorial," *Charleston (S.C.) News and Courier*, October 21, 1928.

72. K. L. Cox, *Dixie's Daughters*, 50, 67.

73. Codieck, "Keepers of History," 9.

74. G. M. Turner, *Florida Railroad History*, 78–80.

75. Florida Association of Museums, *Florida Civil War Heritage Trail*, 22.

76. Ibid.

77. "Report of Kirby Smith Chapter, U.D.C., No. 202, Gainesville, Florida," July 3, 1904, *Gainesville Daily Sun*; "Kirby Smith Chapter #202, Gainesville Florida–Accomplishments," ca. 1927, UDC Scrapbook, carton 8, FSA.

78. *The Blue and the Gray*, 37.

79. Ibid.

80. Ibid., 8.

81. Grissom, *Zinc Sculpture*, 653.

82. "Deposited in Monument," *Gainesville Star*, January 19, 1904.

83. "Monument Is Here," January 12, 1904, untitled announcements, January 15, 1904, "Unveiling Exercises," January 19, 1904, and "Unveiling of the Monument," January 22, 1904, all in *Gainesville Star*; "Report of Kirby Smith Chapter, U.D.C., No. 202, Gainesville, Florida," July 3, 1904, *Gainesville Daily Sun*; "Confederate Soldier Monument," Alachua County Library District Heritage Collection, accessed November 9, 2012, http://heritage.acld.lib.fl.us/1301-1350/1326.html.

84. *Confederate Soldier* [Gainesville], sculpture by John G. Segesman, 1904, *National Art Inventories*, Smithsonian American Art Museum, accessed March 5, 2012, http://www.siris.si.edu; "Large Figure Sculpture in Front of the Old Alachua County Courthouse—Gainesville, Florida," 1971, image no. C033588AL, FPC. In the photograph of the statue, the bayonet still shows clearly on the rifle.

85. "[UDC] Convention Disposes of Much Routine Work," *Pensacola Journal*, May 5, 1905; "Vandals Smash Statue of Confederate Soldier," *St. Petersburg Times*, July 23, 1965; Gary Kirkland, "In for Spring Cleaning; Weathered Rebel Soon Will Return," *Gainesville Sun*, May 15, 1993.

86. Confederate Monuments and Memorials Collection, Record of Memorials–Ocala, Fla., Mrs. Fannie R. Gary, ca. 1908, Museum of the Confederacy; "Let Others Follow Suit," September 19, 1907, *Tampa Morning Tribune*; "Mrs. Mathews Entertains the Daughters" March 20, 1908, *Ocala Banner*; "Meeting of the Confederate Veterans," January 8, 1908, "Monument Unveiling April 25," March 2, 1908, "The Confederate Monument," April 9, 1908, and "U.D.C. Meeting," April 11, 1908, all in *Ocala Evening Star*.

87. "Program for the Unveiling Ceremonies," April 14, 1908, and "Unveiling the Monument," April 25, 1908, *Ocala Evening Star*; "In Memoriam, 1861–1865; A Beautiful Granite Monument Dedicated to the Memory of the South's Heroes by Dickison Chapter United Daughters of the Confederacy with Imposing Ceremonies," May 1, 1908, *Ocala Banner*.

88. "Address of Hon. F. E. Harris; At the Unveiling of the Confederate Monument, Saturday, April 25," April 28, 1908, "Address of Dr. Nunnally; At the Unveiling of the Confederate Monument, Saturday, April 25," April 29, 1908, and "Address of Col. Jno. M. Martin; At the Unveiling of the Confederate Monument, Saturday, April 25," April 29, 1908, *Ocala Evening Star*.

89. "Johnny Reb" [Ocala], sculpture, McNeel Marble Works, ca. 1908, *National Art Inventories*, Smithsonian American Art Museum, accessed November 4, 2012, http://www.siris.si.edu.

90. Clarence Pottorff, "Marion [County] Seeks Offer to Move Confederate Soldier Monument," *FTU*, September 22, 1965; Clarence Pottorff, "UDC Dragoons Defeat Marion Board in Statue Site Battle," *FTU*, November 4, 1965; "Ocala Blacks Rebel over Confederate Monument," *Daytona Beach News-Journal*, July 9, 1991; "Voters League Wants Rebel Statue Replaced," August 6, 1991, and "1965–1969," January 1, 2003, *Ocala Star-Banner*; Joe Byrnes, "Marion County Moving Confederate Monument to New Spot at Courthouse," October 26, 2007; Christopher Curry, "Officials Debate Confederate Statue's Place," August 21, 2008, Bill Thompson, "Johnny Reb Statue Moving to Veterans Park," January 20, 2010, and Carlos E. Medina, "Johnny Reb Rededicated at New Site," April 16, 2011, all in *Ocala Star-Banner*; UDC, "Division News: Florida," September 1991, 31; Prominski, "A Long Hot Summer," 16.

91. Blight, *Race and Reunion*, 122.

92. Florida Association of Museums, *Florida Civil War Heritage Trail*, 36.

93. "Monument to Be Unveiled," June 17, 1909, "Unveiling Monument," June 24, 1909, and "Monument Dedicated," July 1, 1909, all in *Madison Enterprise-Recorder*.

94. "Soldiers' Monument, Madison, Florida," postcard, canceled 1911, image no. MA0864, FPC.

95. Ibid.

96. "City Park Madison, Fla.," ca. 1945, photo postcard, author's collection.

97. Confederate Monuments and Memorials Collection, Record of Memorials–Lakeland, Fla., Mrs. D. J. Browning, ca. 1910, Museum of the Confederacy; "South Florida," June 13, 1908, and "Erection of Monument," March 31, 1910, *Tampa Morning Tribune*; "Florida News," *Gainesville Daily Sun*, August 10, 1908; Martha F. Sawyer, "Polk's Past: Polk's Confederate Monument," *Lakeland Ledger*, October 13, 1993; Tindle, "A Lone Confederate," 14.

98. "Lakeland Plans a Big Celebration," May 18, 1910, and "Lakeland Unveils Con-

fed Monument," June 4, 1910, *Tampa Morning Tribune*; Remillard, *Southern Civil Religions*, 97.

99. Confederate Monument [Lakeland], sculpture, McNeel Marble Works, ca. 1910, *National Art Inventories*, Smithsonian American Art Museum, accessed March 9, 2012, http://www.siris.si.edu; "Confederate Monument—Lakeland, Florida," 1911, image no. PC1999, and "Members of the United Daughters of the Confederacy, Seated around a Confederate Monument in Munn Park—Lakeland, Florida," 1915, image no. N033917, FPC.

100. "Members of the United Daughters of the Confederacy, Seated around a Confederate Monument in Munn Park—Lakeland, Florida," 1915, image no. N033917, FPC.

101. Lakeland Public Library, Lakeland, Fla., Digital Special Collections, "Fountain and Confederate Monument in Munn Park, Lakeland, Florida," 1936, image no. P0127; Martha F. Sawyer, "Polk's Past: Polk's Confederate Monument," *Lakeland Ledger*, October 13, 1993; Tindle, "A Lone Confederate," 14.

102. Florida Association of Museums, *Florida Civil War Heritage Trail*, 62.

103. Crosby, "Memoria in Aeterna," 16.

104. "From All Parts of Florida," *Gainesville Daily Sun*, November 3, 1909; "Monument Appropriation," September 7, 1910, and "U.D.C. Erecting a Fine Monument," January 28, 1911, *Tampa Morning Tribune*; "Memoria in Aeterna, 1911: Hillsborough County's Confederate Monument," Tampa Historical Society historical marker text, 1997.

105. "Daughters Will Unveil Monument," February 8, 1911, and "5,000 Attend the Unveiling of Handsome Confederate Monument," February 9, 1911, *Tampa Morning Tribune*.

106. *Memoria in Aeterna* [Tampa], sculpture, ca. 1911, *National Art Inventories*, Smithsonian American Art Museum, accessed March 9, 2012, http://www.siris.si.edu.

107. "Improvement Work on Public Square Begun," *Tampa Morning Tribune*, August 26, 1911.

108. "Florida: Confederate Memorial Is Knocked Down," *Daytona Beach Morning Journal*, October 29, 1946; "Hillsborough County Courthouse on Franklin Street—Tampa, Florida," 1940s, image no. RC04004, FPC; "Sailor Is Fined for Damaging Statue in Tampa," *St. Petersburg Times*, October 30, 1946; "Peterson Lauds Patriotism of Civil War Southerners," *Tampa Morning Tribune*, June 4, 1949.

109. "Memoria in Aeterna, 1911: Hillsborough County's Confederate Monument," Tampa Historical Society historical marker text, 1997; Larry Dougherty, "Confederate Statue Repairs Quietly Okayed," *St. Petersburg Times*, February 2, 1995; Crosby, "Memoria in Aeterna," 17.

110. UDC, Florida Division, Annie Coleman Chapter, "The Confederate Monument, Eola Park, Orlando, Florida," one-page undated manuscript; Andrews, "Visiting the Orlando Area?" 1.

111. Andrews, "Visiting the Orlando Area?" 1.

112. Confederate Monuments and Memorials Collection, Record of Memorials–Orlando, Fla., Mary Agnes Person, ca. 1911, Museum of the Confederacy.

113. "Story of an Epitaph," *Confederate Veteran* 1, no. 1 (January 1893): 3.

114. "View of Orange County Court House, Soldiers' Monument, Elks Club and San

Juan Hotel, Orlando, Fla.," ca. 1915, image no. N036386, FPC; "Confederate Monument Orlando, Fla.," ca. 1915, postcard, author's collection.

115. "South Florida Social Notes—Orlando," *Tampa Sunday Tribune*, January 21, 1917; Andrews, "Visiting the Orlando Area?" 1, 15; "Confederate Monument and Petunia Flower Beds—Eola Park," ca. 1920, image no. PC2533, FPC.

116. Southern Cross Chapter #796, Miami—Outstanding Work Accomplished, ca. 1927, UDC Scrapbook, carton 8, FSA; "Will Ask Preference of Monument Site," July 31, 1913, and "Confederate Monument for the City Cemetery," August 20, 1913, *Miami Herald*; "Court House Square to Hold the Confederate Monument," *Miami Metropolis*, September 4, 1913.

117. Confederate Monuments and Memorials Collection, Record of Memorials–Court Square, Miami, Fla., ca. 1914, Museum of the Confederacy; "Court House Square to Hold the Confederate Monument," September 4, 1913, and "Dedicate Shaft to Memory of Heroic Dead Who Fought for South," June 3, 1914, *Miami Daily Metropolis*; "Confederate Monument Unveiling This Afternoon," June 3, 1914, and "Confederate Monument Was Unveiled Here Yesterday," June 4, 1914, *Miami Herald*.

118. "Court House Square to Hold the Confederate Monument," *Miami Daily Metropolis*, September 4, 1913; "Memorial to Confederate Heroes, Erected by Daughters Decade Ago, Observes Day beneath Shed Stair," *Miami Daily News*, April 25, 1926.

119. "Memorial to Confederate Heroes, Erected by Daughters Decade Ago, Observes Day beneath Shed Stair," April 25, 1926, and "Simple, Impressive Rites Mark South's Memorial Day," April 27, 1941, *Miami Daily News*; Silverman, "Rediscovered History," 31.

120. *Monument to the Confederacy* [Miami], sculpture, 1913, *National Art Inventories*, Smithsonian American Art Museum, accessed March 9, 2012, http://www.siris.si.edu; Grace Wing, "Confederate Marker Wears Storm Scars," *Miami Daily News*, April 25, 1954.

121. UDC, Florida Division, *Florida's Confederate Monuments*, "Dade County," 29.

122. Florida Association of Museums, *Florida Civil War Heritage Trail*, 61.

123. Carlotta, "United Daughters of the Confederacy—The Florida Division," 516–17; UDC, *Minutes of the Twenty-Third Annual Convention*, 350.

124. "Confederate Shaft to Be Unveiled on June 3," *Tampa Morning Tribune*, May 27, 1916.

125. "Loring Monument Is Unveiled in the Ancient City," *FTU*, December 31, 1920.

126. "Correction of Injustice" and "Scientific, Practical Psychologic Reading," *St. Augustine Evening Record*, January 14, 1921.

127. "Ashes of Gen. Wm. Loring Rest under Monument," *St. Augustine Evening Record*, July 7, 1920; Florida Legislature, "Act to Aid Anna Dummett Chapter," *Regular Session 1921*, 157–59.

128. "Ashes of Gen. Wm. Loring Rest under Monument," *St. Augustine Evening Record*, July 7, 1920.

129. Mrs. Allan Cleare, chapter historian, to Mrs. F. L. Ezell, Florida Division historian, Report from Stephen R. Mallory Chapter, May 3, 1924, UDC Scrapbook, carton 3, FSA; "Key West Is to Unveil Arch Soon," *St. Petersburg Independent*, January 14, 1924; "Memorial Unveiled at Bayview Park," *Monroe Tattler* (Key West), January 1924.

130. "Key West Women—Their Interests," *Miami News-Metropolis*, December 10, 1923; "C. G. Bailey Is Dead at Home; Was Long Ill," *Key West Citizen*, November 19, 1930.

131. Cleare to Ezell, May 3, 1924, FSA; "Confederate Memorial in Municipal Park, Key West, Florida," postcard, ca. 1930s, author's collection; "Key West Women—Their Interests," *Miami News-Metropolis*, December 10, 1923.

132. Florida Association of Museums, *Florida Civil War Heritage Trail*, 68.

133. "Bradentown Women Order Confederate Monument for City," *Tampa Morning Tribune*, March 11, 1924 (the "w" was dropped in 1924 for the current city name of Bradenton).

134. "Foundation Base Has Been Completed for Confederate Statue," *Tampa Morning Tribune*, June 7, 1924.

135. "Huge Crowd Witnesses Unveiling of Monument," *Tampa Morning Tribune*, June 23, 1924; "Unveiling Exercises, Confederate Monument," Manatee County Public Library, Historical Image Digital Collection.

136. Tim W. McCann, "Confederate Monument; Council Debates Home of Marker," *Bradenton Herald*, May 11, 2003; Sara Kennedy, "Landscaping, Renovations Will Revitalize Historic Manatee Courthouse," June 17, 2013, and Sara Kennedy, "Historic Manatee County Courthouse Grounds Makeover Under Way," *Bradenton Herald*, July 16, 2013.

137. Florida Association of Museums, *Florida Civil War Heritage Trail*, 48.

138. Margary Neal Nelson, "Memories," *Putnam County Courier Journal*, October 29, 1986.

139. "Palatka Honored Its Heroes with Pretty Ceremony," *FTU*, November 12, 1924.

140. Margary Neal Nelson, "Memories—The Day They Unveiled the Monument," *Putnam County Courier Journal*, November 5, 1986; "Unveiling of [Palatka] Memorial Monument to Our Confederate Heroes [Program]," 1924, R. M. Burt Papers, folder 3, Florida Historical Society.

141. Margary Neal Nelson, "Memories—The Day They Unveiled the Monument," *Putnam County Courier Journal*, November 5, 1986; "Unveiling of [Palatka] Memorial Monument to Our Confederate Heroes [Program]," 1924, R. M. Burt Papers, folder 3, Florida Historical Society.

142. Margary Neal Nelson, "Memories," *Putnam County Courier Journal*, October 29, 1986; *The Blue and the Gray* (Mullins Company catalog).

143. Margary Neal Nelson, "Memories," *Putnam County Courier Journal*, October 29, 1986.

144. "In Putnam [County]: Horse Landing Fight Told by Lawyer," *Daytona Beach Morning Journal*, March 1, 1961; Federal Writers' Project, *Florida*, 354; "Putnam County Courthouse—Palatka, Florida," 1925, image no. RC03413, FPC.

145. "Marking the Dixie Highway," *Confederate Veteran* 34, no. 5 (May 1926): 205.

146. First planned in 1914 to boost automobile tourism between the Midwest and the South, the Dixie Highway was constructed from 1915 to 1927. The "Cotton Belt Route" was initially considered for its name, but Dixie Highway was eventually chosen to honor the "Fifty Years of Peace" since the end of the Civil War.

147. Scott and McLeod, *History of Anna Jackson Chapter*, 75–79; "Program: The Unveiling and Dedication of the Robert E. Lee Marker On-the-Dixie Highway," 1927, UDC Scrapbook, carton 12, file folder 63, FSA; "Unveiling of Lee Memorial," *Tallahassee Daily Democrat*, October 1, 1927; "Lee Tablet Dedicated on Dixie Highway," *FTU*, October 1, 1927.

148. Scott and McLeod, *History of Anna Jackson Chapter*, 75; "Program: The Unveiling and Dedication of the Robert E. Lee Marker On-the-Dixie Highway," 1927, UDC Scrapbook, carton 12, file folder 63, FSA; Green, "Florida Marker Dedication Recalled," 15; "Unveiling of a Monument Dedicated to Robert E. Lee—Tallahassee, Florida," 1927, image no. N046318, FPC; Archaeological Consultants, Inc., *Cultural Resource Assessment Survey*, 6-15 through 6-16; Gerald Ensley, "Lee Monument on Thomasville [Road] Erected in 1926," *Tallahassee Democrat*, July 24, 2013.

149. Scott and McLeod, *History of Anna Jackson Chapter*, 85, 88, 115; Green, "Florida Marker Dedication Recalled," 15; Florida Board of Parks and Historic Memorials, "Minutes, June 29, 1964, Robert E. Lee Historic Memorial," FSA; UDC, "Division News: Florida," April 1966, 13; UDC, Florida Division, *Minutes of the Seventy-First Annual Convention*, 89; "Lee Monument Found; Leon [County] to Assist Statue Restoring," April 15, 1964, "Marker Rededication for Lee Wednesday," January 16, 1966, and "Old Marker Rededicated; Happy Birthday to Robert E. Lee," January 20, 1966, all in *Tallahassee Democrat*.

150. UDC, Florida Division, Anna Jackson Chapter no. 224, Executive Board Minutes, December 13, 2003, FSA; Harrell, "The Dixie Highway," 18.

151. UDC, *Annual Convention Minutes 1925*, 194; cover of *Confederate Veteran* 34, no. 1 (January 1926); "Our 'Massachusetts Confederate,'" *Confederate Veteran* 37, no. 1 (January 1929): 5.

152. "Unveiling of a Monument Dedicated to Robert E. Lee—Tallahassee, Florida," 1927, image no. N046318, FPC; "Program; the Unveiling and Dedication of the Robert E. Lee Marker On-the-Dixie Highway," 1927, UDC Scrapbook, carton 12, file folder 63, FSA.

153. UDC, Florida Division, *Minutes of the Thirty-Third Annual Convention*, 88–89; "View of Road 15—Nassau County, Florida," May 7, 1953, image no. Dot1381, FPC.

154. Personal communications with John H. Hendricks, West Nassau Historical Society, February 6 and December 30, 2013; "Historians Search for Missing Land Markers," *Nassau County Record*, February 14, 2013.

155. "Memorial to Gen. E. M. Law," *Confederate Veteran* 40, no. 7 (July 1932): 246.

156. "Maj. Gen. Evander McIver Law, C.S.A.," *Confederate Veteran* 22, no. 4 (April 1914): 178–79; Proctor, "The South Florida Military Institute," 28–29.

157. Proctor, "The South Florida Military Institute," 29; Johnston, *Oak Hill Cemetery*, 8-5 through 8-6.

158. "Dwelling of Major General Evander McIver Law," after 1932, image no. FR0478, FPC.

159. "Site of King House [Law Home]," Bartow Historical Trail, Polk County, Florida (© 2005, Steve Rajtar), accessed April 29, 2013, http://www.reocities.com/yosemite/

rapids/8428/hikeplans/bartow/planbartow.html; "Francis S. Bartow Chapter History," Florida Society of the Military Order of the Stars and Bars, accessed November 8, 2012, http://www.mosbfl.org.

160. UDC, Florida Division, *Minutes of the Fortieth Annual Convention*, 76; UDC, Florida Division, *Florida's Confederate Monuments*, "Memorial Fountain," 54; Scott Callahan, "Working the Graveyard Shift," *Leesburg Daily Commercial*, May 18, 2012.

161. UDC, "Division News," January 2006, 30.

162. Florida Association of Museums, *Florida Civil War Heritage Trail*, 69.

163. Ibid.

164. UDC, Florida Division, *Minutes of the Forty-Second Annual Convention*, 64.

165. K. L. Cox, *Dixie's Daughters*, 154–56.

166. "Jackson Highway Named by Cone; Terminus Here," *St. Petersburg Evening Independent*, January 11, 1940.

167. "Notables Gather Here for Marker Dedication," *St. Petersburg Evening Independent*, January 22, 1940; UDC, Florida Division, *Minutes of the Forty-Fifth Annual Convention*, 54, 105.

168. UDC, Florida Division, *Minutes of the Forty-Fifth Annual Convention*, 54, 105.

169. UDC, Florida Division, *Minutes of the Forty-Fourth Annual Convention*, 20; UDC, Florida Division, *Minutes of the Forty-Fifth Annual Convention*, 105.

170. Paul Davis, "Our Town—Jackson Route," *St. Petersburg Evening Independent*, June 10, 1963; Paul Davis, "Our Town—Jackson Road Marker Reset," *St. Petersburg Evening Independent*, March 14, 1964.

171. Davis, "Our Town—Jackson Route"; Davis, "Our Town—Jackson Road Marker Reset."

172. UDC, Florida Division, *Minutes of the Forty-Fifth Annual Convention*, 53–54; UDC, Florida Division, *Minutes of the Forty-Sixth Annual Convention*, 73–74; Cowger, "Stonewall Jackson Highway," 26–27; Scott and McLeod, *History of Anna Jackson Chapter*, 165–67; UDC, "Division News," January 1994, 33–34.

173. UDC, "Gen. Stonewall Jackson Honored 1950," 10; "Stonewall Jackson Memorial Highway," in UDC, Florida Division, *Minutes of the Fifty-Fifth Annual Convention*, 56.

174. Burkhardt, *History of Thomas Benton Ellis Chapter*, 16, 19; "U.D.C. Raising Funds for Memorial Shaft," *Palm Beach Post*, May 9, 1936; UDC, Florida Division, *Minutes of the Forty-Sixth Annual Convention*, 110.

175. Knight, *Stone Mountain*, 12, 92; UDC, "Confederate Monument, West Palm Beach 1986," 12.

176. Knight, *Stone Mountain*, 12.

177. "Confederate Monument Dedicated at Ceremony in Oakdale Cemetery," *DeLand Sun News*, November 24, 1959; "Confederate Memorial Monument Dedicated," *Daytona Beach Morning Journal*, November 24, 1959; UDC, Florida Division, *Minutes of the Sixty-Fifth Annual Convention*, 35.

178. "Confederate Monument Dedicated at Ceremony in Oakdale Cemetery," *DeLand Sun News*, November 24, 1959; "Confederate Memorial Monument Dedicated," *Daytona Beach Morning Journal*, November 24, 1959.

179. "Memorial to Civil War Dead Dedicated by United Daughters of Confederacy," *Daytona Beach Morning Journal*, April 27, 1961; UDC, Florida Division, *Minutes of the Sixty-Sixth Annual Convention*, 35; UDC, "Division News," August 1961, 24.

180. "Memorial to Civil War Dead Dedicated by United Daughters of Confederacy," *Daytona Beach Morning Journal*, April 27, 1961; UDC, Florida Division, *Minutes of the Sixty-Sixth Annual Convention*, 35; UDC, "Division News," August 1961, 24.

181. Widener, *Confederate Monuments*, 32; "Memorial to Civil War Dead Dedicated by United Daughters of Confederacy," *Daytona Beach Morning Journal*, April 27, 1961; UDC, "Division News," August 1961, 24.

182. Bickel, "Lee in Florida," 59.

183. Florida Association of Museums, *Florida Civil War Heritage Trail*, 66.

184. Laetitia Ashmore Nutt Chapter #1447, Ft. Myers, Mrs. Katie Lloyd Gwynne, chapter recording secretary, to Mrs. Townes Randolph Leigh, Florida Division historian, January 29, 1927, UDC Scrapbook, carton 9, FSA; "Daughters of Confederacy Active," *Tampa Tribune*, October 23, 1915; "Haldeman Depicts a Country United in the Highest Ideals . . . at Lee Memorial Hospital Dedication at Fort Myers," *Tampa Sunday Tribune*, January 20, 1918.

185. UDC, "Division News: Florida," August 1966, 15–16; Pete Packett, "Lee Monument Dedicated after 50-Year Effort," *Fort Myers News-Press*, January 20, 1966.

186. *Robert E. Lee Memorial* [Fort Myers], sculpture by Aldo Pero, 1965, *National Art Inventories*, Smithsonian American Art Museum, accessed August 5, 2012, http://www.siris.si.edu; "Robert E. Lee Bust" at *Art Southwest Florida*, created by Tom Hall, accessed August 5, 2012, http://www.artswfl.com.

187. Tammy Ayer, "Refurbished Lee Bust Returns," *Fort Myers News-Press*, December 4, 2003; "Lee Statue Gets New Coat of Paint," *Fort Myers News-Press*, August 20, 2007; "Downtown Statue Gets Needed Repairs," WINK-TV, February 12, 2012, accessed April 14, 2012, http://www.winknews.com.

188. "Reunions," Center for Civil War Research, University of Mississippi, accessed October 18, 2012, http://www.civilwarcenter.olemiss.edu/reunions.html; "Confederate Veterans Reunited for Group Portrait—Franklin County, Florida," ca. 1900, image no. RC05122, "Reunited Confederate Veterans Near East Front of Capitol–Tallahassee, Florida," ca. 1902, image no. RC11577, "Confederate Veterans Reunited for Group Portrait–Crawfordville, Florida," 1904, image no. RC05118B, "Reunion Parade of Confederate Veterans—Lakeland, Florida," 1914, image no. RC11579, "Civil War Veterans Reunion on August 31, 1917—Madison, Florida," 1917, image no. MA0292, "United Confederate Veterans' Reunion—Marianna, Florida," 1927, image no. N046321, "Confederate Veterans Reunited for Group Portrait—Monticello, Florida, 1910s, image no. RC11564, "Civil War Veteran Reunion at Forty Oaks," 1890s, image no. RC11549, and "Confederate Veterans Reunion—Wakulla County, Florida," 1900s, image no. RC04405, all in FPC.

189. "News from All Parts of Florida," *Gainesville Daily Sun*, October 22, 1909.

190. Musgrove, *Images of America*, 30–31; "State Convention of the United Confederate Veterans, 1909—Live Oak, Florida," 1909, image no. N029614, "Confederate Veterans Reunited for Group Portrait," 1909, image no. RC05119, and "Street Scene

during a United Confederate Veterans Convention—Live Oak, Florida," 1909, image no. RC18247, FPC.

191. "United Confederate Veterans on Kentucky Avenue—Lakeland, Florida," 1914, image no. RC08021, and "Confederate Veterans Reunion—Lakeland, Florida," 1914, image no. RC11580, FPC.

192. "Florida Confederate Reunion," *Confederate Veteran* 13, no. 1 (January 1905): 10.

193. "Among the Dealers" (1910), 9.

194. Allardice, *More Generals in Gray*, 78.

195. "Monument for Veterans," November 22, 1912, "A Worthy Cause," November 26, 1912, "For the Monument," December 1, 1912, "Bond of Officials Approved by Board," December 4, 1912, "Selection of a City Hall Site Goes Over," December 18, 1912, "Entertainment for Gen. Lee's Birthday," January 11, 1913, and "Asks for Promised Money," April 23, 1913, all in *Tampa Morning Tribune*.

196. "U.C.V. Monument Is Ready to Be Unveiled," May 13, 1913, "Monument to Be Unveiled Today," May 18, 1913, and "Woodlawn Monument Unveiled Yesterday," May 19, 1913, all in *Tampa Morning Tribune*.

197. "A Worthy Cause," November 26, 1912, "Monument to Be Unveiled Today," May 18, 1913, "Woodlawn Monument Unveiled Yesterday," May 19, 1913, and "Pay Homage to Dead Comrades," April 27, 1929, all in *Tampa Morning Tribune*.

198. "Benefit at Greeson's for Confederate Vets," *Tampa Morning Tribune*, June 29, 1913.

199. Mills, "Gratitude and Gender Wars."

200. Ibid.

201. "Florida Asks Aid to Build Woman's Monument," *Confederate Veteran* 18, no. 11 (November 1910): 519; "Veterans Working Hard for Their Monument to Honor Confederate Women of Florida," *Miami Metropolis*, October 18, 1911; Florida Legislature, "Act to Make Available an Appropriation of Fifteen Thousand Dollars," *Regular Session 1911*, 54–55.

202. Florida Legislature, "Act to Aid the Florida Division of Confederate Veterans," *Laws of the State of Florida . . . Regular Session 1913*, 104–5; Florida Legislature, "Act to Make an Appropriation for the Putting and Keeping in Order of the Grounds," *Regular Session 1915*, 334–37; "From the Tool Chest," 29; "Business Brevities," 146.

203. "Great Tribute to Women of Fla. Planned," February 29, 1912, and "Monument to Women of Confederacy Planned," March 24, 1912, *FTU*; "McNeel Marble Co. Awarded $24,000 Monument Contract," *Marietta (Ga.) Journal and Courier*, August 8, 1913; "The Woman's Monument in Florida," *Confederate Veteran* 23, no. 4 (April 1915): 147; *Encyclopedia Americana*, 1922 ed., s.v. "Newman, Allan [*sic*] George"; Dearinger, *Paintings and Sculpture*, 368.

204. Mitchell, *Art of the Bronze Founder*, 17.

205. "State News Notes," *Miami Herald*, May 1, 1913; "Dedication in May," *Tampa Morning Tribune*, March 15, 1914; "Dignan Park Changed to Confederate Park," October 10, 1914, and "Monument to the Women of the Confederacy Now Ready to Be Unveiled in Confederate Park," April 2, 1915, *FTU*.

206. "Great Throng to Attend the Unveiling of Memorial to Women of the Confed-

eracy" and "Tuesday Declared Holiday by Mayor Bowden Yesterday," October 24, 1915, "All Arrangements Made to Unveil Monument to Women of Confederacy," October 25, 1915, "Unveiling of Memorial to Women of the Confederacy in Confederate Park 3 P.M.," October 26, 1915, and "Flags of Re-United Nation about Memorial Figure Will Remind All of Past Glories," October 27, 1915, all in *FTU*; H. Holt, "From State to State: Florida," 301.

207. "Flags of Re-United Nation about Memorial Figure Will Remind All of Past Glories" and "Unveiling of Memorial to Women of the Confederacy," *FTU*, October 27, 1915; "Senator Fletcher Delivers Fine Address at Unveiling," *Miami Herald*, October 27, 1915; "Women of the Confederacy Are Honored in Unveiling of Tribute of Devotion," *Manatee River Journal* (Bradenton), October 28, 1915.

208. *Florida's Tribute to the Women of the Confederacy*, sculpture by Allen George Newman, 1914, *National Art Inventories*, Smithsonian American Art Museum, accessed March 9, 2012, http://www.siris.si.edu; "Among the Dealers" (1912), 5.

209. "Florida Monument to Confederate Women," *Confederate Veteran* 20, no. 5 (May 1912): 203.

210. Mills, "Gratitude and Gender Wars," 196.

211. "Florida Monument to Confederate Women," 203.

212. Parkinson, "Florida's Tribute," 21.

213. "Proposed Monuments" (1912), 10.

214. "Confederate Vets' Park Rites Mark Lundy's Birth," *St. Petersburg Independent*, January 19, 1958; "Confederate Park Opened with Impressive Ceremony," *Okaloosa News Journal*, January 23, 1958.

215. Ann Spann, "Memorial Dedicated 38 Years Ago," *Okaloosa County Citizen Review*, February 29, 1996; Marvel, "The Great Imposters," 32–33; Serrano, *Last of the Blue and Gray*, 126–33.

216. B. S. Curenton and Patten, *Crestview*, 432.

217. "City Keeps Confederate Flag Flying," *Ocala Star-Banner*, February 28, 1996; Isaac Sabetal, "Confederate Flag Raises Controversy," *Northwest Florida Daily News*, June 1, 2002; Brian Hughes, "New Flag Flying at Confederate Park," *Northwest Florida Daily News*, November 7, 2010; Matthew Brown, "Crestview Council Seeks Public Input on Confederate Flag," *Crestview News Bulletin*, September 11, 2013; Brian Hughes, "Council Adjourns without Action on Lundy Memorial Flag Issue," *Crestview News Bulletin*, November 16, 2013.

Chapter 3. Remembering the Union Soldier and Sailor

1. Dearing, *Veterans in Politics*, 70.
2. Ibid., 69–71.
3. Ibid., 58.
4. Ibid., 68–69.
5. Ibid., 308–51.
6. Gannon, *The Won Cause*, 21.
7. Ibid., 15.

8. "Reunions," Center for Civil War Research, University of Mississippi, accessed October 18, 2012, http://www.civilwarcenter.olemiss.edu/reunions.html.

9. "History," Ladies of the Grand Army of the Republic, accessed August 1, 2013, http://suvcw.org/LGAR/History.html; "Guide to the Woman's Relief Corps," Northwest Digital Archives, accessed October 20, 2012, http://nwda.orbiscascade.org/ark:/80444/xv69430; Stahura and Gibson, *History of Sons of Union Veterans of the Civil War*, 10–11 and 17; "About Us," Daughters of Union Veterans of the Civil War, 1861–1865, accessed August 1, 2013, http://www.duvcw.org/index.php/about-us.

10. Beck and Lees, "U.S. Sanitary Commission Camp Inspections."

11. "Resident Population and Apportionment of the U.S. House of Representatives—Florida," U.S. Census Bureau, accessed November 14, 2012, http://www.census.gov/dmd/www/resapport/states/florida.pdf.

12. Walters, "Union Colony," 1–12.

13. "GAR Florida Research," Sons of Union Veterans of the Civil War, Department of Florida, accessed October 20, 2012, http://www.dofsuvcw.org/garfloridaresearch.html.

14. Gannon, *The Won Cause*, 202.

15. "GAR Florida Research," Sons of Union Veterans of the Civil War, Department of Florida, accessed October 20, 2012, http://www.dofsuvcw.org/garfloridaresearch.html.

16. Walters, "Union Colony," 74.

17. Ibid., 38–40.

18. "Philander H. Fitzgerald," City of Fitzgerald, accessed October 20, 2012, http://fitzgeraldga.org/index.php?option=com_content&task=view&id=53&Itemid=104.

19. Walters, "Union Colony," 39–43.

20. "Zephyrhills," History of Pasco County, accessed October 20, 2012, http://www.fivay.org/zephyrhills.html.

21. Florida Secretary of State, *Report 1913*, 528.

22. "GAR Florida Research," Sons of Union Veterans of the Civil War, Department of Florida, accessed October 20, 2012, http://www.dofsuvcw.org/garfloridaresearch.html.

23. Walters, "Union Colony," 63–70.

24. Florida Association of Museums, *Florida Civil War Heritage Trail*, 57; Merritt, "St. Cloud," 26–27.

25. "GAR Florida Research," Sons of Union Veterans of the Civil War, Department of Florida, accessed October 20, 2012, http://www.dofsuvcw.org/garfloridaresearch.html.

26. Walters, "Union Colony," 45–46; Bell, "Florida's Monument"; Harold Bell, "Memorial to Union Soldiers Provides Reminder of Lynn Haven's Birthright," *FTU*, March 11, 1962; Ann Vick, "In Lynn Haven, a Curious Memorial," *Panama City News-Herald*, May 28, 1972.

27. Walters, "Union Colony," 92–97.

28. Ibid., 192–93.

29. "GAR Florida Research," Sons of Union Veterans of the Civil War, Department of Florida, accessed October 20, 2012, http://www.dofsuvcw.org/garfloridaresearch.html.

30. Dearing, *Veterans in Politics*, 272.

31. "The Memorial Services," *FTU*, May 25, 1891; Grand Army of the Republic, *Journal of the Twenty-Sixth National Encampment*, 201; Johnston, *Evergreen Cemetery*, 7-9 through 7-10 and 8-9; Grissom, *Zinc Sculpture*, 511.

32. "Rev. Samuel D. Paine," *National Tribune*, February 18, 1892; "To Raise a G.A.R. Monument in the South," *New York Daily Tribune*, July 15, 1889.

33. "The Dedication; Pensacola's Confederate Monument Given to History," *Pensacola Daily News*, June 18, 1891.

34. "Advertisements for Monumental Bronze Company," Pennsylvania USGenWeb Archives, accessed January 13, 2014, http://www.usgwarchives.net/pa/1pa/tscarvers/monumental-bronze/monumental-bronze/advertisements.htm.

35. Ibid.; Grissom, *Zinc Sculpture*, 509–11.

36. "Historic Greenwood Cemetery; History Is Buried Here," Greenwood Cemetery, St. Petersburg, accessed October 29, 2012, http://www.historicgreenwood.com/pages/exhibit.html.

37. See chapter 2 for information regarding the joint dedication ceremony.

38. "Zephaniah Phillips," Anne Healy's Genealogy, accessed March 18, 2012, http://www.annefield.net/zephaniahphillips2.htm; "Historic Greenwood Cemetery; History Is Buried Here," Greenwood Cemetery, St. Petersburg, accessed October 29, 2012, http://www.historicgreenwood.com/pages/exhibit.html. In addition to his service in the Twentieth Illinois Infantry, as noted on his tombstone, Phillips also served in the First Illinois Cavalry, the Fifty-Sixth Illinois Infantry, and the U.S. Navy during the Civil War (see cited Healy Web site earlier in this note).

39. Woman's Relief Corps, *Journal of the Twentieth National Convention*, 202; St. Petersburg Museum of History, Historic Photo Archives, "Greenwood Cemetery—Dedication of a Civil War Memorial," 1900.

40. Grand Army of the Republic, *Journal of the Forty-Fifth National Encampment*, 110.

41. Hinder and Stokes, *Greenwood Cemetery*, 8-1 through 8-2.

42. "Once Again the Grand Army Honors Its Fallen Heroes," *St. Cloud Tribune*, May 31, 1917.

43. "Glory Has No Grave, Fifty-First Annual Observance of Memorial Day in Saint Cloud, Program at City Park," *St. Cloud Tribune*, June 5, 1919.

44. "Regular Meeting of L. L. Mitchell W.R.C.," July 1, 1915, "Regular Meeting of L. L. Mitchell Corps," July 15, 1915, "Business Meeting of Woman's Relief Corps," August 5, 1915," and "Grand Army and Navy Union on Memorial Day Did Honor to Soldier and Sailor Dead," June 1, 1916, all in *St. Cloud Tribune*; City of St Cloud, "City Unveils Unknown Soldier Monument," 1.

45. Walters, "Union Colony," 193; Grissom, *Zinc Sculpture*, 653; "The Lynn Haven Monument," City of Lynn Haven, accessed March 27, 2011, http://cityoflynnhaven.com/history/memorial.htm.

46. Weber, "Grand Army of the Republic Monument," 178; "Dedication of Monument," *Panama City Pilot*, February 17, 1921; "A Splendid Monument to Civil War Veterans in Florida," *Bay County Beacon-Tribune*, April 12, 1921.

47. Walters, "Union Colony," 195; Bell, "Florida's Monument"; Harold Bell, "Memo-

rial to Union Soldiers Provides Reminder of Lynn Haven's Birthright," *FTU*, March 11, 1962; Ann Vick, "In Lynn Haven, a Curious Memorial," *Panama City News-Herald*, May 28, 1972.

48. A photo copy of the "Believe It or Not" newspaper panel featuring the Lynn Haven monument is held in the Bay County Library Local History Collection, but the date of publication is not recorded. We were unable to determine a date of publication, but reference to this panel in the May 28, 1972, *Panama City News-Herald* places it prior to that date.

49. "Dedication of Monument," *Panama City Pilot*, February 17, 1921.

50. "A Splendid Monument to Civil War Veterans in Florida," *Bay County Beacon-Tribune*, April 12, 1921.

51. Harold Bell, "Lynn Haven Claims Only Monument to Union Veterans," *Pensacola News Journal*, February 11, 1962.

52. The 1866 Union monument in Key West was funded with the sale of government property, and other Union monuments are located in cemeteries.

53. Baruch and Beckman, *Civil War Union Monuments*.

54. Ann Vick, "In Lynn Haven, a Curious Memorial," *Panama City News-Herald*, May 28, 1972; Ludelle Brannon, "Monument Recognized in New Dedication Ceremony," *Panama City News-Herald*, May 15, 1994; Bell, "Florida's Monument."

55. Ann Vick "In Lynn Haven, a Curious Memorial," *Panama City News-Herald*, May 28, 1972.

56. "Grant Permit for Monument with Conditions," *Tampa Morning Tribune*, May 17, 1922.

57. "Memorial Shaft of G.A.R. Is Unveiled," *Tampa Morning Tribune*, February 13, 1924.

58. Dedication ceremony brochure "G.A.R. Monument Dedicated April, 12, 1939, Miami, Florida," author's collection; Writers' Program of the WPA, *Miami and Dade County*, 70.

59. Dedication ceremony brochure "G.A.R. Monument Dedicated April, 12, 1939, Miami, Florida," author's collection; "Grand Army of Republic Dedicates Monument" and "Annual G.A.R. Session Nears End Here Today," *Miami Daily News*, April 13, 1939.

60. Dedication ceremony brochure "G.A.R. Monument Dedicated April, 12, 1939, Miami, Florida," author's collection.

61. We are uncertain of the reason for this change in plans.

CHAPTER 4. REMEMBERING HALLOWED GROUND

1. Holbrook, *Narrative*, 119.

2. These camps are an unrecognized memorial to the sacrifice of the private soldier trying to survive far from hearth and home. The story of this life that could be pieced together by thoughtful study by archaeologists is in too many places being systematically silenced by thoughtless turning of the soil in search of a few relics.

3. Sellars, "Pilgrim Places," 42–44.

4. Zipf, "Marking Union Victory," 27–28.

5. Sellars, "Pilgrim Places," 35.

6. Zipf, "Marking Union Victory," 27–31.

7. K. L. Cox, "The Confederate Monument at Arlington," 149–50.

8. Florida Association of Museums, *Florida Civil War Heritage Trail*, 39–40; Nulty, *Confederate Florida*. The battle that occurred here in February 1864 was referred to in reports by the Union as the Battle of Olustee and by the Confederacy as the Battle of Ocean Pond. By the time of the battle's commemoration, it was generally known as the Battle of Olustee by the public.

9. Sam Hodges, "Yankee Tribute Stalled; Donations Scarce in Enemy Territory," *Orlando Sentinel*, September 23, 1989; personal communications with Jeff Grzelak, Seventh Connecticut Infantry Reenactment Group, April 25, May 9, and December 2, 2013.

10. "Cathey House Hotel—Lake City, Florida," 1890s, image no. RC06009, FPC.

11. Thompson, "U.D.C. Work in Florida," 442; "To Our Civil War Heroes; Program Dedicating Monument to Memory of Olustee Dead," *Lake City Citizen-Reporter*, January 4, 1901; "The Olustee Monument," *Florida Index* (Lake City), January 4, 1901.

12. "Macon Furnishes Monument," *Macon (Ga.) Telegraph*, January 1, 1901.

13. "History of Government Furnished Headstones and Markers," U.S. Department of Veterans Affairs, National Cemetery Administration, accessed July 17, 2013, http://www.cem.va.gov/cem/history/hmhist.asp.

14. Castile and Rosenblatt, "Florida Sentinel," 24; Lancaster, *Early Years*, 60; Florida Legislature, "Act to Make an Appropriation in Aid of a Monument Commemorative of the Battle of Olustee," *Regular Session 1899*, 213–14.

15. "Ladies Displeased at Clark; Daughters of Confederacy Will Work against a Candidate," *Atlanta Constitution*, January 28, 1900.

16. Ibid.; "Olustee in the Campaign," *Bradford County Telegraph*, February 16, 1900.

17. Florida Legislature, "Act to Amend Section 1 of an Act," *Regular Session 1901*, 207–8; "The Olustee Monument," *Weekly True Democrat* (Tallahassee), March 2, 1906.

18. Hunt, "Proposed Monuments and Monumental Views," 20; Florida Division of Elections, carton 46, Executive Office Appointments, Olustee Monument Commission, August 14, 1903, June 30, 1904, FSA; Florida Secretary of State, "Commissioners to Aid in the Erection of Confederate Monument at Olustee," in *Report 1904*, 13, *Report 1906*, 13, *Report 1909*, 10, *Report 1911*, 13, and *Report 1913*, 14.

19. "The Olustee Monument," *Live Oak Daily Democrat*, May 4, 1907; "Differ as to Site of Olustee Monument," May 14, 1907, "Put the Olustee Monument at Olustee," May 21, 1907, and "Olustee Monument Bill," May 21, 1907, all in *Morning Sun* (Tallahassee); "Third Day [Florida UDC Convention]," *Pensacola Journal*, June 2, 1907; "The Olustee Monument," *Ocala Evening Star*, July 22, 1907; Lancaster, *Early Years*, 61.

20. Florida Department of Environmental Protection, *Olustee Battlefield Unit Management Plan*, A1-1.

21. "Olustee Monument Soon Ready to Dedicate," August 15, 1911, "Monument Unveiling Is Postponed," February 22, 1912, and "State News Notes," September 19, 1912, all in *Miami Herald*; "Unveiling of Olustee Monument Postponed," February 11, 1912, "Veterans Will Meet at Lake City Oct. 23," September 26, 1912, "Floridian Will Unveil Monument at Olustee," October 15, 1912, and "Low Excursion Rates Via Seaboard

[Railroad]," October 22, 1912, all in *Tampa Morning Tribune*; "Veterans Ready to Unveil Handsome Olustee Monument," *FTU*, October 23, 1912.

22. "Handsome Olustee Monument Unveiled and Turned Over to State of Florida," *FTU*, October 24, 1912.

23. "Graven in Granite," October 11, 1909, *Ocala Evening Star*; "Bartow Social Notes, Father Ryan Chapter UDC," *Tampa Morning Tribune*, June 3, 1912.

24. Florida Legislature, "Act to Make an Appropriation for the Putting and Keeping in Order of the Grounds," *Regular Session 1915*, 51; "Report of Custodian of Olustee Monument," *Tampa Sunday Tribune*, August 5, 1917.

25. UDC, Florida Division, *Minutes of the Ninety-Ninth Annual Convention, 1994*, 237; UDC, "Division News: Florida 1995," 37.

26. Florida Association of Museums, *Florida Civil War Heritage Trail*, 25.

27. Florida Legislature, "Act to Make an Appropriation for a Suitable Monument," *Regular Session 1927*, 107–8; "Confederate Monument Commission," Florida Secretary of State, *Report 1929*, 29; "Commission Named to Honor Veterans, State to Raise Memorial to Confederate Soldiers," June 29, 1927, and "Committee Working," *Tampa Morning Tribune*, July 26, 1927.

28. "Governor to Unveil Lake City Monument," *Tampa Sunday Tribune*, December 25, 1927; "Olustee Monument to Be Unveiled on January 18," *Union County Times*, January 13, 1928; O. S. Wodrich, "Summerall and Martin Are Guests at Lake City, High Officials Present for Unveiling of Olustee Battle Monument," *FTU*, January 19, 1928; "Battle of Olustee Monument Unveiled Yesterday at Lake City," *Tallahassee Daily Democrat*, January 19, 1928; "Thousands Participate in City's History-Making Event Here 18th" and "Banquet at the Blanche Hotel Notable Event," *Lake City Reporter*, January 20, 1928; "Gen. Summerall Welcomed Home, Unveils Monument to Confederate Dead at Lake City," *Tampa Morning Tribune*, January 20, 1928.

29. O. S. Wodrich, "Summerall and Martin Are Guests at Lake City, High Officials Present for Unveiling of Olustee Battle Monument," *FTU*, January 19, 1928; "Colonel Thomas Jefferson Appleyard and Florida Governor John Martin," 1928, image no. N046311, and "Memorial of the Civil War Battle of Olustee—Lake City, Florida," 1960, image no. RC15636, FPC.

30. UDC, Florida Division, *Minutes of the Forty-First Annual Convention*, 39.

31. UDC, Florida Division, *Minutes of the Fifty-Fifth Annual Convention*, 48; "UDC Honors Gen. Finegan with Marker," *FTU*, March 6, 1951; Shepherd, "Florida Division Unveils Marker," 19, 23, 26.

32. Florida Association of Museums, *Florida Civil War Heritage Trail*, 39; Williams, "The Battle of Olustee Forever Remembered," 25.

33. Florida Association of Museums, *Florida Civil War Heritage Trail*, 17; D. Cox, *The Battle of Marianna*.

34. Towns, "Honoring the Confederacy," 211; UDC, Florida Division, "Report of Marianna Monument Committee," *Minutes of the Twenty-Sixth Annual Convention*, 89–91; Florida Legislature, "Act Making an Appropriation to Assist in the Erection of a Monument," *Regular Session 1921*, 163–64; "U.D.C. [to] Unveil Monument," October 11, 1921, and "To Unveil Confederate Monument at Marianna," October 21, 1921, *Miami*

Herald; "Big Unveiling at Marianna on Nov. 2nd," *Tallahassee Daily Democrat*, October 21, 1921.

35. Towns, "Honoring the Confederacy," 211; "The Confederate Monument at Marianna, Fla.," *Confederate Veteran* 30, no. 1 (January 1922): 5; "Shaft to Heroes of 1864 Unveiled," *Miami Herald*, November 3, 1921; "New Monument Is Dedicated," *Tampa Morning Tribune*, November 3, 1921.

36. "In Memoriam; the McNeel Marble Company," *Confederate Veteran* 29, no. 8 (August 1921): 320.

37. Florida Association of Museums, *Florida Civil War Heritage Trail*, 34; D. Cox, *The Battle of Natural Bridge*.

38. Scott and McLeod, *History of Anna Jackson Chapter*, 71, 75; "Contract for a Monument Is Let by Commission," *Tallahassee Daily Democrat*, October 21, 1921.

39. Suber and Fletcher, *Fletcher Family*, 245–46; "The Monument," Natural Bridge Historical Society, accessed July 24, 2011, http://www.nbhscso.com/gpage.html; Arbuthnot, Marks, and Cripps, *Archaeological and Historical Investigation*, 5-17 through 5-18; "Portrait of Confederate Soldier John B. Fletcher—Tallahassee, Florida," ca. 1910, image no. PR10759, "Helen McKeown Beside a Monument, Before Covering with Mortar—Natural Bridge Battlefield, Florida," ca. 1919, image no. PR10757, "Monuments on the Road to Natural Bridge—Woodville Region, Florida," 1920s, image no. PR15001, and "View Looking Down the Public Road Between the Monuments at Natural Bridge Battlefield Historic State Park—Leon County Florida," 1956, image no. RC20291C, all in FPC.

40. "Monument Erected at Natural Bridge to Memory of Tallahassee Defenders," *Tallahassee Daily Democrat*, July 7, 1919.

41. "To Dedicate Monument on 55th Anniversary Battle [of] Natural Bridge," February 13, 1920, and "[To] Celebrate Battle of Natural Bridge, Second Monument Is Unveiled," March 11, 1920, *Tampa Morning Tribune*; Scott and McLeod, *History of Anna Jackson Chapter*, 22.

42. Florida Legislature, "Act to Make an Appropriation to Assist in the Erection of a Monument and Establishing a Park," *Regular Session 1921*, 142–43.

43. "Memorial Day Exercises, April 26, 1922, Unveiling of Monument at Natural Bridge," Senator William C. Hodges Papers, Goodwood Museum and Gardens, Tallahassee; "Confederate Monument Unveiled to Heroes at Natural Bridge," *Tallahassee Daily Democrat*, April 27, 1922; "State Honors Heroes of War, Monument to Defenders of Natural Bridge, Fla., Is Unveiled," *St. Petersburg Times*, April 27, 1922; "Dedication of the Natural Bridge Memorial—Natural Bridge Battlefield, Florida," 1922, image no. PR10756, FPC.

44. "Select Monument Site," October 20, 1921, and "Contract for a Monument Is Let by Commission," October 21, 1921, *Tallahassee Daily Democrat*.

45. Florida Secretary of State, "Secretary Detzner Announces Restoration of Historic Natural Bridge Monument Eagle," March 2, 2012; "Natural Bridge's Copper Eagle to Be Restored," *Tallahassee Democrat*, March 3, 2012.

46. "Entrance to Natural Bridge Battlefield Historic State Park—Woodville, Florida," 1959, image no. FPS00872, FPC; Hallie Boyles, "99 Years Ago: Clash at Natural Bridge

Kept Capital Confederate," *Tallahassee Democrat*, March 1, 1964. We were unable to locate any primary source documents detailing exactly when and why the two 1919 Fletcher pillar monuments were dismantled, although one secondary source (Arbuthnot, Marks, and Cripps, *Archaeological and Historical Investigation*, 6-5) indicates that they were not totally removed until the 1970s.

47. "Natural Bridge Battlefield Historic State Park Monument in Leon County, Florida," 1967, image no. RP06048, FPC; Arbuthnot, Marks, and Cripps, *Archaeological and Historical Investigation*, 6-5, 6-6.

48. "Battle of Natural Bridge Centennial Is Observed," March 8, 1965, *Tallahassee Democrat*; Arbuthnot, Marks, and Cripps, *Archaeological and Historical Investigation*, 5-17, 6-5.

49. Florida Association of Museums, *Florida Civil War Heritage Trail*, 35.

50. Silpa, "Historical Archaeology Research Designs for Gamble Plantation," 29–30; Florida Department of Environmental Protection, *Gamble Plantation Unit Management Plan*, 17, A1-1.

51. Silpa, "Historical Archaeology Research Designs for Gamble Plantation," 30.

52. "Shaft to Be Unveiled Tomorrow, Tribute to 117 of Nation's Dead," *Key West Citizen*, November 10, 1930; State of New York, Report of the New York Monuments Commission, 1930, 49–50.

53. State of New York, *Legislative Documents 1921*, 197; Lord, Correspondence, "New York Assemblyman Bert Lord to Edward Griffin, Counsel to the Governor of New York, December 12, 1927"; State of New York, Executive Department, New York Monuments Commission, "For the Acquisition at Key West," *Laws*, 1928, 1132.

54. "New York's $12,000 Key West Memorial," November 23, 1928, and "Shaft to Be Unveiled Tomorrow, Tribute to 117 of Nation's Dead," November 10, 1930, *Key West Citizen*; "Site Is Chosen for New York's War Monument," *Miami Daily News*, February 17, 1929; "Charles Kappes Will Build New York Monument at Key West, Florida," *Gettysburg Compiler*, March 9, 1929; State of New York, Report of the New York Monuments Commission, 1930, 51; Lord, Correspondence, "Charles A. Shaw, Chairman of New York Monuments Commission to New York Assemblyman Bert Lord, June 3, 1929, September 26, 1929, and November 3, 1929."

55. "Immense Throng Sees New York Monument to Soldiers Unveiled," *Key West Citizen*, November 11, 1930.

56. Ibid.; "Charles A. Shaw Pays Tribute to New York Heroes Buried Here" and "Men Who Died Here Unsung Heroes of War, Byrne Asserts," *Key West Citizen*, November 11, 1930; "New York Monument Dedicated in Florida," *New York Times*, November 12, 1930; State of New York, Report of the New York Monuments Commission, 1930, 51–53.

57. Schmidt and Schmidt, "Key West Post Cemetery," 1.

58. Florida Association of Museums, *Florida Civil War Heritage Trail*, 41.

59. Federal Writers' Project, *Florida*, 352; "Old Burial Site Offers Few Clues after Years of Obscurity," *FTU*, February 2, 1958; Debra Buehn, "Respectability after Disrepair for Restored Civil War–Era Cemetery in Green Cove Springs," *FTU*, February 24, 2011; Spencer, *They Are Here*, 221.

60. "Answer to Hitler," December 11, 1941, and "Civil War Leader Escaped through Sarasota," *Sarasota Herald-Tribune*, June 26, 2011; "Answer to Hitler," *Miami Daily News*, November 12, 1941; "Confederate Statesman [to Be] Honored by Dedication," *St. Petersburg Times*, January 2, 1942.

61. "Holland and Peterson Will Join in Tribute to Benjamin," January 18, 1942, "Benjamin Relative to Join in Dedication Ceremonies," January 21, 1942, and "Governor Holland Dedicates Benjamin Marker Here to a 'Great American,'" January 23, 1942, all in *Sarasota Herald-Tribune*.

62. "Benjamin Relative to Join in Dedication Ceremonies," January 21, 1942, "Governor Holland Dedicates Benjamin Marker Here to a 'Great American,'" January 23, 1942, and "Message Sent by Churchill to Ceremony," January 23, 1942, all in *Sarasota Herald-Tribune*.

63. Elmo Scott Watson, "History in the News—Honors to an Exile," *Scandia (Kans.) Journal*, January 15, 1942.

64. "Confederate Memorial Dedication Set Jan. 25," January 16, 1955, and "'Mother of Good Roads' Marks 81st Birthday," January 13, 1957, *Sarasota Herald-Tribune*.

65. Florida Association of Museums, *Florida Civil War Heritage Trail*, 45.

66. UDC, Florida Division, *Minutes of the Fifty-Fifth Annual Convention*, 47–48; Shepherd, "Marker Erected at Historic Florida Fort," 6, 24; Waber, *Evaluation of Yellow Bluff Fort*, 4–6; Florida Department of Environmental Protection, *Yellow Bluff Fort Unit Management Plan*, A1-1.

67. The UDC chapters listed on the monument are Martha Reid Chapter, Jacksonville Chapter, Annie Perdue Sebring Chapter, Alexander H. Stephens Chapter, Mary Holland McLeary Chapter, and Robert E. Lee Chapter.

68. Ray Huard, "Residents Fight to Save Yellow Bluff Fort Site," *Florida Times-Union and Journal* (Jacksonville), January 10, 1981.

69. In 1998 a monument sponsored by the City of Fort Myers was dedicated to the U.S. Colored Troops who fought at the 1865 Battle of Fort Myers; see chapter 5.

70. Randall and Donald, *Civil War and Reconstruction*, 5.

71. Waters and Edmonds, *A Small but Spartan Band*.

72. Sheppard, *By the Noble Daring of Her Sons*.

73. Ibid., 207–11.

74. Jacobson, *McGavock Confederate Cemetery*, 23–32.

75. "McGavock Confederate Cemetery," *Confederate Veteran* 7, no. 1 (January 1899): 26; Jacobson, *McGavock Confederate Cemetery*, 32–33; Emerson, *Historic Southern Monuments*, 305–7.

76. Jacobson, *McGavock Confederate Cemetery*, 38; Bassett, "McGavock Confederate Cemetery," 16; "History," McGavock Confederate Cemetery, accessed March 2, 2013, http://www.mcgavockcemetery.org.

77. S. M. Turner, "Rearguard of the Confederacy," 5–37; Waters and Edmonds, *A Small but Spartan Band*, 12–28.

78. S. M. Turner, "Rearguard of the Confederacy," 35–58; Waters and Edmonds, *A Small but Spartan Band*, 29–40.

79. Confederated Southern Memorial Association, *History of the Confederated Memo-*

rial Associations, 316–17; Linda Wheeler, "Confederate Cemetery Preserves Memories of the Fallen," *Washington Post*, January 18, 2007.

80. Jones, "Editorial Paragraphs," 349–52.

81. "A Rouss Subscription, to Winchester Monument to Florida Confederate Dead," July 24, 1901, and "Michael Bassett Dead [Winchester, Va., News]," February 5, 1902, *Richmond Dispatch*; "Tennessee and Florida Monuments," *Richmond Times*, June 3, 1902.

82. "Confederate Memorials Unveiled in Winchester," *Richmond Dispatch*, June 7, 1902.

83. Waters and Edmonds, *A Small but Spartan Band*, 29–30.

84. Janney, *Burying the Dead*, 1; Sedore, *Virginia's Confederate Monuments*, 108.

85. Alexander, "Report of Bull Run Monument," 232–33; "Confederate Monument," August 28, 1904, and "Monument Unveiled," September 1, 1904, *Richmond Times-Dispatch*.

86. "History and Culture," Chickamauga and Chattanooga National Military Park, accessed November 18, 2012, http://www.nps.gov/chch/historyculture/index.htm.

87. Sheppard, *By the Noble Daring of Her Sons*, 74–91.

88. Ibid.

89. Florida Legislature, "Act to Provide for a Monument to Be Erected on the Battlefield of Chickamauga," *Regular Session 1907*, 223–24; Florida Secretary of State, *Report 1909*, 11, *Report 1911*, 14, *Report 1913*, 14, and *Report 1915*, 17; "Florida to Be Represented by Monument at Chickamauga," May 26, 1912, and "State News Notes," November 8, 1912, *Miami Herald*; "Florida's Dead at Chickamauga," *Tampa Morning Tribune*, October 27, 1912; U.S. War Department, *Annual Reports 1913*, 178.

90. Florida Legislature, "Act to Make Available an Appropriation of Fifteen Thousand Dollars," *Regular Session 1911*, 56.

91. *Florida State Monument* [Chickamauga], sculpture by L. Milinn [*sic*], 1912–1913, *National Art Inventories*, Smithsonian American Art Museum, accessed March 9, 2012, http://www.siris.si.edu; Defebaugh, "New Chattanooga Monuments," 28; "$15,000 Monument to Be Built by McNeel," *Marietta (Ga.) Journal and Courier*, June 14, 1912; "Weather Man Is Good to Veterans, Monuments Are Dedicated," *St. Petersburg Evening Independent*, May 28, 1913; "Dead Heroes Honored by Two States," *San Antonio Light*, May 28, 1913.

92. Parkes, *Sculpture of To-Day*, 205; Levy, "Milione, Louis," 556.

93. "Among the Dealers" (1912), 5.

94. Sedore, *Virginia's Confederate Monuments*, 235.

95. Waters and Edmonds, *A Small but Spartan Band*, 139–68.

96. "Ladies' Memorial Association of Petersburg," *Richmond Times-Dispatch*, June 30, 1912; "Soldiers' Monument," *Richmond Dispatch*, June 8, 1890; Confederated Southern Memorial Association, *History of the Confederated Memorial Associations*, 288–90; Sedore, *Virginia's Confederate Monuments*, 235–36; Neville, *Blandford Cemetery*, 8-17 through 8-18.

97. Neville, *Blandford Cemetery*, 8-18; Sedore, *Virginia's Confederate Monuments*, 236; Robarts, "Florida Soldiers Buried at Blandford Cemetery, Virginia," 106.

98. "Plea for Old Blandford Church," *Confederate Veteran* 15, no. 12 (December 1907):

553; Confederated Southern Memorial Association, *History of the Confederated Memorial Associations*, 291; Janney, *Burying the Dead*, 183–88.

99. "Florida Window Unveiling Monday," *Richmond Times-Dispatch*, June 23, 1912; "Pensacola (Fla.) Memorial Association; Florida Window Unveiled in Blandford Church," *Confederate Veteran* 20, no. 9 (September 1912): 406; "Civil War Memorial Window, at Blandford Church—Petersburg, Virginia," post-1912, image no. PR01739, FPC.

100. Sheppard, *By the Noble Daring of Her Sons*, 122–27.

101. "Florida Memorial," Vicksburg National Military Park, accessed February 8, 2011, http://www.nps.gov/vick/historyculture/florida-memorial.htm; Vicksburg National Military Park Archives, "Dedication of Confederate Monument, Florida Circle," Vicksburg National Military Park, April 17, 1954; UDC, "Florida Dedicates Vicksburg Monument 1954," 3, 39; "Plan Monument," *Tampa Sunday Tribune*, October 7, 1923; "Florida UDC Division to Unveil Monument," *Delta Daily Democrat* (Greenville, Miss.), April 5, 1954; "Memorial Honors Florida's Troops," *Miami Daily News*, April 12, 1954; "Vicksburg to Entertain Civic-Patriotic Groups," *Delta Democrat-Times* (Greenville, Miss.), April 13, 1954; "Florida Memorial Unveiled in National Park Saturday," *Sunday Post-Herald* (Vicksburg, Miss.), April 18, 1954.

102. Vicksburg National Military Park Archives, Memorandum from James R. McConaghie, Park Superintendent, to Regional Director, Region One, April 22, 1954; "Florida Memorial," Vicksburg National Military Park, accessed February 8, 2011, http://www.nps.gov/vick/historyculture/florida-memorial.htm.

103. Waters and Edmonds, *A Small but Spartan Band*, 66–72.

104. Ibid., 73–79.

105. Florida Legislature, "Act to Authorize the Governor to Appoint a Commission," *Regular Session 1895*, 271; "Florida Commission," *Gettysburg Compiler*, July 9, 1895; Gettysburg National Military Park Commission, *Annual Report 1905*, *Report 1908*, and *Report 1911*.

106. Florida Legislature, "Act Providing for the Erection of a Monument on the Battlefield of Gettysburg," *Regular Session 1963*, 514–15; "Young Lawyer Battled for Perry Marker," *Gettysburg Times*, June 27, 1963.

107. "Rep. Gibbons Dedicates Fla. Shaft," *Gettysburg Times*, July 5, 1963.

108. *Florida State Memorial* [Gettysburg], sculpture by J. B. Hill, ca. 1963, *National Art Inventories*, Smithsonian American Art Museum, accessed March 9, 2012, http://www.siris.si.edu; Hawthorne, *Stories of Men and Monuments*.

109. Busey and Martin, *Regimental Strengths and Losses at Gettysburg*.

110. Waters and Edmonds, *A Small but Spartan Band*, 79.

111. *Florida State Memorial* [Gettysburg], sculpture by J. B. Hill, ca. 1963, *National Art Inventories*, Smithsonian American Art Museum, accessed March 9, 2012, http://www.siris.si.edu; "Gettysburg Memorial," *Tallahassee Historical Society Newsletter*, October 1988, 1.

112. Florida Legislature, "Act Relating to the Construction of a Memorial," *Regular Session 1965*, 1018; Hawthorne, *Stories of Men and Monuments*; "500 Witness Dedica-

tion of Confederate Memorial On Battlefield Wednesday," *Gettysburg Times*, August 26, 1965.

113. Sedore, *Virginia's Confederate Monuments*; various Virginia cemetery Web sites.

114. Sedore, *Virginia's Confederate Monuments*; various Virginia cemetery Web sites.

115. D. W. Holt, *American Military Cemeteries*, 306–7; "Confederate Mound at Oak Woods Cemetery, Chicago, Illinois," National Park Service—National Cemeteries, accessed May 7, 2013, http://www.nps.gov/history/nr/travel/national_cemeteries/Illinois/Confederate_Mound_Oak_Woods_Cemetery.html.

116. "Confederate Cemetery," Depot of Prisoners of War on Johnson's Island, Ohio, accessed December 14, 2013, http://www.johnsonsisland.org/history/war_cemetery.htm.

117. K. L. Cox, "The Confederate Monument at Arlington," 149–60.

118. Ibid., 158, 160.

119. Ibid., 149–60.

120. Ibid.

CHAPTER 5. MONUMENTS ERECTED AFTER THE CIVIL WAR CENTENNIAL

1. "United Sons, Confederate Veterans," *Confederate Veteran* 4, no. 8 (August 1896): 258.

2. "What Is the Sons of Confederate Veterans?" Sons of Confederate Veterans, accessed December 12, 2012, http://www.scv.org/whatis.php.

3. "MOS&B Chapter Handbook," Military Order of the Stars and Bars, accessed November 8, 2012, http://www.militaryorderofthestarsandbars.org.

4. Confederate Sons Association of Florida, accessed November 8, 2012, http://www.csaflorida.org.

5. "How We Got Started," Order of Confederate Rose, Florida Society, accessed November 8, 2012, http://florida-scv.org/OCR.

6. UDC, "Division News: Florida; Florida Dedicates New Monument," September 1968, 17; UDC, Florida Division, *Minutes of the Seventy-Third Annual Convention*, 116; "Memorial Day Ceremony Set," April 25, 1968, and "Confederate Memorial Dedicated by UDC Chapter," May 2, 1968, *Bradford County Telegraph*; Dan Hildebran, "Daughters of Confederacy Rededicate Monument," *Bradford County Telegraph*, May 17, 2012.

7. UDC, "Division News: Florida," August 1974, 11; UDC, Florida Division, *Minutes of the Seventy-Ninth Annual Convention*, 91; UDC, "Division News: Florida," January 1986, 10.

8. Hinder, *Oaklawn Cemetery*, 8-2 through 8-3.

9. VanLandingham, "Oaklawn Cemetery Ramble," 107.

10. Harris, "Dedication Address," 8; Martha F. Sawyer, "Polk's Past: Bartow Supplied Several Civil War Generals," June 30, 1982, and Martha F. Sawyer, "Polk's Past: More on Bartow's Rich History," *Lakeland Ledger*, September 20, 1995.

11. Richard Savid, "Fort Meade Lowballs Election Day Highballs [Fort Meade news]," *Lakeland Ledger*, January 26, 1983.

12. Loftin, "Dedication of a Confederate Monument," 18–19; Scott and McLeod, *History of Anna Jackson Chapter*, 141.

13. UDC, Florida Division, *Florida's Confederate Monuments*, "Pinellas County," 69; UDC, Florida Division, *Minutes of the Ninety-Eighth Annual Convention*, 253.

14. UDC, "Sanders Chapter," in *Patriot Ancestor Album*, 39; Scott and McLeod, *History of Anna Jackson Chapter*, 171; UDC, "Division News: Florida," January 1995, 36; Grady Turnage, "UDC to Dedicate Monument Honoring Gun Boat Crew," *Twin City News* (Chattahoochee), May 19, 1994; Grady Turnage, "Dedication of Monument to Dead Crewmen Is Set for Friday," *Twin City News*, May 26, 1994; "Memorial Dedication Held Friday," *Twin City News*, June 2, 1994.

15. In 2001 the Confederate Naval Museum moved to a new and larger facility in Columbus, Georgia, and was renamed the National Civil War Naval Museum.

16. G. Turner and Mulford, *Fort Myers*, 112; Karen Feldman, "Local Spots Pay Tribute to Veterans," *Fort Myers News-Press*, May 29, 2000.

17. Gerald Ensley, "Confederate Memorial Dedication Saturday," *Tallahassee Democrat*, December 10, 1999.

18. Robison and Fisk, *Images of America*, 127.

19. "Capt. Mooney Cemetery," Jacksonville Genealogical Society, accessed February 23, 2011, http://jaxgen.home.comcast.net/~jaxgen/cptmoony.htm; Lammons and Cowger, "Camp Captain Mooney Cemetery," 12–13; Sandy Strickland, "Marker Lets People Stand at Civil War Battle Site," *FTU*, September 17, 2005.

20. Brendan Farrington, "Group Raises Large Confederate Flag in North Florida," *Ocala Star-Banner*, February 16, 2002.

21. Susan Jacobson, "Plans for Confederate Monument Stir Debate," *Orlando Sentinel*, September 26, 2001.

22. Kay Hall, "Alachua Monument Memorializes Deceased Veterans," *Gainesville Sun*, December 26, 2002.

23. UDC, Florida Division, *Florida's Confederate Monuments*, "Indian River County," 49; UDC, "Division News: Florida," January 2005, 33.

24. UDC, "Division News: Florida," February 2007, 41.

25. Robert Niepert, "In the News: Confederate Monument Placed in St. Cloud," *Florida Reenactors*, May 2006, accessed July 29, 2012, http://www.floridareenactorsonline.com/MayMag12006.htm.

26. UDC, "Division News: Florida," Annie H. Darracott Chapter 791, Lakeland, January 2008, 30.

27. "Oxford Confederate Veterans Memorial," Find a Grave Memorial, accessed November 27, 2013, http://www.findagrave.com/cgi-bin/fg.cgi?page=gr&GRid=98244668.

28. "Dedication Ceremony Set [for] Saturday," *Perry News-Herald*, August 24–25, 2007.

29. "New Battle of Marianna Monument," *Civil War Florida*, blog by Dale Cox, January 9, 2008, accessed March 12, 2012, http://civilwarflorida.blogspot.com/2008/01/new-battle-of-marianna-monument.html.

30. "Dedication Ceremony Held at All Veterans Memorial Saturday," *Dixie County Advocate*, November 15, 2007.

31. Taylor, "Cow Cavalry," 196–98.

32. Ray Reyes, "Civil War Monument Troubles Plant City," *Tampa Tribune*, Novem-

ber 15, 2007; Ray Reyes, "Cow Cavalry Memorial Leads Plant City to Rein in Group," *Tampa Tribune*, December 12, 2007; Jan Hollingsworth, "Cracker Calvary Herded History," *Tampa Tribune*, February 20, 2008; Ben Montgomery and Catherine Shoichet, "Confederate Memorial Creates a Stir," *St. Petersburg Times*, November 18, 2007.

33. Wilkinson, "Confederate Cemetery—Tullahoma, Tennessee," 21; Dr. Michael Brady, "The First Confederate Cemetery?" Sons of Confederate Veterans, Tennessee Division, Dr. J. B. Cowan Camp, accessed December 13, 2012, http://www.tennessee-scv.org/camp155/Dr%20Bradley,Civil%20War/cwrc/firstcem.html; Sheppard, *By the Noble Daring of Her Sons*, 109–21.

34. "52 Florida Confederate Soldiers to Be Memorialized at Cemetery," *Tullahoma (Tenn.) News*, February 29, 2008; "Invitation to Confederate Monument Dedication, Tullahoma Confederate Cemetery," UDC Florida Division, accessed December 13, 2012, http://www.floridadivisionudc.com/Tullahoma.pdf.

35. Jan Wesner and Andrew Meacham, "Huge Confederate Flag Is Raised Early along I-75 and I-4," *St. Petersburg Times*, June 4, 2008; Andrew Meacham, "Confederate Flag Rises at I-75 and I-4, and It Will Rise Again," *St. Petersburg Times*, June 15, 2008; Mike Salinero, "Larger Confederate Flag Unfurled Near I-75 in Hillsborough," *Tampa Tribune*, October 13, 2008.

36. Jessica Vander Velde, "Confederate Flag Draws Tears, Cheers in Tampa," *St. Petersburg Times*, April 26, 2009.

37. Bill Varian, "Hard Feelings Unfurl with Huge Confederate Flag," *St. Petersburg Times*, June 5, 2008; Andrew Meacham, "Confederate Flag Will Still Fly," *St. Petersburg Times*, July 27, 2008; "Confederate Flag Again Stirs Racial Tension in Tampa Area," *Sarasota Herald-Tribune*, June 5, 2008; Thomas Becnel, "Beneath an Infamous Rebel Flag in East Tampa," *Sarasota Herald-Tribune*, October 27, 2010; Mike Salinero, "Huge Rebel Flag Up for Good, Site Owner Says," *Tampa Tribune*, September 4, 2008.

38. "Fallen Confederates Honored Saturday," *Gilchrist County Journal*, April 29, 2010.

39. Karen Voyles, "Tri-County Area Dedicates Confederate Monument," *Gainesville Sun*, April 25, 2010.

40. Stephen Kindland, "County Dedicates Civil War Marker," *Clay Today*, February 16, 2011.

41. Audrey Parente, "Confederate Re-enactment Marks 150th Anniversary," *Daytona Beach News Journal*, April 14, 2011.

42. Yvette C. Hammett, "Ground Breaks for 'War Between the States' Memorial," *Tampa Tribune*, April 23, 2013.

43. Timothy O'Hara, "Call to Service for 126 Black Soldiers; Hambright Wants Memorial for the Civil War Soldiers from Key West," *Key West Citizen*, December 22, 2013.

44. "Olustee Monument," Sons of Union Veterans of the Civil War, Department of Florida, accessed December 17, 2012, http://www.dofsuvcw.org/olusteemonument.html; "Proposed Union Monument at Olustee Battlefield Historic State Park Planning Process and Recommendations," Florida Division of Recreation and Parks position statement, November 25, 2013; "Act Now! To Help Olustee Battlefield," Michael Givens, Commander-in-Chief, Sons of Confederate Veterans, October 16, 2013, accessed

November 8, 2013, http://www.sonsofconfederateveterans.blogspot.com/2013/10/act-now-to-help-olustee-battlefield.html.

45. "Battle Lines Drawn over Union Monument at Olustee," WTEV-TV, Jacksonville, November 6, 2012, accessed November 7, 2013, http://www.actionnewsjax.com; Margie Menzel, "Proposed Civil War Monument Sparks Outrage," News Service of Florida, December 3, 2013, accessed December 4, 2013, http://www.bizjournals.com/jacksonville/news; Cindy Swirko, "Battle Brews over Push to Install Union Monument at Olustee," *Gainesville Sun*, December 5, 2013.

46. Bill Thompson, "Baxley Working on Bill Aimed at Planned Olustee Union Memorial," December 9, 2013, and Bill Thompson, "Baxley Targets Park Monuments," January 9, 2014, all in *Ocala Star-Banner*.

CONCLUSION

1. Other out-of-state monuments that commemorate Florida along with all of the other Confederate states are mentioned in chapter 4 but are not included in this total.

2. Johnston, *Evergreen Cemetery, Jacksonville*, 8-25 through 8-26; Ayers, *Southern Crossing*, 261–62; Foster, *Ghosts of the Confederacy*, 167–68; "Phenomenal Record of the McNeel Marble Company," *Confederate Veteran* 18, no. 2 (February 1910): 96.

3. "About SOS!" Heritage Preservation, accessed December 26, 2012, http://www.heritagepreservation.org/programs/sos/aboutsos.htm.

4. Shackel, "Heyward Shepherd," 138–46.

BIBLIOGRAPHY

PRIMARY SOURCES

ARCHIVES AND COLLECTIONS

Bay County Public Library, Panama City, Florida. Local History Collection.

Burt, R. M. Papers. Florida Historical Society, Cocoa, Florida.

City of Pensacola. Code of Ordinances. Pensacola Historical Society, Pensacola.

Confederate Monuments and Memorials Collection. Eleanor S. Brockenbrough Archives. Museum of the Confederacy, Richmond, Virginia.

Florida Board of Parks and Historic Memorials. Minutes, 1958–1969. Series 2257, Record Group 510. Florida State Archives, State Library of Florida, Tallahassee.

Florida Division of Elections. Oaths and Bonds, 1884–2000. Series 622, Record Group 156. Florida State Archives, State Library of Florida, Tallahassee.

Florida Photographic Collection. Florida State Archives, State Library of Florida, Tallahassee. Contains numerous historic photographs of Florida's Civil War monuments from as early as the 1870s.

Hodges, Senator William C. Papers. Goodwood Museum and Gardens, Tallahassee.

Lakeland Public Library, Lakeland, Florida. Digital Special Collections. Includes historic photographs and postcards of the 1910 Lakeland Confederate monument.

Library of Congress, Washington, D.C. Prints and Photographs Division. Historic photographs of several of Florida's Civil War monuments from as early as the 1880s.

Lord, Bert. Correspondence of Hon. Bert Lord of Afton, New York. Copies of correspondence, 1921–1931. Monroe County Public Library, Florida History Department, Key West. (Originals on file at Cornell University Library, Ithaca, New York.)

Manatee County Public Library, Bradenton, Florida. Historical Image Digital Collection. Includes ceremony program and historic photographs of the 1924 Bradenton Confederate monument dedication.

Monroe County Public Library, Key West, Florida. Florida History Department Images. Includes historic photographs dating from the late nineteenth and early twentieth centuries of the 1866 Key West Union monument, as well as later photographs of the 1924 Key West Confederate monument and the 1930 New York State Union monument.

Pensacola City Clerk's Office. Records. Pensacola Historical Society, Pensacola, Florida.

Sarasota County History Center, Sarasota, Florida. Historic Photographs Collection. Includes historic photographs of the Judah P. Benjamin Escape monument, including 1942 monument unveiling.

Stoney, Thomas P. (Thomas Porcher), 1889-1973. Correspondence with James H. Tomb, 1926-1928. (Coll. no. 43/2187). South Carolina Historical Society Archives, Charleston.

St. Petersburg Museum of History, St. Petersburg, Florida. Historic Photo Archives. Includes historic photograph of the 1900 dedication ceremony of Civil War monuments in Greenwood Cemetery.

United Daughters of the Confederacy, Florida Division. Anna Jackson Chapter no. 224. Papers. Series M76-131. Florida State Archives, State Library of Florida, Tallahassee.

United Daughters of the Confederacy Scrapbooks, 1930–1986. Series M89-26. Florida State Archives, State Library of Florida, Tallahassee.

Vicksburg National Military Park Archives, Vicksburg, Mississippi.

GOVERNMENT DOCUMENTS

City of Pensacola. *Code of Ordinances of the City of Pensacola.* Prepared by John B. Jones, City Attorney. Pensacola: H. S. White, Printer, Ruler and Binder, 1902.

Florida Legislature. Act Relating to the Construction of a Memorial on the Battlefield of Gettysburg; Authorizing the State of Florida to Participate in the Erection of Such Memorial; Providing an Appropriation Therefor; Providing an Effective Date. *Regular Session 1965 General Acts and Resolutions Adopted by the Legislature of Florida at Its Fortieth Regular Session (April 6th to June 4th, 1965) under the Constitution of A.D. 1885, vol. I, part 1.* Chapter 65-291-An, 1018–19. Tallahassee: State of Florida, 1965.

———. Act Providing for the Erection of a Monument on the Battlefield of Gettysburg in Memory of the Soldiers of Perry's Florida Brigade Who Took Part in That Battle; Providing for an Appropriation; Providing an Effective Date. *Regular Session 1963 General Acts and Resolutions Adopted by the Legislature of Florida at Its Thirty-Ninth Regular Session (April 2nd to June 19th, 1963) under the Constitution of A.D. 1885, vol. I, part 1.* Chapter 63-226-An, 514–15. Tallahassee: State of Florida, 1963.

———. Act Authorizing the Removal by the County Commissioners of Walton County, Florida, of the Confederate Monument Now Located at Eucheeanna, Florida; Making an Appropriation for Said Purpose and for the Maintenance and Care of Said Monument. *Regular Session 1927 General Acts and Resolutions Adopted by the Legislature of Florida at Its Twenty-First Regular Session (April 5 to June 3, 1927) under the Constitution of A.D. 1885, vol. II.* Chapter 11818, 108–9. Tallahassee: T. J. Appleyard Inc., 1927.

———. Act to Make an Appropriation for a Suitable Monument to Mark the Graves of Confederate Soldiers Who Were Killed at the Battle of Olustee and Who Are Buried at Lake City, Florida. *Regular Session 1927 General Acts and Resolutions Adopted by the Legislature of Florida at Its Twenty-First Regular Session (April 5 to June 3,*

1927) under the Constitution of A.D. 1885, vol. II. Chapter 11817, 107–8. Tallahassee: T. J. Appleyard Inc., 1927.

———. Act Making an Appropriation to Assist in the Erection of a Monument at Marianna to Commemorate the Battle of Marianna. *Regular Session 1921 General Acts and Resolutions Adopted by the Legislature of Florida at Its Eighteenth Regular Session (April 5 to June 3, 1921) under the Constitution of A.D. 1885*. Chapter 8447, 163–64. Tallahassee: T. J. Appleyard, Printer, 1921.

———. Act to Aid Anna Dummett Chapter, Daughters of the Confederacy, Incorporated, of St. Augustine, Florida; in the Completion of Payment for the Loring Memorial, Erected in St. Augustine, Florida, in Honor of General William Wing Loring, Distinguished Son of Florida; and for the Curbing, Railing and Concrete Work Around the Said Loring Memorial for Its Proper Protection; to Make an Appropriation Therefor, and to Provide for the Payment of Such Appropriation. *Regular Session 1921 General Acts and Resolutions Adopted by the Legislature of Florida at Its Eighteenth Regular Session (April 5 to June 3, 1921) under the Constitution of A.D. 1885*. Chapter 8443, 157–59, Tallahassee: T. J. Appleyard, Printer, 1921.

———. Act to Make an Appropriation to Assist in the Erection of a Monument and Establishing a Park on the Battle Field of Natural Bridge, in Leon County, Florida. *Regular Session 1921 General Acts and Resolutions Adopted by the Legislature of Florida at Its Eighteenth Regular Session (April 5 to June 3, 1921) under the Constitution of A.D. 1885*. Chapter 8433, 142–43. Tallahassee: T. J. Appleyard, Printer, 1921.

———. Act to Aid the Florida Division of United Confederate Veterans in Erecting in This State a Monument or Memorial in Honor of the Women of the Southern Confederacy in Memory of Their Heroism, Devotion and Self-Sacrifice during the Civil War, 1861–1865, and Making an Appropriation Therefor in Addition to and Supplementary of the Appropriation made by Chapter 6437, Acts of 1913. *Regular Session 1915 General Acts and Resolutions Adopted by the Legislature of Florida at Its Fifteenth Regular Session (April 6 to June 4, 1915) under the Constitution of A.D. 1885, vol. I*. Chapter 6947, 334–37. Tallahassee: T. J. Appleyard, State Printer, 1915.

———. Act to Make an Appropriation for the Putting and Keeping in Order of the Grounds Adjacent and Belonging to the Site of the Olustee Monument, and for the Proper Care and Protection of the Monument Itself; and to Provide for the Payment of Such Appropriation. *Regular Session 1915 General Acts and Resolutions Adopted by the Legislature of Florida at Its Fifteenth Regular Session (April 6 to June 4, 1915) under the Constitution of A.D. 1885, vol. 1*. Chapter 6824, 50–51. Tallahassee: T. J. Appleyard, State Printer, 1915.

———. Act to Aid the Florida Division of Confederate Veterans in Erecting in This State a Monument or Memorial in Honor of the Women of the Southern Confederacy, in Memory of Their Heroism, Devotion and Self-sacrifice during the Civil War, 1861–1865, Making an Appropriation Therefor, and Repealing Chapter 6142, Acts of 1911. *Laws of the State of Florida Adopted by the Legislature of Florida at Its Regular Session 1913 under the Constitution of A.D. 1885*. Chapter 6437, 104–5. Tallahassee: T. J. Appleyard, State Printer, 1913.

———. Act to Make Available an Appropriation of Fifteen Thousand Dollars Made by an Act Approved May 27, 1907, Entitled an Act to Provide for a Monument to be Erected on the Battlefield of Chickamauga in Memory of the Soldiers of Florida Who Took Part in That Battle. *Regular Session 1911 General Acts and Resolutions Adopted by the Legislature of Florida at Its Thirteenth Regular Session (April 4 to June 2, 1911) under the Constitution of A.D. 1885*. Chapter 6143, 56. Tallahassee: T. J. Appleyard, State Printer, 1911.

———. Act to Aid the Florida Division of Confederate Veterans to Erect in This State a Monument or Memorial in Honor of the Women of Florida and of the South in Memory of Their Heroism, Devotion and Self-sacrifice during the Civil War in 1861–1865, and to Appropriate Five Thousand Dollars Therefor. *Regular Session 1911 General Acts and Resolutions Adopted by the Legislature of Florida at Its Thirteenth Regular Session (April 4 to June 2, 1911) under the Constitution of A.D. 1885*. Chapter 6142, 54–55. Tallahassee: T. J. Appleyard, State Printer, 1911.

———. Act to Provide for a Monument to Be Erected on the Battlefield of Chickamauga in Memory of the Soldiers of Florida Who Took Part in That Battle. *Regular Session 1907 Acts and Resolutions Adopted by the Legislature of Florida at Its Eleventh Regular Session (April 2 to May 31, 1907) under the Constitution of A.D. 1885*. Chapter 5711, 223–24. Tallahassee: Capital Publishing Co., State Printer, 1907.

———. Act to Amend Section 1 of an Act Entitled an Act to Make an Appropriation in Aid of a Monument Commemorative of the Battle of Olustee, and to Provide for a Commission to Expend Said Appropriation, Approved June 2, 1889. *Regular Session 1901 Acts and Resolutions Adopted by the Legislature of Florida at Its Eighth Regular Session (April 2 to May 31, 1901) under the Constitution of A.D. 1885*. Chapter 5053, 207–8. Tallahassee: Tallahasseean Book and Job Office, 1901.

———. Act to Make an Appropriation in Aid of a Monument Commemorative of the Battle of Olustee, and to Provide for a Commission to Expend Said Appropriation. *Regular Session 1899 Acts and Resolutions Adopted by the Legislature of Florida at Its Seventh Regular Session, under the Constitution of A.D. 1885*. Chapter 4815, 213–14. Tallahassee: Tallahasseean Book and Job Office, 1899.

———. Act to Authorize the Governor to Appoint a Commission to Aid in Locating the Positions and Movements of Florida Troops at the Battle of Gettysburg, and to Provide Funds to Pay the Expenses of Said Commission. *Regular Session, 1895. Acts and Resolutions Adopted by the Legislature of Florida, at Its Fifth Regular Session, under the Constitution of A.D. 1885*. Chapter 4489, 271. Tallahassee: Tallahassean Book and Job Office, 1895.

Florida Secretary of State. *Report of the Secretary of State of the State of Florida, for the Period Beginning January 1, 1927, and Ending December 31, 1928*. Marianna, Fla.: Florida Industrial School for Boys Printing Dept., 1929.

———. *Report of the Secretary of State of the State of Florida, for the Period Beginning January 1, 1913, and Ending December 31, 1914, Part 1*. Tallahassee: T. J. Appleyard, State Printer, 1915.

———. *Report of the Secretary of State of the State of Florida, for the Period Beginning*

January 1, 1911, and Ending December 31, 1912. Tallahassee: T. J. Appleyard, State Printer, 1913.

———. *Report of the Secretary of State of the State of Florida, for the Period Beginning January 1, 1909, and Ending December 31, 1910.* Tallahassee: Typographical Union, 1911.

———. *Report of the Secretary of State of the State of Florida, for the Period Beginning January 1, 1907, and Ending December 31, 1908.* Tallahassee: Typographical Union, 1909.

———. *Report of the Secretary of State of the State of Florida, for the Period Beginning January 1, 1905, and Ending December 31, 1906.* Tallahassee: Capital Publishing Co., State Printer, 1906.

———. *Report of the Secretary of State of the State of Florida, for the Period beginning January 1, 1903, and ending December 31, 1904.* Tallahassee: Capital Publishing Co., State Printers, 1904.

———. "Secretary Detzner Announces Restoration of Historic Natural Bridge Monument Eagle." Press release. March 2, 2012.

Florida Supreme Court. *Reports of Cases Argued and Adjudged in the Supreme Court of Florida at Terms Held in 1871–'2–'3–'4.* Volume 14. Reported by Wm. Archer Cocke, Attorney General. Tallahassee: Office of the Floridian, 1874.

Gettysburg National Military Park Commission. *Report of the Gettysburg National Military Park Commission.* Washington, D.C.: Government Printing Office, 1911.

———. *Report of the Gettysburg National Military Park Commission.* Washington, D.C.: Government Printing Office, 1908.

———. *Annual Reports of the Gettysburg National Military Park Commission to the Secretary of War, 1893–1904.* Washington, D.C.: Government Printing Office, 1905.

State of New York. *New York Legislative Documents, One Hundred and Forty-Fourth Session, 1921, Vol. 26, Nos. 90–92 Incl.* Albany: J. B. Lyon Co., 1921.

———. Appropriations for Fiscal Year. Executive Department, New York Monuments Commission. For the acquisition at Key West in the state of Florida, of a site and the erection thereon of a monument, suitably inscribed, in memory of the civil war veterans from this state who are buried in that city. *Laws of the State of New York Passed at the One Hundred and Fifty-First Session of the Legislature.* Chapter 520, Part 1, 1132. Albany: J. B. Lyon Co., 1928.

———. Report of the New York Monuments Commission. *Annual Report of the Adjutant General for the Year 1930.* Major General Franklin W. Ward, the Adjutant General. Appendix C, 48–53. Albany: J. B. Lyon Co., 1931.

U.S. War Department. *Official Records of the Union and Confederate Navies in the War of the Rebellion.* 30 vols. Washington, D.C.: Government Printing Office, 1894–1927.

———. *War Department Annual Reports, 1913.* Vol. 3. Washington, D.C.: Government Printing Office, 1914.

———. *The War of the Rebellion: A Compilation of the Official Records of the Union and Confederate Armies.* 128 vols. Washington, D.C.: Government Printing Office, 1880–1901.

SECONDARY SOURCES

"After the Burning of Bagdad." Letter from Alexander C. Blount to Governor John Milton, April 8, 1862. *Mill Times: Publication of the Bagdad Village Preservation Association* 10 (September 2012): 5.

Alexander, Mrs. J. E. "Report of Bull Run Monument." In *Minutes of the Fourteenth Annual Convention of the United Daughters of the Confederacy Held in Norfolk, Virginia, November 13–16, 1907*, 232–36. Opelika, Ala.: Post Publishing Co., 1908.

Allardice, Bruce S. *More Generals in Gray*. Baton Rouge: Louisiana State University Press, 1995.

"Among the Dealers." *The Reporter: Devoted to the Granite and Marble Monumental Trade* 43, no. 3 (March 1910): 7–11.

"Among the Dealers." *The Reporter: Devoted to the Granite and Marble Monumental Trade* 45, no. 7 (July 1912): 5–9.

Andrews, Phyllis. "Visiting the Orlando Area? Don't Miss This Hidden Gem." *Orange Blossom Banner* (Newsletter of the UDC, Florida Division) 17, no. 2 (Winter/Spring 2009–10): 1, 15.

Arbuthnot, Michael A., Brian S. Marks, and Adam Cripps. *Archaeological and Historical Investigation of the Natural Bridge Battlefield Historic Site, Leon County, Florida*. Florida Master Site File, Florida Division of Historical Resources, Tallahassee, 2010.

Archaeological Consultants, Inc. *Cultural Resource Assessment Survey, SR 61 (Thomasville Road) from Amber V. Road to the Georgia State Line, Leon County, Florida*. Florida Master Site File, Florida Division of Historical Resources, Tallahassee, 1994.

Ayers, Edward L. *Southern Crossing: A History of the American South, 1877–1906*. New York: Oxford University Press, 1995.

Baruch, Mildred C., and Ellen J. Beckman. *Civil War Union Monuments*. Washington, D.C.: Daughters of Union Veterans of the Civil War 1861–65, 1978.

Bassett, Nancy W. "McGavock Confederate Cemetery, Franklin, Tennessee." *UDC Magazine* 60, no. 5 (May 1997): 16.

Beck, Monica L., and William B. Lees. "U.S. Sanitary Commission Camp Inspections in Civil War Florida." Paper presented at Annual Conference of the Florida Historical Society, Jacksonville, Florida, 2011.

Bell, Harold. "Florida's Monument to the North." *All Florida Weekly Magazine*, October 18, 1959.

Bickel, Karl A. "Robert E. Lee in Florida." *Florida Historical Quarterly* 27, no. 1 (July 1948): 59–66.

Blight, David W. *Race and Reunion: The Civil War in American Memory*. Cambridge: Belknap Press of Harvard University Press, 2001.

Bloomfield, Max. *Bloomfield's Illustrated Historical Guide, Embracing an Account of the Antiquities of St. Augustine*. St. Augustine, Fla.: Published by author, 1883.

The Blue and the Gray: Statues in Stamped Copper and Bronze. Salem, Ohio: W. H. Mullins Co., 1913.

Brock, R. A., ed. "The Ceremonies Attending Unveiling of the Monument to Confederate Dead of Florida at Jacksonville, Florida, June 16, 1898." *Southern Historical Society Papers* 27 (1899): 109–31.

Brown, Canter, Jr. *Tampa in Civil War and Reconstruction*. Tampa: University of Tampa Press, 2000.

Brundage, W. Fitzhugh. "'Woman's Hand and Heart and Deathless Love': White Women and the Commemorative Impulse in the New South." In *Monuments to the Lost Cause: Women, Art, and the Landscapes of Southern Memory*, edited by Cynthia Mills and Pamela H. Simpson, 64–84. Knoxville: University of Tennessee Press, 2003.

Buker, George E. *Blockaders, Refugees, and Contrabands: Civil War on Florida's Gulf Coast, 1861–1865*. Tuscaloosa: University of Alabama Press, 1993.

Burkhardt, Sue Pope. *History of Thomas Benton Ellis Chapter No. 1816, United Daughters of the Confederacy, West Palm Beach, Florida, 1922–1974*. West Palm Beach: Privately published, 1974.

Busey, John W., and David G. Martin. *Regimental Strengths and Losses at Gettysburg*. 4th ed. Hightstown, N.J.: Longstreet House, 2005.

"Business Brevities." *Stone: A Monthly Publication Devoted to the Stone Industry in All of Its Branches* 35, no. 3 (March 1914): 146.

Carlotta, Sister Esther. "United Daughters of the Confederacy—The Florida Division." *Confederate Veteran* 24, no. 11 (November 1916): 516–17.

Castel, Albert. *The Presidency of Andrew Johnson*. Lawrence: Regents Press of Kansas, 1979.

Castile, Nora Faye, and Linda Rosenblatt. "Florida Sentinel, the Confederate Monument at Olustee." *UDC Magazine* 69, no. 1 (January 2006): 24.

"City Unveils Unknown Soldier Monument [Walkway] during Centennial Year." *Dateline: City of St. Cloud Monthly Newsletter*, November 2009, 1.

Codieck, Barrett. "Keepers of History, Shapers of Memory: The Florida Division of the United Daughters of the Confederacy, 1895–1930." Master's thesis, Florida State University, 2012.

Coles, David J. "Far from Fields of Glory: Military Operations in Florida during the Civil War, 1864–1865." Ph.D. diss., Florida State University, 1996.

Collins, Ann Taylor. "Pensacola's Confederate Monument." *UDC Magazine* 40, no. 1 (January 1987): 30–31.

Confederated Southern Memorial Association. *History of the Confederated Memorial Associations of the South*. New Orleans: Graham Press, 1904.

Confederate Veteran. Vols. 1–40. 1893–1932.

Cowger, Sue F. "The Stonewall Jackson Highway in Florida." *UDC Magazine* 57, no. 1 (January 1994): 26–27.

Cox, Dale. *The Battle of Marianna, Florida*. Expanded ed. Published by author, 2011.

———. *The Battle of Natural Bridge, Florida: The Confederate Defense of Tallahassee*. Expanded ed. Published by author, 2010.

Cox, Karen L. "The Confederate Monument at Arlington, a Token of Reconciliation." In *Monuments to the Lost Cause: Women, Art, and the Landscapes of Southern Memory*, edited by Cynthia Mills and Pamela H. Simpson, 149–62. Knoxville: University of Tennessee Press, 2003.

———. *Dixie's Daughters: The United Daughters of the Confederacy and the Preservation of Confederate Culture*. Gainesville: University Press of Florida, 2003.

Crosby, Gail Lowman. "Memoria in Aeterna: Honoring the Gallant Men of the South." *UDC Magazine* 70, no. 1 (January 2007): 16–17.

Curenton, Betty Sanders, and Claudia Garrett Patten. *Crestview: The Forkland*. Privately published, 2002.

Curenton, Mark. "Walton County Confederate Monument." *Walton Relations: Walton County Genealogical Society Newsletter* 3, no. 3 (January 2012): 2–4.

Davis, T. Frederick. *History of Jacksonville, Florida, and Vicinity, 1513 to 1924*. St. Augustine: Florida Historical Society, 1925.

Davis, William Watson. *The Civil War and Reconstruction in Florida*. New York: Columbia University, 1913.

Dearing, Mary R. *Veterans in Politics: The Story of the G.A.R.* Baton Rouge: Louisiana State University Press, 1952.

Dearinger, David B., ed. *Paintings and Sculpture in the Collection of the National Academy of Design, 1826–1925*. Manchester, Vt.: Hudson Hills Press, 2004.

Defebaugh, E. H. "New Chattanooga Monuments." *American Stone Trade* 13, no. 6 (January 5, 1914): 28–29.

Dickison, John J. "Military History of Florida." In *Confederate Military History*, vol. 11, part 2, edited by Clement Evans. Atlanta: Confederate Publishing Co., 1898.

Emerson, Mrs. Bettie Alder Calhoun, comp. *Historic Southern Monuments: Representative Memorials of the Heroic Dead of the Southern Confederacy*. New York: Neale Publishing Co., 1911.

Eppes, Susan Bradford. *Through Some Eventful Years*. Macon, Ga.: J. W. Burke Co., 1926.

Fahs, Alice, and Joan Waugh. *The Memory of the Civil War in American Culture*. Chapel Hill: University of North Carolina Press, 2004.

Faust, Drew Gilpin. *This Republic of Suffering: Death and the American Civil War*. New York: Vintage Books, 2008.

Federal Writers' Project, Works Project Administration. *Florida: A Guide to the Southernmost State*. New York: Oxford University Press, 1939.

Florida Association of Museums. *Florida Civil War Heritage Trail*. Tallahassee: Florida Division of Historical Resources, 2011.

Florida Department of Environmental Protection, Division of Recreation and Parks. *Judah P. Benjamin Confederate Memorial at Gamble Plantation Historic State Park Unit Management Plan*. Tallahassee, 2003.

———. *Olustee Battlefield Historic State Park Unit Management Plan*. Tallahassee, 2008.

———. *Yellow Bluff Fort Historic State Park Unit Management Plan*. Tallahassee, 2004.

Foner, Eric. *Reconstruction: America's Unfinished Revolution, 1863–1877*. New York: Harper and Row, 1988.

———. *A Short History of Reconstruction, 1863–1877*. New York: Harper and Row, 1990.

Foster, Gaines M. *Ghosts of the Confederacy: Defeat, the Lost Cause, and the Emergence of the New South, 1865–1913*. New York: Oxford University Press, 1987.

"From the Tool Chest." *The Reporter: Devoted to the Granite and Marble Monumental Trade* 47, no. 2 (February 1914): 29–31.

Galbraith, Christine, and Barbara Miller. *Historical Documentary Research Project, 1902 Florida Capitol Restoration, Third and Final Report*. Florida Master Site File, Florida Division of Historical Resources, Tallahassee, 1979.

Gallagher, Gary W. "Shaping Public Memory of the Civil War: Robert E. Lee, Jubal A. Early, and Douglas Southall Freeman." In *The Memory of the Civil War in American Culture*, edited by Alice Fahs and Joan Waugh, 39–63. Chapel Hill: University of North Carolina Press, 2004.

Gannon, Barbara A. *The Won Cause: Black and White Comradeship in the Grand Army of the Republic*. Chapel Hill: University of North Carolina Press, 2011.

Gardner, Charles. *Gardner's New Orleans Directory for 1866*. New Orleans: Charles Gardner, 1866.

Giuliano, Tara M. "Legend of the Field Stones in Old Bethel Cemetery: Using Archaeology to Explore Social Memory." Master's thesis, University of West Florida, 2012.

Grand Army of the Republic. *Journal of the Forty-Fifth National Encampment, Grand Army of the Republic, Rochester, New York, August 24 and 25, 1911*. Boston: Griffith-Stillings Press, 1911.

———. *Journal of the Twenty-Sixth National Encampment, Grand Army of the Republic, Washington, D.C., September 21st and 22d, 1892*. Albany, N.Y.: S. H. Wentworth, 1892.

Grant, Ulysses S. *Personal Memoirs of Ulysses S. Grant*. Vol. 2. New York: Charles L. Webster and Co., 1886.

Green, Mrs. T. S. "Florida Marker Dedication Recalled." *UDC Magazine* 27, no. 8 (August 1964): 15.

Grissom, Carol A. *Zinc Sculpture in America, 1850–1950*. Newark: University of Delaware Press, 2009.

Hacker, J. David. "A Census-Based Count of the Civil War Dead." *Civil War History* 57, no. 4 (December 2011): 307–48.

Harrell, Annette C. "The Dixie Highway." *UDC Magazine* 74, no. 1 (January 2011): 17–18.

Harris, William Lloyd. "Dedication Address." *Polk County Historical Quarterly* 11, no. 3 (December 1984): 8.

Hawthorne, Frederick W., comp. *Gettysburg: Stories of Men and Monuments as Told by Battlefield Guides*. Hanover, Pa.: Sheridan Press, 1988.

Heidler, David S., and Jeanne T. Heidler, eds. *Encyclopedia of the American Civil War: A Political, Social, and Military History*. 5 vols. New York: Norton, 2000.

Hinder, Kimberly. *National Register of Historic Places Registration Form—Oaklawn Cemetery, Tampa, Florida*. Florida Master Site File, Florida Division of Historical Resources, Tallahassee, 1999.

Hinder, Kimberly, and Sherrie Stokes. *National Register of Historic Places Registration Form—Greenwood Cemetery, Orlando, Florida*. Florida Master Site File, Florida Division of Historical Resources, Tallahassee, 1998.

Historical and Commercial Philadelphia. New York: A. F. Parsons, 1892.

Holbrook, Wm. C. *A Narrative of the Services of the Officers and Enlisted Men of the 7th*

Regiment of Vermont Volunteers (Veterans), from 1862 to 1866. New York: American Bank Note Co., 1882.
Holt, Dean W. *American Military Cemeteries*. 2nd ed. Jefferson, N.C.: McFarland, 2010.
Holt, Hamilton, ed. "From State to State: Florida." *Independent* 84 (October–December 1915): 301.
Hunt, A. M., ed. "Proposed Monuments and Monumental News." *Granite* 10, no. 3 (March 1, 1900): 20.
Jacobson, Eric A. *The McGavock Confederate Cemetery, a Revised and Updated Compilation*. Nashville: Vaughan Printing, 2007.
Janney, Caroline E. *Burying the Dead but Not the Past: Ladies' Memorial Associations and the Lost Cause*. Chapel Hill: University of North Carolina Press, 2008.
Johnston, Sidney. *National Register of Historic Places Registration Form—Evergreen Cemetery, Jacksonville, Florida*. Florida Master Site File, Florida Division of Historical Resources, Tallahassee, 2010.
———. *National Register of Historic Places Registration Form—Oak Hill Cemetery, Bartow, Florida*. Florida Master Site File, Florida Division of Historical Resources, Tallahassee, 2002.
Jones, Reverend J. William, ed. "Editorial Paragraphs." *Southern Historical Society Papers* 7, no. 7 (July 1879): 349–52.
Josephy, Alvin N. *The Civil War in the American West*. New York: Knopf, 1991.
Knight, Lucian Lamar. *Stone Mountain, or The Lay of the Gray Minstrel: An Epic Poem in Twenty Four Parts*. Atlanta: Johnson-Dallis Co., 1923.
LaBree, Ben, ed. *The Confederate Soldier in the Civil War, 1861–65*. Louisville: Prentice Press, 1897.
Lammons, Johnny, and Sue F. Cowger. "Camp Captain Mooney Cemetery." *UDC Magazine* 66, no. 1 (January 2003): 12–13.
Lancaster, Cathryn Garth. *Early Years of the Florida Division UDC, 1896–1921*. Winter Park, Fla.: Privately published, 1983.
Langdon, Loomis L. "The Dead of Olustee." In *History of the First Regiment of Artillery from Its Organization in 1821, to January 1st, 1876 to Which Is Added a Series of Communications from Officers, Now or Formerly of the Regiment*, compiled by William L. Haskin, 461–63. Portland, Maine: B. Thurston and Co., 1879.
Lanier, Sidney. *Florida: Its Scenery, Climate, and History*. Philadelphia: Lippincott, 1875.
Levy, Florence N., ed. "Milione, Louis." *American Art Annual* 14 (1917): 556.
Loftin, Dorothy Council. "Dedication of a Confederate Monument." *UDC Magazine* 51, no. 1 (January 1988): 18–20.
Long, Ellen Call. *Florida Breezes; or, Florida, New and Old*. Jacksonville: Ashmead Bros., 1882.
Marvel, William. "The Great Imposters." *Blue and Gray* 8, no. 3 (February 1991): 32–33.
McKinnon, John L. *History of Walton County*. Atlanta: Byrd Printing Co., 1911.
McQuade, James. *Cruise of the Montauk to Bermuda, the West Indies and Florida*. New York: Thomas R. Knox and Co., 1885.

McRory, Mary Oakley, and Edith Clarke Barrows. *History of Jefferson County, Florida*. Monticello, Fla.: Kiwanis Club, 1935.

Merrill, Peter C. *German Immigrant Artists in America: A Biographical Dictionary*. Latham, Md.: Scarecrow Press, 1997.

Merritt, Mary Lou. "St. Cloud: Home to Sugar and Soldiers." *Yesterday in Florida*, no. 16 (March/April 2004): 25–27.

Mills, Cynthia. "Gratitude and Gender Wars: Monuments to the Women of the Sixties." In *Monuments to the Lost Cause: Women, Art, and the Landscapes of Southern Memory*, edited by Cynthia Mills and Pamela H. Simpson, 183–200. Knoxville: University of Tennessee Press, 2003.

Milton, George Fort. *The Age of Hate: Andrew Johnson and the Radicals*. Hamden, Conn.: Anchor Books, 1965.

Mitchell, William Donald. *The Art of the Bronze Founder*. New York: Press of Gibbs and Van Vleck, 1916.

Moore, James E. "The Battle over the Confederate Monument." *North Florida Living*, March 1984, 48–50.

Musgrove, Eric. *Images of America: Suwannee County*. Charleston, S.C.: Arcadia, 2011.

Neff, John R. *Honoring the Civil War Dead: Commemoration and the Problem of Reconciliation*. Lawrence: University of Kansas Press, 2005.

Neville, Ashley M. *National Register of Historic Places Registration Form—Blandford Cemetery, Petersburg, Virginia*. Virginia Department of Historic Resources, Richmond, 1992.

Nulty, William H. *Confederate Florida: The Road to Olustee*. Tuscaloosa: University of Alabama Press, 1990.

Osborne, Ray. "The President Is Coming." *Indian River Journal* 5, no. 2 (Fall/Winter 2006): 19–24.

Parkes, Kineton. *Sculpture of To-Day*. Vol. 1. New York: Scribner, 1921.

Parkinson, Meta Rowe. "Florida's Tribute to the Women of the Confederacy, Confederate Park, Jacksonville, Florida." *UDC Magazine* 71, no. 1 (January 2008): 20–21.

Pearce, George F. *Pensacola during the Civil War: A Thorn in the Side of the Confederacy*. Gainesville: University Press of Florida, 2000.

Penton, Daniel T., and William L. Leigh III. *A Reconnaissance-Level Archaeological Assessment of the Olustee Battlefield Vicinity*. Florida Master Site File, Florida Division of Historical Resources, Tallahassee, 1994.

Pollard, Edward A. *The Lost Cause: A New Southern History of the War of the Confederates*. New York: E. D. Treat and Co., 1867.

Proctor, Samuel. "The South Florida Military Institute (Bartow): A Parent of the University of Florida." *Florida Historical Quarterly* 32, no. 1 (July 1953): 28–40.

Prominski, Betty L. "A Long Hot Summer." *UDC Magazine* 55, no. 1 (January 1992): 16.

"Proposed Monuments." *The Reporter: Devoted to the Granite and Marble Monumental Trade* 45, no. 11 (November 1912): 10.

Randall, J. G., and David H. Donald. *The Civil War and Reconstruction*. Lexington, Mass.: D. C. Heath, 1969.

Remillard, Arthur. *Southern Civil Religions: Imagining the Good Society in the Post-Reconstruction Era*. Athens: University of Georgia Press, 2011.

Richardson, James D. *A Compilation of the Messages and Papers of the Presidents, 1789–1902*. Vol. 6. Washington, D.C.: Bureau of National Literature and Art, 1903.

Richardson, Wade H. *How I Reached the Union Lines*. Milwaukee: Milwaukee Telegraph Publishing Co., 1896.

Robarts, James N. "Florida Soldiers Buried at Blandford Cemetery, Virginia." *Florida Genealogist* 21, no. 3 (1998): 106.

Robertson, James I., Jr. *The Civil War*. Washington, D.C.: U.S. Civil War Centennial Commission, 1963.

Robison, Jim, and Robert A. Fisk. *Images of America: St. Cloud*. Charleston, S.C.: Arcadia, 2002.

Rogers, George A., and R. Frank Saunders Jr. *Swamp Water and Wiregrass: Historical Sketches of Coastal Georgia*. Macon, Ga.: Mercer University Press, 1984.

Rotundo, Barbara. "Monumental Bronze: A Representative American Company." In *Cemeteries and Gravemarkers: Voices of American Culture*, edited by Richard G. Meyer, 263–92. Logan: Utah State University Press, 1989.

Sammartino, Therese T. *National Register of Historic Places Registration Form—Barrancas National Cemetery, Pensacola, Florida*. Florida Master Site File, Florida Division of Historical Resources, Tallahassee, 1997.

Schafer, Daniel L. *Thunder on the River: The Civil War in Northeast Florida*. Gainesville: University Press of Florida, 2010.

Schmidt, Lewis G., and Janeth E. Schmidt. "Key West Post Cemetery." *Florida Keys Sea Heritage Journal* 12, no. 4 (Summer 2002): 1, 14.

Scott, Effie Morrison, and Stephen A. McLeod. *Centennial History of Anna Jackson Chapter No. 224, Tallahassee, Florida, 1898–1998, United Daughters of the Confederacy*. Tallahassee: United Daughters of the Confederacy, 1998.

Sedore, Timothy S. *An Illustrated Guide to Virginia's Confederate Monuments*. Carbondale: Southern Illinois University Press, 2011.

Sefton, James E. *Andrew Johnson and the Uses of Constitutional Power*. Boston: Little, Brown, 1980.

Sellars, Richard W. "Pilgrim Places: Civil War Battlefields, Historic Preservation, and America's First National Military Parks, 1863–1900." *CRM, the Journal of Heritage Stewardship* 2, no. 1 (Winter 2005): 22–52.

Serrano, Richard A. *Last of the Blue and Gray: Old Men, Stolen Glory, and the Mystery That Outlived the Civil War*. Washington, D.C.: Smithsonian Books, 2013.

Shackel, Paul A. "Heyward Shepherd: The Faithful Slave Memorial." *Historical Archaeology* 37, no. 3 (Fall 2003): 138–48.

Shepherd, Rose. "Florida Division Unveils Marker on Olustee Battlefield, Honoring General J. E. Finegan." *UDC Magazine* 14, no. 7 (July 1951): 19, 23, 26.

———. "Marker Erected at Historic Florida Fort." *UDC Magazine* 14, no. 4 (April 1951): 6, 24.

Sheppard, Jonathan C. *By the Noble Daring of Her Sons: The Florida Brigade of the Army of Tennessee*. Tuscaloosa: University of Alabama Press, 2012.

Shofner, Jerrell H. *History of Jefferson County*. Tallahassee: Sentry Press, 1976.

———. *Jackson County, Florida: A History*. Marianna, Fla.: Jackson County Heritage Association, 1985.

Silpa, Felicia Bianca. "Historical Archaeology Research Designs for Gamble Plantation, Ellenton, Florida." Master's thesis, University of South Florida, 2008.

Silverman, Scott J. "Rediscovered History: The 1904 Dade County Courthouse Confederate Monument." *11th Judicial Circuit Historical Society* (Fall 2007): 28–31.

Spencer, Elizabeth R. *They Are Here: Cemeteries of Clay County, Florida, and a Brief History of Clay County and Northeast Florida*. Orange Park, Fla.: Privately published, 1973.

Stahura, Barbara, and Gary L. Gibson. *History of Sons of Union Veterans of the Civil War*. Paducah, Ky.: Turner Publishing Co., 1996.

Suber, Isabelle, and Hentz Fletcher. *History of the Joseph "Little Joe" Fletcher Family*. Privately published, 1991.

Taylor, Robert A. "Cow Cavalry: Munnerlyn's Battalion in Florida, 1864–1865." *Florida Historical Quarterly* 65, no. 2 (October 1986): 196–214.

Thompson, Mrs. S. B. "U.D.C. Work in Florida." *Confederate Veteran* 10, no. 10 (October 1902): 442.

Tindle, Sheila. "A Lone Confederate Stands Guard in Lakeland." *UDC Magazine* 66, no. 1 (January 2003): 14.

Towns, W. Stuart. "Honoring the Confederacy in Northwest Florida: The Confederate Monument Ritual." *Florida Historical Quarterly* 57, no. 2 (October 1978): 205–12.

Turner, Gregg M. *A Journey into Florida Railroad History*. Gainesville: University Press of Florida, 2008.

Turner, Gregg, and Stan Mulford. *Images of America: Fort Myers*. Charleston, S.C.: Arcadia Publishing, 2000.

Turner, Shane M. "Rearguard of the Confederacy: The Second Florida Infantry Regiment." Master's thesis, Florida State University, 2005.

United Daughters of the Confederacy. "Confederate Monument, West Palm Beach, Florida." *UDC Magazine* 49, no. 1 (January 1986): 12.

———. "Division News: Florida." *UDC Magazine* 71, no. 1 (January 2008): 30.

———. "Division News: Florida." *UDC Magazine* 70, no. 2 (February 2007): 41.

———. "Division News: Florida." *UDC Magazine* 64, no. 1 (January 2006): 30.

———. "Division News: Florida." *UDC Magazine* 68, no. 1 (January 2005): 32–33.

———. "Division News: Florida." *UDC Magazine* 59, no. 9 (October 1996): 32.

———. "Division News: Florida." *UDC Magazine* 58, no. 1 (January 1995): 36, 37.

———. "Division News: Florida." *UDC Magazine* 57, no. 1 (January 1994): 33–34.

———. "Division News: Florida." *UDC Magazine* 54, no. 8 (September 1991): 31–32.

———. "Division News: Florida." *UDC Magazine* 49, no. 1 (January 1986): 10.

———. "Division News: Florida." *UDC Magazine* 38, no. 8 (August 1974): 11.

———. "Division News: Florida; Florida Dedicates New Monument." *UDC Magazine* 31, no. 9 (September 1968): 17.

———. "Division News: Florida." *UDC Magazine* 29, no. 8 (August 1966): 15–17.

———. "Division News: Florida." *UDC Magazine* 29, no. 4 (April 1966): 13.

———. "Division News: Florida." *UDC Magazine* 24, no. 8 (August 1961): 24.

———. "Florida Dedicates Vicksburg Monument." *UDC Magazine* 17, no. 7 (July 1954): 3, 39.

———. "Gen. Stonewall Jackson Honored as U.D.C. Dedicates Marker." *UDC Magazine* 13, no. 5 (May 1950): 10.

———. *Minutes of the Thirty-Second Annual Convention of the United Daughters of the Confederacy Held in Hot Springs, Arkansas, November 17–21, 1925*. N.p., 1925.

———. *Minutes of the Twenty-Third Annual Convention of the United Daughters of the Confederacy Held in Dallas, Texas, November 8 to 11, 1916*. Raleigh, N.C.: Edwards and Broughton Printing Co., 1917.

———. *Patriot Ancestor Album*. Paducah, Ky.: Turner Publishing Co., 1999.

United Daughters of the Confederacy, Florida Division. *Florida's Confederate Monuments and Markers*. Privately published, 2004.

———. *Minutes of the Ninety-Eighth Annual Convention September 23–26, 1993 Pensacola, Florida, and Minutes of the Ninety-Ninth Annual Convention October 6–8, 1994 Jacksonville, Florida*. N.p., 1993–94.

———. *Minutes of the Seventy-Eighth Annual Convention Tallahassee, Florida, October 9–11, 1973 and Minutes of the Seventy-Ninth Annual Convention Jacksonville, Florida, October 8–10, 1974*. N.p., 1973–74.

———. *Minutes of the Seventy-Second Annual Convention Held at Clearwater, Florida, October 10–12, 1967 and Minutes of the Seventy-Third Annual Convention Held at Orlando, Florida October 1–3, 1968*. N.p., 1967–68.

———. *Minutes of the Seventieth Annual Convention Held at West Palm Beach, Florida, October 5–7, 1965 and Minutes of the Seventy-First Annual Convention Held at Jacksonville, Florida, October 4–6, 1966*. N.p., 1965–66.

———. *Minutes of the Sixty-Sixth Annual Convention Held at Orlando, Florida, October 3–6, 1961*. N.p., 1961.

———. *Minutes of the Sixty-Fifth Annual Convention Held at Miami, Florida, October 6–8, 1960*. N.p., 1960.

———. *Minutes of the Fifty-Fifth Annual Convention Florida Division United Daughters of the Confederacy Held in Orlando, Florida, October 10, 11, 12, 1950*. Kissimmee, Fla.: Cattleman Press, 1950.

———. *Minutes of the Forty-Sixth Annual Convention Florida Division United Daughters of the Confederacy Held in Tallahassee, Florida, October 14–16, 1941*. Jacksonville: Drew Press, 1941.

———. *Minutes of the Forty-Fifth Annual Convention Florida Division United Daughters of the Confederacy Held in Pensacola, Florida, October 15–17, 1940*. Orlando: Ferris Printing Co., 1940.

———. *Minutes of the Forty-Fourth Annual Convention Florida Division United Daugh-*

ters of the Confederacy Held in Jacksonville, Florida, October 17–19, 1939. Orlando: Ferris Printing Co., 1939.
———. *Minutes of the Forty-Second Annual Convention Florida Division United Daughters of the Confederacy Held in Miami, Florida, October 20–21, 1937.* N.p., 1937.
———. *Minutes of the Forty-First Annual Convention Florida Division United Daughters of the Confederacy Held in Lakeland, Florida October 20–22, 1936.* Gainesville: Pepper Printing Co., 1936.
———. *Minutes of the Fortieth Annual Convention Florida Division United Daughters of the Confederacy Held in Daytona Beach, Florida, October 15–17, 1935.* N.p., 1935.
———. *Minutes of the Thirty-Third Annual Convention Florida Division United Daughters of the Confederacy Held in Tallahassee, Florida, October 17–19, 1928.* Tallahassee: T. J. Appleyard, 1928.
———. *Minutes of the Twenty-Sixth Annual Convention Florida Division United Daughters of the Confederacy Held in Pensacola, Florida, May 4–6, 1921.* N.p., 1921.
VanLandingham, Kyle S., ed. "Oaklawn Cemetery Ramble—1996." *Sunland Tribune: Journal of the Tampa Historical Society* 22 (November 1996): 105–8.
Waber, Andrew. *An Evaluation of Yellow Bluff Fort State Historic Site, Jacksonville, Fla.* Florida Master Site File, Florida Division of Historical Resources, Tallahassee, 2007.
Walters, Glenda Jane. "Union Colony in the Confederate South: Lynn Haven, Florida, 1910–1920." Ph.D. diss., Florida State University, 1995.
Warren, Robert Penn. *The Legacy of the Civil War.* Lincoln: University of Nebraska Press, 1961.
Waters, Zack C., and James C. Edmonds. *A Small but Spartan Band: The Florida Brigade in Lee's Army of Northern Virginia.* Tuscaloosa: University of Alabama Press, 2010.
Weber, Jessie Palmer, ed. "Grand Army of the Republic Monument to Memory of Union Soldiers Erected in Lynn Haven, Florida." *Journal of the Illinois State Historical Society* 14, nos. 1–2 (April–July 1921): 178.
Widener, Ralph W. *Confederate Monuments: Enduring Symbols of the South and the War between the States.* Washington, D.C.: Andromeda Associates, 1982.
Wilkinson, Joyce. "Confederate Cemetery—Tullahoma, Tennessee." *UDC Magazine* 58, no. 5 (May 1995): 21.
Williams, Alice Timmons. "The Battle of Olustee Forever Remembered." *UDC Magazine* 55, no. 1 (January 1992): 24–25.
Willis, Lee L. *Southern Prohibition: Race, Reform, and Public Life in Middle Florida, 1821–1920.* Athens: University Press of Georgia, 2011.
Woman's Relief Corps. *Journal of the Twentieth National Convention of the Woman's Relief Corps, Auxiliary to the Grand Army of the Republic, Washington, D.C., October 9th and 10th, 1902.* Boston: Griffith-Stillings Press, 1902.
Woolson, Constance Fenimore. "The Ancient City: In Two Parts—Part I." *Harper's New Monthly Magazine* 50, no. 295 (December 1874): 1–25.
Writers' Program of the Work Project Administration. *Planning Your Vacation in Florida: Miami and Dade County.* Northport, N.Y.: Bacon, Percy and Daggett, 1941.

Wynne, Lewis N., and Robert Taylor. *Florida in the Civil War*. Charleston, S.C.: Arcadia, 2002.
Zenzen, Joan M. *Battling for Manassas: The Fifty-Year Preservation Struggle at Manassas National Battlefield Park*. University Park: Pennsylvania State University Press, 1998.
Zipf, Catherine W. "Marking Union Victory in the South: The Construction of the National Cemetery System." In *Monuments to the Lost Cause: Women, Art, and the Landscapes of Southern Memory*, edited by Cynthia Mills and Pamela H. Simpson, 27–45. Knoxville: University of Tennessee Press, 2003.

INDEX

Page numbers in italics indicate illustrations.

Adams, Lt. Isaac, 280

African Americans: on Bradenton monument, 125; burial and graves of, 29, 230; on Crestview Lions Club monument, 161–62; on Ocala monument, 94; on Plant City monument, 283; suffrage and rights of, 24; as Union veterans, 166–67. *See also* U.S. Colored Troops

Alachua monument, 2002, 275–76

American Tribune Soldier's Colony Company, 167

Amnesty, 22–23

Appleyard, Col. Thomas Jefferson, *203*

Arlington National Cemetery monument, Virginia, 1914, 254; dedication of, *256*, 257; Florida soldiers listed at, 255–56, 257; nature and makeup of, 256–57; reconciliation theme in, 256–57; UDC and, 256, 257

Army of Northern Virginia, 232, 257; Florida soldiers in, 295; military engagements of, 235, 243–44

Army of Tennessee, 232, 257, 295

Artisans, 297–99. *See also specific artisans*

Association of Confederate Soldiers, 257

Barrancas National Cemetery, 27–28

Barrett, Anthony, 38, 311n55

Bartow, Brig. Gen. Francis Stebbings, 6, 307n6

Bartow, Maj. Gen. Law monument, 1932: inscription, 135; Law background and, 133–35; nature and makeup of, 135; of UDC, 133

Bartow monument, 1982, 289, 290; inscription on, 264, *265*; nature and makeup of, 264, *265*; from SCV, 264–65

Battlefields: burial on or near, 190–91; commemoration of, 190; as hallowed ground, 190, 230; UDC in marking, 87. *See also* Hallowed ground and hallowed ground monuments; *specific battles or battlefields*

Battle of Chickamauga, 239–40

Battle of First Manassas, 238

Battle of Franklin, Tennessee, 233

Battle of Gettysburg, 31, 249. *See also* Gettysburg Battlefield monument, Pennsylvania, 1963, 1965

Battle of Marianna: Confederate and Union armies in, 208; Florida recognizing, 208–9; location of, 211; military engagement in, 208, 230

Battle of Marianna monument, 1921, *209*; dedication of, 209–10; funds and fundraising for, 208–9; inscription on, 211; nature and makeup of, *210*, 210–11; from UDC, 208–10, 211

Battle of Natural Bridge: Confederate and Union armies in, 211–12; location of, 211; military engagement in, 211–12, 230–31

Battle of Natural Bridge monument, 1922, 212, *213*; dedication of, 214, *215*, 216; from Fletcher, John, 213–14, 217, 330n46; funds for, 214; inscription on, 216–17; nature and makeup of, *213*, 213–14, *216*, 216–17; from UDC, 212–13, 218
Battle of Olustee: Confederate and Union armies in, 192–93; Florida monuments to, 33–34, 192–208, *193*, *195*, *198*, *199–200*, *201*, *203*, *204*, *206*, *207*, 230; as hallowed ground, 230; military engagement at, 192–93; naming of, 328n8; Union soldiers' buried from, 28, 29, 33, 230
Battle of Rowlett's Station, 5
Battle of Vicksburg, 246–47
Beard, Lt. Col. William H., 25
Beaufort National Cemetery, 29
Benjamin, Judah P., 137–38, 218; hallowed ground monument to, 223–26, *224*, *225*, 231; World War II and monument to, 302
Blandford Cemetery and Church, 1912, 1917-1919, Petersburg, Virginia, *245*, 257–58; Confederate dead at, 243; dedication, 246; fund-raising, 246; inscriptions at, 244, 245; LMA involved in, 244, 246; nature and makeup of, 244–45
Bloedner, Christian Friedrich August, 5–6
Bradenton, Florida, 122
Bradenton monument, 1924, *122*, *124*; dedication, 123, 124–25; fund-raising, 122–23; inscription, 123; location, 125; nature and makeup of, 123–24; of UDC, 122–23
Bravery and valor: monuments to, 76–77, 79, 80, 82, 110, 127, 199; in southern commemoration, 12, 231
Breckinridge, John C., 20
Brooksville, Florida, 114
Brooksville monument, 1916: dedication, 114; inscription, 114, 116; nature and makeup of, 114, *115*, 116; UDC and, 114, 116
Burial and graves: battlefield, 190–91; care in, 32, 33–34, 191–92; Civil War end and, 30–32; of Confederate soldiers, 11–12, 26–29, 31–32, 176–77, 178, 191–92, 196–97, 233–39, 243–49, 251–58, 276–77, 277; federal government, Confederate soldiers, and, 31–32, 191–92, 196–97; federal government national cemeteries for, 191; of Florida soldiers, 12, 26–28; GAR on, 163; Loring, 116, 118; mass and unknown, 191, 196, 205, 244, 245; race and, 196, 230; in Reconstruction-era South, 11; of Union soldiers, 11, 28, 29, 31, 33–34, 176–77, 178, 191, 222, 223, 230, 276–77, 277; of USCT, 29, 230. *See also* Cemeteries; Commemoration

Call, Wilkinson, 43–44
Camps, 189–90, 327n2
Cannons and cannonballs: in Palatka monument, 128; in Pensacola monument, 69; Tampa Woodlawn Cemetery monument with, 151, 152–53; at Yellow Bluff Fort monument, 227–28
Care, burial, 32, 33–34, 191–92
Carlotta, Sister Esther, 106
Casey, Edward Pearce, 220, 221
Cedar and McGirt Creek skirmishes, *273*, 273–74
Cemeteries: Florida soldiers in Virginia, 254–56; national, 31, 191; soldiers buried in Florida, 28–29; Union monuments in Florida, 187–88. *See also specific cemeteries*
Centennial, Civil War. *See* Monument or monuments, post-Centennial
Charleston, SC, 84–85
Chattahooche, 267–69, *268*
Chattahoochee monument, 1994: *Chattahoochee* explosion and, 267–69; dedication of, 267–68; financial cost of, 267; inscription, 268; nature and makeup of, *268*, 268–69; from UDC, 267–68
Chickamauga Battlefield monument, Georgia, 1913, 239, *241*, 258; commission for oversight of, 240–41; dedication of, 241–42; funds and fund-raising for, 240–41; inscription on, 243; nature and makeup of, *242*, 242–43
Civil War: death in, 1, 9–10, 12, 26–27, 29–32; economic impact of, 25–30, 166; ending of, 17–21, 30–32, 166; as "felt" history, 259; Florida in, 10, 12, 25–30, 34, 52, 58, 66–67, 73, 77, 88, 96, 102, 114, 119, 122, 125, 137, 145–46,

202, 223, 226, 293; Florida soldiers in, 162, 232, 238, 240, 243–44, 249, 250, 251, 257; Gamble Plantation after, 218–19, *219*; GAR as veterans association after, 11; monument organizations' connection to, 293–94; monuments built during, 5–9; monuments for soldiers and impact of, 7; monuments to legacy or aftermath of, 92–93, 294; northern sentiment of cost of, *14*; reunification at end of, 10; soldiers' experience after, 10; Union officer organizations during and after, 164; Union strategy in Florida, 20. *See also* Military engagement; Monument or monuments, Civil War
Clark, Frank, 197
Clearwater monument, 1993, 267
Climate, 189–90
Codieck, Barrett, 87
Colquitt, Brig. Gen. Alfred H., 205
Commemoration: of battlefields, 190; bravery in southern, 12, 231; GAR influence on, 11; LMAs in southern, 11–12; through monuments, 32, 289–90; of sacrifice, 12–13; of Stonewall Jackson Highway monument, 140–41; UCV in, 11–12, 51
Community monuments, 12; Confederate cause vindication in, 87–88, 92–93; diversity of, 13; Gainesville monument as, 88–91, *89*, *90*; to general sacrifice, 13; Lost Cause narrative in, 162; nature and function of, 162; from UDC, 86–99, *89*, *90*, *93*, *95*, *96*, *98*, *100*, *101*, 101–3, *104–5*, 105–14, *108–9*, *110*, *111–12*, *115*, 116, *117*, 118–25, *120*, *121*, *122*, *124*, *126*, 127–47, *129*, *131*, *133–34*, *136*, *137*, *139*, *140*, *142*, *144*, *146*; Union, 170–88, *172*, *175*, *176*, *177*, *179*, *180*, *182*, *184*, *185*, *186*. *See also* Grand Army of the Republic; United Daughters of the Confederacy
Cone, Fred P., 138
Confederate army: in Battle of Marianna, 208; in Battle of Natural Bridge, 211–12; in Battle of Olustee, 192–93; economic impact of, 25–26; in Florida, 25–26, 58, 62, 66–67, 145–46; Florida soldiers in, 232, 295; surrender of, 17–18, 19–21. *See also* Military engagement
Confederate cause, symbols, or words: community monuments for vindicating, 87–88, 92–93; controversy surrounding, 294–95, 303–5; death of Davis, Jefferson, and Lee in, 72–73; misappropriation of, 294, 303–4; monuments to, 32, 52, 68, 71–73, 76–77, 86, 92–93, 142, 291, 296–97, 301, 303–5; UDC in vindication of, 51, 86, 291. *See also* Lost Cause narrative
Confederate leaders: amnesty, reconstruction, and, 22–23; Confederate cause and death of, 72–73; in new South origin story, 12. *See also* Davis, Jefferson; Lee, Gen. Robert E.
Confederate Memorial Day, 49, 174
Confederate monument or monuments: to Confederate cause, 32, 52, 68, 71–73, 76–77, 86, 92–93, 142, 291, 296–97, 301, 303–5; to Confederate soldiers, 123–25, 127–28, 143, 160–62, *161*, 194–208, 226–28, *227*, 233–49, *237*, *250*, 251–58, *256*, 285, 287, *288*, 289, 301; to Confederate veterans, 143–44, *144*, 148, *149*, 276–77, *277*, *278*, 278–79, 281, 285–86, *286*; to Confederate women, 153–60, *156*, *157*, *158*, *159*; dedication dates for, 174; to Dickison, 147, 150, *150*; in Florida, 295–96; to Florida soldiers, 15, 26–27, 40, 42, 45, 54, 65, 66, 80, 233–49, *237*, *250*, 251–58, 283–84, *284*; function, nature, and message of, 4, 300–303; to hallowed ground, 229–30; Jacksonville, 77–80, *78*, *81*, 82, 84–86, *85*; Marianna, 58–60, *59*, *60*, *61*, 62, 208–11, *209*, *210*; Monticello, 73, *74–75*, 75–77; Pensacola, 66–73, *70*, *71*, *72*; from private individuals, 51, 77–80, *78*, *81*, 82–86, *83*, *84*, *85*; Quincy, 62–63, *63*, *64*, *65*, 66; relocation of, 303–4; St. Augustine, 42–45, *43*, *44*, *46*, *47*; in St. Petersburg, 82–84, *83*, *84*; Tallahassee, 52–58, *53*, *55*, *57*; time period for building, 86–87; UCV, 147–48, *149*, *150*, 150–60, *152*, *156*, *157*, *158*, *159*; Walton County, 38, *39*, 40, *41*, 42. *See also* Community monuments; United Confederate Veterans; United Daughters of the Confederacy; *specific Confederate monuments*

Confederate Mound at Oak Woods Cemetery, Chicago, Illinois, 255
Confederate navy, 84–86
Confederate soldiers: burial and graves of, 11–12, 26–29, 31–32, 176–77, 178, 191–92, 196–97, 233–39, 243–49, 251–58, 276–77, *277*; Civil War death of, 1; Confederate monuments to, 123–25, 127–28, 143, 160–62, *161*, 194–208, 226–28, *227*, 233–49, *237*, *250*, 251–58, *256*, 285, 287, *288*, 289, 301; federal government and burial of, 31–32, 191–92, 196–97; honoring dead, 49; in Lost Cause narrative, 50. *See also* Florida soldiers
Confederate Sons Association of Florida, 260
Confederate States of America, 9–10
Confederate Veteran, 158
Confederate veterans: Confederate monuments to, 143–44, *144*, 148, *149*, 276–77, *277*, *278*, 278–79, 281, 285–86, *286*; at Jacksonville Hemming monument dedication, 78–79; at Pensacola monument, *71*; post-Centennial monuments to, 290. *See also* Sons of Confederate Veterans; United Confederate Veterans
Congress: Johnson conflicting with, 23, 309n22; Lincoln's Annual Message to, 17; during reconstruction, 23–24, 30
Controversy: Confederate cause or symbol, 294–95, 303–5; Lost Cause narrative, 304; over Crestview Lions Club monument, 161–62; Pensacola monument, 70–71; from Plant City monument, 283, 294; Tallahassee monument, 54–55, 56, 301–2; from Tampa monument, 2008, 285
Cow Cavalry, *282*, 282–83, 294
Cox, Karen L., 86–87
Crawfordville monument, 1987: dedication of, 266–67; nature and makeup of, *266*, 266–67; from UDC, 267
Crestview Lions Club monument, 1958: African Americans and controversy over, 161–62; to Confederate soldiers and Lundy, 160, *161*; inscription, 160; location, 160–61; nature and makeup of, 160
CSS *David*, 85–86
Dade City monument, 2006, 276–77
"Daughters of the Confederacy," 50
Daughters of Union Veterans of the Civil War, 264
Davis, Jefferson: Civil War cost and, *14*; in Civil War end, 20–21; Confederate cause and death of, 72–73; on Confederate women, 153; Miami monument, 1914, and, 113; monuments to, 123, 124–25
Davis, Robert W., 197
Daytona Beach monument, 1961: changes to, 145; dedication, 144–45; inscription, 145; nature and makeup of, 145; of UDC, 144–45
Dead, Civil War: Confederate Memorial Day and honoring, 49; Confederate soldiers as honored, 49; federal government on, 14; monuments to, 193–214, *215*, 216–49, *234*, *237*, *239*, *241*, *242*, *245*, *247*, *250*, 251–58, *252*, *253*, *256*, 280, 295, 301–2; soldier, 1, 307n4; unknown, 191, 196, 205, 244, 245. *See also* Burial and graves
Death: in Civil War, 1, 9–10, 12, 26–27, 29–32; Confederate cause and Confederate leader, 72–73; from disease, 34–35; home and, 30–31; of Lincoln and reconstruction, 19–21, 309n20; new South origin and Confederate leaders, 12. *See also* Burial and graves; Sacrifice
Dedication: Arlington National Cemetery, *256*, 257; Battle of Marianna monument, 1921, 209–10; Battle of Natural Bridge monument, 214, *215*, 216; Blandford Church, 246; Bradenton monument, 123, 124–25; Brooksville monument, 114; Chattahoochee monument, 267–68; Chickamauga Battlefield monument, 241–42; Confederate monument dates for, 174; of Crawfordville monument, 266–67; Daytona Beach monument, 144–45; DeLand monument, 144; Dixie Highway monument, 128–30, *129*; Fort Myers monument, 1998, 271, 332n69; of Gainesville monument, 88, 90–91; Gamble Plantation monument, 1937, 138; Gettysburg Battlefield monument, 252;

Havana monument, 271; Jacksonville Confederate Park monument, 155–56; of Jacksonville Hemming monument, 77–79, 82; Jacksonville monument, 2001, 273; of Jacksonville Union monument, 171; of Key West, New York Regimental Monument, 221; Key West monument, Bayview Park, 120; Lakeland monument, 99, 101; Leesburg monument, 135, 136–37; of Lynn Haven Union monument, 179–80; Madison monument, 1909, 97; Madison monument, 1996, 269–70; for Marianna monument, 1881, 58; of Miami Union monument, 183–84, *184*, 185, 187; Ocala monument, 92, *93*; of Old Town monument, 281; of Olustee Battlefield monument, Finegan, 1951, 206, *207*; of Olustee Battlefield monument 1912, 196, *198*, 198–99, *199*, 302; of Olustee Confederate Dead 1901, 194–95, 196; of Olustee Confederate Dead 1928, 202–3; Orlando monument, 107; Palatka monument, 125, 127; Pensacola monument, 67; of Quincy monument, 62–63; to reunification, 79, 82; St. Augustine Loring monument, 116; of St. Cloud monuments, 272, 278; of St. Petersburg Greenwood Cemetery monument, 82, *83*, 84; of St. Petersburg Union monument, 174; of Sarasota monument, 223–25, *224*, 226; Sebastian monument, 276; of Starke monument, 261; of Stonewall Confederate Cemetery, 235–36; of Stonewall Jackson Highway monument, 138, 141; of Tallahassee monument, 53–54, 58; Tampa monument, 1911, 103, 107; of Tampa Union monument, 182–83; Tampa Woodlawn Cemetery monument, 151; of Union Dead monument, Magnolia Springs Cemetery, 223; Vicksburg Battlefield monument, 247–48
DeLand monument, 1959: dedication, 144; inscription, 143–44; nature and makeup of, 143–44; of UDC, 143
Democrats, 24–25
Dickison, Capt. John J., 1, 79, 147, 150, *150*, 171
Dimitry, John, 108–9
Disease: death from, 34–35; Key West, 34–35; yellow fever, 220
Diversity, community monument, 13
Dixie Highway monument, Bradfordville, 1927: dedication, 128–30, *129*; inscription on, 131–32; to Lee, 128–29, *129*, 130–31, *131*; location, 130; nature and makeup of, 130–31, 319n146; of UDC, 128, 129, 131
Dixie Highway monument, Nassau County, 1928: dedication, 132; to Lee, 132; location, 132; nature and makeup of, 132, 319n146; of UDC, 132

Economy, Florida: Civil War impact on, 25–30, 166; Confederate army impact on, 25–26; Union veterans' impact on, 166, 167–68
Elder, John Adams, 67–68
Emancipation Proclamation, 20
End or ending: of Civil War, 17–21, 30–32, 166; reunification and Civil War, 10; of slavery, 20
Eppes, Susan Bradford, 56, 129
Ezekiel, Moses, 256, 257

Federal government: battlefield commemoration by, 190; on Civil War dead compared to veterans, 14; Confederate soldier burials and, 31–32, 191–92, 196–97; monuments for, 7–8, 308nn8–9; national cemeteries from, 191
"Felt" history, 259
Fifteenth Amendment, 24
Financial cost: of Chattahoochee monument, 267; Fort Myers monument, 1966, 147; of Fort Myers monument, 1998, 271; of Gainesville monument, 88; Havana monument, 271; of Jacksonville Confederate Park monument, 154–55; of Jacksonville Hemming monument, 78; of Key West, New York Regimental Monument, 221; of Miami monument, 1914, 111; of Quincy monument, 63; of Stonewall Jackson Highway monument, 138–39; of Tallahassee monument, 52–53; of Vicksburg Battlefield monument, 247; of

Financial cost—*continued*
Walton County monument, 38; of Yellow Bluff Fort monument, 227
Finegan, Brig. Gen. Joseph, 206–7
Finley, Brig. Gen. Jesse J., 58
Fitzgerald, Philander H., 167
Flagler, Henry, 166
"Flags across Florida" monuments: as post-Centennial monuments, 290–91; Tampa monument, 2008, among, 285; White Springs monument among, *274*, 274–75
Fletcher, Duncan U., 199
Fletcher, John B., 213–14, 217, 330n46
Florida: Battle of Marianna recognized in, 208–9; Civil War end and, 18–19, 166; Civil War in, 10, 12, 25–30, 34, 52, 58, 66–67, 73, 77, 88, 96, 102, 114, 119, 122, 125, 137, 145–46, 202, 223, 226, 293; Confederate army in, 25–26, 58, 62, 66–67, 145–46; Confederate monuments in, 295–96; economy of, 25–30, 166, 167–68; GAR in, 166–67, *168*, 169; Gettysburg Battlefield monument and commission from, *250*, 251; hallowed ground in, 192–214, *193*, *195*, *198*, *199–200*, *201*, *203*, *204*, *206*, *207*, *209*, *210*, *212*, *213*, *215–16*, 216–31, *219*, *222*, *224*, *225*, *227*; immigration to, 166, 194; Johnston, Gen. Joseph, surrender impact on, 19; Lost Cause narrative in, 187, 296–97; population, 162, 166, 194, 232, 293; post-Centennial monuments in, 260–62, *263*, 264–92; soldiers buried in cemeteries of, 28–29; Union army in, 18–19, 34, 42, 52, 58, 66–67, 77, 145–46, 232; Union monuments in, 15, 33–35, *36–37*, 38, 82–84, *83*, 163, 187–88, 228–29, 264, 289, 293, 295, 300; Union strategy in, 20; Union veterans in, 15, 166–70, *168*, *170*; USCT enlisted in, 18–19. *See also* Economy, Florida; Geography, Florida; Monument or monuments, Florida; Real estate, Florida; Reconstruction-era Florida; Society, Florida; *specific towns and cities*
Florida soldiers: burial and graves of, 12, 26–28; in Civil War, 162, 232, 238, 240, 243–44, 249, *250*, 251, 257; in Confederate army, 232, 295; Confederate monuments to, 15, 26–27, 40, 42, 45, 54, 65, 66, 80, 233–49, *237*, *250*, 251–58, 283–84, *284*; population of, 162, 232; social impact of death of, 26, 29; UDC in monuments to, 257–58; in Virginia cemeteries, 254–56
Forrest, Nathan Bedford, 289
Fortifications, 34, 310n51
Fort Meade monument, 1983: to Jackson, 265–66; nature and makeup of, 265–66; from SCV, 265–66
Fort Myers, Florida, 145–46
Fort Myers monument, 1998: dedication, 271, 332n69; financial cost of, 271; nature and makeup of, *270*, 271; to USCT, *270*, 270–71, 289, 290, 332n69
Fort Myers monument, 1966, 145; financial cost of, 147; fund-raising, 146; inscription, 147; to Lee, 302–3; of UDC, 146–47, 302–3
Fourteenth Amendment, 23, 24
Funds and fund-raising: for Battle of Marianna monument, 208–9; Battle of Natural Bridge monument, 214; Blandford Church, 246; for Bradenton monument, 122–23; for Chickamauga Battlefield monument, 240–41; Fort Meyers monument, 146; Gettysburg Battlefield monument, 251, 254; Jacksonville Confederate Park monument, 159; for Jacksonville Union monument, 171; for Key West, New York Regimental Monument, 220; of Key West monument in Clinton Square, 327n52; for Lynn Haven Union monument, 181; for Miami Union monument, 184, *185*; for Monticello monument, 73; Ocala monument, 92; for Olustee Battlefield monument 1912, 197–98, 201; for Olustee Battlefield Union monument, 194; for Olustee Confederate Dead 1928, 202; for Pensacola monument, 67; St. Augustine Loring monument, 118; for Tallahassee

monument, 53–55, 56; Tampa monument, 102–3; for Union monuments, 187

Gainesville, Florida, 88
Gainesville monument, 1904: as community monument, 88–91, *89*, *90*; dedication of, 88, 90–91; financial cost of, 88; inscription, 91; nature and makeup of, 88–90, 91; restoration to, 91
Gamble, Maj. Robert, 137–38
Gamble Plantation: after Civil War, 218–19, *219*; in Civil War, 137
Gamble Plantation, 1937: dedication, 138; inscription, *137*; of UDC, 138
Gamble Plantation monument, 1925, 218–19, 231
Gannon, Barbara A., 164–65
GAR. *See* Grand Army of the Republic
Geography, Florida, 26
George N. Clark Company, 298–99
Gettysburg Battlefield monument, Pennsylvania, 1963, 1965: dedication of, 252; Florida commission for, *250*, 251; Florida soldiers in, 249, *250*, 251, 252, 253, 258; funding of, 251, 254; inscription on, 251–52, 254; nature and makeup of, 251–52, *252*, *253*; restoration of, 253
Gilchrist, Albert W., 199
Grand Army of the Republic (GAR): on burial and graves, 163; in commemoration, 11; community monument building time period, 170–71; on Confederate soldier burial, 31–32; in Florida, 166–67, *168*, 169; formation of, 164; in Jacksonville Union monument, 171, 173; LGAR and WRC in, 165; in Lynn Haven, 169, *170*, 178–79; Lynn Haven Union monument and, *179*, 179–80, 181; in Miami Union monument, 183–84, 185, 187; national encampments of, 165; nature and function of, 164; organizational structure, 165; in Orlando Union monument, 175–77, *176*; as post-Civil War veterans association, 11; race in, 164–65; reconciliation monuments involving, 82–83; St. Cloud monument, 2000, from, 272, *272*; in St. Cloud Union monument, 1915, *177*, 177–78; in St. Petersburg Union monument, 174; in Tampa Union monument, 182–83; UDC conflict with, 196–97; Union monuments and, 187–88; on Union soldier burial, 31; for Union veterans, 11, 166–67; veterans colonies in South, 170
Grant, Lt. Gen. Ulysses S.: on African-American rights, 24; in Civil War end, 17; presidency of, 24–25
Graves. *See* Burial and graves
Green Cove Springs, Florida, 223
Green Cove Springs monument, 2011, 287
Groveton Cemetery, Manassas Battlefield, Virginia, 1904, 257–58; Confederate dead at, 238; nature and makeup of, 238–39, *239*; UDC and, 238
Groveton monument, *9*

H. L. Hunley, 84–85
Hallowed ground and hallowed ground monuments: battlefields as, 190, 230; Battle of Olustee as, 230; to Benjamin, 223–26, *224*, *225*, 231; Confederate monuments to, 229–30; in Florida, 192–214, *193*, *195*, *198*, *199–200*, *201*, *203*, *204*, *206*, *207*, *209*, *210*, *212*, *213*, *215–16*, 216–31, *219*, *222*, *224*, *225*, *227*; Lincoln on, 189; post-Centennial, 289–90; from UDC, 229; union monuments to, 228–29. *See also* Dead, Civil War
Harris, Frank, 92–93
Harris, J. V., 35
Havana monument, 1999, 271
Hazen, Gen. William, 6
Heiple, Roger, 166
Hemming, Charles C., 78, 80
Hemming, Lucy, 78
Heyward Shepherd monument, 304–5
Holbrook, Col. William C., 189–90
Home, 30–31
Human loss, 6

Immigration, Florida, 166, 194
Inscriptions. *See specific monuments*

Jackson, Gen. Thomas "Stonewall," 45, 47; monuments to, 79–80, 123, 124–25, 138–41, *139*, *140*, 265–66; Stonewall Confederate Cemetery to, 26–27, 235–38, *237*, 257; Stonewall Jackson Highway to, 138–41, *139*, *140*
Jacksonville, Florida, 77, 80, 82
Jacksonville monument, Confederate Park, 1915: to Confederate women, 153–60, *156*, *157*, *158*; dedication, 155–56; financial cost of, 154–55; fund-raising, 159; inscription, 157, 158; nature and makeup of, 156–58, *157*; UCV in, 153–55, 157
Jacksonville monument, Evergreen Cemetery, 1973, 262
Jacksonville monument, Evergreen Cemetery, 1910: to Dickison, 150; inscription, 151; nature and makeup of, 150–51; UCV in, 150, 151
Jacksonville monument, Evergreen Cemetery, 1928: to CSS *David*, *85*, 86; inscription, 86; from private individuals, 84–86, *85*
Jacksonville monument, Hemming Plaza, 1898: dedication of, 77–79, 82; financial cost of, 78; inscription, 79–80; Jacksonville fire and, 80, 82; nature and makeup of, 79–80, 82; private individuals in, 77–80, *78*, *81*, 82
Jacksonville monument, Riverside Park, *159*, 159–60
Jacksonville monument, 2001: to Cedar and McGirt Creek skirmishes, *273*, 273–74; dedication, 273; inscription, 274; from UDC, 273
Jacksonville Union monument, 1891: dedication of, 171; funds for, 171; GAR in, 171, 173; inscription on, 173; nature and makeup of, 171–73, *172*
James Bennitt or Bennett farm, 17, 308n4
Johnson, Andrew, 22–25, 30, 309n22
Johnson's Island, 255
Johnston, Gen. Albert Sidney, 108–9
Johnston, Gen. Joseph E.: in Civil War end, 17–18, 19, 20–21; surrender of, 19–21
Jones, Maj. Gen. Sam, 19
Key West, Florida: in Civil War, 34, 119; disease in, 34–35; fortifications at, 34; Union army in, 34
Key West, New York Regimental Monument, 1930: dedication of, 221; financial cost of, 221; funds for, 220; inscription on, 221; location of, 220–21; nature and makeup of, 221–22, *222*; as state monument, 220; yellow fever and, 220
Key West monument, Bayview Park, 1924, *120*; changes to, 120–21; dedication, 120; inscription, 120; location, 121; nature and makeup of, 120–21, *121*; of UDC, 119–21
Key West monument, Clinton Square, 1866: fence surrounding, 35; as Florida monument, 34–35, *36–37*, 38; funding of, 327n52; nature and makeup of, 35; from Navy Club of Key West, 35, 38
Kissimmee monument, 2002, 275
Knight, Lucian Lamar, 142–43

Ladies' Memorial Associations (LMAs), 290; in Blandford Cemetery and Church, 244, 246; Confederate Memorial Day from, 49; in confederate soldier burial, 32; as "Daughters of the Confederacy," 50; in Florida monuments, 15, 38, 42–43, 44–45, 47–48, 49–50, 51–60, *53*, *55*, *57*, *59*, *60*, *61*, 62–63, *63*, *64*, 65–73, *70*, *71*, *72*, *74–75*, 75–77; in Lost Cause narrative, 50; in Marianna, 58; Monticello, 73; in monument building, 49–50, 51–60, *53*, *55*, *57*, *59*, *60*, *61*, 62–63, *63*, *64*, 65–73, *70*, *71*, *72*, *74–75*, 75–77; monuments as sculpture for, 297–98; Pensacola, 67, 69–70; Quincy, 62–63; after Reconstruction, 49; St. Augustine monument, 1872, 42–43, 44–45, 52; in southern commemoration, 11–12; Stonewall Confederate Cemetery and, 235–36; in Tallahassee monument building, 52–58, *53*, *55*, *57*; Walton County in, 1, 38
Ladies of the Grand Army of the Republic (LGAR), 165
Lake City, Florida, 202
Lakeland monument, 1910, *101*; dedica-

tion, 99, 101; inscription, 102; nature and makeup of, 101–2; of UDC, 99, *100*
Lakeland monument, 2007, 279
Landscaping, Florida monument, 300
Law, Maj. Gen. Evander McIver, *133*, 133–35, *134*
Lee, Gen. Robert E.: in Civil War end, 17; Confederate cause and death of, 72–73; military engagements involving, 243–44; monuments to, 79–80, 124–25, 128–29, *129*, 130–31, *131*, 145–47, *146*, 148, 289, 302–3
Leesburg monument, 1935: dedication, 135, 136–37; inscription, 136, 137; nature and makeup of, 136; of UDC, 135, *136*
LGAR. *See* Ladies of the Grand Army of the Republic
Lincoln, Abraham: on Civil War end, 17; on Civil War Florida, 20; on hallowed ground, 189; monuments to, 183; reconstruction and death of, 19–21, 309n20
Littlefield, A. W., 131–32
Live Oak monument, 1909: inscription, 148; location, 148; nature and makeup of, 148; UCV in, 148
LMAs. *See* Ladies' Memorial Associations
Location, Florida monument, 299–300. *See also specific monuments*
Loring, William Wing: background and burial of, 116, 118; monument from, 116, *117*, 118–19
Loring Camp, 151–52, 153
Lost Cause narrative, 49; in community monuments, 162; Confederate soldiers in, 50; controversy surrounding, 304; Davis, Jefferson, and Lee death in, 72–73; in Florida, 187, 296–97; LMAs in, 50; monuments to, 32, 50, 65, 95–96, 98–99, 153, 296–97; after World War I, 297
Lundy, William "Uncle Bill," 160, *161*
Lynn Haven, Florida, 169, *170*, 178–79
Lynn Haven Union monument, 1921, 178, 327n48; dedication of, 179–80; fund-raising for, 181; GAR in, *179*, 179–80, 181; inscription on, 181; nature and makeup of, *180*, 180–81; vandalism of, 181
Madison, Florida, 96
Madison monument, 1909: dedication, 97; nature and makeup of, 97–98; UDC and, *96*, 97, 98–99
Madison monument, 1996: dedication of, 269–70; inscription, 269–70; nature and makeup of, *269*, 269–70
Magnolia Springs Cemetery Union Dead monument, Green Cove Springs, pre-1939, 223
Mallory, Stephen R., 68, 119–20
Manassas: Battlefield, 6, *6*, 7–8, *8*, 9; monument at, 12–13
Marianna, Florida, 58
Marianna monument, 1881: dedication ceremony for, 58; as Florida monument, 58–60, *59*, *60*, *61*, 62; inscription, 59–60, 62; LMA in building, 58; nature and makeup of, 59–60, 62. *See also* Battle of Marianna monument, 1921
Marianna monument, 2007, 280, *281*
Martin, Col. John M., 92, 93
Martin, John W., 214
Marvin, William, 23
McCook, Brig. Gen. Edward M., 19
McElroy, John, 168–69
McGavock Confederate Cemetery, Franklin, Tennessee, 1890, 27, 257; Confederate dead at, 233–35, *234*; inscriptions at, 234–35; nature and makeup of, 233–35; UDC and, 235
McNeel Marble Company, 155, 156, 241, 298
McNeill, Capt. Archibald, 137–38
Meade, Lt. George, 266
Memoria in Aeterna monument, 296–97
Message, monument: of Confederate monuments, 4, 300–303; Reconstruction context in understanding, 303; of Union monuments, 188, 300
Miami monument, 1914: financial cost of, 111; inscription, 113–14; location, 111, *111*, 113; nature and makeup of, 111–14, *112*; of UDC, 111–12, 113–14
Miami Union monument, 1939, 188; dedication of, 183–84, *184*, 185, 187; fund-raising for, 184, *185*; GAR in, 183–84, 185, 187;

Miami Union monument—*continued*
inscription on, 184, 186–87; nature and makeup of, 185–87, *186*; WRC in, 185, 187
Milione, Louis, 241
Military engagement: of Army of Northern Virginia, 235, 243–44; Battle of Chickamauga, 239–40; in Battle of Franklin, Tennessee, 233; at Battle of Gettysburg, 249; in Battle of Marianna, 208, 230; in Battle of Natural Bridge, 211–12, 230–31; at Battle of Olustee, 192–93; at Battle of Vicksburg, 246–47; in Fort Meyers, 145–46; in Gainesville, 88; at Green Cove Springs, 223
Military government, 23–24
"Military History of Florida" (Dickison), 1
Military Order of the Stars and Bars, 260
Monticello, Florida, 73
Monticello monument, 1899: as Florida monument, 73, *74–75*, 75–77; fund-raising for, 73; inscription, 76; LMA in building, 73; nature and makeup of, 73, 75–76; Quincy monument compared to, 76
Monumental Bronze Company, 173
Monument companies, 297–99. *See also specific companies*
Monument or monuments, Civil War: to bravery and valor, 76–77, 79, 80, 82, 110, 127, 199; Civil War impact on soldiers through, 7; to Civil War legacy or aftermath, 92–93, 294; commemoration through, 32, 289–90; for community, 12–13; to Confederate cause, 32, 52, 68, 71–73, 76–77, 86, 92–93, 142, 291, 296–97, 301, 303–5; current relevance of, 16; to Davis, Jefferson, 123, 124–25; to dead, 193–214, *215*, 216–49, *234*, *237*, *239*, *241*, *242*, *245*, *247*, *250*, 251–58, *252*, *253*, *256*, 280, 295, 301–2; for federal government, 7–8, 308nn8–9; function and importance of, 4–5, 16; to Hazen's Brigade, 6, *7*; to Jackson, 79–80, 123, 124–25, 138–41, *139*, *140*, 265–66; to Lee, 79–80, 124–25, 128–29, *129*, 130–31, *131*, 145–47, *146*, 148, 289, 302–3; to Lincoln, 183; to Lost Cause narrative, 32, 50, 65, 95–96, 98–99, 153, 296–97; of major events, 87; at Manassas Battlefield, 6, *6*, 7–8, *8*, 9; monument organizations and connection to, 293–94; private individuals building, 51, 77–80, *78*, *81*, 82–86, *83*, *84*, *85*; to reconciliation, 78–79, 82–84, *83*, 174, 224–25, 256–57; sacrifice reflected in, 10, 12–13, 62; "surrender," 7, 303n8; to Thirty-Second Indiana, 5, *5*; ubiquity of, 5–6, 10; UDC placement strategy for, 110; to unknown, 244, *245*, *281*; from veterans, 38. *See also* Community monuments; Confederate monument or monuments; Hallowed ground and hallowed ground monuments; Union monument or monuments; *specific monuments*
Monument or monuments, Civil War, building of: during Civil War, 5–9; LMAs in, 49–50, 51–60, *53*, *55*, *57*, *59*, *60*, *61*, 62–63, *63*, *64*, 65–73, *70*, *71*, *72*, *74–75*, 75–77; time period for Confederate, 86–87
Monument or monuments, Florida: artisans and monument companies of, 297–99; "Flags across Florida," *274*, 274–75, 285, 290–91; to Florida soldiers, 15, 26–27, 40, 42, 54, 65, 66, 80; inscriptions on, 296–97; Jacksonville, 77–80, *78*, *81*, 82, 84–86, *85*, 150–51, 153–60, *156*, *157*, *158*, *159*, 171–73, *172*, 262, 273, 273–74; Key West, 34–35, *36–37*, 38, 119–21, *120*, *121*, 220–22, *222*, 327n52; landscaping around, 300; LMAs involvement in, 15, 38, 42–43, 44–45, 47–48, 49–50, 51–60, *53*, *55*, *57*, *59*, *60*, *61*, 62–63, *63*, *64*, 65–73, *70*, *71*, *72*, *74–75*, 75–77; location of, 299–300; Marianna, 58–60, *59*, *60*, *61*, 62, 208–11, *209*, *210*, 280, *281*; Monticello, 73, *74–75*, 75–77; national tragedy and, 4; nature and function of, 3–4, 295–96, 297–98, 305; Olustee Battlefield, 33–34, 192–208, *193*, *195*, *198*, *199–200*, *201*, *203*, *204*, *206*, *207*, 230; Pensacola, 66–73, *70*, *71*, *72*; physical condition and restoration of, 299; post-Centennial, 260–62, *263*, 264–92; from private individuals, 51, 77–80, *78*, *81*, 82–86, *83*, *84*, *85*; public buildings or

grounds and, 305; Quincy, 62–63, *63*, *64*, 65–66; Reconstruction-era Florida and building of, 13, 32–35, *36–37*, 38, *39*, 40, *41*, 42–45, *43*, *44*, *46*, 47–48; regimental, 283; St. Augustine, 42–45, *43*, *44*, *46*, 47, 116, *117*, 118–19, 301; St. Petersburg, 82–84, *83*, *84*, 174–75, *175*; as sculpture, 297–98; Tallahassee, 52–58, *53*, *55*, *57*; tourism and, 47, 179–80; UDC, 15, 296–97; Union, 15, 33–35, *36–37*, 38, 82–84, *83*; Union community monuments in, 170–88, *172*, *175*, *176*, *177*, *179*, *180*, *182*, *184*, *185*, *186*; Walton County, 38, *39*, 40, *41*, 42. *See also* Community monuments; United Daughters of the Confederacy; *specific monuments*

Monument or monuments, post-Centennial, 15–16; to Confederate veterans, 290; to Cow Cavalry, *282*, 282–83, 294; "Flags across Florida," 290–91; in Florida, 260–62, *263*, 264–92; hallowed ground commemorated in, 289–90; organizations involved in, 259–60, 289, 290–92; proposed, 291; regarding slavery, *269*, 269–70; Starke, 260–61, *261*; Union, 187, 291–92; to USCT, *270*, 270–71, 289, 290, 332n69. *See also specific monuments*

National Association of the Daughters of the Confederacy, 50

National cemeteries: from Federal government, 191; of U.S., 31

National tragedy, 4

Natural Bridge Battlefield Historic State Park, 212

Natural Bridge Road, 212

Navy Club of Key West, 35, 38

Newman, Allen G., 155

Ninetieth and Ninety-First New York Infantry Regiments, 220–22, *222*

North, Civil War sentiment of, *14*

North Carolina, 22–23

Northrup, William J., 167

Nunnally, G. A., 92, 93

Ocala monument, 1908: dedication, 92–93, *93*; fund-raising, 92; inscription, 94, 95–96; locations for, 94–95, *95*; nature and makeup of, 93–94; UDC and, 92

Old Town monument, 2007, 291; to Confederate veterans, 281; dedication of, 281

Olustee Battlefield Historic State Park, 208; Union monument controversy, 291–92

Olustee Battlefield monument, Colquitt, 1936: inscription on, 205–6, *206*; location of, 205; nature and makeup of, 205–6, *206*

Olustee Battlefield monument, Confederate, 1912: dedication of, 196, *198*, 198–99, *199*, 302; funds and fund-raising for, 197–98, 201; inscription on, 200–201, 202; location of, 197–99; nature and makeup of, *200*, 200–201, *201*, 202; politics and, 197; from UDC, 196–97, 198, 201, 202; Union soldiers and, 196–97

Olustee Battlefield monument, Finegan, 1951: dedication of, 206, *207*; inscription on, 206–7; from UDC, 206–7

Olustee Battlefield monument, 1991, 267; funds and fund-raising for, 194; inscription on, 194

Olustee Battlefield monument, Union, 1866, 295; as Florida monument, 33–34, 192–94, *193*

Olustee Confederate Dead monument, Lake City, 1901: dedication of, 194–95, 196; inscription on, 195–96; nature and makeup of, 195–96; of UDC, 194, *195*

Olustee Confederate Dead monument, Lake City, 1928, *203*; dedication of, 202–3; funds for, 202; inscription on, 204–5; location of, 202–3; nature and makeup of, *204*, 204–5

Olustee Monument Commission, 291

Order of Confederate Rose, 260

Organizations, monument: Civil War connection to, 293–94; in post-Centennial monuments, 259–60, 289, 290–92. *See also specific organizations*

Orlando Greenwood Cemetery, 176–77

Orlando monument, 1911, *108*; dedication, 107; inscription, 108–9; location of, *109*, 109–10, *110*; nature and makeup of, 107–8; of UDC, 108, 110

Orlando Union monument, 1910: GAR in, 175–77, *176*; inscription, 175–76, 177; nature and makeup of, 175–76, *176*
Ormond Beach monument, 2011, 287, *288*, 289
Oxford monument, 2007, 279

Paine, Rev. Samuel D., 171
Palatka, Florida, 125
Palatka monument, 1924, *126*; cannonballs in, 128; dedication of, 125, 127; inscription, 127–28; nature and makeup of, 127; of UDC, 127–28
Pensacola, Florida, 66–67
Pensacola monument, 1891: cannonballs in, 69; Confederate cause in, 71–73; Confederate veterans at, *71*; controversy, 70–71; dedication, 67; as Florida monument, 66–73, *70*, *71*, *72*; fund-raising for, 67; inscription, 68–69; LMA in building, 67, 69–70; modification of, 69–71; nature and makeup of, 67–68, 69; UDC and, 69–70
Perry, Brig. Gen. Edward A., 63
Perry, Capt. Edward Aylesworth, 68–69
Perry monument, 2007: inscription on, 279; nature and makeup of, 279–80, *280*; from SCV, 279–80
Phillips, Gen. Zephaniah, 82–83, 174
Physical condition, of Florida monuments, 299
Plant, Henry, 166
Plant City monument, 2007: controversy from, 283, 294; to Cow Cavalry, 282, 294; nature and makeup of, *282*, 282–83; as regimental monument, 283; UDC and, 282
Pollard, Edward R., 49, 65
Population, of Florida, 162, 166, 194, 232, 293
Post, Kit Carson, 82–83
Private individuals: Jacksonville monument from, 77–80, *78*, *81*, 82, 84–86, *85*; monuments built by, 51, 77–80, *78*, *81*, 82–86, *83*, *84*, *85*; St. Petersburg monument from, 82–84, *83*, *84*
Public buildings and grounds, 305

Quincy, Florida, 28–29, 62
Quincy monument, 1884: dedication of, 62–63; financial cost of, 63; as Florida monument, 62–63, *63*, *64*, 65–66; inscription, 65; LMA in building, 62–63; location of, 63; Monticello monument compared to, 76; nature and makeup of, 63, 65–66

Race: burial, graves and, 196, 230; GAR on, 164–65; UDC Union monument opposition based on, 302. *See also* African Americans; U.S. Colored Troops
Real estate, Florida, 167–68
Reconciliation: monuments to, 78–79, 82–84, *83*, 174, 224–25, 256–57; World War I and, 297
Reconstruction: amnesty, Confederate leaders, and, 22–23; Congress during, 23–24, 30; Democrats in, 24–25; for Johnson, 22–25, 30; Lincoln's death impacting, 19–21, 309n20; LMAs after, 49; monument message through context of, 303; Radical, 30; Republicans in, 23–25; St. Augustine monument, 1872, and, 301; slavery and, 23, 24; state government in, 22–25
Reconstruction-era Florida: Lincoln's strategy for, 20; monument building in, 13, 32–35, *36–37*, 38, *39*, 40, *41*, 42–45, *43*, *44*, *46*, 47–48; state government in, 23, 24–25
Reconstruction-era South: burial and graves in, 11; difficulties in, 13–14; military government in, 23–24
Regimental monuments, 283
Relevance, of monuments, 16
Republicans, 23–25
Restoration: Florida monuments physical condition and, 299; to Gainesville monument, 91; of Gettysburg Battlefield monument, 253
Reunification: Civil War end and, 10; dedications to, 79, 82
Reunions, UCV, 148, 155, 241–42
Robertson, Jr., James I., 293
Rose, Capt. Charles J., 183–84, *184*, 187
Ryan, Abram J., 60, 91, 108, 116

Sacrifice: commemoration of, 12–13; community monuments to general, 13; of Confederate women, 158; monuments reflecting, 10, 12–13, 62
St. Augustine monument, 1872: as Florida monument, 42–45, *43*, *44*, *46*, 47; inscription of, 45, 47; LMA involvement in, 42–43, 44–45, 52; location of, 43–45, 52; nature and makeup of, 44, 45, 47; Reconstruction and, 301; as tourist attraction, 47
St. Augustine monument, William Wing Loring, 1920, *117*; dedication, 116; fundraising, 118; inscription, 118–19; nature and makeup of, 118–19; of UDC, 116, 118, 119
St. Cloud, Florida: GAR in, *168*, 169; soldiers colony in, 168–69
St. Cloud monument, 2000: dedication of, 272; GAR, 272, *272*; nature and makeup of, 272, 272–73
St. Cloud monument, 2006: to Confederate veterans, *278*; dedication of, 278; inscription on, 278–79; from SCV, 278
St. Cloud Union monument, 1915, *177*, 177–78
St. Petersburg, Florida, 138, 140
St. Petersburg monument, Greenwood Cemetery, 1900: dedication of, 82, *83*, 84; inscription, 83; nature and makeup of, 82–83; from private individuals, 82–84, *83*, *84*
St. Petersburg Union monument, 1900: dedication of, 174; GAR in, 174; inscription, 175; nature and makeup of, 174–75, *175*; reconciliation in, 174
Sarasota monument, Judah P. Benjamin Escape Monument, 1942: dedication of, 223–25, *224*, 226; inscription on, 225–26; nature and makeup of, *225*, 225–26; reconciliation at, 224–25; from UDC, 223, 224, 226
Scott, Kate Dilworth, 73, 75
Sculpture, Florida monuments as, 297–98
SCV. *See* Sons of Confederate Veterans
Sebastian monument, 2004: dedication and inscription, 276; SCV and UDC in, 276
Secession, 9–10
Segesman, John G., 88–90, 178–79
Sherman, Maj. Gen. William Tecumseh, 17–18, 20–21
Skinner, Porter V., 185, 187
Slavery: Confederate symbols and, 304; post-Centennial monuments on, *269*, 269–70; reconstruction and, 23, 24; Thirteenth Amendment abolishing, 20
Smith, Gen. Edmund Kirby, 79
Society, Florida: Civil War impact on, 25–30; Florida soldiers' deaths and, 26, 29
Soldiers: camps for, 189; dead, 1, 307n4; Florida cemeteries and burial of, 28–29; monuments for Civil War impact on, 7; post-Civil War experience of, 10. *See also* Confederate soldiers; Florida soldiers; Union soldiers
"Soldier's Cemetery," Quincy, 28–29
Soldiers or veterans colonies: Lynn Haven, 169; St. Cloud and, 168–69; South and GAR, 170; Union veteran, 167–69; in Zephyrhills, 167–68
Soldiers' Rest Confederate Cemetery, 27
Sons of Confederate Veterans (SCV), 98; Alachua monument of, 275–76; Bartow monument of, 264–65; Confederate symbol controversy and, 294–95; in Dade City monument, 276–77; Fort Meade monument from, 265–66; Havana monument from, 271; Kissimmee monument from, 275; Perry monument from, 279–80; in post-Centennial monuments, 259, 260, 289, 290–92; post-Centennial Union monument opposition from, 291–92; St. Cloud monument, 2006, from, 278; Sebastian monument and, 276; in Tampa monument, 2008, 285; Trenton monument from, 285–86; in Tullahoma monument, 283–84; UDC and UCV cooperation with, 147; White Springs monument from, 275
Sons of Union Veterans of the Civil War (SUVCW), 291
South, new: Confederate leaders' deaths in, 12; GAR veterans colonies in, 170

Sprague, Col. John T., 42–43
Starke monument, 1968: dedication of, 261; inscription, 261; nature and makeup of, 261; from UDC, 260–61
State government: Key West, New York Regimental Monument, from, 220; in reconstruction, 22–25
Stonewall Confederate Cemetery, Winchester, Virginia, 1902, 26–27, 257; dedication of, 235–36; Florida soldiers at, 237–38; inscription on, 237; LMA involved in, 235–36; nature and makeup of, 236, 237, *237*
Stonewall Jackson Highway monument, St. Petersburg, 1940, *139*; dedication of, 138; financial cost of, 138–39; inscription, 139; location of, 138, 140; nature and makeup of, 139–40; of UDC, 139
Stonewall Jackson Highway monument, Jefferson County, 1950, *140*; dedication of, 141; inscription, 141; location of, 141; nature and makeup of, 141
Stonewall Jackson Memorial Highway commemorative markers, 141–42
Stovall's Brigade, 240
Submarines and torpedo boats, 84–86
Suffrage, 24
Surrender: of Confederate army, 17–18, 19–21; of Johnston, Gen. Joseph, 19–21; Lincoln's death and terms of, 19–20, 21
"Surrender monument," 7, 308n8
SUVCW. *See* Sons of Union Veterans of the Civil War

Tallahassee, Florida, 52
Tallahassee monument, 1881: controversy surrounding, 54–55, 56, 301–2; dedication ceremony for, 53–54, 58; financial cost of, 52–53; as Florida monument, 52–58, *53*, *55*, *57*; fund-raising for, 53–55, 56; inscription, 54; LMAs in building, 52–58, *53*, *55*, *57*; location of, 55, 56–57; nature and makeup of, 54
Tampa, Florida, 102
Tampa, Woodlawn Cemetery monument, 1913: cannonballs at, 151, 152–53; dedication of, 151; inscription, 152, 153; location, 153; nature and makeup of, 151–53, *152*; UCV in, 151
Tampa monument, 1911, *104–5*; dedication, 103, 107; fund-raising, 102–3; inscription, 105, 106; location, 106–7; nature and makeup of, 103, 105–6; of UDC, 102–3, 106
Tampa monument, 2008: controversy surrounding, 285; as "Flags across Florida" monument, 285; inscription, 285; SCV in, 285
Tampa monuments, Oaklawn Cemetery, 1975, 1976, and unknown date, *262*; inscription on, 262, *263*, 264; nature and makeup of, 262, *263*, 264; Union monument in, 264
Tampa Union monument, 1924, *182*; dedication of, 182–83; GAR and WRC in, 182–83; inscription on, 183; location, 183; nature and makeup of, 183
Third Army Corps Union, 164
"Third System" of fortifications, 34, 310n51
Thirteenth Amendment, 20
Thirty-Second Indiana Volunteer Infantry, 5, *5*, 307n5
Time and time period, 86–87, 170–71
Tomb, James Hamilton, 85–86
Torpedo boats. *See* Submarines and torpedo boats
Tourism, 47, 179–80
Trammel, Park, 107
Trenton monument, 2010, 285–87, *286*
Tullahoma monument, Tennessee, 2008, 283–84, *284*

U.S. *See* United States
U.S. Colored Troops (USCT), 229; burial and graves of, 29, 230; post-Centennial monuments to, *270*, 270–71, 289, 290, 332n69; UDC opposition to Union monuments and, 302; Union army in Florida and enlistment of, 18–19
UADF. *See* Union Army District of Florida
UCV. *See* United Confederate Veterans
UDC. *See* United Daughters of the Confederacy
Union: navy, 25; officer organizations and

societies, 164, 167; prisoners, 13–14; strategy, 20
Union army: in Battle of Marianna, 208; in Battle of Natural Bridge, 211–12; in Battle of Olustee, 192–93; in Florida, 18–19, 34, 42, 52, 58, 66–67, 77, 145–46, 232. *See also* Military engagement
Union Army District of Florida (UADF), 193–94
Union monument or monuments: community, 170–88, *172*, *175*, *176*, *177*, *179*, *180*, *182*, *184*, *185*, *186*; Florida, 15, 33–35, *36–37*, 38, 82–84, *83*, 163, 187–88, 228–29, 264, 289, 293, 295, 300; in Florida cemeteries, 187–88; funds and fund-raising for, 187; GAR and WRC in, 187–88; to hallowed ground, 228–29; message, nature, or purpose of, 188, 300; post-Centennial, 187, 291–92; St. Petersburg, 82–84, *83*, *84*; SCV and UDC opposition to, 291–92, 302; time period for community, 170–71; to Union soldiers, *177*, 178, 193, 220–23, *222*, 287, *288*, 289; to Union women, 177; vandalism to, 181. *See also specific Union monuments*
Union soldiers: burial and graves of, 11, 28, 29, 31, 33–34, 176–77, 178, 191, 222, 223, 230, 276–77, *277*; Olustee Battlefield monument, 1912, and, 196–97; Union monuments to, *177*, 178, 193, 220–23, *222*, 287, *288*, 289. *See also* Union veterans
Union veterans: African American, 166–67; economic impact of, 166, 167–68; in Florida, 15, 166–70, *168*, *170*; GAR for, 11, 166–67; in real estate, 167–68; soldiers colonies for, 167–69; Union officer organizations for needs of, 164, 167
United Confederate Veterans (UCV), *203*; commemoration from, 11–12, 51; Confederate monuments from, 147–48, *149*, *150*, 150–60, *152*, *156*, *157*, *158*, *159*; Confederate women honored by, 153–54, 159; in Jacksonville Confederate Park monument, 153–55, 157; in Jacksonville monument, 1928, 150, 151; in Live Oak monument, 148; Loring Camp of, 151–52, 153; nature and mission of, 51; reunions, 148, 155, 241–42; SCV and UDC cooperation with, 147; in Tampa Woodlawn Cemetery monument, 151
United Daughters of the Confederacy (UDC), 304; Arlington National Cemetery and, 256, 257; Bartow Law monument of, 133; in battlefield marking, 87; Battle of Marianna monument from, 208–10, 211; Battle of Natural Bridge monument from, 212–13, 218; Bradenton monument of, 122–23; Brooksville monument and, 114, 116; Chattahoochee monument from, 267–68; Clearwater monument from, 267; community monuments of, 86–99, *89*, *90*, *93*, *95*, *96*, *98*, *100*, *101*, 101–3, *104–5*, 105–14, *108–9*, *110*, *111–12*, *115*, 116, *117*, 118–25, *120*, *121*, *122*, *124*, *126*, 127–47, *129*, *131*, *133–34*, *136*, *137*, *139*, *140*, *142*, *144*, *146*; Confederate cause vindication for, 51, 86, 291; Confederate monument building time period of, 86–87; Crawfordville monument from, 267; Dade City monument and, 276–77; Daytona Beach monument of, 144–45; DeLand monument of, 143; Dixie Highway monument of, 128, 129, 131, 132; Florida monuments of, 15, 296–97; in Florida soldier monuments, 257–58; Fort Myers monument, 1966, and, 146–47, 302–3; Gamble Plantation monument, 1937, and, 138; Gamble Plantation monument, 1925, from, 218–19, 231; GAR conflict with, 196–97; Groveton Cemetery and, 238; hallowed ground monuments from, 229; Jacksonville monument, 1973, from, 262; Jacksonville monument, 2001, of, 273; Key West monument, Bayview Park of, 119–21; Lakeland monument, 1910, and, 99, *100*; Leesburg monument of, 135, *136*; Madison monument, 1909, and, *96*, 97, 98–99; McGavock Confederate Cemetery and, 235; Miami monument of, 111–12, 113–14; monument placement strategy of, 110; nature and goals of, 50–51; Ocala monument and, 92; Olustee Battlefield monument, 1951, from, 206–7; Olustee Battlefield monument, 1912, from, 196–97,

198, 201, 202; Olustee Confederate Dead, 1901, 194, *195*; Orlando monument and, 108, 110; Palatka monument and, 127–28; Pensacola monument and, 69–70; Plant City monument and, 282; in post-Centennial monuments, 259, 289, 290–92; St. Augustine Loring monument from, 116, 118, 119; Sarasota, Benjamin Escape Monument, from, 223, 224, 226; SCV and UCV cooperation with, 147; Sebastian monument and, 276; southern commemoration from, 11–12; Starke monument from, 260–61; Stonewall Jackson Highway monument from, 139, 140–41; Tallahassee monument and, 301–2; Tampa monument, 1911, of, 102–3, 106; in Tullahoma monument, 283–84; Union monument opposition from, 291–92, 302; Vicksburg Battlefield monument and, 247–48; West Palm Beach monument from, 141, 143; Yellow Bluff Fort monument from, 227, 228, 231

United Sons of the Confederacy of Dixie County, 281

United States (U.S.): in Confederate soldier burial, 31–32, 191–92, 196–97; national cemeteries of, 31; "Third System" of fortifications of, 34, 310n51. *See also* Federal government

Unknown: dead, 191, 196, 205, 244, 245; monuments to, 244, 245, *281*

Valor. *See* Bravery and valor

Vandalism, 181

Vandervoort, Rev. Harry G., 179–80

Veterans, Civil War, 14, 38. *See also* Confederate veterans; Soldiers or veterans colonies; Union veterans

Vicksburg, Mississippi, 246–47

Vicksburg Battlefield monument, Mississippi, 1954, 246, *247*, 258; dedication of, 247–48; inscription, 248; location of, 248–49; nature and makeup of, 248; UDC and, 247–48

W. H. Mullins Company, 298–99

Walton County Female Memorial Association, 1, 38

Walton County monument, 1871, 1, *2*; current location of, 3, 40; financial cost of, 38; as Florida monument, 38, *39*, 40, *41*, 42; inscription, 38, 40; location dispute over, 40, 300–301; nature and makeup of, 38, 40; from Walton County Female Memorial Association, 1, 38

Warren, Robert Penn, 259

West Palm Beach monument, 1941: Confederate cause in, 142; inscription, 142–43; nature and makeup of, 141–42, *142*; from UDC, 141, 143

White Springs monument, 2002: as "Flags across Florida" monument, *274*, 274–75; nature and makeup of, *274*, 274–75; from SCV, 275

Woman's Relief Corps (WRC): within GAR, 165; in Miami Union monument, 185, 187; in St. Cloud Union monument, 1915, *177*, 177–78; in Tampa Union monument, 182–83; Union monuments and, 187–88

Women, of Confederacy: Confederate monuments to, 153–60, *156*, *157*, *158*, *159*; sacrifice of, 158; UCV honoring, 153–54, 159. *See also* United Daughters of the Confederacy

Women, of Union, 177

World War I, 125, 127, 297

World War II, 224–25, 231, 302

WRC. *See* Woman's Relief Corps

Yellow Bluff Fort, 226

Yellow Bluff Fort monument, 1951, *227*; cannons at, 227–28; financial cost of, 227; inscription on, 228; land donation for, 226–27; nature and makeup of, 228; from UDC, 227, 228, 231

Yellow fever, 220

Zephyrhills, Florida, 167–68

WILLIAM B. LEES is executive director of the Florida Public Archaeology Network at the University of West Florida. A former president of the Society for Historical Archaeology, his interest in Civil War monuments was kindled when he did a survey of Oklahoma monuments while working for the Oklahoma Historical Society in the early 1990s.

FREDERICK P. GASKE served as director of the Florida Division of Historical Resources, as Florida state historic preservation officer, and as executive director of Goodwood Museum and Gardens in Tallahassee. He is the editor and coauthor of the *Florida Civil War Heritage Trail* produced by the Florida Association of Museums.